The International Library of Sociology

THE SOCIOLOGY OF RELIGION

Founded by KARL MANNHEIM

The International Library of Sociology

THE SOCIOLOGY OF RELIGION
In 8 Volumes

I	The Economic Order and Religion (The above title is not available through Routledge in North America)	*Knight and Merriam*
II	Islam and the Integration of Society	*Watt*
III	Religious Behaviour	*Argyle*
IV	The Sociology of Religion (Part 1): Established Religion	*Stark*
V	The Sociology of Religion (Part 2): Sectarian Religion	*Stark*
VI	The Sociology of Religion (Part 3): The Universal Church	*Stark*
VII	The Sociology of Religion (Part 4): Types of Religious Man	*Stark*
VIII	The Sociology of Religion (Part 5): Types of Religious Culture	*Stark*

THE SOCIOLOGY OF RELIGION

A Study of Christendom

Part Two
Sectarian Religion

by

WERNER STARK

First published in 1967
by Routledge

Reprinted 1998, 1999, 2000, 2001
by Routledge
2 Park Square, Milton Park, Abingdon, Oxon, OX14 4RN
or
270 Madison Avenue, New York, NY 10016

First issued in paperback 2010

Routledge is an imprint of the Taylor & Francis Group

British Library Cataloguing in Publication Data
A CIP catalogue record for this book
is available from the British Library

Sociology of Religion: Part Two - Sectarian Religion
ISBN 978-0-415-17590-6 (hbk)
ISBN 978-0-415-60559-5 (pbk)
The Sociology of Religion: 8 Volumes
ISBN 978-0-415-17823-5
The International Library of Sociology: 274 Volumes
ISBN 978-0-415-17838-9

Publisher's Note

The publisher has gone to great lengths to ensure the quality of this reprint but points out that some imperfections in the original may be apparent

CONTENTS

Preface

The present publication needs no long introduction. All I have to emphasize is that it forms a whole with the volume which preceded it under the subtitle 'Established Religion', and with the volume which will succeed it under the subtitle 'The Universal Church'. The three books together represent a comprehensive study of the relationships, within the orbit of Christendom, between religious organizations on the one hand and the inclusive society on the other.

W. STARK

Acknowledgments

As in volume I, we list here, with thanks, the publishers who have been good enough to permit us to quote from books under their imprint. The authors' names are given in brackets.

Abingdon Press (Cameron, R. M.); The Bodley Head (Avvakum); Cambridge University Press (Braithwaite, W. C.); The Carey Kingsgate Press (Underwood, A. C.); Columbia University Press (Curtiss, J. S.; Shaw, P. E.); The Cresset Press (Huehns, G.); John Day Company (Whalen, W. J.); Doubleday & Co. (Harris, S.; Herberg, W.); Gerald Duckworth & Co. (Sumner, B. H.); The Epworth Press (Wilkinson, J. T.); Harper & Row (Montross, L.); Harvard University Press (Conybeare, F. C.); B. Herder Book Company (Algermissen, K.); Holt, Rinehart & Winston (Turner, F. J.; Wright, J. F. C.); Little, Brown & Co. (Whitney, J. P.); Longmans, Green & Co. (Lloyd, A.); Meridian Books (Niebuhr, R.); Thomas Nelson & Sons (Sandall, R.); Oxford University Press (Bridenbaugh, C.; Knox, R.); Philosophical Library (Church, L. F.); Princeton University Press (Melcher, M. F.); Putnam's & Coward-McCann (Hinshaw, D.); Charles Scribner's Sons (Dakin, E. F.); Martin Secker & Warburg (Cohn, N.); Turnstile Press (Holloway, M.); University of California Press (Wilson, B. R.); University of Pennsylvania Press (Milyukov, P.). Also Collins-Knowlton-Wing, Inc. (Whiting, J.P.); Paul R. Reynolds, Inc. (Whalen, W.J.)

Introduction

The law of life which ordains that every enjoyment shall have its price and every possession its proper burden, applies as much to the field which we are studying in this work as it does to all others. Whenever and wherever a religion sheds its lustre over the society within which it is established, that society is sure to cast back its shadow over the religion with which it is connected and by which it is glorified. The assertion that the existing institutions are God-given and God-willed has its appeal to those who are at peace with the world in which they live; but to those who are not, it will appear unacceptable, nay, repulsive and outrageous – an impious mockery of all that is sacred. To those who are content already, the merging of church and state, and the ideas and ideologies which this merger calls forth, will give an even deeper contentment; but in those who, for whatever reason or reasons, feel rebellious, the sanctification of things secular will evoke an even stronger rebelliousness. Indeed, in cultures whose general thought-patterns are attuned to an underlying metaphysic, who tend to see everything in religious terms, the concepts of religion will – not unnaturally – be the prime medium in which social tensions become conscious and formulated and harden into fighting fronts. It could not be otherwise. Established religions are, as we have seen, embodiments of the principle of conservatism; but if this is so, then the revolutionary forces in a society must form their own religious organizations, parallel but antagonistic embodiments of the principle of revolt. These organizations, born of a negative attitude to the contemporary established socio-economic and political system, are traditionally called sects. 'A church,' Benton Johnson has recently written, 'is a religious group that accepts the social environment in which it exists. A sect is a religious group that rejects the social environment in which it exists.'[1] And Richard Niebuhr, in his much-read and much-appreciated little book, *The*

[1] Johnson, B., 'On Church and Sect,' *American Sociological Review*, 1963, p. 542.

Social Sources of Denominationalism,[1] has taught us to see the sect as a religious 'conflict society' which has arisen in opposition to an 'institutional church'.

We shall have to investigate later whether Johnson's unqualified use of the word 'church' is justified in this context, and whether Niebuhr's qualification – 'institutional' – is adequate. There are churches – even institutional ones – which do not appear to give rise to widespread sectarianism. For the moment, our main attention must be directed to the fact that sects are conflict societies. When Professor Asher studied the Molokane, he found that they called the state church 'Russian' and its adherents 'Russians', 'as if they themselves were foreigners'.[2] This is highly characteristic. Typical sectarians are *in* their country rather than *of* their country; and while their sectarian spirit is yet in undiminished spate, they are even, as a rule, *against* it. It is no accident that the names by which they are traditionally known in the English-speaking world are terms which express deviation from the norm: separatists, dissenters, nonconformists. In other languages, words of even stronger disapproval, not to say opprobrium, are often used.

As the sequel is going to show, the initial tension between sect and surrounding society has, in the great majority of cases, evinced a tendency to diminish, until in the end there is often very little difference left between the values and volitions of the once revolutionary body and those of the wider social world. The sect runs through a whole gamut of moods, from comparative wildness all the way to comparative mildness. But even at their inception, some sects are far more aggressive and anarchistic than others. We could rank them on a continuum, from such formations as the Skoptsy at the one end, a group who thought little of inflicting pain or even death, to the Moravians on the other, who harmed nobody, and whose disapproval of the rest of humanity was only expressed by being, in all quietness, different from them. This great variety makes it very difficult to give a coherent and realistic picture of sectarianism as a whole. Yet this is precisely what we must attempt to do. A book like the present, which is typological in its aim, must speak of the sect rather than of sects. But, of

[1] First published in 1929. Cf. paperback ed., New York 1957, pp. 18, 125, 224.

[2] Cf. Conybeare, F. C., *Russian Dissenters,* Cambridge, Mass. 1921, p. 314.

course, the abstract type can be seen only in and through its concrete embodiments. Our method will therefore be to present the decisive facets and features which, in various combinations, constitute sectarianism, and to append to each of them a number of factual illustrations taken, now from this movement, now from that, always choosing the most revealing characteristics which have come to our knowledge.

I · THE ORIGIN OF SECTS

The last root of all sectarianism lies in the alienation of some group from the inclusive society within which it has to carry on its life. It is a kind of protest movement, distinguished from other similar movements by the basic fact that it experiences and expresses its dissatisfactions and strivings in religious (rather than political or economic or generally secular) terms. The causes of alienation can be many, but hunger and humiliation easily come first. All through history, the lowest ranks of society have been the prime recruiting ground of heresies and schisms. Marxists are, by and large, within their rights when they claim that sect movements are phenomena of an ongoing class struggle in societies within which the class conflict as such has not yet become conscious. Writing mainly of the history of Protestantism, but enunciating a far wider truth, Niebuhr has well said that 'the sect has ever been the child of an outcast minority, taking its rise in the religious revolts of the poor'.[1]

The undoubted causal connection between material poverty on the one hand and religious protests on the other must not, however, be regarded – as it has sometimes been regarded – as a sufficient explanation of the whole phenomenon. Even if we are to remain in the area of class contrast, we soon find other important contributing factors. One is presented to us, on the grandest possible scale, by the history of Indian spirituality. We do not think, nowadays, of Buddhism and Jainism as sects. But at their inception they were just that, religiously conceived protest movements against an inclusive society and its inherent religiosity. After the northern invaders had settled down on the subcontinent and made themselves masters of the aboriginal population, the country's inhabitants were divided into four classical castes: the Brahmins or priests; the Kshatriyas or princes; the Vaisyas or commoners; and the Sudras or serfs. The relations between these castes were determined by the degree of ritual (Max Weber said: magical) purity which was respectively attributed to them: the Brahmins, for instance, were at the apex of the social pyramid because their touch would defile nobody, while they could easily be defiled. Buddhism

[1] Niebuhr, loc. cit., p.19.

and Jainism arose in opposition to this principle of social stratification as soon as it came to be regarded as invidious and objectionable. There is thus no background of material poverty to these religious formations, and, characteristically, the founder of the one, the Buddha or Siddartha, was a ruler's son, the founder of the other, the Jina or Mahavira, a high-ranking aristocrat. Both were technically Kshatriyas; and as such both resented the privileged position of the Brahmin caste. Their religious reorientation sought to break it. Such opposition or such protest must exist for a sect to arise, even a revolutionary sentiment and situation, but by no means always economic deprivation or exploitation.

Sometimes, indeed, the attempt to track down the origins of a sect leads, not into the arena of class struggle, but towards other causes of social division and human disaffection. The basic tension may lie between national and racial groups; it may lie between geographical regions or town and country; it may lie between the sexes or the generations; and it may lie outside the area of sociality properly so called, in purely individual character traits, some personal property or problem which induces a man to shun the altars where his socially and emotionally integrated neighbours worship. Needless to say, often these factors cut across and complement each other in a complex pattern of causation in which it may just be possible to distinguish the contributory strands, but impossible to say how much each or any of them is responsible for the total effect. We shall encounter them all as we look at the historical facts, or rather the few of them which we have found in our limited field of observation.

THE MAIN SOCIAL CAUSE OF SECTARIANISM

When all is said and done, the fact remains that the chief reason for men getting together in order to form sectarian groupings has been their unhappiness in, and revolt against, a social system within which their position – the position of their class – was, in Veblen's terminology, humilific, for instance because their livelihood was insecure or their wages low, or their status (Max Weber's 'estimation of honour') unsatisfactory. An eye-opening detail in this respect is the predominant, not to say dominant, place of textile workers in the history of European sectarianism which must surely strike any student who concerns himself with these matters.

Whether we follow the thread of time or consider the canvas of geography, we find representatives of this industry at every nodal point.

One of the first occasions on which trouble began to brew in the Middle Ages was the communal insurrection at Cambrai in the year 1077. A priest called Ramihrdus preached radical religious reformation and roused the city's artisan population. Most of them must have been weavers, for Cambrai was above all a textile town, as the term cambric (still used for fine linens) testifies. The great reform pope Gregory VII was in sympathy with Ramihrdus who attacked the local, very much unreformed, bishop, rather than the Church. The unrest at Milan known as the Pataria was of the same kind. The main protagonists were also textile workers; its targets were the noblemen-bishops supported by the Emperor, and, under the influence of St. Peter Damian, it finally gave its support to the papal reform party. But the turbulent waters did not always remain within the Church's well-dug bed. A little later St. Bernard (who was born in 1090) came across rebellious and renegade clerics 'to his horror sitting bearded and untonsured at the looms alongside men and women weavers'. Here we are already face to face with more heretical movements like the Brethren of the Free Spirit, the Cathari and the Waldensians. All of them were to a large extent recruited from the operatives of the textile industry. 'In 1157, a synod gave its attention to certain heretics who were active within the ecclesiastical province of Rheims which included most of northern France and the Low Countries. These *pifres* or *pifles* (as they were called in French) were weavers . . . When Eckbert [of Schönau] later came to write a tract against the various heretics [of the "Free Spirit" variety] whom he had encountered along the Rhine, he pointed out that many of them were weavers . . .' The Cathari, too, tended to appear wherever looms were humming, and it is highly significant that at Arras (another classical textile town) they were habitually referred to as the *textores*. What Arras was in the north, Lyons was in the south, and the Waldensians who started there as the 'Poor Men of Lyons' were headed by a cloth-merchant who had repented of his trade as well as of his sins.[1]

[1] Cf. Cohn, N., *The Pursuit of the Millenium*, Fairlawn, New Jersey 1957, pp. 34, 35, 91, 153, 154; *also* 148, 162, 220. Cf. further Honigsheim, P., in *Versuche zu einer Soziologie des Wissens*, ed. Scheler, M., München and Leipzig 1924, pp. 335 and 336.

Thus there was started a tradition which was never to break off. One of the most dramatic figures of sixteenth-century religious unrest was Thomas Müntzer. While he himself was what Max Weber would have called a pariah intellectual, he owed his chiliasm to a fuller, Nikolaus Storch, and it was in Storch's home-town that he made his main bid for men's souls, and in Storch's trade that he had his greatest success. 'A few months after he arrived in Zwickau, Müntzer became a preacher at the very church where the weavers had their special altar, and he used the pulpit to utter fierce denunciations . . . In April 1521, the Town Council intervened and dismissed the turbulent new-comer; whereupon a large number of the populace, under Storch's leadership, rose in revolt... Many arrests were made, including, significantly enough, more than fifty weavers.'[1] In the seventeenth century, George Fox, commonly regarded as the father of Quakerism, was a weaver's son, and some of the most important local leaders, such as Steven Crisp at Colchester and Thomas Symonds at Norwich, were themselves weavers.[2] In the eighteenth century, Methodism, while appealing to all the factory proletariat, had a special message for the textile workers. For instance, the way in which it got a footing in Dublin is characteristic. 'In 1747 Charles Wesley . . . saw an opportunity of preaching to the weavers, if only he could get some place for regular ministration. In Cork Street he went to the Weavers' Store, where the looms were kept, and there preached to more than five hundred. Encouraged by his reception, he decided to buy Dolphin's Barn, which had been used as a weavers' shop. The ground floor was converted into a preaching-room.'[3] Again the men at the loom as the main contingent! Of Nottingham, John Wesley reported that 'most of our society are of the lower class [and] chiefly employed in the stocking manufacture'.[4] And even in the nineteenth and twentieth centuries, this copious source of sectarianism still flowed. The founder of the 'Nazarenes', Johann Jakob Wirz (who died in 1856), and the founder of 'Shepherd and Flock', Friedrich August Hain (who died in 1927), were both weavers.

As this brief survey has already shown, great textile centres had

[1] Cohn, loc. cit., pp. 252, 254, 255.

[2] Braithwaite, W. C., *The Beginnings of Quakerism,* 2nd ed., Cambridge, England 1955, pp. 28, 163, 382.

[3] Church, L. F., *The Early Methodist People*, New York 1949, pp. 52 and 53.

[4] Ibid., p. 4.

a tendency to generate great sect movements, and with the local shifts of the textile industry there were also shifts in the main venues of sectarianism. A look at the religious map will confirm this picture. Few of those who know England will deny that East Anglia is still the most Protestant part of the country; even its Anglicanism is sharply profiled in this way. And few of those who know Germany will doubt that Silesia ever was, and still is, the heartland of Pietism. But both East Anglia and Silesia bear the imprint of the textile industry. 'Here were the most important export centres' of the wool industry, writes G. Huehns, in her study of *Antinomianism in English History*, of the 'Eastern Counties'. Here, too, 'the New Drapery found its first home. Hence there were more hands, relatively speaking, dependent there on "the estate of clothing" than elsewhere'. With the Civil War, the self-same Eastern Counties emerged as the main assailants of the traditional, king-centred religiosity of feudal England. Already in 1642, Parliament expressed its thanks to Essex for the great support given to the anti-royalist cause and religion, and in 1643 John Williams published his *London's Love to Her Neighbours* in which East Anglia is addressed in the following terms: ''Twas you that first sought to prevent them [i.e. Charles's friends] of their purposes . . . your monies that maintained wars against them; . . . [and you] were the first movers in the way of reformation . . .'[1] This inclination to the religious left has remained with the 'six associated counties', and its origin is not unconnected with the once prevailing trade. The case of Silesia is perhaps best illustrated by a reference to her greatest modern writer, Gerhart Hauptmann. His moving drama, *Die Weber*,[2] brought the sufferings of the Silesian textile workers on to the stage, and his great novel, *Der Narr in Christo Emanuel Quint*,[3] showed how many of them found solace in a deep, if brooding, religiosity.

Casting about for an explanation of this curious interconnection between a certain type of work and a certain type of thought, Paul Honigsheim has suggested that the type of work concerned tended to produce a 'definite nervous condition' which in turn tended to evoke the sectarian type of thought.[4] He points to the relative isolation of the operatives (the textile industry was for centuries a domestic industry), to their absorption in and by the work which

[1] Huehns, loc. cit., London 1951, p. 76. [2] *The Weavers*, published in 1892.
[3] *The Fool in Christ Emanuel Quint*, published in 1910. [4] Loc. cit., p. 336.

yet, unlike the work of artisans, did not yield any aesthetic-creative satisfaction, and even to the monotonous droning of the loom, which may have produced a semi-hypnotic state favourable to mystical speculations and experiences. Without denying the presence of these factors in, and their importance for, the causative complex, it would yet seem that the true explanation must be sought, not in psychological, but in socio-economic circumstances. Unlike the typical medieval craftsman who was in direct personal contact with his suppliers and with his customers, who operated on a small, easily overlooked and easily controlled market, who had no masters above him and no permanent proletariat beneath him, and who, for all these reasons, could feel well integrated and hence well contented, the cloth-worker was something of an odd man out. As economic historians have shown,[1] his raw materials came from afar, and his wares had to travel wide to reach their ultimate destination. This dependence on distant markets made it impossible for the small man to stand alone; there was not only room, but even a definite need, for an entrepreneur. The 'Great Industry' was already very early a capitalist industry. And what was worse, any political dislocation, any war, however far away, tended to upset the trade and, in one way or another, by the drying up of the supply lines or the blocking up of the lines of sale, to create under-employment or unemployment, with all the miseries that come in their train. No wonder that the weavers felt aggrieved. The greatest happiness the old world life of Europe could yield for the petty bourgeois – the feeling that he was secure in his little corner – was denied to this type of working man.

But even worse things were in store. Unlike other lines of production, this one was soon deeply disturbed by technological progress. By the twelfth century, the sources begin to contain references to a revolutionary contraption (to a *doubly* revolutionary contraption – revolutionary like a drum, and revolutionary like a *coup d'état*!) – to the *molendinum fullericum*, or fuller's mill. The trampling of cloth in the trough (an essential part of the process of production) was replaced by the beating of it by tilt hammers driven by water-power. However beneficent this improvement may have been in other respects, from a human point of view it was a catastrophe for the textile workers. Typical townsmen, they

[1] Cf. esp. *The Cambridge Economic History of Europe,* ed. Postan, M., and Rich, E. E., Cambridge, England 1952, vol. II, chapter VI (by E. Carus-Wilson).

now saw their industry migrating to the open country, to the flowing rivers which supplied the motive force for the fly-wheels. Their source of livelihood dried up, and a whole train of miseries was set in motion. Gloom descended, and not just gloom, but gloom without a ray of hope. Is it any wonder that eschatological moods and modes of thought spread through Fuller's Row everywhere? They inspired that outcrop of heresies which we find on all sides in the fourteenth, fifteenth and sixteenth centuries. The wool-carders' revolt of Florence in 1378 and the weavers' revolt of Ypres, Ghent and Bruges in 1379 were outward manifestations of an underlying condition which showed itself not only in revolutionary acts but also in revolutionary thoughts, and, given the generally religious character of thinking at the time, especially in sectarian thoughts, the sect being the revolutionary form of religious life.

This, humanly speaking, unhappy history was to repeat itself two hundred years later, in the eighteenth century. The very same phenomenon which had ruined the textile towns was now ruining the textile villages and textile valleys – technological progress. As the fuller's mill had thrown the foot-fuller out of work, and, indeed, out of society, so was the effect of the spinning-jenny on the hand-spinner and the power-loom on the handloom-weaver. Once again, gloom descended, deep, deep gloom; once again, there seemed no ray of hope. Or rather, there was no ray of hope in this world – there was only a ray of hope breaking in from another, higher and lighter sphere, from beyond, the hope which the field preachers were bringing, men like John Wesley and his crew, whose words were balm for many a distressed and despairing heart. As before, there was an underlying condition which led both to politically revolutionary acts, such as the wrecking of machines, and to religiously revolutionary thoughts, such as the great new sect of Methodism.

The case of the 'weavers' heresies'[1] is typical, not to say archetypal. It is only very rarely that the social scientist can come so close to identifying a proper cause-and-effect pattern as here. But the etiology of sectarianism is plain. When a group cannot feel happy and at home within its social matrix; when its position is depressed and its life-experience depressing; then it will strive to

[1] The expression is used by the economic historian Carus-Wilson, loc. cit., p. 399.

withdraw from the mental matrix of the surrounding society, and especially from its basic metaphysical and religious assertions and assumptions. Rejected, it will reject – what could be more logical? what is more easy to understand?

As every society has its own pariah or near-pariah group, so every society has its own variety of religious dissent: the given sects reflect and express the social problems present. In Russia, for instance, it was, up to 1917, the peasant class that constituted the lowest stratum of the population. Its existence was joyless, its work hard and its burdens heavy. Consequently it proved a good recruiting ground for all manner of sectarian movements. 'The adherents of the sects were almost all peasants,' Curtiss reports, 'with a few townsmen, chiefly of humble origin.'[1] This general judgement is borne out by more specific observations. The first historian of the Dukhobortsy, O. M. Novitsky, wrote as follows: 'Wherever they went, it was not the rich, but the poor and humble, the peasantry and the workers, that welcomed their teaching. The educated knew them not, and it was rare even for a merchant to join them.' In the same way, the propaganda of the Molokane was successful mainly 'among the labouring classes'.[2] Sometimes we are even fortunate enough to find something like statistical information, though the word must not be used in a wide sense. A governmental commission appointed in 1733 to study the Khlysty, which reported about its findings in 1739, tracked down and condemned 303 persons. Among them were more than a hundred peasants, eighty monks, presumably also of peasant origin, about fifty artisans and merchants, but only one person of noble status, a white raven mentioned by name. The rest of the group could not be caught, and hence not further described. The drive against the same sect which lasted from 1745 to 1757 netted 454 persons, among them over 300 peasants, 70 monks, nuns, novices and low-placed clergy, about 50 artisans and merchants, but only two noblemen.[3]

In spite of Novitsky's remark about the rarity of merchants among the Russian dissenters, we find this group (as already the

[1] Curtiss, J. S., *Church and State in Russia,* New York 1940, p. 155.

[2] Conybeare, loc. cit., pp. 268 and 316.

[3] Grass, K. K., *Die russischen Sekten,* Leipzig 1905–1914, vol. I, pp. 117, 118, 137, 138. Grass's two volumes, of 716 and 1,016 pages respectively, are the most valuable collection of documents we possess.

figures just quoted have shown) in fact strongly represented in at least some of the sects. Not only are there merchants, but they are often rich merchants, proper capitalists even, such as the Gromovs (in the timber trade) and the Kovylins (in the brick trade)[1]; and not only are they sectarians, but sometimes extreme sectarians, for instance, Skoptsy. 'The Skoptsy are frequently money-changers or petty bankers,' Grass has emphasized. 'They like to carry on the banking business . . . Because of their economic habits of life, their industry and their childlessness, masses of capital easily accumulate in their hands.'[2] Of the Khlysty we are told: 'Having rich merchants among their converts, they never want funds. A single rich convert has been known to rebuild an entire village which had been burned down, merely because there were a few Khlysty in it.'[3] Reports about the Old Believers give a similar picture. In Siberia, around Ekaterinaburg, for instance, we are informed, 'many rich merchants and citizens belong to the sect'.[4]

The Western observer, used to regarding the rich as the upper class *par excellence*, may be inclined to see in these reports a strong disproof of our basic thesis, namely that the sects are the religious expression of social dissatisfaction and sentiments of revolt, outgrowths of the class struggle, organizations of the lower classes, tools of their aggressiveness. But it must be remembered here that in a feudal society capitalists *are* outcasts, in spite of their wealth, and that, just because of their wealth, they are apt to be a particularly rebellious set. 'Our former merchant,' Dostoevsky says in his *Diary*,[5] 'notwithstanding the role which everywhere in Europe capital and the millionaires have played, in Russia, comparatively speaking, occupied a rather insignificant place in the social hierarchy. . . . Only a few individuals from among . . . the merchants [have] found their way into the category of "[the] best men", and the nobility [has] continued to head the nation . . . A general, for instance, was so highly esteemed that even the richest merchant deemed it a great honour to have him in his home for dinner.' And then he adds a sentence which is much more revealing than a whole volume of statistics could possibly be: 'Even recently I read

[1] Conybeare, loc. cit., pp. 132 and 153; cf. also p. 135.

[2] Grass, loc. cit., vol. II, p. 883.

[3] Conybeare, loc. cit., p. 360.

[4] Ibid., p. 104.

[5] Dostoevsky, F., *The Diary of a Writer*, transl. Brasol, B., New York 1949, vol. I, pp. 482 and 484.

an anecdote – which I should not have believed, if I had not known that it was perfectly true – about a Petersburg lady belonging to the *beau monde* who, at a concert, publicly drove from her seat a merchant-woman, worth ten millions, occupied her place, and in addition gave her a scolding – and this occurred only some thirty years ago.'

The merchants, then, were, and had every reason to regard themselves as, a despised and depressed class. Yet their wealth was not without influence on their religious attitudes. When capitalism began to wax strong in the land and the social status of the rich, and even of the *nouveaux riches*, began slowly to improve, while the peasant masses remained in abject poverty and serfdom, a characteristic rift appeared between the two strata. 'In every country, trade and wealth engenders the instinct to uphold church and state,' Conybeare says, and he is right with regard to the Russia that was finally turning from feudalism to capitalism, though less right with regard to the old-style Muscovy. 'One is therefore prepared to learn that it was chiefly among dissenting shopkeepers in Russia that an inclination to pray for the Tsar showed itself. The Russian peasant, on the other hand, remained obdurate. Thus on 23 January 1864, when division of opinion about the matter revealed itself in a general meeting of the Popovtsy [i.e. the Old Believers] . . . only ten persons were in favour of offering up in the liturgy a prayer for the Tsar, the peasants and poorer citizens going against it *en masse* . . .'[1]

From Russia it is most instructive to move to England because the two countries are both characteristically similar and characteristically different. They are similar because they each have produced a great deal of religious dissent; and they are different because Russian society remained largely stagnant through the centuries, while English society ran through several successive developmental phases, each of which had its own discontented minorities and therefore also its own appropriate sectarian movements. But we may, on the way, cast a brief glance at another precapitalist country, seventeenth-century Scotland. Sir Walter Scott, in his great novel, *Old Mortality*, has characterized the situation between the skirmish of Drumclog and the battle of Bothwell Brig, in the struggle between Episcopalians and Covenanters, in the following words: 'The royalists . . . were not

[1] Conybeare, loc. cit., pp. 178 and 179.

numerous, but were respectable from their fortune and influence, being chiefly landed proprietors of ancient descent. . . . On the other hand the towns, the villages, the farm-houses, the properties of small heritors sent forth numerous recruits to the Presbyterian interest.'[1] How neat this confrontation is! yet hardly neater than it was in life. The fighting fronts between religious groupings are rarely less well defined than those between political parties or adversaries in the economic field.

Turning now to England, we can say, with a little harmless simplification, that each succeeding century produced a major sectarian formation, besides, of course, a number of minor ones: the sixteenth, the Baptists; the seventeenth, the Quakers; the eighteenth, the Methodists; the nineteenth, the Salvation Army; the twentieth, the Jehovah's Witnesses. The latter movement, though formally founded in 1872, hardly made its impact before 1900 or even 1910. All these new starts were necessary, not only because sects invariably degenerate and decline, but also because new classes appeared on the scene with grievances of their own which demanded new forms of expression and new doctrines of consolation.

From the sociological point of view, there is a fairly well defined dividing line between the Anabaptists and Baptists on the one hand, and the Quakers, the Methodists and the Salvation Army on the other. The background and framework of the three newer movements is the rapidly unfolding national economy of capitalism, that of the older groupings, however, was still the petty medieval town. Significantly, Quakerism, Methodism and Salvationism are specifically English phenomena, whereas the Baptist movement was not precisely international in the sense in which the word is commonly used, but interlocal, appearing everywhere the class conflicts of medieval urbanism had come to a head. Its centres abroad were such cities as Strassburg, Zürich, Basle, Cologne, Osnabrück, Leyden, and above all Münster whose sorry history in the fifteen-thirties has often been retold. In view of the extravagances which characterized the goings-on in the 'New Jerusalem', the English Baptists have, not surprisingly, evinced a tendency to claim that their origin had little or nothing to do with continental Baptism. This is, however, hardly a thesis which can

[1] Scott, Sir W., *Old Mortality*, chapter XX, *ad finem*. Woodstock ed., New York n.d., p. 186.

be sustained. On the contrary, there was a good deal of coming and going, on the part of the sectarians, between the island and the continent. The joiner Christopher Vitell of Southwark, whose preaching sowed religious revolt all over southern England, was a native of Delft who only later settled in or near London; and although he formally belonged to the 'Family of Love' rather than to the Baptists proper, his message was a rich confusion to which Baptism owed something, if not indeed a great deal. Both John Smyth, the Se-Baptist, or self-baptizer, who started English Baptism, and Thomas Helwys, its other father-figure, spent longish spells in the Netherlands. It was easy then to move from town to town; a townsman was at home in any town; and one reason why this was so, was the presence in all of them of roughly the same social conflicts.

By the end of the Middle Ages, the towns had produced a painful division between the smug and satisfied strata of the merchants and master artisans, called, in Zürich, by a happy term, *die Ehrbarkeit* (the respectability), and the highly dissatisfied journeymen who could no longer hope one day to climb up the social scale, but were to all intents and purposes a permanent proletariat. All urban classes were against the old religion because the city was something of an alien body in the body of feudalism, and the citizens rejected both the – at the time not yet modernized – faith of Rome and the social order with which they saw it co-ordinated. But their attitude to the new religion – to Protestantism – was not the same. It gave the rich all they wanted, but it made the poor feel cheated and betrayed. Luther, and even Zwingli and Calvin, were partisans of order. Luther's was the kings' and princes' Reformation; Zwingli's and Calvin's was in effect, whatever else it may have been in design, the Reformation of the arrived or rising bourgeois classes; there was a need for a poor men's Reformation as well, and that proletarian Reformation was Anabaptism and Baptism.

We have already mentioned that Christopher Vitell was a joiner. 'The Anabaptist leaders... were tailors, smiths, shoemakers and carpenters.'[1] Journeymen-weavers were particularly prominent. In Salzburg, there is talk of a wallet-maker, a girdle-maker, a shoelatchet-maker. Melchior Hoffmann was a skinner; Jan Matthys a baker; Jan Bockelson a tailor who had tried to set up as

[1] Bax, E. B., *The Rise and Fall of the Anabaptists*, London 1903, pp. 330 and 331.

a cloth-merchant and gone bankrupt. Hans Brödli in Zollikon, near Zürich, and Simon Stumpf in Basle preached mainly on the Pauline precept that all should earn their bread by the work of their hands. To men of this mark, infant baptism, administered by learned predicants, appeared to be no more than a formal reception into an unredeemed society; the baptism of adult believers, on the other hand, bestowed by anybody, was a demonstrative separation from a wicked world, a revolutionary rite in a religious form. Bernt Rothmann of Münster, an intellectual himself, but the son of a smith, taught in his *Restitution, or Setting up anew of just and wholesome Christian Doctrine, Faith and Life* (October 1534) that only the lowly and unlearned had a messianic mission to fulfil; Luther and Zwingli were to him no better than Erasmus, a bookman and Catholic.

The development of lower-class religiosity in England ran parallel to that on the Continent, though there was a lag of about two generations. 'Towards the end of Elizabeth's reign, small groups appeared,' writes the historian of the English Baptists, 'who had come to feel how hopeless it was to stay within the State Church. . . . They reverted to the sect-type of Christianity and maintained that the Church should consist of men and women who had consciously dedicated themselves to Christ and His service', in contrast to the 'parish churches of which men were members from their birth or baptism as infants'.[1] Many of these sectarian groupings ended up in the fold of Congregationalism, but some also in the fold of Baptism. While the remarkable leader of the latter, Thomas Helwys (of Broxtowe Hall in Nottinghamshire) was a person of quality, his immediate successor, John Murton, was a furrier.[2] Of yet later leaders of the 'General Baptists', Henry Adis was an upholsterer and John Belcher a bricklayer, of the 'Particular Baptists' John Spilsbury a cobbler and William Kiffin a brewer, a trade which he himself termed 'a very mean calling'.[3] Other equally mean callings encountered among the early Baptist preachers are tailors, leather-sellers, soap-boilers, weavers, and tinkers. One tract written against them refers sarcastically to 'Mr. Patience, an honest glover, Mr. Griffin, a reverent taylor, Mr. Knowles, a learned "scholler", Mr. Spilsby, a renowned cobbler, Mr. Barber, a button-maker, and divers others', and another tract

[1] Underwood, A. C., *A History of the English Baptists*, ed. London 1956, p. 32.
[2] Ibid., p. 48. [3] Ibid., pp. 48, 91, 94, 60.

to 'Greene the felt-maker, Spencer the horse-rubber, Quartermine the brewer's clarke', all of them 'ignorant coxcombes', yet 'mighty sticklers in the new kind of talking trade',[1] i.e. sectarian preaching. As far as social provenance and human type are concerned, the English Baptists were very much the same people as the continental Anabaptists.

Structurally, the situation around the middle of the seventeenth century was similar to that prevailing a hundred years earlier. Again there are three layers, as it were, on top the Anglicans, comparable to the Catholics on the Continent, in the middle the Presbyterians and Independents, parallel to the Calvinists abroad, a group, according to Clarendon's *History*, 'followed by the most substantial and wealthy citizens',[2] and underneath a dark, simmering mass of discontent, recruited from the lowest social stratum of the day, but particularly strong and vocal in the Cromwellian army. 'The Presbyterians,' so Selbie has summed up the situation, 'were all for the maintenance of the monarchy, and were generally on the side of the gentry and the established order. They looked on the army as representing sectarianism and democracy in the most objectionable form. . . . But meanwhile feeling in the army was getting out of hand. The religious spirit there . . . became more and more intolerant of the royal delays and deceits on the one hand, and the mild measures proposed by the Presbyterian majority in Parliament on the other. Certain regiments broke out into open mutiny.'[3] There were the Fifth Monarchy Men and the Ranters and the Levellers and the Diggers and a whole host of others, but when the first fermentation was over and the new nonconformity settled down into more abiding forms, it was the Society of Friends, *vulgo* the Quakers, who emerged as the prime incarnation of this age's spirit of religious (and social!) revolt.

Gooch has given a graphic description of the conditions in the country around 1649, those conditions which plagued the broad masses everywhere, even though the outcry about them came mainly from the rankers in the army. 'Though the working classes had stood aloof from the great struggle,' i.e. the Civil War, he

[1] Ibid., pp. 76 and 86.

[2] Clarendon, Edward Earl of, *The True Historical Narrative of the Rebellion and Civil Wars in England,* book X, p. 175, ed. Macray, W. D., *The History of the Rebellion,* Oxford 1888, vol. IV, p. 311.

[3] Selbie, W. B., *English Sects,* n.d., pp. 89, 90, 91.

writes, 'they shared the general expectation that the establishment of the Republic would usher in the era of reform. The rise of prices . . . was followed but slowly by the increase of wages. And the hardship was heightened by the monopoly prices demanded for many of the necessities of life. To these chronic evils was added, during the fifth decade of the century, that of a series of unusually bad harvests. The war, too, had brought with it on the one hand a large increase of taxation, and, on the other, the intolerable vexation of free quarter. And though the miserable condition of the poor was constantly discussed . . . no improvement was being effected.'[1] 'At this very day poor people are forced to work for 4d. a day, and corn is dear. And the tithing priest stops their mouth and tells them that "inward satisfaction of mind" was meant by the declaration "the poor shall inherit the earth",' Gerard Winstanley wrote in *The Curse and Blessing that is in Mankind*. It was not so that he understood the Gospel promise: 'I tell you, the scripture is to be really and materially fulfilled. . . . You jeer at the name of Leveller. I tell you, Jesus Christ is the head Leveller.'[2]

Of all the incarnations of this levelling spirit which dreamt of, and aimed at, a radical democratization of England, the Quakers had the most lasting impact. They were the reservoir, so to speak, in which all the turbulent waters finally collected and found form and rest. The first fact that strikes the observer about this movement is its national character – not, of course, in the sense of nationalism, for in an age in which the national state, the Leviathan, was in the ascendant, internationalism, in the sense of pacifism, was a natural plank in a revolutionary platform, but national in the sense of all-English, not narrowly confined to the towns and not closely paralleled abroad. Capitalism was now ready to develop in the whole island, and its centres were often in industrial villages rather than in towns – on the open Yorkshire fells rather than within the walls of York; and it was ready to develop as yet only in this island and not yet in other countries abroad. It was this situation – its emergence from a half-formed proletariat of a half-formed capitalism – which set its mark on the early Quaker meetings.

To those who know our Quakers today – a progressive group

[1] Gooch, G. P., *The History of English Democratic Ideas in the Seventeenth Century*, Cambridge 1898, pp. 212 and 213.
[2] Cit. ibid., p. 220.

indeed, but by no means revolutionary, and above all very, very well-to-do – it may seem strange that we should try to depict them as originally a typical lower class, indeed, lowest class, movement. Yet Pagitt's assertion, in his *Heresiography*, that they were 'made up of the dregs of the common people',[1] though harsh, is not entirely unjustified. A remarkable list of London Quakers married in 1680 gives the following professions: 'Mariner, weaver, farmer, cordwainer, clothier, shoemaker, schoolmaster, tallow-chandler, joiner, bricklayer, rope-maker, merchant, strong-water seller, yeoman, blacksmith, labourer, salter, ironmonger, cheesemonger, cooper, fellmonger, pin-maker, wire-drawer, silk-stocking frame-work knitter, plasterer, baker, glazier, fruiterer, haberdasher, car man, timber-merchant, dyer.'[2] In this list only the clothier and the merchant look at all like more substantial men; the rest of the bridegrooms are decidedly small fry. 'Friends were drawn principally from the trading and yeomen classes, though there were also some artisans and labourers, a fair number of merchants and a few gentry,' their own historian, W. C. Braithwaite, has written. 'When Margaret Fell wrote to the King about the Fifth Monarchy imprisonments, she pointed out the loss to the nation, "If you continue and go on to take so many thousands of poor husbands and tradesmen from their husbandry and callings . . ." These classes supplied the main strength of Quakerism, and the movement, with its plainness of speech and dress, seemed a low and mean thing to persons of education or position.'[3] Elsewhere in the book,[4] Braithwaite speaks of 'prosperous yeoman stock', and this would put a somewhat different complexion upon the matter. But quite apart from the fact that yeomen were no gentry, i.e. were not members of England's ruling rural class, the sympathies of the Quaker founder, Fox, were with an even lower stratum: 'He saw the abuses that resulted from the power which the justices then possessed of fixing agricultural wages . . . The Statute of Apprentices (1563) had required the justices to do this every year at the Easter quarter-sessions, and, in so far as it was put in force, it lent itself to great oppression, although originally intended to bring the statutory wages into correspondence with the increasing cost of living . . . At Mansfield he spoke to the justices against the oppression

[1] Cit. Gooch, p. 272.
[2] Lloyd, A., *Quaker Social History*, London 1950, p. 77.
[3] Loc. cit., p. 512. [4] Ibid., p. 154.

caused by fixing a legal wage for farm-labourers below what was equitable.'[1]

But what specious proof do we need for the revolutionary character of Quakerism? If ever there was a group that openly demonstrated its condemnation of the class division of society, it is this. Men who do not doff their caps even to the richest and most respectable, who will say 'thee' and 'thou' to anybody, who will be kicked and beaten rather than pay hat-honour or word-honour to anybody, are as egalitarian as anybody has ever been, latter-day Communists not excluded.

All in all, the casual entry against Malton in the Episcopal Returns for 1669 – 'Quakers very numerous, mean quality' – seems to state the facts fairly and squarely.[2] But a low social status does not necessarily imply a low standard of living, and the Quakers seem, by and large, to have had what it takes to keep body and soul together. Their rebelliousness appears to have been due more to political than to economic underprivilege. In this respect, the situation around 1750 was different from that around 1650. One cannot but shudder when one reads the following passages from John Wesley's pen: 'I have known one [woman] picking up from a dunghill stinking spratts, and carrying them home for herself and her children. I have known another gathering bones which the dogs had left in the streets and making broth of them to prolong a wretched life.'[3] By now the first wave of capitalism had gone across the country and produced that system of domestic industry which is its early classical embodiment. On the human plane it meant misery for thousands, above all long hours of work and low wages for it. But not only was the system of domestic industry a hard one, it was also unstable. As the century wore on, a series of great mechanical inventions came to undermine it, culminating in the steam engine which spelled the end of production in small isolated homesteads and the beginning of production in large integrated workshops. As Max Weber has expressed it, manufacture was ousted by machinofacture. The former process was reversed: industry migrated back from villages to towns, producing those monstrous conurbations of miserable hovels which still disfigure, for instance, the north of England. 'Working men,

[1] Ibid., pp. 522 and 49. [2] Ibid., p. 77, note 3.

[3] Cit. Cameron, R. M., *Methodism and Society in Historical Perspective,* New York and Nashville 1961, pp. 65 and 66.

drawn from the most distant quarters, were agglomerated by thousands in great towns, bound to their employers by no other tie than that of interest, exposed to the fever of an immensely stimulated competition, and to the trying ordeal of sudden, rapid, and unforeseen fluctuations in their wages and their employments.'[1] Thus to a low standard of living was added a high degree of insecurity, and between them they produced what Lecky has termed 'restless discontent', 'most dangerous symptoms of revolution'.[2]

One feature which particularly characterized – indeed, disfigured – this age was the almost total human estrangement between the various strata of society. Lecky's great book speaks of a 'movement of disintegration, breaking the ties of sympathy' – he might have said: the last ties of sympathy – 'between class and class'.[3] And he quotes a source which truly deserves to be quoted. When Countess Selina of Huntingdon, a most extraordinary person, joined the Methodists and told her friends about it, the Duchess of Buckingham wrote to her: 'I thank your ladyship for the information concerning the Methodist preachers. Their doctrines are most repulsive and strongly tinctured with impertinence . . . It is monstrous to be told that you have a heart as sinful as the common wretches that crawl the earth. This is highly offensive and insulting and I cannot but wonder that your ladyship should relish any sentiments so much at variance with high rank and good breeding.'[4]

We can, in these symptomatic sentences, touch, almost physically, the root-cause of all sectarianism. When they were written, the Duchess of Buckingham and those whom Rowland Hill described as 'a ragged legion of preaching barbers, cobblers, tinkers, scavengers, draymen and chimney-sweepers'[5] were as yet members of one religious body, the Church of England. But what meaning was there left in this association? It is almost a definition of a church to say that those who belong to it acknowledge that their hearts are equally sinful. But this the Duchess of Buckingham would not do. Social division had burst, nay abolished, religious community, and it was but a logical step, however reluctantly taken, for the Methodists to start a religious organization of their own.

[1] Lecky, W. E. H., *A History of England in the Eighteenth Century*, New York 1878, vol. II, pp. 692 and 693.
[2] Ibid. [3] Ibid. [4] Cit. ibid., p. 671. [5] Cit. ibid., p. 651.

So highly charged was the atmosphere with religious rebelliousness that even some decaying sectarian movements experienced a remarkable renascence. The 'General' Baptists of the 'New Connexion' appeared and made headway in the lace and hosiery towns of the Midlands, and the woollen and cotton towns of Yorkshire and Lancashire.[1] In the main city of the latter county, in Manchester, the Quakers gave birth to the Shakers, another protest movement of the wretchedly poor. Their prophetess, Ann Lee, as a girl worked in a cotton mill and later as a cutter of hatter's fur. Like herself, 'the early Shakers came mainly from the lower middle class groups. They were rooted in revolt: revolt against smugness and bigotry in religion, revolt against social and economic evils, revolt against the uglier side of human nature'.[2] But neither the New Connexion variety of the General Baptists nor the Shaker variety of the Quakers had the right message: the right message, the 'right' religion for the new proletariat, had to be the diametrical opposite of the 'wrong' religion of the upper classes. And as this was a religion of the head, it had to be a religion of the heart. This was precisely what Methodism provided. To the social gulf which was fixed between affluence and poverty, there soon corresponded a mental chasm between rationalizing and emotional religiosity.

The recruiting ground of early Methodism can almost be identified on contemporary urban maps. Where the toilers dwelt, there the chapels came to be. Apart from the ever-important textile districts, there were, for instance, the mining regions. 'All subterraneous places belonged to them,' declared Sidney Smith.[3] 'The weavers of Bristol, the miners of Kingswood, the colliers and keelmen of Cornwall and Staffordshire and Wales – these were the groups whence Methodism drew most of its converts.'[4] As for Staffordshire, it was, however, less the mining and the transport industries than the manufacture of china and earthenware goods that was affected; the pottery towns became almost exclusively abodes of Wesleyanism, and its presence and influence are still felt in the picture drawn of them in Arnold Bennett's *Old Wives' Tale* (1908). But there is no need to run through the different districts and industries; the voice of John Wesley was no stranger to any of

[1] Cf. Underwood, loc. cit., p. 157.

[2] Melcher, M. F., *The Shaker Adventure*, Princeton 1941, p. 5.

[3] Lecky, loc. cit., p. 655.

[4] Niebuhr, loc. cit., p. 60.

them. It is more the common denominator of all the various workers' groupings that matters here, and that common denominator was impecuniousness. When it was suggested that every Methodist should pay a penny a week towards the costs of the class meetings, there were objections: a penny a week was much too much . . .[1]

It is true that Wesley succeeded in catching, here and there, a member of the upper classes. As Cowper proudly announces:

> 'We boast some rich ones whom the Gospel sways,
> And one who wears a coronet and prays.'[2]

But that one (Lord Dartmouth) did not make a crowd, any more than one swallow makes a summer. The facts can best be elucidated if we distinguish within Methodism (the broader movement) the three narrower streams running side by side which tended increasingly to separate themselves from each other: Evangelicalism, Calvinistic Methodism, and Wesleyanism in the proper sense of the word. Evangelicalism embraced not a few moneyed people, like the so-called Clapham Saints, but – characteristically, *most* characteristically! – it remained in the Church of England. Calvinistic Methodism – 'Lady Huntingdon's Connexion' – was socially more mixed, but it was Wesleyanism, far and away the most numerous group – not without reason very often simply identified with Methodism – which attracted and embraced the indigent and is thus the sectarian movement of the eighteenth century *par excellence*. 'You are a low, insignificant people,' Wesley said to his followers. 'You are poor almost to a man, having no more than the plain necessaries of life.'[3] And so indeed it was.

Wellman J. Warner has done excellent research into the social composition of the group which can be described as the spearhead of the Wesleyan–Methodist movement, and his results show exactly the pattern which, on general grounds, one has to expect. Among the early class-founders and class-leaders he encountered the following types: a poor pedlar, an impoverished widow, a family servant, a carpenter, a schoolmaster–shepherd, a retired

[1] Cameron, loc. cit., p. 41, note 17.

[2] 'Truth', lines 377 and 378. *The Poetical Works of William Cowper, ed.* Milford, H. S., London 1959, p. 39.

[3] 'Advice to the People called Methodists', *Works*, ed. Emory, J., New York 1853, vol. V, p. 250.

soldier, an upholsterer, a tailor, a tanner, a piecemaker, a handloom weaver, a cordwainer, a cooper, a grocer–breadbaker, a brazier; among the early local preachers a collier, a brass cutter, a toy-maker, a farmer, a baker, a cabinet-maker, a printer, a schoolmaster; among the regular preachers, a survey of sixty-three biographies revealed that six were farmers' sons, three the sons of labourers, two each the sons of clothiers, shopkeepers, building workers and publicans, and one each of members of the following trades: woollen manufactory, pilchard fishery, masonry, tanning, carpentry, shoemaking, cutlery and other similar occupations. 'Practically all of the regular preachers,' Warner concludes, 'were drawn from a single social stratum, located between unskilled labour and the middle class.'[1]

The last words, though strictly true, are apt to be misinterpreted. Cameron, for instance, comments as follows: 'Almost none of the regular preachers came from the upper classes, and, contrary to the current opinion, none from the lowest.'[2] Yet other writers have gone still further and concluded that there was, from the beginning, something almost middle-class-ish about the Methodists, and they have even suggested, on the strength of such impressions, that 'not all sects originate in the lower classes'.[3] Such assertions, however, betray, so far as the Methodists are concerned, a lack of historical perspective. That many of the early Methodists (and Quakers and Baptists, etc.) had skills, does not mean that they were above the lowest classes; it means rather that, in the circumstances, they were among the lowest classes. Unskilled persons have existed at all times, and at all times they have been ranked beneath the skilled. But, in the eighteenth century, they were not yet the numerous, widespread and compact class which they became when the development of the factory system made skills unnecessary. The domestic industry presupposed skill on the part of the operatives; to be a proletarian meant to be an *artisan* working for a capitalist employer – working for him at home, with one's own tools, not in his workshop and at his machines. Perhaps

[1] Warner, W. J., *The Wesleyan Movement in the Industrial Revolution,* London 1930, pp. 263, 259, 260, 249, 250.

[2] Cameron, loc. cit., p. 41. Cf. also the interesting list of the Trustees of the New Chapel in London, given, with occupations, in Church, loc. cit., pp. 82, 83.

[3] Cf. Lincoln, C. E., *The Black Muslims in America,* Boston 1961, p. 215, and the literature adduced ibidem, p. 267, note 9.

the facts can best be expressed in the language of the eighteenth century itself. The Methodists belonged to the third estate which was the basis and the bottom of the social structure. As yet there was no fourth estate to give it a relatively higher ranking. When that fourth estate appeared, all was changed. But then a new sect movement was needed to cater for the new poor, for the poor, we might say, who had come to be beneath the poor – beneath those poor who had opened their hearts to John Wesley's call.

Another hundred years on, and this capitalist situation, the stage of classical capitalism, has been reached. William Booth, the father of the Salvation Army, started life as a Methodist preacher, but he found it impossible to contact the strata in which he was interested within and through the Methodist movement – not even within and through those parts of it which had least fallen victim to advancing respectability. Perhaps we are not unduly over-simplifying when we say that Methodism as a whole had by now become identified with the lower or lowest middle class, while the new proletariat, and especially the *Lumpenproletariat*, was beyond its reach. What Booth's 'Christian Mission', founded in the East End of London in 1865, set out to do was to evangelize the semi- and un-skilled factory workers, especially those in casual employment, especially also those to whose wages there was no minimum line. Booth himself has described the social circumstances out of which the Salvation Army arose in his unspeakably depressing book *In Darkest England* (1890); but Marx's *Capital*, vol. I, published in 1867, also reflects them to perfection. As yet, the 'New Unionism' which, after 1871, organized the hitherto unorganized and secured tolerable, and indeed progressively favourable, conditions even for those whose life had been intolerable, did not exist; as yet, the birthrate among the poorest was so high that no wage-earner could be above the poverty-line while he had a young family; as yet, there was no social legislation which would have cared for the sick and the old. Well might the *East London Evangelist* write in January 1869: 'Day by day, the mass of pauperism is becoming intensified. Hunger and misery reign supreme . . . .'[1]

They certainly reigned supreme among the silk-weavers of Spitalfields and Bethnal Green, many of whom were descended from Huguenot immigrants and hence had a sectarian tradition

[1] Cit. Sandall, T., *The History of the Salvation Army*, vol. I, London and Edinburgh 1947, p. 118.

behind them. Their *Communauté*, later called 'The Christian Community', provided a first and fundamental block of supporters for William Booth. Around these starvelings collected all the other flotsam and jetsam of the great metropolis – figures so low in status that nobody wanted to be associated with them. 'The converts came from all the lowest classes.' Addressing a Wesleyan body, Booth formulated his basic principle as follows: 'We go to the common people, to the publicans, the harlots, and thieves. We do not fish in other people's waters. No, out of the gutter we fish up our converts; and if there is one man worse than another, our people rejoice the most over the conversion of that man.'[1] These words are hardly over-dramatic. The Midnight Meeting Movement, for instance, started by Mrs. Booth in 1859, did indeed cast out its net for the 'fallen . . . women inmates of low lodging-houses in Spitalfields'.[2] But there were, of course, more substantial, and, so to speak, more regular sources of membership supply for the Salvation Army, such as the coal-heavers, the dockers and the navvies, three types of workers who had no skills but were essentially human beasts of burden. What was worst in their lives was perhaps not even the low standard of living with which they were afflicted – it was the dreadful insecurity of their livelihood. A docker, for instance, could never be sure in the morning that there would be work for him that day on the waterfront, a state of affairs which came to an end only under the Attlee Government's 'decasualization' legislation in the forties of this century.

For people of this description, the places of worship of the established religion had no attraction whatsoever. Lord Shaftesbury estimated in 1860 that not even 2 per cent of the working population of London attended any church. 'We found,' Booth wrote, 'that . . . the aversion of the working classes to churches and chapels was so strong as could readily be conceived.' Unfortunately the estrangement was mutual. The historian of the Salvation Army tells of a nonconformist minister, one W. Tyler, who was 'a man of the widest sympathies'; yet even he 'did not go further than to undertake to affiliate revival converts with his church as a branch fellowship. For "respectable" congregations to accept them as full fellow-members was another matter'. Here was a case where the

[1] Cit. Coates, Th. F. G., *The Prophet of the Poor,* New York 1906, pp. 90, 119, 120.

[2] Sandall, loc. cit., p. 25.

prophet had to go to the mountain; the mountain assuredly would not come to the prophet. Booth and his fellow-workers descended into the morass where alone they could catch the coal-heavers and the navvies. They preached in places like the Oriental Theatre in Poplar, 'a dirty, draughty and comfortless place of the lowest description', full of 'grievous stenches' – the sort of place 'decent people won't come to'.[1] As the Methodist Chapel had once displaced the Quaker Meeting House, so the Salvationist Citadel was now displacing the Methodist Chapel as the centre of the most popular form of religion, and both shifts were equally the reflection of social rather than of purely religious evolutions.

With the progressive chastening of capitalism – the coming of effective trade unions, the coming of the small family pattern, the coming, too, of far-reaching labour and welfare legislation – the social scene accepted a new look, and the old sources of sectarianism began to flow less copiously. Yet they did not dry up altogether. During the 1930s, when the economic crisis spread gloom through the working classes, fresh dissenting groups were beginning to spring up or to spread out. Such was the Elim Foursquare Gospel Church. 'It arose [in Ireland] in an atmosphere of insecurity . . . and it spread, by use of revivalist techniques, in England and Wales in the period of economic unrest and depression . . . These were times when hopes and aspirations were transferred from this world to the next, or when the sudden termination of this dispensation by cataclysmic events was a more congenial prospect than it could ever be in prosperous times.' This kind of 'pentecostalism is predominantly the religion of working-class and poor people. . . . There are few who have attained much in the world who are drawn to Pentecostalism; it is a religious expression of those who might be termed "disinherited" . . . Elim's converts . . . are drawn from the lower social classes . . . Elim people . . . are prepared usually to recognize themselves as "the low and the least", and rejoice in the many biblical promises made to this class'.[2] Clearly, Elim is yet another link in the chain reaching down from the early Baptists, a chain which will not come to an end until all misery and degradation is eradicated.

Still, the misery and degradation which is the ever-active cause

[1] Sandall, loc. cit., pp. 53, 69, 74.

[2] Wilson, B. R., *Sects and Society*, London and Berkeley 1961, pp. 15, 42, 105, 106, 107.

of sectarian sentiments and organizations has, in all probability, ceased to be mainly social and economic, and has become progressively personal and psychological. It is now less the hungry than the lonely who long for the consolations which are offered by the special religiosity of the deprived and depressed. Besides low social status and bad living conditions, other factors have always played their part, and some of them appear to be rising into greater prominence. We must give them all due attention. But before we do so, we must make sure that the socio-economic aspect is not unduly undervalued There has recently been a tendency in this direction which should be carefully examined.

CHRISTIAN SCIENCE: AN INSTRUCTIVE SPECIAL CASE

In a book of unusual merit, *Sects and Society*, Bryan R. Wilson has taken up the discussion of Christian Science, and though he agrees that, in general, 'the frequently posited relationship between socio-economic conditions and religious expression' – and, more specifically, between poverty and sectarianism – is supported by the data,[1] he would make an exception here. He speaks of 'a basically hedonistic faith . . . concerned almost entirely with this-worldly well-being', and asserts that 'it accepts . . . the institutionalized value-system', and that 'its ethos is one of contentment with the established order of political and economic arrangements'.[2] There is no doubt whatever that Christian Science has in fact become what Dr. Wilson says it is; there can be no quarrel about the present condition. But the question arises whether it has always been as we find it now: the analysis of origins is vitally important. And if we go to the root of the phenomenon, we see that it is a confirmation of, and not an exception to, the rule that sects are basically religious groupings which *reject* the social environment in which they come to life.

First of all, the Christian Science movement took its rise, not in the rich and sophisticated city of Boston to which it later migrated, but in the poverty-stricken and utterly un-sophisticated shoe-manufacturing town of Lynn. Both the first patients and the first pupils of Mrs. Eddy were 'mostly humble shoe workers from the factories of that town . . . with horizons somewhat bounded by the

[1] Wilson, loc. cit., p. 317.

[2] Ibid., pp. 319, 320 and 179. Cf. also the clear summing-up on p. 317.

little world they moved in'. Among her early favourites, Richard Kennedy was a box-maker, George Tuttle a seaman, Daniel Harrison Spofford first a farmhand and then a shoe-operative, Hiram S. Craft also a shoe-operative, Edward J. Arens a carpenter, Calvin Frye a machinist, and even Asa G. Eddy had had, as a boy, to learn 'how to run the family loom' and rose no higher as a grown man than to being a sewing-machine agent in East Boston. 'In later years,' Mrs. Eddy's biographer reports, 'she took pride in the wealth of her congregation; and poverty in one of her followers came to be regarded as an error as serious as sickness or sin.' But at Lynn he sees her 'in the midst of . . . young artisans'.[1] Even as late as 1920, George Santayana, in *Character and Opinion in the United States*, ranked Chistian Science among the 'forms of popular religion' which he stigmatized as 'thoroughly plebeian'.[2]

But not only was Christian Science geographically the product of a proletarian environment, it was also historically the continuation of a sectarian tradition. The medical man has ever been an upper class figure, part and parcel of the establishment; in Victorian times, complete with top-hat and *favoris*, he was even something of an embodiment of respectability. To have healers of their own class was a not entirely unnatural desire of the lower strata. Characteristically, George Fox had pondered whether it would be better to become a preacher or a medical practitioner. 'In one of his first "openings", he records, the hidden virtues of all creation were made visible to him and all nature felt to be of good odour. He then debated with himself whether he should not apply this knowledge to the healing of the bodies of men and become a physician. He decided, however, that to minister to their souls was of greater importance and began his evangelical labours.'[3] Yet these labours did not prevent him from occasionally acting the healer, for we are told that he 'cured a deformed boy at Hawkshead by laying his hands on him and speaking to him'.[4] If George Fox thus anticipated Mrs. Eddy's profession, Mrs. Eddy, for her part, followed his general philosophy – a very sectarian one, it would seem.

For our third argument in support of the idea that Christian

[1] Dakin, E. F., *Mrs. Eddy,* ed. New York 1930, pp. 83, 86, 116, 70, 139, 173, 121, 120, 115, 88.

[2] Santayana, G., op. cit., New York 1920, p. 189.

[3] Huehns, loc. cit., p. 139.

[4] Braithwaite, loc. cit., p. 247. Cf. also pp. 341, 391, 565.

Science does not invalidate the thesis that sects, at their inception, are movements of the depressed, we have to anticipate a little (which will do no harm). Not only the poor were socially disadvantaged in Mrs. Eddy's day, but also the female sex, which may therefore be considered in this context as a class as well as a biological category. But the feminism of the Christian Science movement is one of its most striking attributes: it was part and parcel of what Basil Ransom, in *The Bostonians*, complainingly calls 'damnable feminization'.[1] If it was revolutionary in no other respect, it was revolutionary in that it tried to wrest the leadership in the religious sphere from the male powerholders and give it to the hitherto powerless, those whom St. Paul had bidden to be silent in churchly matters. 'We are witnessing the transfer of the Gospel from male to female trust,' said the Rev. George B. Day, C.S.B., in a sermon. 'Eighteen hundred years ago Paul declared that man was the head of the woman; but now, in *Science and Health*, it is asserted that "woman is the highest form of man".'[2] A transvaluation of values indeed! The last are made first. Here again Mrs. Eddy continued a well-defined sectarian tradition. It was one of the fundamental beliefs of the Shaker community that the deity was bi-sexual, and that its complete revelation and incarnation had therefore to be twofold: once in a male form, and once in a female. The male form was Jesus, the female Ann Lee. Mrs. Eddy met with these beliefs in her girlhood and had only one doubt, namely that it was Ann Lee who was the Saviour's female self.[3] While somewhat inhibited, she yet played with the idea that she herself was what the Shakeress had claimed to be; and this led to the illustration to be found in the first edition of Mrs. Eddy's poem, *Christ and Christmas* (1893), which showed her side by side with Christ. Not surprisingly, even her disciples found this a little embarrassing, and the edition was withdrawn.[4]

This feminism, not to say anti-masculinism, of Mrs. Eddy is all the more significant because it showed itself not only in religious-phantasmagoric, but also in practical-political forms: as Dr. Wilson

[1] James, H., op. cit., ed. The Modern Library, Random House, New York, 1956, p. 343 (ch. 34).

[2] Dakin, loc. cit., p. 194.

[3] Ibid., pp. 13, 192, 193, 194; Peel, R., *Christian Science*, New York 1958, pp. 24–9.

[4] Dakin, loc. cit., p. 539.

himself notes, she campaigned for women's votes.[1] Even if one underplays the fact that she was associated with underprivileged proletarians (which, however, she had been while at Lynn), one cannot overlook her siding with the underprivileged sex. But important as this argument is, the next (our fourth) is still more so. Around the year 1875, when *Science and Health* first appeared, American society was dominated by a rather rough and tough entrepreneurial and commercial class. This class had two opponents in the field: on the one hand, the working people of the kind you could find at Lynn, and on the other hand, the non-working, but also non-enterprising people you could find at Boston. There existed a small, but self-confident and vocal stratum which could economically be characterized as a *rentier* class and intellectually as a class of aesthetes, figures parallel to the Pre-Raphaelites or the Oscar Wilde set in England, who looked askance at the dominance of the country by the money-grabbers and countered the prevailing materialism by a hyper-idealism, or, to use the technical term, by a transcendentalism, which was as much anti-capitalist as any proletarian ideology. The greatest figure of this group was Ralph Waldo Emerson, but Bronson Alcott, too, was a leading representative. Now, Alcott befriended Mary Glover (as she then was known)[2] and thereby opened her eyes to the fact that she could catch fatter fish than the lean ones in the Lynn pond. Her decision to move to Boston was the consequence. This move was the making of her and her whole endeavour. Sociologically, a radical redirection now occurred. The erstwhile sub-bourgeois movement became supra-bourgeois: the already-since-a-while-rich replaced the never-to-be-rich; but the *rejection* of existing society remained; neither Mrs. Eddy's old friends at Lynn nor her new friends at Boston liked the just-becoming-rich, the *nouveaux riches* in the egg-shell. They were too money-mad for both of them.

That the reorientation, though radical, was relatively easy to accomplish, can be seen from the fact that even some of her poor disciples at Lynn had a sympathy for the rich refined set at Boston, as the proletarian ideologists *à la* Marx had a sympathy for the conservative-romantical ideologists *à la* Sismondi. About ten years before she met Alcott, 'Mrs. Glover had met a young shoe factory employee called Hiram S. Crafts who . . . had . . . come to Lynn . . . to follow his trade. . . . Shoemaker as he was, he had read

[1] Wilson, loc. cit., p. 179.

[2] Peel's book explores this friendship.

something of Emerson, had become interested in the idealistic philosophy of transcendentalism, and found hints in some of the things Mrs. Glover told him about [her mentor in spiritual healing] Quimby which made him want to learn more'.[1] Here, then, was a bridge which could quickly be crossed. What seems decisive in our discussion is the fact that the attitude to which Mrs. Eddy crossed over was a definitely anti-capitalist attitude.

Wilson's sentence which is most difficult to accept occurs on page 323 of his otherwise very penetrating book: 'Even the religious protest of Christian Science is not a protest against society as a whole.' Perhaps we can best show this assertion to be unjustifiable by holding against it a quotation from Santayana who called Christian Science 'a groan at the perpetual incubus of business'.[2] And Peel, too, is to be cited here. He is right, as is Santayana. 'Mrs. Glover,' he writes, 'lived for one purpose only: to bring her revelation of reality to a world sunk in materialism.'[3] In so far as contemporary capitalism was through-and-through materialistic – and who would deny that it was?! – Mrs. Glover's, i.e. Mrs. Eddy's, super-idealistic philosophy, like that of Emerson or Alcott (or Ruskin or Wilde), was anti-capitalistic.

It was precisely her association with a rentier class, a well-to-do but increasingly deposed and decomposed, and therefore disgruntled and alienated, set, which made Mrs. Eddy what Dr. Wilson shows her to have become – the prophet who appealed most 'to those who have blessings to enjoy in the world'.[4] The rentier is he who wants to enjoy in peace: the entrepreneur wants, not to enjoy, but to conquer. He accepts, he has to accept, war. And he cannot spend – he must save, for what else is capitalism but the formation, use, *and* preservation of capital? The capitalist class properly so called needs a hard ethos, an ethos of sustained effort and equally sustained discipline: it has therefore ever been Calvinist in outlook. But nothing is more anti-Calvinist than Christian Science. 'Those reared in the orthodox theology of the nineteenth century,' writes Dakin where he tries to explain Mrs. Eddy's success, 'had been brought up in fear and trembling before a God . . . whose worship was properly carried on only by denying oneself every natural human joy and pleasure. A release from such a God was for many people a greater boon than [even] release from

[1] Dakin, loc. cit., p. 70.
[2] Santayana, loc. cit.
[3] Peel, loc. cit., p. 66.
[4] Wilson, loc. cit., p. 212.

disease.'[1] This release *Science and Health* afforded in rich measure. But by displacing the God who commanded much work and no fun, it helped to knock away one of the supports on which contemporary society rested and relied. We would say, therefore, against Dr. Wilson, that precisely the religious protest of Christian Science was a protest against the surrounding society as a whole – against the ethos on which that society was established.

Of course, as the years passed, Christian Science became increasingly adjusted to its surrounding society, as other sects do and ever have done. Dr. Wilson rightly describes it as being now an upper-middle class and suburbanite denomination.[2] Other sects rise up in the world: Christian Science had first risen up and was later sinking down again. Its final resting place was, however, with and within the satisfied strata. The adjustment did not take place without its characteristic crises, and a brief glance at the most poignant of them will help to confirm our analysis. Probably Mrs. Eddy's most able as well as most devoted disciple was Mrs. Augusta Stetson, head of the movement in New York City. Her loyalty to headquarters was intense: yet she was expelled, hardly knowing what for. *We* know what for. The tension which sprang up between Mrs. Stetson and Mrs. Eddy was the tension between Boston and New York, old respectability and new, not always respectable, wealth. This one-time animosity has by now become a joking matter, but it was by no means entirely overcome in 1909 when the 'loving child Augusta' was excommunicated by her 'precious leader, teacher and guide'.[3] The issue, entrepreneurial-creative *versus* rentier-consumptive capitalist was still alive, and its very existence goes to show that even Christian Science (of the Eddy-Bostonian variety at any rate) was something of a protest movement in opposition to an established top-ranking class and its values and beliefs.[4]

[1] Dakin, loc. cit., p. 197.

[2] Cf. Wilson, esp. pp. 199 and 201.

[3] Dakin, pp. 494, 485, 489.

[4] We have inserted this excursus here because it helps us to develop and delineate our main thesis. But there is a more general problem involved, to which we would draw attention. Many sociologists, and not the worst of them by any means, when they come up against a phenomenon which is difficult to explain on the basis of current conceptions, abandon these conceptions and seek for new ones, instead of investigating whether what is needed is not simply a more judicious use of the old ones. Existing tools should not be lightly thrown away; they should rather be made sharper, if this is

ANOTHER INSTRUCTIVE SPECIAL CASE: THE CHRISTADELPHIANS

Besides the Christian Scientists, Dr. Wilson has singled out the roughly contemporaneous Christadelphian movement for close investigation. In this selection he has shown a very happy hand, for here we have indeed a particularly interesting sect formation. The excellent descriptive material put at our disposal can form the basis of a somewhat more daring analytical effort.

As all the facts go to prove, the Christadelphians were not just a proletarian grouping, but a grouping drawn from the *lowest* strata of the proletariat. At times the coffers were empty 'consequent on the large drain in relief of the poor' among the brethren; at times the ranks would thin out owing to the emigration of the more desperate. A writer in *Macmillan's Magazine* of August 1890, who sought them out in 'one of the most desolate and depressing of our London districts', noted that they were 'a little more gaunt' than their fellows, and called an 'expression of despondency habitual to many of them'. Their own leader F. G. Jannaway dubbed them, perhaps not without the characteristic inverted sectarian pride, 'despised and rejected of men', people 'outside the pale of social recognition'.[1] No wonder that they were filled with rebelliousness. 'Christadelphianism offered something of the same kind of ultimate goal as revolutionary socialism,' says Dr. Wilson, and the most prominent Christadelphian, Robert Roberts, admitted, at least by implication, that many of his friends had turned to the sect more for negative than for positive reasons: 'Such small headway as the truth has made in our day has been mainly among the poor and democratic, to whom the aggressive aspects of the truth's mission has presented more attraction than those that have to do with . . . spiritual excellence.'[2]

[1] Wilson, loc. cit., pp. 300–2.

[2] Ibid., p. 303.

at all possible. A case in point, in addition to the one discussed in the text, is Norman Cohn's assertion about the Skoptsy: 'Here is a millenarian movement which quite clearly cannot be interpreted in terms of class conflict.' (Cf. 'Medieval Millenarism', *Millennial Dreams in Action,* ed. Thrupp, S. L., The Hague 1962, pp. 40–1.) A closer consideration of the circumstances would soon teach Dr. Cohn that it can in fact very largely be interpreted in these terms. Cf. above, p. 13.

But against whom was this aggressiveness directed? It is the answer to this question that reveals why Christadelphianism is so interesting for the sociologist of religion. It was directed, not only against the rich, not only against the employers, but also, and as much, against the aristocracy of labour, against the well-to-do craftsmen, the factory foremen and the like. Besides London, the British city in which Christadelphianism has flourished most is Birmingham,[1] and Birmingham has a 'distinctive tradition . . . in labour relations. . . . The skilled workers of Birmingham enjoyed amicable relations with their employers . . . This,' Wilson rightly says, but probably understating the case, 'may have been unsatisfactory to the unskilled from among whom many Christadelphians were recruited . . . The absence of a revolutionary movement in economic and political spheres' due to the relatively contented outlook of the top layer of the local labour force, 'may have promoted interest in a religious expression which was essentially revolutionary' in the bottom layer of that force.[2]

Even the skilled workers of Birmingham came predominantly from families who had had their day of religious revolt. They were often Methodists and Baptists, and for this reason Christadelphianism assumed features which were in contrast, not only to the tenets of conservative religion, i.e. Anglicanism, but even to those of the cooled-down denominations which we have just named. Two such features which can be clearly discerned are its anti-emotionalism and its relative anti-feminism. 'The [theological] schema outlined by Dr. Thomas and his followers is intended as a rational presentation of what the Bible teaches, with a strong emphasis on empirical tests,' Wilson writes on the first point. 'Thus the concepts of heaven, hell, soul and devil are rejected on dual counts of being unscriptural, and also unreasonable – ideas not empirically proven.'[3] This bespeaks a surprising rationalism. But the group's anti-emotionalism is best seen in their attitude to conversion: 'The individual is converted by reasoning and Scripture, and its promise, rather than by an impulsive desire for security and salvation . . .

[1] The difficulties between the London and Birmingham branches about which Dr. Wilson reports could be explained, *mutatis omnibus mutandis,* along similar lines as the difficulties between the Boston and New York variants of Christian Science.

[2] Wilson, loc. cit., pp. 296 and 297.

[3] Ibid., pp. 229 and 230.

Immediate and instantaneous conversion is not looked for . . .'[1] What a difference from, for instance, the Salvation Army with its Methodist tradition! No storm in the soul here, but cool consideration, not heart religion, but religion of the head.

The maleness of the movement is no less noticeable, and no less characteristic, than its anti-emotionalism. 'The ecclesias are dominated by men,' Dr. Wilson reports. 'Christadelphianism has no distinctive appeal to women. It offers them no important roles . . . and in general favours no form of feminism . . . Christadelphianism . . . tends to be patriarchal in most things.'[2] This emphasis, too is in contrast to the sectarian tradition in general. True, male predominance and privilege are present everywhere in the Christian dispensation, except in an odd group here and there, such as Shakerism or Christian Science. But one of the tendencies which set the classical sects off from Calvinism and Lutheranism, the religions of post-Reformation respectability, was their somewhat more positive attitude to womanhood. And against this somewhat more positive attitude of the Methodists and Salvationists, for instance, the Christadelphians assumed a more decidedly anti-feminist position. As sociologists we cannot but assume that the relative pro-feminism of the groups of the skilled and comfortable workers helped to evoke the relative anti-feminism of this group of unskilled and decidedly uncomfortable workers. In this way, a sect is not only a protest movement, but it may even be a protest against a protest. Wheels are within wheels, and all that can be said is that the inspiration of dissenting attitudes is always a religiously conceived condemnation of the social set-up and those who benefit from it.

THE MINOR SOCIAL CAUSES OF SECTARIANISM

By and large, then, it would appear that the traditional opinion, according to which sects are religious expressions of socio-economic dissatisfactions, is well justified. But dissent may be due to other kinds of discontent as well. As a class may protest, and clothe its protest in religious forms, so may a nation or a race, or a sex group, or an age group, or this and that type of disadvantaged individuals. What all these cases have in common is the opposition,

[1] Ibid.

[2] Ibid., pp. 298 and 297.

in society, of honorific and humilific elements, the presence of invidious distinctions, as Veblen also expressed it – the presence of inferiorities which cry for compensation, and are compensated for, or over-compensated for, by the formation of sectarian types of life and thought.

Of the first of these relatively minor causes of sectarianism – of the religious protest of a nation which regards itself as wronged – the history of Bohemia, later Czechoslovakia, affords good examples. Hussitism was from its inception a nationalistic movement, but one which conceived itself in religious rather than in political or cultural terms.[1] When nationalism re-awoke in the nineteenth century, the ill-will of the Czechs against Austria was also directed – to some extent at any rate – against the Church, for though the parish priests in Czech villages were invariably Czech, the hierarchy was on the whole drawn from the German-speaking districts. The archbishopric of Prague changed hands as soon as the revolution of 1918 broke out; nevertheless an appreciable part of the population decided to sever its ties with Rome. The resulting heresy and schism, inspired by an aggressive nationalism, lost ground again when the demand for a Czech-recruited bishops' bench was fully met; but that it could break out at all is a proof that the religious sphere can be the scene of a national as well as a socio-economic revolt.

This general observation is well borne out by Russian history. 'The three sects [of the Dukhobortsy, Molokane and Stundists],' writes Conybeare, 'are as characteristically Little Russian in their origin and provenance as the Raskolniks [or Old Believers] are Great Russian.' The former had their centre in Kiev, the latter in Moscow.[2] The Skoptsy were a fierce sect everywhere, but they were particularly so in the Finnish parts of the empire, for there national rebelliousness was added to social discontent, producing a high degree of fanaticism.[3]

In the British Isles, it is in particular Wales which illustrates

[1] In so far as Bohemia was in the fifteenth century economically a more highly developed country than Germany, in so far as, for instance, there was a flourishing mining industry and a large mining proletariat, the social factor in the narrower sense of the word was also important. What we distinguish conceptually, was one in reality.

[2] Conybeare, loc. cit., pp. 261 and 9. Cf. also Curtiss, loc. cit., pp. 178, 179, concerning the Uniats.

[3] Cf. esp. Grass, loc. cit., vol. II, pp. 544 et seq.

our present point. Though the Anglican communion has numerous adherents, to be truly Welsh has come to mean to be a Welsh Methodist (or possibly Baptist), and it is significant that the Church of England, under nationalistic pressures, has had to have itself 'disestabished' in the Principality. The question which traditionally greets a new-comer: 'Are you church or chapel?' – a question not necessarily welcoming in spirit – does not only mean: are you Anglican or Dissenter? It also means: are you Tory or Labour? And it further means, at least *subintelligendo*: are you for 'alien domination' or for home rule? In this way, the social, political, and national attitudes are fused with the religious and expressed by preference in the language of religion.

If a nation like the Welsh is dominated by resentment against the English because it regards its own position as humilific and that of the supposed betters as honorific, it is not surprising that the black-skinned races should be dominated by super-resentment against the white-skinned ones, for the invidious discrimination which human narrowness has built up in the latter case is vastly more pronounced, and hence hurtful, than in the former. Indeed, at the present moment, the most copious source of sect development is the depression, human and psychological, of certain racial groups and their desperate need to overcome that depression. Africa, the West Indies, and the Negro ghettos of America have in recent years produced more sectarian growths than the rest of the world rolled into one, from pacific groupings who will do no more than claim that Simon of Cyrene was a coloured person, to highly militant ones whose votaries carry revolvers and are ready to use them. Just to give one example, let us mention the Ras Tafarians, because, centred in Jamaica, they form a link between the North American Negro and the African Continent. The basic doctrines of the movement, according to George E. Simpson's excellent summary, are: 'First, black men [are] reincarnations of the ancient Israelites . . .; second, the wicked white man is inferior to the black man; third, the Jamaican situation is hopeless Hell; fourth, Ethiopia is Heaven; fifth, Haile Selassie is the Living God; sixth, the invincible Emperor of Abyssinia will soon arrange for expatriated persons of African descent to return to the Homeland; and seventh, in the near future black men will get revenge by compelling white men to serve them.' 'Despite the hostility of the Ras Tafarians towards ministers and their congregations,' Simpson adds, 'the cult may be regarded as a pseudo-religious movement. Passages of the Bible are read or quoted at meetings and interpreted in ways which give support to Rastafarian doctrines, and many of the cult's songs are adaptations of Methodist or Baptist hymns. For many . . . the movement can be regarded as a functional equivalent of orthodox and revivalist religions, political parties, and a variety of social organizations.'[1]

If the contrast between the races is the obvious explanation of the fact that racially mixed societies produce more sectarianism than racially homogeneous ones, the reason that towns sometimes have more dissent than villages, and villages sometimes more than towns, large towns sometimes more than small ones and small towns than large ones, are by no means obvious. Yet the observation that there are appreciable differences has often been made. Wilson has come across the fact in his study of the Elim Foursquare Gospel Church. 'In market towns and country places there is often a culturally deprived population,' he says, 'which, once aware of its own cultural retardment, is prepared to capitalize its difference from city dwellers by exalting necessity into virtue, and by giving religious value to the limitations which circumstances alone impose . . . This hypothesis might account for the existence of two Elim churches at Bournemouth, and for the churches at Hove, Worthing and Southport – all centres where the social influence of the middle and upper classes is predominant, where in consequence the lower class might more intensely require special religious accommodation.'[2] The conjecture would appear entirely justified. Yet the whole subject-matter of this paragraph would deserve more careful consideration than it has received. Generally speaking, there appear to be two contradictory tendencies at work: in large conurbations, life is more impersonal, and hence there are the depressions and frustrations of human isolation which may, and often do, generate a longing for belonging, for the warmth and comfort of a sect; in small towns, on the other hand, life is more personal, and hence there are the depressions and frustrations which arise when rich and poor, honoured and despised, are forced to enter into direct contact and have, willy-nilly, to compare their respective fortunes in life, and which therefore generate

[1] 'The Ras Tafari Movement in Jamaica in its Millennial Aspect', *Millennial Dreams in Action*, as quoted above, p. 160.
[2] Wilson, loc. cit., p. 99.

sharper resentments and the wish for an ideology that will counterbalance and an organization that will counteract them, as at Bournemouth or Hove or Worthing or Southport. Thus it is that statistically town and country may at times appear to be equally afflicted with religious dissent, while analytically the two situations are rather different.

The next cause of sectarianism we have encountered already: the sex division of society, the underprivileged position of one of the sex groups. That women predominate numerically in most sects is a matter of common knowledge, and the sociologist must be excused if he does not accept the physiological and physio-psychological explanations, for instance along Freudian lines, which are sometimes given for the fact. The appearance of a woman-led religious movement like Christian Science is not unconnected with the appearance, at the same time, of a feminist political movement such as the Suffragettes. Both come from the same etiological complex: the combination of rightlessness descended from the past with a determination not to let it continue into the future. Mrs. Pankhurst's physical propaganda was cousin-german to Mrs. Eddy's metaphysical one. The Suffragette movement parallels the civil-rights organizations of the Negroes, Christian Science their religious movements. The physical fact of colour is as little responsible for the Negro forms of revolt as the physical fact of gender for the feminists. Both are protests against discriminatory valuations; one could almost say, against the treatment of natural groupings as if they were essentially (lower) social classes.[1]

More intriguing than the predominance of women in nonconformist circles is the predominance of certain age groups, for instance adolescents. Yet the case is no different, basically, from that of the female and coloured classes: even the young can be, and are, a painfully placed, unhappy and alienated stratum. The activation of the sex urge is apt to predispose a young man or woman towards sectarianism for it brings, in our culture at any rate, feelings of guilt, and the doctrines of many sects give meaning to these feelings and teach how they can be dealt with. As important, however, is the new-found awareness of one's own actual and potential independence, of one's own judgement and of one's own will. It leads regularly to a condemnation of established society, to what is known as the teen-age revolt, but revolt can end up in two ways:

[1] For Russia, cf. Conybeare, loc. cit., pp. 189, 190, 191.

either in a purely negative attitude, in the attempt to throw off the shackles imposed on the individual by society, or in a negative-positive attitude, the attempt to live according to better, higher and finer principles than the grown-up world whose weaknesses and shams are now recognized. This idealistic possibility inherent in the teen-age revolt, when it gains the upper hand, can inspire a stern morality and a live religiousness, such as many sectarian groupings offer.[1]

It is not in our own society, however, that we can best study how a contrast between the age groups can generate sectarian forms of life and thought. The reason is that in our society the opposition between the young, e.g. the unmarried, and the older people, e.g. the married, is not too sharp and therefore not too conscious and not too meaningful. It is different in other societies where the age groupings play much more the kind of role which in our setting is played by socio-economic classes. One instance is offered by the Germanic tribes of Europe in the first millennium. The older, married men owned and worked the land; the younger, unmarried men formed war-expeditions and filled their time, and gained their keep, by booty and conquest. The chief god of staid society was Tiwaz (Zeus, deus) – the god of the heavens, hence of order and also vegetation, i.e. of all the elements that are important to a settled agricultural life. But Tiwaz had little meaning for the braves. They wanted a warrior-god, and they found him in Woden, leader of the host of the dead, who, ranking originally under Tiwaz, was raised by his votaries up above him. The cult of Woden was an ecstatic cult, his worship the frenzied enactment of his deeds and the deeds of his fearsome associates – the very word Woden is philologically kindred to the German word *Wut*, which means fury. No respectable landholder would go in for such berserk activities – property as well as age bring coolness and collectedness. But a young warrior will feel his ardour kindled by them, while the formalism of Tiwaz-worship will appear to him empty and meaningless. Here we have a far more sharply-profiled religious revolt of the young than is ever to be expected under modern conditions. The development we have sketched out had world-historical consequences, for wherever Germanic war-bands made permanent conquests, as in England, they established their own god, Woden, and not

[1] Cf. Wilson, loc. cit., p. 117.

the god of the stay-at-homes, Tiwaz. And in so far as Woden was essentially a leader in battle to whom his followers owed faith and fidelity, this was not without importance for the waning of the tribal, and the coming of the feudal, system and all that it stood for.[1]

The causes of rebelliousness on the part of the young are partially social, partially psychological. The two aspects are not, in life, divided, indeed, they are hardly divisible even in theory. It is only the clumsiness of our concepts that forces us to make an artificial distinction between them. But what is true of the young, is true of all. And the psychological factor can be so strong that it overbalances the sociological factor. There are cases where a man's social circumstances, his wealth for instance, should make for a conservative attitude and would seem to predispose him for membership in some established church, but where his personality structure is such that he will become estranged from respectable society, drift into alienation and revolt, and end up in some sect, even a sect of the poor. This point is of crucial importance in our analysis. Whenever the thesis supported in these pages is presented – namely that sects are essentially manifestations of social dissatisfactions – somebody is sure to object and to point to a sect leader who was not poor or deprived in any way, who was, on the contrary, from an upper and satisfied stratum. This argumentation overlooks the fact that society may reject and humiliate a rich person as well as a poor one. In Victorian times, for instance, an old maid was regularly rated as a failure, even if she had millions; she was both pitied and ridiculed – what wonder that she fled at times from the company of her own set into the arms of the poor? There are a thousand and one ways in which one can be unsuccessful in society, a thousand and one reasons for the causal chain which leads from rejection to rebelliousness and from rebelliousness to sectarianism. And all these many ways and reasons are similarly circumstanced, not to say identical in structure. The failure of a personality to integrate itself harmoniously in established society is always a social phenomenon as well as a psychological one, due as much to qualities of the common life as to qualities, or lack of qualities, in a personal character. Often supposedly a-typical sectarians, on closer investigation turn out to be the archetypal exceptions which confirm the rule.

[1] Cf. Höfler, in *La Regalità Sacra*, Rome 1959, pp. 696–9.

A good case in point is Bernhardt Knipperdollinck, whose name looms large in the annals of the Anabaptist movement at Münster. He was no poor clothworker, but, on the contrary, a rich cloth-merchant, not an exploited proletarian, but rather an exploiter of proletarians. Does his appearance, even his very existence, disprove the assertion that sects are formed and joined by the down-and-out? By no means. One does not have to look very far for the reason why he became a co-engineer of the Anabaptist revolt. He had failed to become elected to the patrician town-council – failed to achieve the place in the social order to which he aspired and thought himself entitled. It is understandable that he turned against his fellow-patricians and threw in his lot with the proletarians (who promptly elected him Mayor in 1534). He *was* down and out under the old dispensation – not in the labour market, but in the political ring, and this made his position and psychology parallel to, indeed, near-identical with, any proletarian who could not manage to secure for himself a satisfactory job or standing in society. The cases of the patricians Konrad Grebel in Zürich and Eitelhans Langenmantel in Augsburg may well have been similar to Knipperdollinck's at Münster. We do not know their backgrounds because often the sources are incomplete, and it is only by accident that we sometimes learn of the truth. It is puzzling, for instance, to find goldsmiths mentioned in early Quaker records, for goldsmiths, like cloth-merchants, belonged to the top layer. But one life-history reveals the secret – that of the Londoner Humphrey Bache whose shop was 'at the sign of the snail in Tower Street'. 'At the beginning of the Civil War his trade had fallen off, and he had obtained employment under the Commonwealth, being at first engaged at three shillings a day as one of the overseers of the work on the city fortifications.'[1] It was, therefore, not the rich, but the impoverished Humphrey Bache who explains why men turned towards the Quaker sect.

A steep descent down the social ladder has propelled many a man towards sectarianism. A splendid example is William Booth whose father had originally been very well-to-do, but had then lost all that he had had. Booth himself has told the story: 'My family, by one of those strange destinies to which Nottingham was subject in those days, was reduced to absolute poverty. I had to be taken from school at a very early age, and was placed under

[1] Braithwaite, loc. cit., p. 517.

very unfavourable circumstances.... My life seemed to be blighted at its very commencement. But then religion, the right kind of religion, came into my heart and turned my opinions, lifted me up from the depths into which I was in danger of falling, and made me General of the Salvation Army.'[1] This is a valuable and insightful statement, and it spells strong support for the general way in which we see the co-ordination of the social and personal reasons which may drive a man towards dissent.

Many a time there is, between these reasons, even conceptually, only a difference in degree, but none in kind; that is to say, the pressures which drive a certain man in the direction of a sect are the same as those which influence his class-mates, but they impinge upon him with greater force. In the history of the Strict and Particular Baptists, the name of John Warburton has an abiding place. As a Lancashire weaver, he was certainly typical of his trade; but he had not even a cottage of his own, as so many other domestic workers did; he 'worked his loom in a cellar, and was so desperately poor that only the kindness of the deacons of an Independent church to which he [at first] belonged, saved him from being turned out of his cellar and sent, with his wife and young family, to the work-house'.[2] The repulsion and revulsion from the world was doubly strong in this weaver, but it was the same sentiment as that which other weavers also felt. Sometimes, however, social and personal reasons can be more clearly distinguished – distinguished by kind, and not only by degree. George Whitefield, the pioneer of Calvinistic Methodism, had plenty of social reasons for turning away from respectable society: son of an innkeeper-woman, potboy in his youth, he could get through his Oxford education only by working as a servitor, which was very humiliating. But he had a personal reason also – a reason so clearly and exclusively personal as we shall rarely find one: nature had inflicted on him cross-eyes, a squint of no common proportion. This physical feature made life even more of a misery for him than it would have been, had he had normal sight. His excessive asceticism, his fierce fasts, his emotional instability, his rapid changes from measureless depression ('I am a dead dog') to equally measureless exultation ('My heaven has already begun') are equally due

[1] Cit. Coates, pp. 17 and 18. The case of Gerard Winstanley was strikingly similar. Cf. Gooch, loc. cit, p. 221.
[2] Underwood, loc. cit., p. 186.

to his social *and* his personal disadvantages, to his dire poverty and to his ugly face.

What moves a man off centre, need not, however, be a physical feature as in Whitefield's case; it may be a personality trait whose origin is so obscure that we cannot say whether it was social, psychological or somatic. George Fox had no squint, but, as we hear again and again, his eyes were terrible to behold. The founder of the Skoptsy, Selivanov, seems to have had a similarly devastating look.[1] These 'burning men' are a phenomenon which probably belongs to psychology rather than sociology: but neither ridiculous nor unbearable eyes would, by themselves, have made a sect or a sectarian. They merely reinforced tendencies which arose from the social situation of the times.

THE ROLE OF THE SECT LEADER

Intensifiers rather than initiators of sectarian sentiments, these more individual factors have great importance for the study of the sect leaders. Here as everywhere, the leader must, almost by definition, have more intensity than the led, and this extra-intensity is as a rule provided by the extra tension between self and society which a physical feature or a personal life-history may generate.

This brings us to the role of the charismatic personality, and in the little that we have said so far about it, there is already an implied rejection of Max Weber's conceptions on this head. For Weber, who was an out-and-out individualist, the prophet is first, and the religious movement is only secondary. For us, the discontent-producing constellation, which bears in it the germ of the movement, is first, and the leader is only secondary. Differently expressed: Weber tends to see the great man as unique; we see him as a case among many, distinguished from his followers only by his extra energy. It can happen that the depressed stratum is so abject and wretched that it has not even the strength to protest and rebel. If so, we have before us a somewhat special case, and the leaders are apt to come from outside, for instance, from a stratum that is just a little less abject and wretched than the common run. But this hardly changes the principle. The principle is that the movement as such is the child of an objective situation, not, as Weber preferred to think, of a subjective will. This at any rate is

[1] Cf. Braithwaite, loc. cit., pp. 411 and 475; Conybeare, loc. cit., p. 366.

how we see the matter. Our attitude is more truly sociological than Weber's, his is more personalistic. All of Weber's philosophy is involved, and we cannot discuss it in its depth and breadth here.[1] We can only point to the facts which bear out our contention. Sometimes there is hardly a prophet at all, certainly not one who could claim super-normal charisma; and yet there is a movement. For instance, 'Anabaptism in England . . . lacked a real leader';[2] yet it produced Baptism. Sometimes the apparently unique founder-figure turns out, on closer consideration, to be not at all unique. To the half-informed, George Fox appears as the father of Quakerism: to those who know the facts, he is no bigger than, say, James Nayler. If Nayler had not disgraced himself, history might have awarded the prize to him. It was Fox's rationality, not his irrational charisma, which allowed him to emerge as the victor in the contest for leadership. 'The swift response to the message of Fox was not only due to the young prophet's fervour and sincerity,' says the Friends' historian. 'It came because the message answered the expectations of . . . earnest spiritually-minded groups,' and those who have brought Braithwaite's work up to date go even further in asserting that 'he was spokesman for a spontaneous movement which unconsciously rested on many precedents and predecessors'. Indeed, with typical Quaker sincerity they admit that Fox's pre-eminence may owe something to stage management and machinations.[3]

Studying more recent evolutions, Bryan Wilson has asserted that 'Elim churches are not mainly a spontaneous demonstration of religious dissatisfaction by people sufficiently able and enterprising to build up a church life for themselves . . . they are a response to a call from a leader.' But where he widens his survey, he tells a different story: 'Historical circumstances and factors intrinsic to the nature of Pentecostalism itself delayed the crystallization of the movement into a denominational form. No one leader had been responsible for the new teaching . . .'[4]

Perhaps we come nearest to the truth when we say that the

[1] Much of what we have said in criticism of his theory of elective affinity in our *Sociology of Knowledge* would be relevant in an extended discussion.

[2] Underwood, loc. cit., p. 27. Cf. also Niebuhr, loc. cit., p. 48.

[3] Braithwaite, loc. cit., pp. 514, 546, 547; cf. also pp. 60 and 65, and, for the competition between Fox and Naylor, pp. 247 and 248.

[4] Wilson, loc. cit., pp. 108 (also 37) and 33.

function of a leader is to make a latent conflict conscious, to give form to a pre-existing movement, to impart direction to its energies, and to help it to focus on definite ends. All this makes him an important figure, but it does not make him a founder, if the word be taken in its fullest meaning. If a catalyst is immersed into a chemical solution, it brings out – it activates and actualizes – what is contained in it. But the potentiality and power must be there before he sets to work, and without the right substances and setting his intervention would be entirely without avail.

POSSIBLE SHIFTS IN THE CAUSES OF SECTARIANISM

One last aspect of the co-existence of more social and more personal reasons for sectarian developments remains to be considered: the possibility that their mixture may change, and in particular that social reform may progressively get the better of social discontents and thus block one source of the stream which has flowed so fully and freely in the past. Actually, the world is as yet nowhere near this state of affairs, and even the British welfare state has not dried everybody's tears. Yet it is fair to say that hunger has in all probability declined in relative importance within this syndrome everywhere: but if hunger has declined, humiliation has not, nor have all the other causes, great and small, which may lead to the alienation of individuals and groups from their society. Only the disappearance of all discontents would finally close this chapter in the history of the human race.

An interesting study of recent developments has been published under the title 'Jehovah's Witnesses as a Proletarian Movement',[1] and this would seem to indicate that the author found the members of that sect to be predominantly of working-class origin. But this is not so, because the word 'proletarian' is used here in an unusual sense – 'to describe a movement [i.e. any movement] which lives in, but is not of, a given society'.[2] The common identification of 'proletariat' and 'wage-earners' is therefore not implied. What the author did in fact find was that the members showed personal character-traits which set them in contrast to the rest of society, to those who are usually regarded as 'normal individuals'. The key concept which he uses in analysing the typical Witness is the

[1] Werner Cohn, in *The American Scholar,* 1955, pp. 281 et seq.

[2] Ibid., p. 282.

Durkheimian concept of *anomie*.[1] In a similar vein, Father McCluskey has described the following as the chief candidates for the Witnesses: 'the bitter from whom life has stolen hope, the malcontent or anarchical who are eaten up with disgust at government, the business failures who have been bruised in competition . . . the simple, the illiterate, the dejected, the novelty seekers, the underprivileged and the genuinely hungry for God . . .'.[2] Thus we are not confronted, in this case, with an outgrowth of the class conflict; we are confronted, rather, with a group of people whose hostility to society at large is due to a personal inability to feel at home and at ease in it, and the explanation of this sectarian formation would seem to lie in individual biographies, not in economic conditions, in men's inner and not their outer lives.

But though the Witnesses were not, to all appearances, as a rule recruited from the working classes, they were very well aware of the fact that the working classes are always, even today, a particularly propitious field for sect propaganda – which is significant, too. One acute observer asserts that their (now abandoned) habit of inviting matyrdom, for instance, parading outside Catholic churches with banners reading 'religion is a racket' on a Sunday morning, was due to the belief that any attack on them would, almost automatically, bring the masses, especially the wage-earning masses – in spite of higher wages and shorter hours – to their side. 'A fistfight or arrest [would] put the Witnesses in the category of the persecuted while the provocation was forgotten. Drawing [perhaps better: hoping to draw] its new blood from those elements in society which made up the dispossessed and the proletariat, the [Watch Tower] Society would bring itself to their attention by such incidents. Here were simple people being oppressed by the same clerical and political powers which oppress me, thought the bystander with proletarian tendencies. . . . The Witnesses wore the cloak of the underdog with a measure of eagerness.'[3] And well they might.

Purely personal reasons for joining a sect have, of course, always existed. Why did Darcy Brisbane, Lady Maxwell, become a Methodist? 'She lost her husband in less than two years after their

[1] Ibid., pp. 297 and 298.

[2] McCluskey, N. G., *Who are Jehovah's Witnesses?*, New York 1956, pp. 15 and 16.

[3] Whalen, W. J., *Armageddon around the Corner*, New York 1962, p. 190.

most happy marriage. Six weeks after his death her little son died, and she was left a lonely widow at nineteen years of age.'[1] Here we have a rudely disturbed personal equilibrium which was re-established in and through the emotional warmth of a sectarian fold. In a study of the white people who sought refuge in the 'heavens' of that black 'god', Father Divine, an acute observer found four categories of typical cases: First, old maids; despised by the outside world because of their ill success in the marriage-market, they found themselves appreciated, and, in view of the sect's emphasis on virginity, honoured, in this protective enclosure; secondly, women who had not been able to enjoy or even to bear married life and who longed for an environment in which sex and all it implies was tabooed; thirdly, men who found existence in the rough-and-tumble of contemporary society too wearing – effeminate types, for instance, sometimes types with heavy over-mothering in childhood, who were simply lost when their mothers died and left them orphans; and finally homosexuals, both male and female.[2] It is difficult to imagine that social reform, however comprehensive and intelligent in design, however successful even in execution, will completely remove these and similar causes of personal estrangement from established society, and the longing, arising from it, to find in a sect-like environment that integration which the world at large had been unable or unwilling to give. Dr. Wilson has laid his finger on the salient fact when he writes that 'intense religious experience is one way' – perhaps the main way – 'of adding depth to lives otherwise shallow, insecure and difficult'.[3]

Considering a specific pentecostal grouping against the background of the British welfare state, Wilson makes a number of observations which are of general, not to say universal, bearing. Social security as established by law, he points out, is related specifically to economic poverty; but 'it is gradually being recognized that material want is not the only severe and chronic complaint which men suffer in society: they can, in the increasing impersonality of modern urban life, and whilst enjoying plenty, suffer severely from social isolation . . . an affliction of considerable

[1] Church, loc. cit., p. 112.

[2] Harris, S., *Father Divine, Holy Husband*, Garden City, N.Y. 1953, pp. 283, 292, 293, 306, 307, 308.

[3] Loc. cit., p. 100.

dimension in our society... The Elim church does effectively combat loneliness, anxiety and fear; it releases tensions, offers catharsis ... and ... persuades the individual to integrate himself into a community ... The role of the emotional sect may be changing with changing social conditions,' our witness concludes on another page, 'but the sect also recruits new members, and for them the role of the sect may not be specifically socio-economic compensation ... The sect may have important ... functions for the individual long after the relation of religious expression and socio-economic circumstances has ceased to hold in this case.'[2]

Do these facts force us to abandon the general analysis of the origin of sectarianism which we have offered in the present pages? By no means. Do they demand a serious modification? Hardly. It is still the poor, the unhappy, the down-and-out, who crave for the comforts and consolations which sects have offered down the centuries. If a man has no assured livelihood, he is poor; but if he has no assured friends, he is poor also, if for a different reason, and in either case he will be deprived and alienated, and will tend to form, with his fellows, 'a religious group that rejects the social environment in which it exists'.

RELIGIOUS SECT AND POLITICAL PARTY

It is obvious that a religious group rejecting the social environment in which it exists is comparable to, and kindred to, a political party which feels the same way about the surrounding society. There is, as it were, one current of revolt which can flow in two different channels, one religious, the other political, and this raises the question when and why, in a given situation, the one alternative rather than the other is chosen. Let us note first of all that on occasions men may hesitate at the crossroads. 'At the time of Shays's Rebellion,' we are told in a Shaker history, 'some of the Massachusetts Believers who lived in the vicinity of Springfield, were heard ... to express partisan views. Like most of the early Shakers, they were poor men, well aware of the grievances against which Shays's men were fighting and inclined to sympathize with them.' Should they follow the call of Daniel Shays or the call of James Whittaker? For many the decision may have been in the balance for a while, even though 'Father James'

[1] Ibid., pp. 344, 345, 347, 322, 321.

made it clear to his flock that he who has come 'to feel for one political party more than for another . . . and unites with one evil spirit against another, is off from Christian ground'.[1]

The same problem arose, in a much more poignant form, for those American Negroes who found themselves wooed, simultaneously, by the Civil Rights organizations and by such sects as Father Divine's. The Civil Rights organizations held out the prospect of practical success, but only in the distant future; they knew that the struggle would be long. Father Divine offered the satisfactions of day-dreaming only, but he offered them here and now, with no waiting period in between. When, in 1950, the Miami Beach authorities tried to prevent people of full colour from using the beach facilities, he did not invoke the courts and the Constitution: he asserted instead that disasters would befall those who offended God's creatures: had not the Winecoff Hotel at that segregationist city, Atlanta, Georgia, burnt down with the loss of one hundred and twenty-one lives? Had not tornadoes devastated Texas and Oklahoma? Had not, even at Miami, a 'Red Tide' washed up tons of dead fish whose nauseous stench made all bathing impossible there? Why fight at law if God Himself avenged your wrongs?

In economics there is a law according to which distant and uncertain benefits are rated lower (discounted) in proportion to their distance and uncertainty, so that they appear, even to a rational view, smaller than present and certain benefits, which, in themselves, are merely equal or even inferior. Bread today is better than cake tomorrow. Here we have something similar. The Civil Rights leaders paid in bills on the future; Father Divine paid less, but he paid cash, and that is why so many would rather turn to him. 'Father Divine's Negro followers get more immediate satisfaction from the way their leader attacks discriminatory patterns than the followers of more down-to-earth Negro leaders can ever get from theirs . . . . They, who have been unable to find homes and jobs and food enough for their children to eat, can't be bothered with the long-range planning of practical race-relations agencies. . . . What do they care that, every time Father rejects legal and educational means for attaining civil rights in favour of his retribution, he is opposing the final goal of the Negro in America – complete and equal integration? That final goal for tomorrow is

[1] Melcher, loc. cit., p. 51.

too far off to make sense. . . . They would rather have Father's fantasy today.'[1]

The reason, then, that the spirit of revolt sometimes expresses itself in metaphysical-religious, sometimes in physical-practical-political terms, would seem to lie in the relative hopefulness or hopelessness of the situation when considered with a view to possible reform. If reform is a distinct possibility, a political party rather than a religious sect will appear on the scene; if reform is, or is judged, a virtual impossibility, a religious sect rather than a political party will appear. Much depends on the concrete conditions in which a class or sub-class finds itself. When the well-organized workers of Britain began to secure better standards of living and the ill-organized or un-organized failed in this endeavour, Christadelphianism arose to express the feelings of the latter stratum, and Christadelphianism, understandably, condemned both Trade Unionism and Labour Party from whom its adherents expected little help. F. G. Jannaway's *Ought Christians to be Socialists?* and *Which is the Remedy?* (both of 1909) gave voice to the view that the world is in so hopeless a state that talk about social reform cannot be taken seriously. 'The Christadelphian is in conflict with the prevailing social order, but powerless to organize its overthrow,' the prime student of the sect has written. 'The Christadelphian did not want reform.' Out of a philosophy of sour grapes he asserted that 'he did not want higher status in the world, nor did he want the world to be improved; he wanted the whole order to be thrown into chaos and suffering, and a new order to be established in which [through divine intervention] his superiority and authority would be acknowledged. . . . He was emotionally involved in his predictions for disaster, out of which he, and those with him, would alone emerge triumphant'.[2]

A particularly convincing illustration of the fact that hopefulness turns a man to politics, hopelessness to sectarianism, is afforded by the biography of the founder of the Salvation Army. 'When he was thirteen years old, Feargus O'Connor visited [his home-town] Nottingham, and the great Chartist orator had an enthusiastic disciple in William Booth. He shouted himself hoarse in his approval of the Chartist sentiment. He in his boyish

[1] Harris, loc. cit., pp. 178 and 180.

[2] Wilson, loc. cit., pp. 351 and 352; cf. also pp. 286, 288, 311, 312. Cf., however, below, p. 58, note 2.

enthusiasm subscribed to the Charter.'[1] But Chartism died, and the longing for a new deal remained. If men could not bring it about, what other alternative was there but to expect it from God?

The final proof of our thesis lies, however, in the striking fact that the evolution of powerful labour organizations immediately brought an involution of the sects (or of the denominations which had developed out of the sects). R. F. Wearmouth speaks, in relation to the nineteenth century, of a turn 'from the Bible to the Statute Book',[2] and A. C. Underwood reports as follows: 'In Bradford in 1893 was held a conference of labour and socialistic organizations to co-ordinate local and sporadic efforts in a national organization. Lord Snowdon spoke of it as "the most important political event of the nineteenth century". It was no accident that thereafter the Baptist churches of Bradford [and elsewhere!] lost scores of members and adherents. . . . The pendulum of interest was beginning to swing from religion to politics, and . . . many joined the crusade for social, rather than personal, salvation.'[3]

Nevertheless, it would be wrong to see the radical party in politics only as a competitor and killer of the radical sect in religion: it is as much to be regarded as its child and continuator. The typical sect bears in itself, but thinly disguised, the future form of the typical party. 'Though the Levellers drew strength from the religiosity of their time, they yet remained always primarily a political party,' Huehns writes with truth, if with considerable exaggeration, and a contemporary, Thomas Edwards, indicated in his *Gangraena* (vol. III, p. 20) the same fact: 'Instead of legal rights and the laws and customs of this nation, the sectaries talk and plead for natural rights and liberties such as men have from their birth.'[3] In other words: they propagate the principles of a radical democratic reform. The left, as can be seen, is always the left, whether it prays or plots, whether it is too weak to fight and turns utopian and religious, or strong enough to fight and turns realistic and political.

Even the Russian Revolution of 1917 was actively prepared by

[1] Coates, loc. cit., p. 14.
[2] Wearmouth, R. F., *Some Working Class Movements in the Nineteenth Century*, London 1948, p. 321.
[3] Underwood, loc. cit., p. 255.
[4] Huehns, loc. cit., pp. 115 and 107.

the dissenting movements. The Old Believers were in the end no longer particularly radical, yet a study of their organ, the *Staro-obryadets*, reveals that they supported the constitutionalist party, urged economic reforms for the improvement of the working and living conditions of the factory proletariat and demanded a modernization of the criminal code. Some of them went much further and raised the banner of the class war. Quoting a source of the year 1877, when Lenin was just learning how to read, Conybeare shows that they were concerned about the conflict between capital and labour and sided with the latter. 'Latterly the Old Believers have discovered that the number of the Beast, i.e. the title of Antichrist, is contained in the word *khozyain*, which means employer.'[1]

If an already stale sect, like the Old Believers, could take a stand of this kind, it is not surprising that newer sects showed this leftishness to an even higher degree. Particularly interesting and important here are the Molokane and the Stundists. A sub-sect called the Communals sprang from the Caucasian Molokane through fission. When they were exiled (because of their propaganda for an egalitarian redistribution of land and wealth) to Eastern Siberia, they organized themselves into collective farms and thus anticipated one of the main ideals which the Communists have tried to press on the Russian people since 1917. In the same way, the Stundists produced the Neo-Stundists who turned from Bible-reading to lay literature and drifted further and further in the direction of full-fledged Communism. The transfer of land-ownership to the peasantry was one of the firmest planks in their platform. The Orthodox missionary in their midst, D. I. Skvortsov, was not wrong when he called their programme 'nothing other than Socialism and Communism'. Indeed, the Bishop of Kherson even asserted that some of them had taken part in the secret movement of the workers of the city of Nikolaev which led to the formation of the Union of Russian Social Democrats.[2] If this assertion is true, and there is every indication that it is, then this is a good instance of the process which has so often transmuted an originally religious into an essentially political protest against a wicked world.

In England, the historical connection between Methodism and

[1] Conybeare, loc. cit., pp. 255, 256, 224.

[2] Milyukov, P., *Outlines of Russian Culture*, ed. Philadelphia 1948, vol. I, pp. 107, 108, 109, 110; Curtiss, loc. cit., pp. 165, 166, 167.

the Labour Party was openly acknowledged by the latter's leaders at a crucial moment in the movement's fortunes. When, after World War II, a bitter power struggle developed during the election campaign of 1945, Winston Churchill asserted that Socialism was thoroughly un-English, having been hatched out in the brain of the German Karl Marx. Not so, Morgan Phillips replied. English Socialism is thoroughly English: it is the political prolongation of the religious awakening called Methodism, a product of the British past. There is much that could be adduced in support of Phillips's contention.[1] A long list could, for instance, be made of the names of men who were both dissenters and Socialists. To mention only one example: Aneurin Bevan, for a long time the strongest personality of the Labour Party's left, was a typical product of the Welsh non-conformist Sunday-school. 'The Welsh Sunday-schools of those years,' so Bevan's biographer tells us, 'were occasionally a cover for incipient political debate. One breakaway group from a Sunday-school class in Tredegar made contact with the Independent Labour Party in Merthyr and secured their aid in forming a Tredegar branch.'[2] Thus Bevan had no need to change over-much when he concentrated his efforts on, and made his career in, the political movement of the proletariat.

A little problem is presented, in this context, by the political attitude of Methodism's founder. John Wesley was a dyed-in-the-wool Tory.[3] Yet the reader of the present book should know already how a puzzle of this kind can be resolved. The Tories of early Hanoverian days were an opposition party: Oxford in particular was stubbornly Jacobite – so much so that a troop of horse had to be sent to the city by George I after his accession. Wesley travelled along the same road as Mrs. Eddy, though in the opposite direction: she from the poor of Lynn to the dwellers in the Bostonian ivory-tower, he from the dwellers in the Oxonian ivory-tower to the poor. Besides, Wesley's Toryism was not without its progressive aspects. He was, for instance, a determined opponent of abuses such as vote-buying and the 'rotten boroughs', which falsified the representation of the British people in their Parliaments and had to be removed by the Reform Bill of 1832.[4]

[1] Cf. Martin, D. A., 'The Denomination', *The British Journal of Sociology*, 1962, p. 12.

[2] Foot, M., *Aneurin Bevan: a Biography*, New York 1963, vol. I, pp. 25 and 26.

[3] Cameron, loc. cit., pp. 42–6.

[4] Ibid., p. 56.

Still, Wesley was on the political right. But, in this point, the movement which he started simply refused to follow him. It bore in itself a latent liberalism, and indeed a latent labourism, which asserted itself with increasing vigour and in the end linked Methodism to the political left, however little its beloved leader might have cherished this bed-fellowship. The man on whom Wesley's mantle fell, Jabez Bunting, still was a High Tory, but 'near the middle of the nineteenth century, the Methodists emerged from under the spell of Wesley's teaching on . . . uncritical adherence to the *status quo* in politics . . . They broke the "pontificate" of Bunting and began to join forces, politically and socially, with the [other] dissenters'.[1] It was the Methodist Richard Oastler who introduced the war-slogan of the radical labour movement, the war-cry 'wage-slavery'; it was another Methodist, Philip Grant, who edited the *Ten Hours' Advocate*; it was yet another Methodist, J. R. Stephens, who first called for the application of violent methods in the class war.[2] A considerable proportion of the early Trade Union leaders were Methodists, and an even more considerable proportion of them were Primitive Methodists.[3] Aneurin Bevan was no maverick. He followed a well-trodden path when he changed from pulpit to platform.

In view of Marx's well-known assertion that religion is the opium of the people, it is not a little instructive to study the speeches of Mrs. Catherine Booth, wife of the Salvation Army General. Her religion was nothing of the kind; it was the people's adrenalin rather than its opium, a stirrer-up, not a quietener-down. Indeed, we can go so far as to say that she fanned the class-hatred which sprang up in her day. 'Mrs. Booth's scathing references to the profligate section of the rich – to "His Grace the Duke of Rackrent, the Right Honourable Woman Seducer, Fitz-Shameless, and the gallant Colonel Swearer", for instance – appealed directly to some of [her] Whitechapel hearers,' Coates reports; he should have said: 'appealed to the class hatred that was in them'. 'Mrs. Booth made constant attacks upon the habits of those [the upper] classes. She declared they led idle and often vicious lives, they were wasting their time, money and health on luxury and lust. She denounced their habits in fierce and exaggerated language. She lashed "society" – especially "fast society" – with the Corellian

[1] Ibid., p. 74. [2] Ibid., p. 79.

[3] For some illustrations, cf. Cameron, loc. cit., pp. 79 et seq.

vehemence to which it became accustomed in later days.'[1] Karl Marx would not have loved Catherine Booth and Catherine Booth might have loathed Karl Marx, but in their hatreds they met all the same; and if it is a question who went further in his attacks, the preacher easily outdoes the politician. If Mrs. Booth's language is considered, we must compare her to Marx's demagogic disciples rather than to Marx himself. But the main point is that sectarian and social movements were equally anti-capitalistic in sentiment and striving.[2]

The fact that the political arena becomes more, the religious less, attractive as the hopes of a group become less utopian and more realistic, can be seen in the changing attitudes and sentiments of the North American Negro population. At first, while equality with the white man was nothing but a vain dream, the coloured man sought relief in purely religious terms: for instance by developing the parallel between the position of the Jews in Egypt and the position of the Africans in America, by telling himself that enslavement does not necessarily mean inferiority, but that, on the contrary, it may mean superiority, as God's people were superior to their owners and tormentors in pre-Mosaic times. Later, when equality began to look more like a practical proposition, there was an edging nearer, as it were, to the political scene. Father Divine's movement – as we have seen – was still a typical sect, yet his temporary flirtation with the Communist Party was not without significance.[3] Later still, the Black Muslims definitely assumed the traits of a pressure group. Still organized as a sect, still to all appearances a religion, they were *de facto* more fond of playing politics than of praying. Even the choice of Islam as an appropriate ideology was largely determined by power-political considerations. True, it was selected because it is a faith radically at variance with the American culture-traditions and thus served as a defiant rejection of the inclusive society, as a flamboyant expression of alienation from all things American. But besides these negative reasons, there were

[1] Coates, loc. cit., pp. 73 and 87.

[2] Cf. also what Wilson says about the kinship between Christadelphians and Communists, loc. cit., pp. 352 and 353; also ibid., pp. 288 and 289. 'Christadelphianism offered something of the same kind of ultimate goal as revolutionary socialism . . . and it brought the force of Scripture to justify the judgment which would be wrought on the rich and powerful of the world' (p. 303).

[3] Harris, loc. cit., pp. 185, 189, 190.

some more positive incentives at work as well. Islam is a fighting creed; its votaries are men who conquer, not men who turn the other cheek. Such a religion must appear more meaningful to a group that can believe it has a fighting chance than a religion that counsels meekness and submission. Indeed, there were even some still more down-to-earth, still more practical-political, reasons for the adoption of Islam: Islam is a world power; the rulers of America must treat the rulers of Egypt and Iraq and all the other Muslim lands with consideration; if the Black Muslims could manage to creep under the mantle of the Muslim governments of the Middle East (and that they tried, for instance, by means of Elijah Muhammad's much-advertised pilgrimage to Mecca), they would gain immeasurably in strength. As can be seen, though the Black Muslims were still in form a radical sect, they were in fact already to a considerable extent a radical party: the two things shade imperceptively into each other. Finally, in 1964, when Malcolm X split the movement and started his own, he shed the remaining religious tints and emerged as a purely political, punch-packing leader. And thus it is that parties displace and replace sects. The case of the American Negro is clearly parallel to that of the English working man about which we have spoken above: as in England the coming of increasingly successful Trade Unions emptied the chapels and filled the meeting halls, so did the increasingly successful effort on the part of the Negro in America to secure civil rights.

RELIGIOUS SECTARIANISM AS AN ANSWER TO RELIGIOUS ESTABLISHMENT

The kinship in type between political parties, especially radical political parties, and religious sects, especially still young and (if the word be permitted) as yet unspoilt sects, also sheds a good deal of light on another problem connected with the origins of sectarianism: the question as to why some societies have produced more religious dissent than others. Statistics of religious affiliation are notoriously unreliable and misleading, but it is an obvious and undeniable fact that England has produced more sects than, say, Austria or Bavaria, and Russia more than, say, Spain. Why should this be so? The explanation lies in the closeness of the tie between State and Church in England and Russia, their near-identity there, and in the looseness, in the near-non-existence, of that tie in Austria, Bavaria and Spain. In general terms it can be said that sects arise above all where there is an 'established' religion, a state church. As this state church is, by nature, by definition, an adjunct of the conservative forces in the country, any and every movement of social dissatisfaction must condemn it as it condemns the existing property or power relations. And as it is easier to contract out of a church than out of an economic or political system, revolutionary sentiment may work itself out, by preference, in the abandonment of the official form of religion and the formation of, and the joining in, sectarian efforts. A church such as the Church of England basks in the light of the Crown; but, just because this is so, it must also share in its shadows. There is a principle of justice involved here: did not the laws of the Germanic tribes who founded the monarchy ordain that 'he who takes the good drop, must take the bad drop also'?

Richard Niebuhr has asserted that the 'associational sect' arises in opposition to an 'institutional church'.[1] But this is an altogether misleading formulation. It is not the *institutional* character of the church that arouses the misgivings and inspires the actions of the sectarian: it is its *established* character, the fact that it is one of the bastions built into the fortress surrounding and protecting the social order which the revolutionary condemns and would like to overthrow. An implicit acknowledgement of this fact is contained in the following words of Edmund Waller, the poet-politician of the mid-seventeenth century: 'Our laws and the present government of the Church are mixed like wine and water. I look on the episcopate as an outwork or barrier and say to myself that if this is stormed by the people and the secret thereby discovered that we can deny them nothing which they demand, we shall have a task no less difficult to defend our property against them than we had lately to preserve it against the prerogative of the Crown.'[2] 'He that takes one stone from the Church,' Charles II of England is reported to have said, 'takes two from the Crown.'[3] The rebellious strata in the country agreed and proceeded accordingly. In order to bring down the Crown, they knew that they had to undermine the Church: in turning away from the Anglican altar, they also, almost

[1] Niebuhr, loc. cit., p. 18.

[2] Cit. Gooch, p. 206.

[3] Pearson, H., *Charles II: His Life and Likeness*, London 1960, p. 136.

automatically, turned away from the Anglican and English throne, and all it stood for in their minds.

It is for this reason that the two classical countries of caesaro-papism, England and Russia, are also the two classical countries of sectarianism.[1] In the Catholic countries, on the other hand, revolutionary movements have had a tendency to be predominantly political: Italy has fewer sects than England, but a lot more Communism; and in so far as atheism is regularly associated with Communism, also, perforce, a lot more unbelief. Not that Catholic countries cannot produce sects: the later Middle Ages prove the contrary. But they will produce sects only under certain circumstances: they will do so whenever and wherever the position of the Church of Rome comes closer to that of the Church of England and the Church of Russia – whenever and wherever she moves too near to the State and is in danger of losing her identity and independence. The sectarianism of the fifteenth century was clearly the consequence of the fact that the Church had entered far too deeply into the feudal system and had now to bear and to share the hostility which the revolutionary rising bourgeoisie felt for that decaying order of life. Had the Church not withdrawn from this perilous, even death-dealing, association, she would not have survived. But the effort at renewal whose driving force was the Society of Jesus and whose consummation was the Council of Trent, brought, on the sociological side, a relative dissociation between throne and altar. Externally it can be seen, above all, in the renewed emphasis on the international nature of Roman Catholicism. Rome's internationalism in an age of ever-increasing nationalism has earned her much hostility and hate, but it has helped her to preserve and to demonstrate her independence of the State. And where the masses feel that Church and State are not one establishment, there they will not be so inclined to visit the sins of the State on the Church. Indeed, it is not too much to say that even many radicals have realized that the association of the Church of Rome with established society was accidental rather than essential, whereas the association of the Churches of England and of Russia with their social matrix was altogether essential. The Church of Rome has ever defined herself as a *societas perfecta*, a perfect society in the sense that it needs no other to lean on. In the same terminology, the Churches of England

[1] The case of America is sociologically very different, however similar it may look to a superficial eye, and has to be treated separately. Cf. below, pp. 333.

and of Russia would of necessity have to be described as *societates imperfectae*, departments, by definition, of a wider social system, organs in an inclusive national organism, and hence connected with that system, with that organism, for better and for worse.

The mentioning, in this context, of internationalism (which indicates, not only a relative independence of a specific state, but also of the socio-economic system sheltered by that state), helps to remind us that Catholicism was not the only church that regarded herself as a *societas perfecta*. For a while at any rate she had a companion and competitor – Calvinism, for Calvin's design was to create a new universal church which would be the equivalent of, and the replacement for, the old: Geneva was to become another Rome, and her ruler was to realize, in changed conditions, the dream which Gregory VII had dreamt: the supremacy of the godly spirit over the worldly powers. This grand plan did not find fulfilment. As Niebuhr, for instance, demonstrates, Calvinism in all its forms soon tended to become, in every sense of the word, but especially in the social sense of the word, a narrow church – a bourgeois church, a church of the middle classes.[1] Yet the principle of the separation of Church and State remained, and for this reason the Calvinist and Presbyterian countries have historically far less sectarianism than the caesaropapist ones. A comparison between Scotland and England is most revealing, not to say downright convincing, in this regard. Even Methodism made only minor inroads into Scotland. And whenever schism appeared in the Scots Kirk, for instance, when the Free Church of Scotland – 'The Wee Free' – split off from the main body, it was due to that very same all-too-close approach to the powers that be which originated the same trouble in the Catholic camp. It was in particular the vexed question of lay control over clerical appointments which burst the unity of the Church of Scotland, for that lay control was in the hands of the upper classes, the land-owners. This would have meant the *de facto* 'establishment' of the Kirk, its subordination to 'respectable society', a consummation which was unacceptable to all those who believed, with Calvin, that God's house should not become a wing in the world's palace, that the communion of saints should never be confounded – even externally – with the state of sinners.

A whole series of facts can be adduced in support of the thesis which we are presenting. The first, if not the foremost, proof of it

[1] Niebuhr, loc. cit., chapter IV.

lies in the point of time at which sectarianism ceases to be marginal, and becomes a central phenomenon of socio-religious life. It is the sixteenth century – the century in which the State ceases to be a loose congeries of often ill-assorted territories and subsocieties and turns into a well-integrated unity with one all-powerful will at its core – a will that claims to be more than merely human; the century in which the State rises up and the Church sinks down, until, in many territories, it becomes the State's servant. The two developments are connected: the latter evoked the former; sectarianism is an answer to caesaropapism; the heresiarch is the counterpart to the king who, in Hobbes's famous frontispiece, wields crozier as well as sword, and who, in Hobbes's still more famous phrase, regards himself as 'a mortal god'. If Ivan IV of Russia and Henry VIII of England had not seen their power as divine or at least as divinely bestowed, their opponents would not have – indeed, could not have – decided to challenge them by preference in the religious field. If Joseph Sanin, if Luther and Cranmer, had not added a halo to the crown, those who wished to change politics and economics would have had no need to revolutionize religion, to split the Church. There may have been amity between Church and State, bishops and kings in the Middle Ages (though often enough there was enmity: remember Gregory VII!), but yet they never became one, and the Church consistently withheld ultimate approval from the State: and therefore those whose life-experience led them to an ultimate disapproval of the State, were not induced, were not constrained, to direct their attack against the Church as well.

'The main stream of medieval heresy flowed from the East, and the inspiration which fed it was something alien to the genius of Europe,' Ronald Knox has written. 'The lesser movements which might seem to foreshadow the Reformation were sporadic and unimportant, freaks of religious history. Enthusiasm [i.e. sectarianism] did not really take shape until the moment when Luther shook up the whole pattern of European theology; did not come out into the open till more than a century later. Not until the days of the Commonwealth can it be studied in its full context.'[1] The statement

[1] Knox, R., *Enthusiasm*, New York and Oxford 1950, p. 4. Those who are inclined to reject Knox as a witness because he was a Catholic, are referred to Norman Cohn's work, loc. cit., pp. 22 and 24. He, too, asserts that mass sectarianism is a modern phenomenon; and he can hardly be suspected of prejudice in favour of the medieval Church!

might be improved. Instead of simply speaking of the East, Knox might have spoken of the Byzantine, i.e. caesaropapist, East; instead of speaking of the genius of Europe, he might have spoken of the Catholic genius of Europe; and instead of referring to Luther's theology *tout court*, he might have mentioned his political theology – his surrender of religion to the princes – as well. But Knox is right: sectarianism acquires importance only after religion has become an official adjunct of the State, and thereby a *pièce de résistance* for the revolutionary forces.

Even more characteristic (if that is possible) than the developments in the West are the parallel and roughly contemporary developments in the East. As already indicated, Russia's Cranmer was Joseph Sanin; Russia's Henry VIII, Ivan the Terrible; Russia's Charles I, Alexey, the second Romanov. Before the middle of the sixteenth century, prince and patriarch were co-ordinate, rather than super- and sub-ordinate, figures in Muscovite life; there were annual occasions, such as Palm Sunday, when the spiritual superiority of the church-dignitary over the secular ruler was openly manifested and acknowledged by the tsar; and as long as this situation existed, the unity of the Russian Church was not in jeopardy. But under the influence of Sanin and his two successors Daniel and Makary the Church was, as historians like to express it, 'nationalized' – as the sectarians preferred to say, it was sold to the government. Immediately there was an impassioned protest. Sanin was opposed by Nil of Sorsk, Daniel by Vassyan, Makary by Arfemy. The latter three lost the battle and thereby the foundations were laid for the great schism which was to erupt a century later, and which shows some historical parallelism (besides a close historical coincidence, i.e. coincidence in period) with the Civil War in England, after which ecclesiastical unity was for ever a lost cause. When Alexey's Archbishop Laud, the Patriarch Nikon, changed the liturgy – a change which the conservative-minded masses regarded less as a fruit of his humanist desire for purer Greek, than as a demonstration of the mad resolution of the governors to reform, i.e. to desecrate, Russia's time-hallowed institutions – the breaking-point was reached. On the surface it looks as if the split was due to some petty disagreements on points of ritual, e.g. the question as to whether the sign of the cross should be made with two or with three fingers, but in reality the reason was the from now on inescapable involvement of the Church in the reforming, or rather revolutionizing, activities of the State which ran counter to the deepest values of the still medieval people of the great motherland. When Nikon later tried to reassert his independence and failed, when he 'met the fate of St. Thomas of Canterbury', as Conybeare has phrased it, and the 'lay papacy of the tsar'[1] became the rock on which both State and Church were to rest until 1917, the opponents of the government had no choice but to condemn the Church along with the State from which it had become indistinguishable.

How the lower classes in Russia felt about the official Church and why they abandoned it, can be seen as clearly from the following words of the outside observer Frederick Conybeare as from any statement from inside the country; the echo is as authentic here as any original voice: 'The Russian clergy preach to the people the indissoluble union of autocracy, orthodoxy and nationality, and deny the form of government to be a thing both human and mutable. This is why the clergy has made itself hated of an oppressed people . . . The Church has really transformed itself into a political institution, and its pastors [are] mere *employés* of the government . . . In its relations with the police you behold it sacrifice sincerity and authority and enslave itself to Babylon . . . The faithful perceive that the religious life of Orthodoxy is reduced to a legalistic formalism . . . and . . . they abandon the temple.'[2] The words are harsh and in all probability somewhat exaggerated. But the main fact stands out and cannot be impugned: it was the official character of the Church, its absorption into the State, that caused the religious revolts which punctuated Russian history for a quarter of a millennium, from 1667 to 1917.

In England and in Russia, the union of Church and State was consummated, and this consummation led to an open and irreparable religious schism. In France, the union of Church and State was not consummated: Gallicanism, as we have seen, was never more than half an Anglicanism. But there was, even in France, a strong tendency towards the formation of a state church, and the more the country moved in that direction, the more religious dissent there was, and the more that dissent gained in definiteness, both intellectually and organizationally. The more likely it became that the future would bring an amalgamation of the body politic and the body ecclesiastical, the more likely it also became

[1] Conybeare, loc. cit., p. 46. [2] Ibid., pp. 256 and 257.

that there would ultimately result an open religious fissure. In the end, the semi-establishment of the Gallican church produced the semi-sectarianism of the Jansenists and the Quietists. They were in the Church; they were not quite of the Church. But when, later on, after the Revolution, the basic tendency was reversed and an ever broader ditch opened between churchmen and power-holders, religious non-conformity disappeared (though atheism gained in strength). And thus it can be asserted that there exists something like a functional relationship (in the mathematical sense of the word) between the rapprochement of Church and State, and the estrangement from the Church of the strata which reject the State and reject the *status quo*.

The thesis which we are labouring here can also be confirmed in a different way – experimentally, as it were. Sect movements which arose in the caesaropapist countries and whose adherents (not being sociologists, and not knowing how hopeless their endeavour was) tried to export them to non-caesaropapist countries, countries with a division of Church and State, failed as a rule to gain a footing there. A good case in point are the excursions of the Quaker propagandists into Scotland. 'Scotland was a country even less receptive than Ireland,' writes the historian of the Friends. 'As had been the case in Ireland, Quakerism found most entrance in the army.'[1] But the army was English, not Irish or Scots. 'As for the Scots,' the *Life* of William Caton reports, 'they could not endure sound doctrine, but turned away their ears fron hearing the truth.' 'Oh, this is a dark nation . . . a stupid, sottish, ignorant people,' Howgill and Robertson wrote after their missionary travels in 1657. 'The way of truth is much dammed up at present,' and Howgill, perhaps even more deeply hurt than his friend, assured George Fox: 'It is a dark and an untoward nation, and little desire after God, and a false-hearted people and a blood-thirsty.'[2] Fox's own experiences north of the border led to the same conviction. 'He was in the Highlands among the clans and remarks, "They were devilish and like to have spoiled us and our horses, and run with pitchforks at us, but through the Lord's power we escaped them."'[3] Altogether, these gentle invaders found the soil of Scotland rather 'stony.'[4] – at least for the seed they had come to sow.

[1] Braithwaite, loc. cit., pp. 226 and 228.
[2] Ibid., pp. 228 and 231. Cf. also p. 352.
[3] Ibid., p. 351. [4] Ibid., p. 408.

Braithwaite's statement that Scotland was even less receptive than Ireland must not be understood to imply that *Catholic* Ireland was more receptive than Calvinist Scotland. He clearly refers here to Ireland as a whole, and such successes as the Quaker missionaries had on the island were concentrated in the Protestant parts, in those counties which, to this day, are split between Catholicism, Anglicanism and Dissent. 'The attempts which were made to carry the Quaker message to Roman Catholic lands,' Braithwaite admits, were 'barren in fruit'.[1] 'In Europe the Quaker success was limited to the Protestant–Puritan areas,' Braithwaite's editors confirm in an additional note,[2] and Catholic Ireland was in this respect no different from the Catholic Continent. Indeed, Braithwaite himself has to record, with sorrow, that the Irish soil was no less 'stony', then as now, than the Scottish.[3]

An attempt to drive the wedge of sectarianism into the body of Catholicism was repeated, two hundred years later, by men far better equipped for the task than the poor and uneducated Quakers. The 'apostles' which the 'Catholic Apostolic Church' – the Irvingites – sent out into the world to warn all and sundry of the impending doom and above all to gather the 144,000 elect of the Apocalypse, were well provided with cash and well versed in the modern languages. Yet those of them whose 'tribes' (or rather mission fields) were within the Catholic culture area came home empty-handed. 'His "tribe" was Italy,' we are told of Apostle Spencer Perceval, 'though little result came thence, and the "sealing" was far short of the required 12,000'. 'He placed a copy of the *Catholic Testimony* in the hands of Prince Metternich for the Emperor of Austria,' we hear of Apostle Francis V. Woodhouse, 'his area or "tribe" being Austria and South Germany (Reuben). Austria, however, was an unfruitful field.' And, of Apostle Frank Sitwell: 'He received as his field Spain and Portugal (Naphtali), but this "tribe" was unpropitious.'[4] It was only in the north of Germany, where the Prussian monarchy with its established *Landeskirche* had created conditions comparable to those in England, that the wooing of these Apostles aroused any response.

Lest it be said that the Irvingites and the early Quakers were peculiar and even scurrilous men who might not interest and

[1] Ibid., pp. 415 and 416. [2] Ibid., 575 [3] Ibid., p. 408.
[4] Shaw, P. E., *The Catholic Apostolic Church, sometimes called Irvingite,* New York 1946, pp. 80, 81, 83.

impress the commonsensical multitudes, let us wind up with a look at Wesley's experience. His appeal was broad, if ever an appeal was, yet in Scotland and in Southern Ireland it fell flat all the same. 'I use the most cutting words, and apply them in the most pointed manner,' the great Evangelist writes in his *Journal* about Edinburgh, 'still they hear, but *feel* no more than the seats they sit upon.' Similar is his comment on the people of Glasgow: 'They hear much . . . and feel nothing.' And in another context he moans: 'I cannot find my way to the hearts of the people at Perth.' The same complaint is made about the people of Armagh and Aghrim: they are 'sermon-proof'. At Dublin, Wesley 'spoke to all that came, but . . . found scarce any Irish among them. At least ninety-nine in a hundred of the native Irish remain in the religion of their fathers'.[1] If this soul-shaker could not shake the souls of the Irish and the Scots, who could? There is only one explanation for his success in England and his failure in Scotland and Ireland: the fact that the English poor were alienated from their Church as well as from their society, the Irish and Scots poor from their society, but not from their Church; and this, in turn, is due to the unity of Church and Society, Church and State, in the one case, and their divorce and distinction in the other.

If we were to look at the contrast between Catholic and Calvinist lands on the one hand, caesaropapist ones on the other, merely with the eyes of the student of religion, we should find ourselves confronted with a paradox. State churches have as a rule shown surprising toleration in so far as dogmas are concerned, Catholicism and Calvinism comparative intolerance. The Church of Russia was throughout the eighteenth century riddled with Lutheran theology, yet little protest was voiced; the Church of England bears even now an Anglo-Catholic and an Anglo-Calvinist wing within herself, and yet there are no official misgivings; church-parties there may be, but no heresy-hunts. And yet the Churches of England and Russia have split again and again, whereas the Church of Rome at any rate has not engendered much sectarianism where she has managed to survive the Reformation period unscathed. The solution of the paradox lies in the simple fact that behind religious dissent there hides socio-political conflict. The sectarian turns away from the official establishment, not so much because he is unable to accept this or that abstruse

[1] Cf. Knox, loc. cit., pp. 516, 517, 459.

doctrine, but rather because he is appalled at the fact that the mantle of religion should have been thrown over the sores of society, that a supposedly godly church should have allied herself with an unmistakably devilish world, and thereby lost the claim to be acknowledged as the proper abode of the pure and the poor. It was not the theology of the Orthodox and Anglican divines which evoked Raskol and Dissent, it was their politics, and for this reason it is the sociologist who can explain the phenomenon of sectarianism, and not the student of religion as such.

We are not asserting here that religious opinions are merely 'mirrorings' of socio-economic or political 'interests', that they are shadows without a substance. All that we are saying at this point is that a social fact (the prevalence of sectarianism in certain societies) is the consequence of a more basic social fact (the merger of church and state in those societies). It was not their craving for a religion of the heart which closed, first the pulpits, and then the church doors, against the Methodists: it was their lack of respectability. When Lord Sidmouth, in 1811, promoted his anti-Methodist bill, he inveighed, not against Arminians or Sentimentalists, but against 'pig-drivers and chimney-sweeps'.[1]

In the verbal war which, throughout the centuries, has raged between the established churches and the non-conformist sects, the preoccupation, on either side, with socio-political issues has often enough come to the surface. Writing to the Town Council in Münster in December 1532, Martin Luther defined the Anabaptists as those 'who are ever inclined towards revolt, interfere in political matters and arrogantly desire to rule'. No doubt, this was the core of his hatred of them, even if he did not like their version of theology (largely Lutheran!) either. Of the period around 1650, Underwood has asserted that 'the term Anabaptist was used in those times generically to denote anyone holding advanced religious or political opinions, pretty much as in recent times such a person was called a "Bolshie"'. This statement is not elegant, but it is certainly correct.[2]

In the Russian sources the same centrality of the political factor can often be traced and proved. In a pathetic letter to the tsar, the Protopope Avvakum, leader of the Old Believers, wrote: 'Nothing

[1] Wilkinson, J. T., *1662 and After*, London 1962, p. 139.

[2] Cf. Tumbült, G., *Die Wiedertäufer*, Bielefeld and Leipzig 1899, pp. 62 and 63, and Underwood, loc. cit., p. 77.

so much engenders schism in the churches as overbearing love of domination on the part of the authorities.' We shall do well if we take his words literally. The leftish sects were inclined to see the Orthodox Church as part of an unholy trinity of which the other two links were Crown and Treasury, and even the milder sects are at times found to designate her as an ingredient in the 'fiscal system'. She 'does duty as a government weapon for the defence of order', the Bezpopovtsy cried – and what neater formulation can we desire?[1] The historians, too, are behind our contention. Uzov, for instance, believed 'that in the Raskol the true driving force was not religion, but other factors, which may be summarized as the struggle against centralization and the growth of Tartar influence', and Conybeare judges that the Schism was 'really a struggle between the democratic elements and the authorities' in both Church and State – or rather in Church-State and State-Church.[2] The conservative writers are not slow to make use of this fact in their justification of police actions which were, again and again, taken against the sects. The Orthodox author of the broad-based *History of the Russian Raskol* (Kazan, 2 vols, 1895, 1897), Ivanovsky, 'strives to show that the dissidents were not punished on account of their religious opinions, but for opposing the tsar's government'.[3] There is a good deal of truth in this statement, even though it was made to justify political persecution. Indeed, Ivanovsky really understates his case. It was not only for opposing the tsar's government that, for instance, the Skoptsy were persecuted, it was for siding with the country's enemies even in a state of war. In 1812, these sectarians were on the side of the invader Napoleon, not on the side of the defender Alexander, and in 1823 and 1824 there was a prophecy current among them, according to which their triumph and the humiliation of the 'Jewish' (i.e. Orthodox) Church would come through Russia's defeat on the battlefield at the hand of foreign powers.[4] During the Crimean War, the Molokane appear to have offered up prayers for the overthrow of the oppressors of 'spiritual christianity'.[5]

As in the East, so in the West. 'There is risen a sect of perilous

[1] Conybeare, loc. cit., pp. 19, 186, 146.
[2] Ibid., pp. 14 and 23. Cf. also pp. 25, 26, 27, 253, 254.
[3] Ibid., p. 104. Cf. also pp. 93, 94, 284, 285.
[4] Grass, loc. cit., vol. II, pp. 200 and 643.
[5] Conybeare, loc. cit., p. 314.

consequences,' Queen Elizabeth wrote to James VI, 'who would have no kings but a presbytery . . . Suppose you or I can tolerate such scandals?' 'All these men tend towards,' Parker assured Burleigh in the same vein, 'is the overthrow of all of honourable quality and the setting a foot . . . a popularity.' James VI himself, when he became James I of England, blew the same trumpet: he described the Puritans as 'ever discontented with the present government, and impatient to suffer any superiority, which maketh the sect unable to be suffered in any well-governed commonwealth'. Even more interesting is the fact that the Puritans, when power fell to them, made judgements about the Quakers very much as Elizabeth and James had about them when they had still been in pursuit of power. 'I think their principles and practices are not very consistent with civil government,' Henry Cromwell opined, and Major-General Philip Skippon agreed: 'Their principles strike both at ministry and magistracy.' The conviction persisted. 'Believe me,' wrote James II to the Prince of Orange yet a generation later, 'it is republicanism which is at the bottom of all these affairs in England, and not religion.'[1] Public reaction to the Methodists was similarly shot through with political attitudes. A Staffordshire magistrate described the preachers of this movement as 'disorderly persons who go about raising riots'; a jury at Cork called them persons of ill fame, vagabonds and common disturbers of H. M. peace'.[2] No reference is made to religious non-conformity at all. It was not their habit of methodical prayer that aroused the men on the bench against the Methodists!

The passages given, to which many others could be added, show conclusively that it is not religious but revolutionary sentiment which sets the sects against established society. And inversely: it is revolutionary, and not religious, activity which, as a rule, sets organized society against the sects. Here as everywhere, hostility and hate are mutual: as the state became the focus of the sects' enmity, so the sect became the focus of enmity on the part of the state. Sects, while they are yet young, have almost invariably borne the yoke of persecution, and under that painful experience they have often defined themselves even more sharply, and differentiated themselves even more decisively, from the social order than at first. This brings us to an important, if distressing phase in their

[1] Gooch, loc. cit., pp. 41, 62, 331, and Braithwaite, loc. cit., pp. 215 and 258.

[2] Lecky, loc. cit., p. 630-

life-cycle: their clash with authority, law and police and the patriotic populace at large.

THE STATE VERSUS THE SECT

The long-drawn-out attempt on the part of the caesaropapist states to repress, and, if possible, to exterminate, sectarianism began already before the Church's national branches had been finally absorbed by the national states, that is, before withdrawal from the Church had become an act of disloyalty to the government; in other words, before religious dissent had become something like treason in the sense which the criminal codes are wont to ascribe to that ugly word. Spain introduced the Inquisition in 1481, and the Inquisition was an institution of the State, even though part of its personnel was provided by the Church. Anti-Spanish propaganda down the centuries has succeeded in branding the Inquisitors as typical heresy-hunters, but historical research shows that they were above all else treason-hunters, one might most say, spy-catchers. The very year 1481 is characteristic: the war against the Moriscos, to be triumphantly concluded in 1492 by the conquest of Granada, was reaching its climax; if it was to be won, the fifth column in the country had to be suppressed; that fifth column consisted mainly of Marranos, also called Conversos, formally Christians but really Jews, who secretly favoured the Moriscos. To find the betrayers and to render them harmless (which, in the circumstances, meant to kill them in such a way as to frighten other would-be agents of the enemy into desisting from their activities and schemes) became part and parcel of the war effort and later of the effort to preserve national security. Religious dissent and political disloyalty were really one thing, yet it is true to say that it was the latter aspect rather than the former that lit the fires of the *autos da fé*.[1]

Much the same thing can be said about the persecution of the sects after Luther, Cranmer and Sanin had succeeded in transforming the Church in their respective countries into departments of the State and thereby in giving religious non-conformity the character of an un-patriotic, anti-social, and occasionally even criminal, attitude. In times of war there was always the suspicion, if not of treasonable activity, then at least of insufficient enthusiasm for the

[1] Cf. Walsh, W. Th., *Isabella of Spain,* New York 1930, *passim*, but esp. pp. 43, 44, 84, 85, 165, 207–11, 281.

national cause – a suspicion greatly strengthened, and to some extent justified, by the widespread sectarian refusal to carry arms. In times of peace there remained the parallel suspicion of plotting against the government, of wanting, if not working for, its overthrow, and this again received support and confirmation by the conduct of the sectarians themselves, many of whom anxiously avoided any kind of behaviour that might be construed as an acceptance of established institutions. To use, for once, the language of organicism, the sects have always been alien bodies within the body social, and every healthy organism has a tendency to reject and to eject elements that do not belong into it. To their conformist and conservative contemporaries, the sects have always appeared as ulcers which had better be lanced.

Such, for instance, was the attitude of the German princes to the Anabaptists. Looking at these wild men, the princes could not but regard them as enemies of law and order, as enemies even of accepted morality, and conclude that it was both their right and their duty to wipe the offenders off the face of the earth. But, owing to the new conditions, owing to the merger of Church and State, their police-action involved, almost automatically, religion, and did so in a double way. On the one hand, the representatives of the State Church could be called upon to justify the persecution by the secular arm: of Luther it could not be said, *ecclesia non sitit sanguinem*; on the other hand, the victims of the persecution, the votaries of sectarianism, could not help being driven, by rebound as it were, even deeper into religious nonconformity: at first they had merely turned their backs on respectable religiosity; now they had to turn around to face and fight their enemy; and thus the sectarians became even more sectarian, at least for a while.

'In 1536, the Landgrave of Hesse asked the opinion of the Lutheran reformers concerning the proper treatment of the Anabaptists. In the *Opinion* which was consequently written by Melanchthon, but was signed also by Luther, the question whether princes are under duty to suppress "the unchristian sect of the Anabaptists", is answered in the affirmative.' The response of the Anabaptists was, in spite of their recent defeat at Münster, sharp and decisive. Under the title 'The preachers of our time do not serve Christ, but the princes', even the mild Menno Simons could write the following words: 'How much ever some of them boast of the Holy Gospel of Christ, yet, it is not preached except in a deformed and useless fashion, and only to the extent that the worldly princes and governments will tolerate and permit. For as the princes are, so are the preachers, and as the preachers are, so is the church: and this is carried so far as one must withdraw from Christ Jesus and His holy apostles and disregard their teaching and adhere to the princes and the theologians and believe their word – all on pain of being broken on the wheel or burned at their hands, or killed and murdered in some other tyrannical way; just as if the preachers should be sent by the princes and not by Jesus Christ.'[1]

Of Russia, it is hardly an exaggeration to say that the roles of priest and policeman came perilously close to each other; in the thinking of the people at any rate they were practically confounded. What Ivan the Terrible had begun and Alexey had carried to formal conclusion, Peter the Great perfected with his characteristic know-how and unlimited ruthlessness: 'The reformer of Russia looked upon the Church as part of the complex mechanism of the State, and linked with its holy duties a policeman's and inquisitor's tasks, utterly out of keeping with the dignity of its character. The priest was charged to draw up an exact list of those who paid the imposts and was obliged, in violation of the secret of the confessional, to draw up a report of political plots or offences. With the change of their character from that of shepherds of souls to inspectors of police, the clergy forfeited the confidence of the people, and the ties which united them with it were snapt for good.'[2] 'If the Raskol reject the official religion,' Volkov explained in his *Lettres à l'Etranger*, 'it is because the priests are servants of an administration which oppresses them . . .'[3]

The circumstances in Russia show that submission, on the part of the clergy, to the central authorities will always tend to find its complement in a similar submission to the local power-holders, and those local power-holders were in all typical cases the direct economic exploiters of the people – landlords and factory owners. 'The weakness of priestly influence was ascribed to failure to side with the peasants against the land-owners, an attitude which at times became almost slavishness before the great and the near-great,' writes Curtiss, and he quotes passages from official Ortho-

[1] Horsch, J., *Menno Simons*, Scottdale, Pa. 1916, pp. 101, 108, 109.
[2] Conybeare, loc. cit., p. 74. Cf. also pp. 69, 72, 73.
[3] Cit. ibid., p. 253. Cf. also Curtiss, loc. cit., pp. 85 and 86.

dox papers which show that their editors knew the right answer to the searching question: 'Why don't they believe us?' 'Who has not noticed what humbleness and even servility the ministers of the Church display before some local bigwig – a landlord, an official, or merely a rich merchant?'[1] The diagnosis was correct, but no remedy could possibly be found as long as caesaropapism lasted. It was unavoidable that the lower classes should seek religious satisfactions and salvation, not with those who sided with their oppressors, but with those who – like themselves – opposed them, with hedge-preachers and hedge-priests.

In a despotic state such as that of the tsars, the persecution of the sects – according to official opinion, enemies of God and man, simply because they were adversaries of the government, of the landowners, and of the capitalists – was bound to assume extreme forms. The Khlysty appeared around 1700 and developed, in the first thirty years of the eighteenth century, into an independent group. Persecution set in immediately: 'The earliest inquisition began . . . in Moscow in January 1733 . . . In all over three hundred were condemned, five of them to death, the rest were knouted or had their tongues cut out, were sent to hard labour in Orenburg and Siberia, shut up in monasteries etc. . . . In 1745–52 followed a fresh inquisition, also in Moscow. . . . Victims were racked every day, searing with hot irons being the most approved method of torture. Five were burnt alive in public. Twenty-six condemned to death [though later merely deported],[2] the rest to the knout, deprivation of their noses, exile etc.'[3] If it can be said in explanation and extenuation of these cruelties that the Khlysty were a dangerous set of men, it is necessary to reply that even the mildest sects did not fare any better. The Molokane or Milkdrinkers were mild, but the government did not hesitate to punish them for their non-conformity by at times depriving them of their children.[4]

How deep-rooted the hatred of non-conformity was, can be seen from the following report: 'In 1896 appeared at Kiev a new journal, the *Missionerskoe Obozrenie* . . . under the patronage of

[1] Curtiss, loc. it., p. 278. Cf. also pp. 65, 69, 357, 358, and *passim*.

[2] Cf. Grass, loc. cit., vol. I, p. 138, concerning this detail.

[3] Conybeare, loc. cit., p. 361.

[4] Curtiss, loc. cit., p. 160. The persecution of the Old Believers is reflected in Leskov's novel *The Cathedral Folk*, trans. Hapgood, I. F., London 1924, part I, chapter V (pp. 37–43).

Pobedonostsev. . . . In tone it was fanatical . . . demanding a crusade against the Raskol which it wished to see suffocated in blood. Even the orthodox clergy learned to detest it.'[1] If the latter statement is true, the paper must have been extreme indeed.

Particularly harsh was the treatment of the sect leaders. They were imprisoned in certain monasteries of which the most notorious were the Spaso-Evfimevsky and the Solovetsky convents – places not too different from the fortresses behind whose walls the more politically inclined opponents of autocracy often disappeared.

As invariably happens, pressure merely evoked counter-pressure. The Khlysty, and no doubt other dissenters as well, came to believe that if the State Church had any supernatural character, it must be satanic: they regarded themselves increasingly as the only true and apostolic church, as the successors to the holy martyrs whom the princely enemies of God had hated and hunted in the days of old, and indeed as successors to Christ Himself, victim of Herod, Caiphas and Pilate, while the Orthodox appeared to them as the successors of the Jews and Pharisees, the perpetrators of deicide on Mount Calvary.[2]

While in Russia the repression of dissent went on, with little diminishing severity, right to 1917,[3] in England it soon lost momentum – partly, of course, because the sects themselves changed, rather rapidly, from true non-conformity to *de facto* near-conformity. Yet for a while it was vigorous enough. The Corporation Act, the Act of Uniformity, the Conventicle Act, the Five-Mile Act and the Test Act, sometimes bracketed together as the 'Clarendon Code', inflicted severe disabilities on the dissenters, and if various forms of relief were granted in the course of time, the Test Act at any rate had a long life and made it impossible for centuries for sons of sectarians to attend the national universities.[4] In addition to these legal enactments, there was also what might be called a policy of pin-pricking. Pin-pricks, taken singly, are not too painful, but when they are inflicted *seriatim*, they can cause con-

[1] Conybeare, loc. cit., p. 250. Cf. also Curtiss, loc. cit., pp. 168 et seq., concerning Pobedonostsev's persecution of the Stundists.

[2] Cf. Conybeare, loc. cit., p. 354.

[3] Cf. esp. Curtiss, loc. cit., pp. 328 et seq.

[4] For a picture of the position at the beginning of the nineteenth century, cf. Selbie, loc. cit., pp. 198 and 199.

siderable irritation. To give but one example: according to the Corporation Act, the Sheriff of the City of London was required to take the Sacrament in an Anglican parish church – which a non-conformist, obviously, could not do. Up to 1767, non-conformists were deliberately and maliciously elected to the office, and when they refused to comply with the religious requirements of the law, they were mercilessly mulcted, the proceeds being used to meet the costs of building the new Mansion House. It is doubtful whether this veiled robbery was any more acceptable to the religious left in England than the double poll tax which Peter I imposed upon the Old Believers in his country.[1] In deference to the truth, it has to be recorded that – mainly as a reaction to the attempt to repress religious non-conformity by means of governmental action – the English 'parson' was no more popular among the lower classes than the Russian 'pope'. The careful investigations of Rowntree and Lavers in *English Life and Leisure* leave us little choice but to see this rejection of official religion and its representatives by the masses as a proven fact.[2] Even the identification of parson and policeman is sometimes encountered. The Christadelphian John Thomas described the clergy as a 'more dignified though less honest kind of policemen than the civil force . . .'[3]

Still, persecution *was* milder in England than it was in Russia, and the advancement of democratic principles, associated as they regularly are with tolerant attitudes, had something to do with it. But we must be careful and truthful: the difference between the democracy of the West and the autocracy of the East should not be exaggerated; it was less pronounced than it might appear at first blush. Two collateral circumstances must be brought into the picture which greatly modify a favourable first impression.

One is the fact that if the persecution of Protestant dissenters was relatively mild, that of Catholic dissenters certainly was not. Even now, some last Catholic disabilities are still in force; a Catholic, for instance, cannot become Prime Minister of England. The reason why the rigour of the law was inflicted on the Catholics rather than on the sectarians is, once again, political rather than

[1] Wilkinson, loc. cit., p. 113; Selbie, loc. cit., pp. 195, 198, 199; Underwood, loc. cit., pp. 95, 96, 118.

[2] Rowntree, B. Seebohm, and Lavers, G. R., *English Life and Leisure*, London 1951, chapter XIII, pp. 339 et seq.

[3] Cit. Wilson, p. 294.

religious. The sectarians were disliked because their patriotism was lukewarm, but they were not suspected of treason: there was no foreign power to which they were beholden. The Catholics, on the other hand, were, rightly or wrongly, always suspected of treason, and therefore they were not merely disliked, but positively hated: had they not a king abroad, the Pope, who dared to think himself higher than the King at home, who was, at the very least, his competitor for a Catholic subject's loyalty? and was the Pope not always allied with Spain or France so that a Catholic's loyalty was necessarily problematical? What the Marranos were to the Spanish, the Catholics were to the English: the criminals who were ready to let the Trojan Horse into the land. The Protestant dissenters greatly gained from the fact that they were judged less bad than somebody else.

The persecution of Catholics was not restricted to official acts and enactments; it was taken up and carried on by the mobs beyond the point where law and law-enforcement ended. The famous and infamous Gordon riots afford a very good illustration. Even after their 'emancipation' in 1829, the Catholics preferred to build their churches in obscure side-streets rather than in the main thoroughfares; even then they could not be certain what would happen. This brings us to our second modifying circumstance: if the laws of England were less severe than the laws of Russia, the mobs of England were more aggressive than the Russian mobs – even towards Protestant dissenters. This, too, is perhaps a consequence of the development towards democracy.

Quakers, Methodists and Salvation Army, all three paid a heavy price for their convictions. Jail was by no means the worst hazard which the early Quaker 'publishers' had to face, for in jail they were at any rate safe. Freedom could be a good deal worse. When the Friends gathered for a meeting in Cambridge on the first Monday of July 1660, an enraged mob fell upon them 'striking at those they could reach, flinging at others . . . and sometimes throwing wildfire and gunpowder into the meeting . . . to . . . weary us out of the place; and when they saw they could not do it by all these means, they brake and battered down the doors and walls next the street with bolt-hammers and other engines, and . . . used us as if our lives were all at their mercies . . . so that very many of us were sorely hurt and bruised, twenty-two had their blood shed, one so lamed that he was left behind unable to walk abroad, and a woman almost killed by their cruel usage'. Oxford vied with her sister in this sorry business. Stoning was tried in several places. At Haverhill, George Harrison and Stephen Hubbersty were dragged out of a private house and the mob most desperately did beat them to the ground, kicking them in a sad manner, driving them along the town, halloing them and stoning them . . . and this did not the townsmen seek to prevent, but set others on'.[1] Harrison died shortly afterwards.

What the mob at Cambridge shouted was, characteristically, the word: rebels, rebels . . . Any conscientious objector to armed service was a rebel. When, a hundred years later, the Methodist John Nelson managed to get his release from the army, 'at Ackham, he was knocked down so often, he could no longer rise, then dragged along the street by the hair of his head, with half a dozen or so trampling upon him "to tread the Holy Ghost out of him",' as his assailants put it. Nelson got away alive; not so the lay preacher William Seward (whose crime was nothing like conscientious objection – merely being a Methodist); he lost his life in 1740.[2] John Wesley was in danger more than once, especially during the Wednesbury riots, when the populace threatened to knock his brains out and showed every sign of determination to carry out the threat.

General Booth's men were even less interested in undermining the security, external or internal, of England than the Methodists, but Coates has this to report of the period around 1882: 'While within a year about seven hundred members of the Salvation Army were seriously assaulted, without one single charge being preferred by them in consequence, nearly a hundred members, a large proportion of whom were women, were sent to prison for alleged obstruction caused in the streets by the processions.'[3]

The story does not stop here. The Jehovah's Witnesses have written and are writing a new chapter. This is not surprising. As long as societies will feel themselves rejected or even threatened by an inner foe (and this is what live sects usually are – consider the attempt of the Jehovah's Witnesses in war-time to spread disloyalty and insubordination in the US army and navy for which twenty-year sentences were inflicted in May, 1918),[4] they will react

[1] Braithwaite, loc. cit., pp. 296, 297, 367, also 354, 473, 474.
[2] Cameron, loc. cit., p. 55; Lecky, loc. cit., p. 628.
[3] Coates, loc. cit., p. 141.
[4] Hébert, G., *Les Témoins de Jéhovah*, Montreal 1960, pp. 46 and 108.

with vigour and determination, for men are no less intent on their survival collectively than they are individually.

An account of the persecution of the sects by the combined powers of church and state would neither be full nor fair if it did not draw attention to the fact that the sectarians not infrequently bring it on themselves by their defiant and at times downright aggressive behaviour. Conybeare reports of the Stundists that 'on Good Friday, even the poorest among them eat meat'.[1] It is difficult not to see in this demonstrative action a challenge to the orthodox majority who harm nobody if, on this their holiest of days, they abstain from flesh-foods. Here again we have a policy of pin-pricking, but this time it is one inflicted by the weaker on the stronger party. We have already mentioned the habit of the Jehovah's Witnesses of yesterday to parade outside the churches of other religious communities with banners and placards reading 'Religion is a racket'. In doing this, they merely continued an old sectarian tradition. Three hundred years earlier, Quakers had nailed this notice on the doors of Anglican 'steeple-houses': 'God is not worshipped here: this is a temple made with hands: neither is this a church, for the church is in God. This building is not in God, neither are you in Him who meets here.'[2] It is clear that sectarian conduct of this kind must poison the atmosphere; it can help to explain, if not indeed to excuse, the aggression, or rather counter-aggression, which the orthodox forces feel and put into action against their ill-intentioned and ill-advised neighbours.

Defiance can, of course, have many forms, large and small, beginning with a simple holier-than-thou attitude (such as that which greatly incensed Charles Dickens against the Methodists)[3] and ending with a direct attack on all of the established decencies, such as public appearance in 'bridal clothes', as the Dukhobors call it – i.e. public appearance in the nude. The Quakers at one time thought this a good way of bearing witness. We have noted that the Friends received a very rough handling at Oxford. This is perhaps less surprising if we take into account the activities in the city of two young Quaker misses, called Fletcher and Leavens. The

[1] Conybeare, loc. cit., p. 334.

[2] Braithwaite, p. 50. Cf. also pp. 53, 68, 279, 280, 282, 288, 289.

[3] Cf. Dickens, Ch., *The Posthumous Papers of the Pickwick Club,* chapters XXVII, XXXIII, LII, Appleton ed., New York 1872, pp. 151–5, 185–91, 297–301, esp. pp. 152, 191, 300, 301.

Quaker historians are as a rule not too keen to go into detail about early 'extravagances'; but here William C. Braithwaite reports as follows: 'Elizabeth Fletcher, then a girl of sixteen, and [according to another Friend, Thomas Camm] "a very modest, grave young woman, yet contrary to her own will and inclination, went naked through the streets as a sign against that hypocritical profession they then made there, being Presbyterians and Independents [i.e. Cromwellians], which profession she told them the Lord would strip them of". Both girls also went into the colleges and churches, preaching repentance and declaring the word of the Lord. Their conduct subjected them to savage treatment from the "black tribe of scholars" and to a whipping from the authorities, the mayor refusing to be a consenting party.' Kindly mayor! No more kindly though than the Mayor of Cambridge who put his own gown on William Simpson when he did what Elizabeth Fletcher did in the other place. The Swarthmore Collection contains a document concerning one William Peares. It is endorsed in Fox's hand: 'died in prison at York about 1654'. When the paper is reversed, the reason for his martyrdom is revealed: 'The cause of his imprisonment was because he was moved to strip himself naked, a figure of all the nakedness of the world . . . It was the naked that suffered for the naked truth, a figure of your nakedness.'[1] Fox approved of such demonstrations, though Braithwaite cannot help qualifying them as 'zealous indiscretions' – admitting, at the same time, that 'such testimonies were more frequent during the early years of the movement than has been commonly allowed'.[2]

For various reasons, chief of them perhaps the simple fear of the consequences, the Russian dissenters did not bear witness in this particular way. Yet the idea came to the Dukhobors spontaneously, and, as it were, naturally, when, after their emigration to Canada, they found themselves in conflict with the government there. In 1929, the penalty for nudism had to be increased to three years in prison, but even this move did not have the desired result: indeed, there was more nudism after it than before! The dusting of itching powder on the bare bodies by the police was equally unsuccessful. On 15 May 1932, no fewer than 254 men and women paraded in their birthday suits!

[1] Braithwaite, loc. cit., pp. 158, 149 and 192. Cf. also pp. 126, 148–51, 189, 372, 373, 432, 433.
[2] Ibid., pp. 126 and 148.

THE 'ECCLESIOLA IN ECCLESIA'

The occurrence of such demonstrations shows that the alienation of a sectarian group from the inclusive society has reached a high pitch, and this in turn indicates that the persecution of the sect was intense, or was at least experienced as intense, by those whom it affected. But what of countries where repression is habitually mild?

A case in point is Prussia. Traditionally Lutheran, she was also caesaropapist and soon developed a religious protest movement known as Pietism. But the King of Prussia conceived of himself as the Supreme War Lord rather than as the Supreme Head of the Church, and so socio-economic conflicts did not find their main formulation in religious terms. The consequence was that half-sects developed, rather than full sects. The label used is often *ecclesiolae in ecclesia* – little churches within the Church. The Pietists informally met for prayer; no doubt they felt themselves to be men set apart; but their protest stopped short of final severance from the State Church. When we speak of *ecclesiolae in ecclesia,* in, say, Silesia, we ought to stress the word 'in' as much or more than the other two.[1]

Yet the division was there, even if it was not driven to the point of open separation. And open separation could not be avoided when the dormant conflict was awakened, so to speak. As soon as Hitler came to power, the people of Silesia and the rest of Lutheran Germany had to make their choice. The patriotic Protestants carried on as before, but the Pietists formed the Confessional Church (*Bekenntniskirche*), an ever more sharply defined entity. Persecution on the part of the police was not long delayed.

Similar developments occurred earlier in history both in England and in Russia. Speaking of the Methodist 'societies', Lecky tells us that 'the design of each was to be a church within a church, a seedplot of a more fervent piety'.[2] 'What may we reasonably believe to be God's design in raising up the preachers called Methodists?', asked an early Conference, and the suggested answer was: 'Not to form any new sect, but to reform the nation, particularly the Church [– the Anglican Church].'[3] To the Pietist prayer meetings corresponded the Methodist love-feasts, night-long sittings with nothing sinister about them, marathons of passionate devo-

[1] Cf. Knox, loc. cit, pp. 398, 401–3.
[2] Lecky, loc. cit., p. 608.
[3] Cameron, loc. cit., p. 26. Cf. also pp. 36, 37, 74.

tion. The last thing Wesley wanted was to break away from the Church of England; all he desired was to 'vary' from it.[1] But his loyalty was of little avail. The Methodists were driven out of the Anglican establishment; they had to become separatists – sectarians in spite of themselves. Characteristically, it was legalism which forced the issue, as we can best see in the case of the Calvinistic Methodists. 'The Countess of Huntingdon's . . . [religious] societies were set up as within the Church of England, and the Countess had no intention of severing herself from it. But she built places of worship, and a legal decision compelled her to register them under the Toleration Act, i.e. as dissenting chapels.'[2] It was Caesar who said: he who is not for me, is against me.

In Russia, a similar fate was inflicted on the Stundists. 'The early Stundists took up no hostile position against the Orthodox Church; their object was merely to moralize its members, just as Wesley, at any rate to begin with, had no idea of founding a separate sect outside the Anglican communion . . . It was only about 1870 that the new Pietists organized themselves into a distinct sect; till then they baptized their children in the Orthodox churches, confessed and received communion in them, kept the Easter fast.' Conybeare, in giving this information,[3] surmises that it was the influence of other dissenting groups which induced the Stundists to turn away from the establishment, but this is a wrong interpretation. His account must be collated with that of Curtiss, if the truth in this matter is to be discovered. Curtiss shows that the State became ever more hostile to the Stundists whose socialist leanings were utterly unacceptable to the power-holders in this semi-feudal country, until the Synod, in 1889, declared the group officially an 'especially dangerous sect'.[4]

THE CONFRONTATION OF SECT AND STATE CHURCH

All that has gone before can be summed up in one basic fact – namely, that the sect is the anti-type of the State Church, as shadow is the anti-type of light, and night of day. We have followed this all-important theme now through many of its socio-political ramifications, but we have not yet seen its formulation in strictly religious terms. The immediately following pages will complete the picture

[1] Knox, loc. cit., p. 506.
[2] Selbie, loc. it., pp. 176, 182–5.
[3] Conybeare, loc. cit., p. 332.
[4] Curtiss, loc. cit., pp. 40 and 41.

presented so far by investigating this particular aspect. From the *sociology* of religion we proceed to the sociology of *religion.*

As the reader will recall, the heart piece of established religiosity is the conception of the ruler as in some sense holy, in extreme cases as a deity of some kind. Logically, then, the heart piece of sectarian religiosity should be the conception of the ruler as in some sense infernal, in cases of consistent elaboration as a devil or even the Devil. Though not all dissenting groups have gone so far, many of them have. Both in Russia and in England the claim of the orthodox that the monarch is Christ-like has been countered by the assertion of the revolutionaries that he is Anti-Christ.

In Russia, the *Book of Faith* which appeared in 1648 – an eschatological text which marked the growing tension between the autocracy that had sanctified itself with the help of Sanin's doctrines and the dissident classes which would not accept that self-sanctification – predicted that in 1666 the Great Russian Church would finally fall away from the truth. Curiously enough, it was in 1666–7 that the breach between State Church and Old Believers became an accomplished and irreparable fact. It was not long after that the office of the tsar was radically reinterpreted: the sun-like countenance became, in the eyes of the sectarians, a devilish mask. At first, it was only Nikon who was regarded as an infernal agent, but when Alexey proved himself a Nikonian worse than Nikon, an increasingly sinister light began to fall on him as well. The great leader of the Old Believers, Avvakum, preached that Nikon – an antitype to John the Baptist, in that he spread the Serpent's gospel of lies, as John had spread the Spirit's gospel of truth – had slain Alexey's soul, and when Alexey died, Avvakum had a vision of him in the fires of hell. It was because he communicated this vision to the new ruler Fedor that he was burnt at the stake.[1]

But where Avvakum saw Alexey merely as a servant of Antichrist, his successors saw Alexey's successors as serial incarnations of Antichrist himself. It was Peter the Great, an innovator far more incisive than his father had been, who became the archetypal tsar-devil, the anti-type to the tsar-saint of the days of old. The Old Believer Avram revised the prophetic time-schedule and came to the conclusion that 1699, and not 1666, would see the coming of Antichrist in person. Five days before the beginning of 1699, Peter returned home from abroad – an ill-omened coincidence. The

[1] Conybeare, loc. cit., p. 99. Cf. also pp. 84, 94–7.

Streltsy – the traditional guards regiment – wanted to bar his entry into Moscow, but the *Reiters* – Peter's new-style, largely German-recruited bodyguard – put them to flight. Foreigners now had the power in the land: Holy Russia was desecrated. When Peter did not stop to salute the ikon of the Iversky Virgin, but hurried to the German suburb to see Anna Mons instead; when, five days later, he did not ask the patriarchal benediction, usual on New Year's day, but went for a drinking bout with Shein; when he did not come out to receive the traditional acclamation of the citizens, it was a foregone conclusion that Satan had ascended the throne of the saints. If he had not been Satan, why should he have avoided the holy relics, the holy places, the holy people?[1]

What is sometimes called Bible Mathematics came to the help of these conceptions. Why did Peter assume the outlandish title of Emperor? He gave himself this title, the sectarians asserted, in order to conceal his identity; he concealed it under the letter m. For if the letter m is omitted, the remaining characters of the word *imperator* sum up, according to the traditional numerical values of the slavonic alphabet, to 666 – the number of the Beast in the Apocalypse of St. John (XIII, 18). What could be clearer, and what more catastrophic?

There is neither need nor room for a closer study of this characteristic doctrine – characteristic above all because it obviously is an inversion of Orthodox ruler-deification. Only two points deserve to be mentioned: firstly, that it persisted; and secondly, that it was fairly general. Both circumstances are illustrated by the same fact: in 1868, the mild and already semi-conservative Old Believers held a council in their Austrian centre at Byelo-Krinits and decided to excommunicate all and sundry who would pray for the powers that be; prayer for the tsar had become the most blasphemous of all acts. Who would pray for Beelzebub himself? Some Old Believers, it is true, allegorized the doctrine: Antichrist is the spirit of the times, a spirit afloat, the spirit of national apostasy. Even then, however, the tsar remained the prime representative (if not the visible incarnation) of that spirit. But other Old Believers stuck to the more primitive conception that Antichrist was a person, the Man of Sin – and where should they find him if not in the hub and centre of all earthly things, in the Kremlin? As for the truly radical sects,

[1] Milyukov, loc. cit., pp. 43–7, 56–9; also Conybeare, loc. cit., pp. 91 and 92.

they had no doubt whatsoever that Russia was being ruled by a hierarchy from hell.[1]

Owing to the steady decline of the royal power in England, which contrasts so strongly with its long survival in undiminished vigour in Russia, we cannot, and we do not, find the same identification of king and devil on English soil. Yet while the Leviathan's might was still great, a tendency to see the figure on the throne in the lurid light of the hellish regions was by no means absent. Brandt's *Reformation in the Low Countries* (ed. 1720, Vol. I, p. 456) speaks of a Scots sermon received on the Continent according to which 'all kings were the children of the devil', and advising 'that it was therefore idle to pray for James'. John Lilburne's *Regal Tyranny Discovered* carries the following passage: 'Since it is an instinct of nature that there is a God, it is rational we should not make gods unto ourselves. But certain monsters of the devil's lineage assume to themselves the very sovereignty, style and office of God. And these monsters are commonly called kings.'[2] The reference to the 'devil's lineage' perfectly matches the caesaropapist concept of a divine, or at any rate Davidic, dynasty. While the court preachers liked to dwell on the kings as the offspring of saintly Edward the Confessor, the sectarian predicants depicted them as 'derived from [the not-so-saintly] William the Conqueror, who was identified with the Little Horn of Daniel's prophesy'.[3]

Lest it be thought that the onward march of democracy and unbelief has made it impossible for anybody and everybody to conceive the powers of this world as infernal in origin, let us quickly cast a glance at the ideas of the Jehovah's Witnesses.[4] They tell us a different story. All political rule is, according to their way of thinking, satanic. In their apocalyptic interpretation of history, the years 1914 and 1918 carry an especial significance. In 1914 Christ ascended His heavenly throne and started to give battle to Antichrist; by 1918 He had defeated the Foe, i.e. cast him and his followers down to earth, their last refuge, where they now – for a while – exercise supreme power, or rather the remnants of power. The Prince of Darkness has three visible agents at present: religion, commerce (note the anti-capitalistic implication here!) and

[1] Conybeare, loc. cit., pp. 175–9, 158.

[2] Gooch, loc. cit., pp. 48, 145, 146.

[3] Braithwaite, loc. cit., p. 484.

[4] The Christadelphians, too, must be mentioned here. Cf. Wilson, loc. cit., pp. 232, 286, 287.

government. With regard to government, the Witnesses see little difference between democracies and dictatorships. They refused to cry: 'Heil Hitler', for this phrase is blasphemous; but they also refuse to salute the Stars and Stripes. Participation in this common American ceremony is declared a mortal sin. The Anglo-American power-block is identified with the 'Beast' of Daniel and the Apocalypse (cf. Daniel VII, 7–8; Apocalypse XVII, 3–18), and the United Nations with the 'Abomination', the 'Disgusting Thing', mentioned by Daniel and Saint Matthew (Daniel XI, 31; Matthew XXIV, 15).[1]

The classical expression of these convictions is to be found in Rutherford's book *Government* and in the anonymous publication *Let God be True* (1946, second revised edition, 1952). The last-named work is studiously moderate, but the hatred of established authority comes through all the same. Quoting from their own *New World Translation of the Christian Greek Scriptures,* the Witnesses refer to Matthew IV, 8 and 9: 'Again the Devil took him [Jesus] along to an unusually high mountain, and showed him all the kingdoms of the world and their glory, and he said to him: "All these things I will give you if you fall down and do an act of worship to me".' 'From this,' the Witnesses conclude, 'it is unreasonable to think anything else than that all world governments were the Devil's property. He was the invisible ruler of them. . . . The Devil's attributes of greed, cruelty and selfishness have characterized every government on earth.'[2]

These words are not meant to be purely theoretical. In another context of the same book, the threat of civil disobedience is consciously, if cautiously, raised, as we can see by simply italicizing half a sentence: 'Since Jehovah has chosen his witnesses out of the world to be ambassadors in behalf of his kingdom to the peoples of earth, they are no part of this world. . . . The time, energy and life of a witness are dedicated exclusively to the service of Jehovah God. . . . Any turning aside from assigned duty so as to engage in *serving another master, to perform other work assigned by the civil state,* and any refraining from preaching because of complying with men's arbitrary commands to stop are in Jehovah's eyes unfaithful. God has declared that those false to agreements are worthy of death (Romans I, 31, 32).'[3]

[1] Cf. Hébert, loc. cit., pp. 122 and 246 (notes 11 and 12).
[2] *Let God be True,* ed. Brooklyn 1952, p. 56. [3] Ibid., p. 236.

THE TRANSITION FROM STATE CHURCH TO SECT: SOME PSYCHOLOGICAL AIDS

The neat confrontation of two conceptions of the ruler – his definition, by the state church, as an agent of heaven, if not (in Hobbes's words) as a mortal god, and his definition, by the sects, as an agent of hell, if not as a live devil on leave, as it were, for an earthly assignment – may be satisfying from the logical point of view; from the psychological point of view it is highly unsatisfactory. If men were fully rational, if their decisions were made on the conscious plane alone, such a black-and-white picture would make it easy for them to come to a final assessment of the two competing religious traditions, to choose the one and to reject the other, and to feel happy ever after. But men are not fully rational, and subconscious ties interfere with their modes of action; and even when they have made up their minds and acted accordingly, doubts arising from the subconscious continue to plague them, to pose and to press the tormenting question: have I done right? A poor man may be driven, by his whole life-experience, into the sectarian camp; yet the internalization of culture, if not positive indoctrination, may make him hesitate, and may make him unhappy after he has crossed the borderline between the state church and some sect. To overcome such difficulties, to put asleep such doubts, life has developed some helpful psychological anodynes, ideologies, which make the transition from a religious patriotism to a religious rebelliousness easy. We find examples in all the main areas of schism.

One rather primitive idea of this kind is the conviction that the king, the good and kindly king, is not to blame for the evils under which the would-be sectarian smarts: if only he knew. . . . But he does not know. He is surrounded by wicked counsellors, and *they* are the infernal agents. To revolt against them cannot be wrong; indeed, it is merely doing what the holy ruler himself would do, if he were a free agent. Moreover: rebellion against the established régime can be construed as an attempt to shift power back into the hands of the holy one. It is clear that speculations of this sort are powerful aids to the development of, and the recruitment for, sects, even sects with downright dangerous leanings.

In the West, the pamphlet known as *The Reformation of the*

Emperor Sigismund argues along these lines.[1] When John Goodwin, on the eve of the Civil War, left the Anglican establishment and went over to Independency, he published a defence of his conduct in which he denied any hostility to the monarch as monarch. 'It is a just prerogative of the person of kings in what case soever to be secure from the violence of men, and their lives to be as consecrated corn, meet to be reaped and gathered only by the hand of God,' he asserted. But while the ruler may be sacred, those around him are not. The people of England had no quarrel with their King; in what they did, even when they took up arms, they were but 'defending his royal person, honour and estate, endangered by his accursed retinue'.[2] About twenty years later, the Quakers still felt, and justified themselves, in the same way. On 29 May 1660, Richard Hubberthorne wrote from London: 'This day did King Charles and his two brethren James and Henry come into this city. Charles is of a pretty sober countenance, but the great pride and vanity of those that brought him in is unexpressable, and he is in danger to be tempted to those things which he, in himself, is not inclined unto.' 'The great excess and abomination that hath been used this day in this city is unexpressable,' Hubberthorne adds; yet he is not prepared to blame the monarch who, like a Friend, 'is of a pretty sober countenance.'[3]

Goodwin and Hubberthorne were rather mild sectarians, as sectarians go; they were not committed to the doctrine that the king is the apocalyptic beast. But even where this wild idea held sway, as in Russia, parallel psychological aids to the loosening of men's ties with the state church made their appearance and proved strong propellants in the direction of sectarianism. Most significant in this context were the legends which spontaneously formed around the figures of Peter I and Peter III.

When Peter the Great behaved as no Russian ruler had ever behaved before; when he did not salute the holy ikons and relics; when he did not ask the Patriarch's blessing; when he did not show himself to the people, the conviction gained ground in wide circles that this man simply *could* not be the legitimate tsar. Two connected rumours sprang up. The one asserted that Peter was not the son of the Tsaritsa Natalia at all, but of the Swiss Lefort and a German girl, in other words, a usurper, a foreigner, a fiend had

[1] Cf. Tumbült, loc. cit., pp. 1 and 2.
[2] Gooch, loc. cit., pp. 132 and 133.
[3] Braithwaite, p. 474.

made himself master of the country, with the nefarious purpose of converting God's people to heresy and thereby driving them into Satan's clutches. The other rumour was the positive counterpart to this. The true Peter, holy scion of a holy house, was still alive, but had gone underground.[1] It was for the faithful to hope and wait for his re-emergence and meanwhile to keep faith with him. But that faith could not be kept in the official Church which had been captured by the forces of Antichrist: to leave the Church was therefore a sacred duty, and not, as might appear, an act of impiety and rebellion. Things had sadly changed. What was wrong before the assumption of power by Peter had become right, what had been right, wrong.

Sixty years later, a similar but more elaborate legend arose and shed a religious glamour on the hapless Peter III. The facts lent themselves to it: Peter had been married (under pressure from the Empress Elizabeth, it would seem) to a German princess, Sophia von Anhalt-Zerbst, who has entered history as Catherine II, the Great (her Orthodox name). The relation of the spouses was from the beginning one of deep dislike, and one summer morning in 1762 the wife deposed the husband – the foreigner deposed the Rurik and Romanov. A few days after, her paramour, Prince Orlov, killed Peter, but this was not, of course, widely known. The general assumption was that the rightful tsar was somewhere in hiding, ready to re-emerge and to possess himself of his legitimate heritage. The woman on the throne was clearly the Devil's appointee, as the man thrust into darkness was God's chosen one. Holy Russia had to go underground with him – there was no other choice.

Not surprisingly, any revolutionary figure emerging from anonymity and leading the people against the government was soon thought to be Peter III. Pugachov, for instance, head of the uprising which erupted in 1773, was seen in this light. He made use of this mystical current, assumed the style and title of the murdered monarch, and thus met and confirmed the people's belief.

But the main impersonator of Peter was the founder of the extreme Skoptsy sect, Selivanov. It was whispered that the Emperor, in order to escape from his pursuers and would-be assassins, had

[1] de Grunwald, C., *Peter the Great*, trans. Garvin, V., London 1956, p. 188. Cf. also Cherniavsky, M., *Tsar and People*, New Haven 1961, pp. 75, 76 and 77, note 12.

changed places with a simple soldier of that name and thus managed to save his life. Henceforth he was not arrayed in splendid robes but in humble garb – but, of course, he had remained what he had been, God's chosen vessel, the Saviour of his people. (This story, curiously enough, was revived in the nineteenth century, Alexander I taking the place of Peter III and the hermit Kuzmich that of Selivanov.)[1] When the 'Crucifiers' (i.e. the police) after 'crucifying' (i.e. knouting) him, deported Selivanov to Siberia, his transport met that of the pretender Pugachov. Immediately, 'the truth' became known. Selivanov's guard was double that of Pugachov's (for even the ungodly are unwitting witnesses of the truth); and when the throng following Pugachov beheld Selivanov, they immediately went over to him (for the holy people cannot be deceived for long). The upshot of this story is clear: the Skoptsy are the Tsar's – or rather the Tsar-Christomimetes's – faithful subjects, the Orthodox his betrayers, traitors unto God and man. There was no deed more meritorious than to become a Skopets – above all, there was no deed more Russian, more truly Russian, more Russian and Christian at the same time.[2]

This powerful ideology which transferred the authority of the official Church to a revolutionary sect and thereby removed any idea that to join the sect was politically and religiously wicked, lived on to 1917. In 1873,[3] it was found to be in full vigour, and there was even a belief that the son and heir of the last tsar had been made a Skopets by a Skopets nurse.[4] It is difficult to know what exactly went on in the minds of these latter-day Skoptsy; perhaps nothing very exact; but the idea seems to have been that a new Peter III was on the way to the throne, in order to reveal once again the splendour and sainthood of a true tsar and to redeem and exalt those who had kept his image – the Christ-tsar-image – pure through long, dark and devilish years.

In the autocratic East, it was the true tsar who had to go underground; in the democratic West, it was the true people. In his revealing study of two proletarian sects, the Elim Foursquare Gospel Church and the Christadelphians, Wilson has found

[1] Cf. Cherniavsky, loc. cit., pp. 146 and 148.

[2] Grass, loc. cit, vol. II, pp. 82–5; cf. also pp. 143–6. Cf. also Cherniavsky, loc. cit., pp. 97 and 98.

[3] Grass, loc. cit., pp. 595 and 596.

[4] Conybeare, loc. cit., pp. 369 and 370.

strong traces of the British–Israel theory among their members.[1] This doctrine, which claims that the Anglo-Saxons of Britain and America are the ten lost tribes of Israel, and that the King of England is therefore of the House of David, is as much an outcrop of established religiosity as the idea that the tsar is the chosen one of God. It has, in consequence, found credence in rather exalted circles.[2] But the same doctrine can also become the basis of a sectarian creed, and the man who first conceived it, Richard Brothers, was very much the kind of wood out of which heresiarchs are made.[3] A distinction can be made between those who do not know what it means to be British and those who do: to the Bible-reading British–Israelites, the difference between the Jews at large, sunk into iniquity, and 'Jahwe's faithful remnant' was, of course, familiar. What had happened to God's people before, had happened again. And as 'Jahwe's faithful remnant' had been the true Jews, the rest not, so the British–Israelites were now the true British, and therefore the true Jews of the lost ten tribes, the others not. The upshot of this way of thinking is that to be a British–Israelite, or an Elim man, or a Christadelphian, is to be, not un-British, but true-British, more British than the common run of Britons. No patriotic scruples will plague the adherent of this set of ideas when he joins a group which otherwise appears to condemn the national values, the whole world of Britishry. At times, indeed, a conflict between the nationalistic and the separatist elements in such a compound ideology can appear, for instance during a war: to serve, or not to serve, in the armed forces, becomes then a difficult question.[4] But, normally, trouble of this kind remains subliminal, and the fact is that the British–Israel doctrine has, for many, smoothed the transition from established religiosity to revolutionary sect.

[1] Cf. Wilson, loc. cit., index, *sub verbo* British-Israelism.

[2] Wilson, loc. cit., p. 55 (note 3).

[3] Cf. *Dictionary of National Biography, sub nomine.* A new study of Brothers, his mission and its consequences, is overdue. The existing literature is mainly taken up with proofs that the British are *not* the lost ten tribes!

[4] Wilson, loc. cit., pp. 88, 89, 255, 256, 264.

2 · THE NATURE AND VARIETY OF SECTS

The negative attitude out of which sects arise, the depreciation of everything that is in, and belongs to, the world, finds its complement and counterpart in a positive attitude, an appreciation of that which is out of, and does not belong to, the world – practically speaking, the sectarians themselves. Sectarians have ever tended to see the human race as covered in darkness, with only one small circle of light within it, and that circle of light is their own circle, their own redeemed and already transfigured souls. This discriminatory evaluation is merely another instance of the common distinction between in-group and out-group so well described by Sumner at the beginning of *Folkways*. What is different in the case of sectarian egocentricity is, of course, the description and definition of the distance between self and other, value and unvalue, in religious and metaphysical terms which tends to make the colours involved – light on the one side, darkness on the other – rather glaring. There are gradations – it is one thing to set saints against sinners, another to speak of angels and devils – but these are no more than variations of the fundamental theme, the contrapuntal contrast between those who are for and those who are against God, the sheep and the goats.

A point at which these gradations and variations become obvious is the question which every sect has to consider – whether or not it has a messianic mission to the rest of mankind. It goes without saying that the state church, according to sectarian conceptions, has no such mission, or would at the very least be incapable of carrying it out, even if it had one: for how can the blind undertake to lead the blind? As the sect sets itself up as an alternative to the state church, one might be inclined to expect that it will regularly claim the redemptive role for itself; in fact, however, this is not so. Only some dissenting groups have cared for the salvation of their fellow-men; others, in all probability the majority, have been content to let the bulk of the race go to perdition.

MESSIANIC AND NON-MESSIANIC SECTS

The first General Baptists of England are a good example of the messianic variety. 'Helwys and his group in Amsterdam became convinced that their flight from persecution had been a mistake,' their historian tells us, 'because, as he said, "thousands of ignorant souls in our own country were perishing for lack of instruction". They therefore returned to London about the end of 1612, knowing perfectly well the dangers they ran. . . . Helwys had accepted Smyth's Arminian opinions . . . holding that in the divine intention Christ died for all men . . . Helwys proclaimed his faith in the title he gave to one of his books: *A Short and Plain Proof, by the Word and Works of God, . . . that all men are redeemed by Christ.*'[1] Similar was the attitude of the contemporary continental Baptists known as Mennonites. Menno Simons himself wrote: 'We seek from our whole heart nothing but that we may effect the salvation of all mankind. . . . We earnestly seek, to the extent of our opportunity, to make known and proclaim to all mankind the grace of God which has appeared, and His great love towards us, that they may experience with us the same joy and renewing of spirit and know and taste with all saints how sweet and good and kind the Lord is to whom we have come.'[2]

Jumping across more than three hundred years, we still find the same friendly attitude in the ranks of the Elim Foursquare Gospel Church. 'The eschatological teachings of the Elim movement blend with its fierce evangelism. . . . The elect is no exclusive élite already chosen, but a company into which all are invited, even though, when all invitations are answered, it will remain an elect body. The movement can thus see itself as an instrument of God, extending to all a chance of salvation. . . . Sermons end with an appeal to the unconverted to come forward and be saved.'[3]

A group which claims to be archetypal in this respect, and whose claim has been widely accepted, are the Quakers. 'Fox and his friends,' Selbie has written, 'were essentially a missionary people. The light of Christ which they knew was, they believed, for all men, and they were compelled to make it known.'[4] Speaking of his early 'openings', i.e. intuitive insights, Fox records: 'I saw the infinite love of God. I saw also that there was an ocean of

[1] Underwood, loc. cit., pp. 46 and 47.
[2] Cit. Horsch, pp. 49–51.
[3] Wilson, loc. cit., p. 27.
[4] Selbie, loc. cit., p. 103.

darkness and death; but an infinite ocean of light and love which flowed over the ocean of darkness . . .' It came to him 'that every man was enlightened by the Divine Light of Christ', and he saw it 'shine through all'. One of his first publications in 1653 is addressed 'to all that would know the way to the kingdom, whether they be in forms, without forms or got above all forms', and his fellow-Friend Farnsworth in the very same year issued a pamphlet entitled: *The General-Good to all People, or the Lord's free Love running forth freely to his own People in these latter days*. In view of these testimonies, Braithwaite has concluded, writing about the first generation Quakers, that 'their primary business . . . was this work of message-bearing, this broadcast sowing of the seed on every soil: the message was regarded by them as one of universal scope, though the spiritual Israel . . . might alone respond to it'.[1]

All this sounds well enough, but Farnsworth's title has an ominous distinction between 'all people' and 'the Lord's own people' which indicates a rather different attitude underneath the surface. The truth is that many sectarians are interested in the salvation of their fellow-men in theory rather than in practice, in words rather than in fact. Outcast and persecuted as they often are, unsuccessful and alienated as they always are, these men are, perhaps understandably, filled by a hatred of those who persecute them, and even of those who are more integrated and comfortable and successful than they are, which frequently kills all real desire to spread the good message and to broaden the road to redemption. Men have never been over-anxious to distribute their privileges far and wide, and religious dissenters are no exception to the rule. And thus there springs up, in many cases, a well-nigh anti-messianic attitude. What if millions upon millions sink into the bottomless pit, into sulphur and brimstone, as long as my friends and I are raised to heaven?

A passage from the Quaker pamphlet *To All who would know the Way to the Kingdom* which Braithwaite has *not* quoted, runs as follows: 'Oh ye rich men and proud men of the earth, weep and howl, for your misery is coming. . . . The fire is kindled, the day of the Lord is appearing. . . .'[2] Words full of threat, but empty of mercy! In the same vein, Robert Rich shouted at the doors of the

[1] Braithwaite, loc. cit., pp. 36, 37, 131, 151. Cf. also pp. 46 and 47.

[2] Cit. Huehns, p. 143. Miss Huehns gives 1654, and not 1653, as the date of publication.

House of Commons (though on a day of particular stress and strain, as we should emphasize): 'The Lord is coming to separate between the sheep and the goats, to gather up the wheat into garners, and to burn the chaff with fire that is not to be quenched.'[1] The day of the Lord is in either case the day of judgement, the day of damnation, not the day of final reconciliation and redemption. How far are Fox and Rich from the sentiments of, say, the Levellers, who never wanted to be anything but fighters for their class and haters of their class enemy? The following passage from *The True Levellers' Standard Advanced* (1649) is not very different in spirit from the Quaker pronouncements which we have transcribed: 'You Pharaohs, you have rich clothing and full bellies, you have your honours and your ease; but know the day of judgement is begun and that it will reach you ere long. If you will find mercy, let Israel go free; break to pieces the bands of property. The poor people you oppress shall be the saviours of the land.'[2]

In a way, Braithwaite himself acknowledges that Quaker messianism was a short-lived affair. He writes: 'A community that is in active dissent from the world round it tends to become a state within the State, and the pressure of persecution strengthens the tendency. The Quaker Publisher had a world wide message, but the Children of the Light who accepted it formed a gathered church that was very clearly separated from the rest of the population, notably . . . by the outward marks of simple dress, plain language, and the refusal of customary ceremonies and marks of social respect . . . the world went one way and the Quaker community another.'[3]

Nevertheless, in this as in all other respects, the Quakers were a particularly philanthropic set of men. But what was merely an occasional mood in them, was a hardened character trait in others. Some sects have been remarkably blood-thirsty, as, for instance, the Anabaptists of Münster and their train. Tumbült has called Jan Matthisson and Cohn Hans Hut 'prophets of vengeance', and this is precisely what these two preachers were. In Hut's world of phantasy, the 'two-edged sword of justice' played a very great role. At Whitsuntide, 1528, he announced, Christ would return to earth to place that sword (along with chains for kings and nobles) into the hands of the re-baptized Saints, to enable them to deal

[1] Braithwaite, loc. cit., p. 263. [2] Cit. Gooch, loc. cit., pp. 216 and 217.
[3] Braithwaite, loc. cit., p. 465.

with Catholics and Protestants, priests and pastors alike. Matthisson claimed a special revelation in which he was expressly bidden to wipe the ungodly from the face of the earth by force of arms. And there is little evidence that in doing so he would have uttered the traditional prayer of the hangman: 'And may God have mercy upon your souls. . . .'[1]

Nowadays the rather complex theology of the Jehovah's Witnesses is not without hope for the penitent. Nevertheless, a certain amount of pleasure is taken in the vision of Armageddon which is central to their system of belief. At that terrific battle, the Witnesses will quietly sit on a hillside and watch the carnage that will be going on down in the plain. Safe from harm, these sectarians at times gloat over the wrath to come. For them 'Jehovah remains a blood-thirsty and arbitrary God who is interested only in the modern "Theocratic Organization" of Jehovah's Witnesses', a student of the movement has stated, 'and condemns to destruction all men who do not belong to it, that is, members of all other churches and religions, and the representatives of all political and economic organizations'.[2] And even of those who are spared, only very few – the 'little flock' of 144,000 – will receive the divine nature and share in the glory. The 'great multitude', though composed of 'consecrated saints' like the 'little flock', will undergo chastisement and then emerge as merely inferior spiritual beings. As for the 'wolves disguised as sheep' . . . Total destruction will be their lot.[3]

Not very different are the opinions of the Christadelphians. They, too, deny that all men were destined by God for the same high end. 'The Christadelphians recapitulate the New England Calvinist idea of the Church; it is not a universal institution, but a church of the chosen and everlasting saints.' Wilson notes a certain element of sadism among these sectaries: 'There is,' he writes, 'an element of satisfaction – expressed particularly by the earlier writers – in the meting out of justice and vengeance to the sinful world. . . . They look forward to a time when the saints will persecute the world, as the world has persecuted the Jews, and, by extension, the Christadelphians.' Indeed, the whole appeal of the Christadelphians is 'an appeal to those who can fervently desire to

[1] Tumbült, loc. cit., p. 33; Cohn, loc. cit., p. 275.

[2] Algermissen, K., *Christian Sects,* New York 1962, p. 95.

[3] Cf. Hébert, loc. cit., pp. 27 et seq.

see this world pass away with great agony for the great majority'.[1] It is sweet for men to see their adversaries punished, be it only in a day-dream, the solace of the impotent.

Hence when sectarians engage in propaganda, their real aim is rarely the conversion of the whole human race, which is the ambition of true apostolicity; it is rather the strengthening of their own rebellious and alienated group. Few of them have ever entertained the ideal of Origen and Leibniz, the *apokatastasis panton*, or salvation of all.

THE SECT AS A RELIGIOUSLY CONCEIVED ÉLITE

Underprivileged in the eyes of the world, the true sectarians regard themselves as overprivileged in the kingdom of God. The following words of a 'Brother' Anderson, a working-man and part-time pastor of a coloured congregation, show the essential conviction in a naïve and, one could almost say, charming form. They were taken down by the Rev. T. K. Beecher just as they came from the speaker's mouth: '. . . I 'member wat I saw las' summer 'mong de bees. . . . De bees kep' a goin' an' a cumin' in de clover: an' dey jes' kep' on a fillin' up de hive till de honey was a flowin' like the lan' ob Canaan. An' I saw all roun' de hives was de ants an' worms an' de black bugs, and dey kep' on de outside. Dey warn' bees. Dey could na make de honey for dar selves. Dey could na fly to de clover an' de honey suckle. Dey jes' hung roun' de bustin' hive an lib' on de drippin's.'[2] Honeybees and black bugs – what neater confrontation can there possibly be?

Needless to say, in most cases, the same conviction is expressed in far more sophisticated terms. Particularly interesting, in the context of this book, is the use of the caesaropapist definition of the ruler as priest (or saint) and king for the self-characterization of the sectarians because it brings out, in an impressive way, the fact that rebellious religiosity is the mirrored image of established religiosity. A passage from the Book of Revelation (V, 9 and 10) greatly helped here. 'And they sung a new canticle, saying: Thou art worthy, O Lord, to take the book and to open the seals thereof: because thou wast slain and hast redeemed us to God, in thy blood, out of every tribe and tongue and people and nation: And

[1] Wilson, loc, cit., pp. 325, 351, 353, 311.

[2] Coates, loc. cit., pp. 124 and 127.

hast made us to our God a kingdom and priests. And we shall reign on the earth.' 'This text is ever on the tip of a Raskolnik's tongue,' Conybeare reports from his personal experience.[1] Among the Russian dissenting groups which he studied, the 'Righthand Brotherhood' of the mid-nineteenth century has left its mark, even though it was only small. Its founder, Ilin, expressed his message in a couplet, and Conybeare has successfully translated it for us:

> 'Nor churches raise of stone, nor altars rear,
> But everywhere God glorify and fear.
> Your priests we own not, rites away we fling,
> With us each brother is a saint and king.'[2]

In the same spirit, Robert Browne asserted in *Life and Manners of All True Christians* (1582) that all true Christians were priests and kings, and John Robinson, pastor, in Holland, to the Pilgrim Fathers, wrote: 'In this holy fellowship, every one is made a king, a priest, a prophet, not only to himself, but to the whole body.'[3]

The reason that this formulation was not more frequently used lies in the fact that the sectarians were, as a rule, so steeped in religious and especially biblical lore that they could take their imagery from no other source. We have already encountered a very widespread assertion, namely, that the members of the sect are the 144,000 white-robed ones of the Apocalypse (VII, 14): 'These are they who are come out of great tribulation and have washed their robes and have made them white in the blood of the Lamb.' The Jehovah's Witnesses are only one of many, many groups who have claimed this identification.

But there are plenty of other possibilities which have been eagerly seized. One occurs in Ezechiel (IX, 2–6): 'Behold six men came from the way of the upper gate which looketh to the north: and each one had his weapon of destruction in his hand. And there was one man in the midst of them clothed with linen, with a writer's inkhorn at his reins . . . And the glory of the Lord of Israel went up . . . and he called to the man that was clothed with linen and had a writer's inkhorn at his loins. And the Lord said to him: Go through the midst of the city, through the midst of Jerusalem, and mark Thau upon the foreheads of the men that

[1] Conybeare, loc, cit., p. 182, note 4.
[2] Ibid., p. 330. Cf. also p. 279.
[3] Gooch, loc. cit., pp. 50 and 76.

sigh and mourn for all the abominations that are committed in the midst thereof. And to the others he said in my hearing: Go ye after him through the city and strike; let not your eyes spare, nor be ye moved with pity. Utterly destroy old and young, maidens, children and women: but upon whomsoever you shall see Thau, kill him not.' The Anabaptists, for instance, believed that *they* had received the holy sign, the symbol of survival and salvation.[1]

Yet another historically important passage is contained in Isaias (XIV, 1 and 2): 'The Lord will have mercy on Jacob and will yet choose out of Israel, and will make them rest upon their own ground. And the stranger[s] shall be joined with them, and shall adhere to the house of Jacob. And the [Jewish] people shall take them and bring them into their place: and the house of Israel shall possess them in the land of the Lord for servants and handmaids. And they shall make them captives that had taken them: and shall subdue their oppressors.' Why these particular verses appealed to the sectarians can best be understood by remembering here the Rastafarians: today the black men are in bondage to the white; tomorrow the white shall be in bondage to the black. The sectarians are the Jews, God's chosen people; their enemies are the Egyptians (cf. the Leveller invective above), or the Babylonians, or the Assyrians, or the Philistines, proud nations, yet heading for a fall, for the Lord is not with them.

The reference to Isaias XIV is only one instance out of many, one might almost say, countless ones, by means of which the dissenters dramatize themselves as the Jews – i.e. the priest-kingly nation – of these latter days. Russia's Righthand Brotherhood, to which we referred not long ago, preached circumcision, demanded Sabbath observance and forbade the eating of pork, while condemning the Jews properly so called as a 'congregation of Satan'. Similar tendencies made their appearance among the Molokane who, in the end, split into two subsects, the Sabbatarians and the 'Sundayites'. Generally speaking, the term 'Judaizer' appears again and again in all discussions of the Russian sects.[2]

In the West, the same ideas are holding sway among the sectarians. From the Quakers to the Jehovah's Witnesses, the proudest name they claim is 'the New Israel'. Sometimes this is a generalized label; sometimes more specific features of the Bible

[1] Horsch, loc. cit., p. 87, note 2.

[2] Cf. Conybeare, loc. cit., pp. 331, 324, 325.

story are singled out for use. Those who know the English scene may have observed that chapels of the Strict and Particular Baptists are often called 'Zoar'. It was to Zoar (Segor) that Lot escaped from Sodom (Genesis XIX, 22). The identification thus claimed is highly characteristic. These sectarians see themselves as the few who will escape the fire and brimstone which will rain down upon, and utterly destroy, the wicked, Sodom-like world.[1]

All these passages are sociologically interesting because they confirm what we have said about the typical sectarian attitude towards the rest of humanity – the fact that they tend to hate rather than to love. Even the place-name 'Zoar' contains an element of this kind, for Zoar or Segor means 'the little one' – only a few will escape! The passages from Ezechiel and Isaias suited the near-sadists particularly well. Ezechiel reports God as saying: 'The iniquity of the house of Israel and of Juda is exceeding great, and the land is filled with blood, and the city is filled with perverseness. . . . Therefore neither shall my eye spare nor will I have pity. . . . Defile the house and fill the courts with the slain. Go ye forth. And they went forth and slew them that were in the city' (IX, 9, 10, 7). Similarly Isaias: 'Howl, O gate: cry, O city. All Philistia is thrown down: for a smoke shall come from the north, and there is none that shall escape his troop. . . . I will make thy root perish with famine, and I will kill thy remnant' (XIV, 31, 30).

The preference for the Old Testament and for the Apocalypse (the part of the New Testament which, with its dependence from, e.g. Daniel, is most like the Old) is in itself highly revealing. The sectarians are frustrated fighters: even those who preached that one should turn the other cheek would have liked to clench the fist instead.[2] Jehovah, the tribal deity, suited them better than Jesus, the lover of all. But some sects have characterized themselves by preference in New Testament terms, and we must survey this material as well. We shall find it no less interesting.

Typologically, we can distinguish here two forms: sects which claim that their *head* is a new incarnation of the deity (be it of God the Father, or of the Son, or of the Holy Spirit), and sects which claim that *all* their members are such incarnations. As usual in this complex life, the two ideas are at times combined, with various degrees of ingenuity, for instance by asserting that the founder is the Father, and his followers are, each of them, the

[1] Cf. Underwood, loc. cit., p. 187. [2] Cf. below, pp. 198 et seq.

Son made flesh. The distinction between divinizers of the leader and divinizers of the group is by no means purely theological, but has important sociological implications as well. Where the first type prevails in its purity, the sectarians appear as a secondary *élite*; they are exalted by virtue of their association with a super-exalted personality, as a king's footman participates, to some extent, in the king's glory. Where the second type is fully developed, the sectarians are a primary *élite*, each bearing the mark of distinction – the highest mark of distinction, namely divinity, or at least deiformity – in himself. It is clearly this latter alternative which marks the *acmé* of sectarian self-appreciation. 'The true Light . . . shows itself through illuminated, i.e. *godded* men, for through such persons the Most High is *manned*,' wrote Henry Nicholas,[1] founder of Familism and forebear of many other groups. Those among our readers who remember our discussion of the Christomimetic King in Vol. I will see immediately that in these conceptions we behold the democratic counterpart of the ruler-deification which is so widespread in the royalist world. There, one was god; here, all are – all, that is, who belong to the sect, who are not associated with the king-devil on the throne.

A good example of a sect whose members see themselves as a secondary *élite* are the Shakers. God came twice to earth: once in a male shape, once in a female: first as Jesus Christ, then as Ann Lee. Here there can be no comparison between sect-leader and sect-follower. Such glory as the latter possesses is derived from the former. Mary Baker Eddy, successor of Ann Lee, saw to it that this would not be forgotten. Witness the following by-law contained in the *Manual of the Mother Church*: 'If the author of the Christian Science textbook call on this Board for household help or a handmaid, the Board shall immediately appoint a proper member of this Church therefor, and the appointee shall go immediately in obedience to the call.' And then follows a very curious passage in which the little word 'me' is transferred from Jesus to Mrs. Eddy – a quotation from Matthew x, 37: '"He that loveth father or mother more than me is not worthy of me."'[2] No doubt the selected servant took great pride in the fact that she was in a sense what those had been who had attended on Jesus, while He was on earth.

Even in the twentieth century, it is by no means rare for a sect

[1] Cit. Braithwaite, p. 23. [2] Cit. Wilson, p. 143.

to form around a supposed incarnation or re-incarnation of God. Fritz Blanke, in his handbook *Kirchen und Sekten*,[1] mentions the following self-styled messiahs as the centre of existing groups: Anton Unternährer, Oskar Ernst Bernhardt, Friedrich August Hain, Count St. Germain, Christus Georg von Montfavet (in fact a postal employee called George Roux), Lou Voorthuizen, Johann Jacob Wirz, Johannes Pertinax (*recte* Schenk), Emil Zehnder, Edwin Züllig, and, of course, George Baker, known as Father Divine.

What is interesting, not only from the point of view of the sociology of religion, but also from the point of view of general sociology, is the way in which groups which regard themselves as primary *élites* are often forced back in the direction of a secondary or derived *élite*. In Russia, the Khlysty got their name for two reasons: the word sounds both like the term for flagellate and like the name of Christ, and the label Khlysty therefore implies the assertion that all these flagellants were Christs. When Selivanov took his Skoptsy out of the parent sect of Khlysty, it was difficult to do him proper honour. No good saying he was a new Christ – everybody was that. So there was no other solution but to teach that Selivanov was an incarnation of God the Father, and the title which came to be settled upon him was 'The Lord Sabaoth'.

What was in this case merely a matter of logic and affection turned in the case of Father Divine into a practical problem, a problem of discipline. Father Divine, when still George Baker, was something of a disciple of a prophet called Samuel Harris. Samuel Harris lived in Allegheny, Pennsylvania. 'On Sundays he served as a lay preacher there. On weekdays he worked as a steel-mill laborer. . . . One night, in the middle of reading the Bible, he came on a verse [verse 16] in the third chapter of First Corinthians that staggered him . . . "Know ye not that ye are the Temple of God, and that the spirit of God dwelleth in you?" the Bible asked. Didn't the Bible speak plain as day that if the spirit of God dwelt in him, and if the Spirit and the Word were one, then God Himself dwelt in him? And if God dwelt in him, then his body was God's body – and he, Harris, was God.' I Corinthians III, 16 had done for him what St. John I, 9 had done for George Fox. (Harris conveniently overlooked I Corinthians III, 2 and 21: 'You are yet carnal . . . Let no man therefore glory in men.') Illuminated, Harris

[1] Zürich 1959, pp. 91–4.

now assumed the name of Father Jehovia, but he was not, it seems, denying that what was true of him was true of others also. One of his followers, St. John the Vine Hickerson, tried to collect around him other deities, but he found that they were unwilling to be mere followers: were they not as much as the Vine was? Who was he to lead them? The Hickerson experiment ended in failure. Baker, who had closely watched it, learned the lesson. He found out that, for a sect to be a success, it must be subject to its master, and therefore he was careful to present himself to the people of Harlem, not as 'God in the Sonship degree', but as 'God in the Fathership degree'. The idea paid off, and Father Divine became one of the twentieth century's most renowned heresiarchs – and a millionaire to boot.[1]

Not all sects, however, have so easily abandoned their democratic constitution. Indeed, many of them have stuck to it and even developed it to the degree to which they developed their inherent anti-authoritarianism. The Russian Dukhobors or Spirit-Wrestlers originally entertained the idea that they were descended from Sidrach, Misach and Abdenago – a legend similar to the self-dramatization of the Strict and Particular Baptists as those who were like Lot, the man who fled from wicked Sodom and survived in godly Segor. In the eighteenth century, however, their leader Pobirohin taught 'that God does not exist by Himself, but is inseparable from man. It is for the righteous in a way to give Him life. . . . Jesus Christ was the spirit of piety, purity, etc., incarnate. He is born, preaches, suffers, dies, and rises again spiritually in the heart of each believer. He is the Son of God, but in the same sense we are also the sons of God. The inward word reveals Him in the depth of our souls. It existed in all ages and enlightens all who are ready to receive it. . . .'[2] Every Dukhobor is The Son; indeed, every Dukhobor is the whole Godhead. 'Through our Memory we are one with the Father; through our Understanding one with the Son, through our Will one with the Spirit; and the three persons are separately symbolized as Light, Life and Peace. Thus every Dukhobor is the Trinity incarnate.'[3]

[1] Harris, loc. cit., pp. 13 and 14.

[2] Summary of Pobirohin's theology in the *Encyclopedia of Religion and Ethics*, ed. New York 1955, article Doukhobors (vol. IV, pp. 865–7). Cf. also Conybeare, loc. cit., pp. 270, 271, 274, 277, 278, 279, 280, 286.

[3] Conybeare, loc. cit., p. 270.

The deep obeisances with which these men salute – indeed, worship – each other are merely the outward signs of this belief in a universal inward Christness. Of course, it was not only the holiness of Jesus which the Dukhobors claimed for themselves: it was also His power. 'When Judgement Day comes,' their leader Peter Verigin the Younger assured them, 'you will see me on one side of God, and Christ on the other. You, the true Dukhobors, will be behind us, the jury. All other people of the world will be out in front, in the prisoners' dock, getting judged.'[1]

The Khlysty achieved the same self-interpretation by developing an adoptionist Christology. Even Jesus was merely a man until His thirtieth year, and even His body decayed after He was laid to rest. One becomes a Christ through adoption by the Father, i.e. through the descent of the Holy Ghost. The great figures of the Old Testament were already Christs; and so are the great figures of the New Dispensation, especially, of course, the Khlysty. By incarnation, these sectarians mean the entry of the Holy Spirit into a human heart, by the virgin birth, education into Christhood, such as Mary gave to Jesus and led Him to the Jordan, i.e. preparation for a spiritual rebirth, by resurrection the re-incarnation of the Holy Ghost in a new human being. The descent of the Holy Ghost into a heart is brought about by a prolonged fast. It is within anybody's and everybody's power. 'Unhappy is he who believes only in one Christ!'[2]

How permeated the Khlysty were, one and all, by this doctrine, can be seen from the following incident which occurred during the legal proceedings against the sectarians in 1849. One of the 'goddesses' swivelled round and addressed the bystanders as follows: 'I have chosen the body of this woman for my dwelling, after having first driven the devils from her inside, and now I say with her lips that the end of the world will soon come to pass. If you will turn to the better, I shall grant you another three years; but if you will not turn to the better, I shall shorten the interval by three years.'[3] Preaching in this style is repeatedly recorded.

The same logic which drove the sectarians in the East forward

[1] Wright, J. F. C., *Slava Bohu*, New York 1940, p. 301. (Note the slight development towards the secondary *élite*-type here!)

[2] Cf. Grass, loc. cit., vol. I, pp. 253, 255–7, 259, 263, 264; Conybeare, loc. cit., pp. 339, 340, 342.

[3] Ibid., Grass, vol. I, p. 182, note. Cf. also pp. 188–9, note 3.

until they reached the very end of the road – self-divinization – also acted on the sectarians of the West. The two variants are essentially one type. The Quakers called themselves 'children of the light, faithful servants of the Lord, witnesses in His name, prophets of the Highest, angels of the Lord,' and these self-assumed epithets show them, not in their most extravagant, but rather in their more sober mood.[1] One phrase to which the Quakers were particularly addicted was the assertion that they were 'the seed'. This sounds harmless enough, but it is essentially the claim that every Friend was the equal of Christ.[2] 'He that has the same spirit that raised up Jesus Christ is equal with God,' Fox said,[3] and whatever construction be put upon these words, however much a careful gloss may reduce their apparent meaning, they stand as a proof of the Quaker tendency to see themselves as being 'godded' or deiform. Braithwaite himself refers to 'extremes of identification with the Divine' and candidly regrets his early co-religionists' 'inadequate recognition of the earthly character of the vessel'.[4]

The whole history of George Fox is punctuated with accusations that he was committing blasphemy by asserting his godhood, and curious and courageous acceptances on his part of these accusations. It is impossible to give more than one or two instances! Speaking of his experiences at Carlisle, some time in the summer of 1653, Fox himself reports how he dealt with the justices at the place. 'They asked me if I were the son of God. I said, "Yes". They asked me if I had seen God's face. I said "Yes" . . . And so they sent me to prison.' The same question was put to Fox at Leicester in February 1655. He replied: 'I said, I was no more; but the Father and the Son was all in me, and we are one.' When he assured Cromwell that he would not draw any 'carnal sword' against him, Fox referred to himself as 'George Fox who is the son of God', and the crucial promise he gave ran as follows: 'And my kingdom is not of this world, therefore with the carnal weapon I do not fight.'[5]

A particularly good piece of evidence is the Preface, almost

[1] Braithwaite, loc. cit., pp. 44 and 206.

[2] Admitted by Braithwaite's editors; cf. ibid., p. 583.

[3] Ibid., p. 109.

[4] Ibid., pp. 109 and 110.

[5] Ibid., pp. 117, 179, 180; cf. also p. 70 (*re* Gainsborough) and pp. 107 and 108 (*re* Lancaster).

certainly from the pen of Fox, to *A Battle-Door for Teachers and Professors to learn Singular and Plural* (1660). Two sentences will suffice for a quotation here: 'All languages on earth is [*sic*] but natural and makes none divine, but that which makes divine is the Word which was before languages and tongues were . . . All languages are to me no more than dust, who was before languages were, and am comed [*sic*] before languages were.'[1] Fox did not have many words, but he was the Word – or so it seemed to him.

The Quakers of today, sobered as they are, are in the habit of drawing a clear distinction between Fox and Nayler. Nayler is condemned for his well-known extravaganza – his riding into Bristol on a donkey, with women running ahead and shouting *hosanna*. Fox, on the other hand, is praised for remaining within the bounds of reason and decorum, even if he had as vivid a sense of Christhood as Nayler. This attitude conveniently forgets that Fox, no less than Nayler, impersonated Christ. On Firbank Fell, there is a commemorative tablet which informs posterity that 'here or near this rock, George Fox preached to about one thousand seekers for three hours on Sunday, June 13, 1652'. A study of the detail leaves no doubt whatever that Fox imitated Christ's Sermon on the Mount, as Nayler did Christ's Entry into Jerusalem.[2] How very unfair life is! Nayler was apprehended and severely punished; Fox got away scot-free. And later generations still make an entirely unjustifiable distinction where in fact there is none. If Nayler can be said to have blasphemed, so had Fox.

Among Nayler's severest critics was Margaret Fell. But this is how she addressed her friend Fox: 'O thou bread of life, without which bread our souls will starve! O for evermore give us this bread, and take pity on us . . . O our life, we hope to see thee again that our joy may be full . . . O thou fountain of eternal life, our souls thirst after thee . . . O thou father of eternal felicity.' In a letter to Nayler, Margaret called Fox 'him to whom all nations shall bow', him to whom has been given 'a name better than every name, to which every knee must bow. . . .'[3] The reference is to Philippians II, 10: 'That in the name of Jesus every knee should bow . . .' If blasphemy there was, or bad taste, or whatever be charged against Nayler, the burden must be borne by

[1] Ibid., pp. 498 and 497.
[2] Ibid., pp. 553, 84 and 85.
[3] Ibid., pp. 105 and 250.

his fellow Friends as well. It does not alter the case to say that 'Margaret Fell's phrases are not intended by her to designate Fox as the Messiah . . . but only as conspicuously foremost in the company of men and women who . . . were "Children of the Light"'.[1] Nayler himself had answered the question whether he was the only Son of God by saying: 'I am the Son of God, but I have many brethren.' The fact of the matter is that with the Quakers we are in midstream between the ruler-deification of pre-democratic and the folk-deification of democratic days, midstream between the Anonymus of York and Guiseppe Mazzini. The Blasphemy Act of 1650 was the official answer to this current in English non-conformity.

Lest it be said that the case of the Quakers was very exceptional in the West, let us adduce another one of different antecedents. 'Roelof Martens, who is better known by the name of Adam Pastor, of Dorpen in Westphalia, was about 1530 priest at Aschendorf . . . Pastor [in his *Contrast between True and False Doctrines*, *c.* 1550] asserts that he does not deny the divine nature in Christ, but nevertheless he holds that He did not exist as the Son of God previous to His coming into the world, and was divine only in the sense that God dwelled in Him.'[2] Here the later sentence completely cancels the earlier: Christ is unique, yet He is not unique; every godly man is godded. We have the same logic as before. Martens-Pastor is clearly on the way to the adoptionist Christology of the Khlysty and all that it implies.

Enough has now been said to illustrate our point, namely that the sects regard themselves as a definite *élite*. There are differences of degree, but the Khlysty and the Quakers show us their self-interpretation in its extreme form. What more can a group assert of itself than that all its members are Christs? Only one detail remains to be mentioned: the sectarian attitude to the Bible. This is an important facet in the present context and will also help to prepare a future discussion – that of the dissenters' tendency towards anti-authoritarianism, even anarchy.

For a man like Luther, who was an authoritarian to the marrow of his bones, the destruction of the authority of the priesthood left a void which he felt to be unbearable, and he filled it by setting up the authority of Scripture in place of that of the Church. He thereby created a condition which the non-conformists with their

[1] Ibid., pp. 251 and 253.
[2] Horsch, loc. cit., pp. 194 and 195.

revolutionary hunger and thirst after freedom could not accept. Thus there arose the contrast of the 'dead' word and the 'living' word which we find in many sectarian theologies. The Bible is but the dead word; the Christ-Voice within is the living word. This was a great bone of contention between Luther on the one hand, and Müntzer, Storch and Schwenkfeld on the other. For Schwenkfeld the Bible was no less 'outward' than the Sacraments of the Old Church, and from him the doctrine wandered, probably *via* such Mennonites as Hans de Ries, to George Fox. In England the presence of the doctrine as early as 1579 can be seen from the fact that the Familists were said in this year to hold 'that the Bible is not the Word of God, but [merely] a signification thereof, and the Bible is but ink and paper, but the Word of God is spirit and life'. Nearer the Quaker era, a Ranter is quoted as saying, with characteristic openness: 'Have not I the Spirit, and why may not I write the Scripture as well as Paul, and what I write be as binding and infallible as that which Paul writ?'[1] For the true sectarians, there can be no half-way house between authority and freedom.

From the Familists and the Ranters it was but a short step to the Quakers. George Fox interrupted a preacher at Nottingham by exclaiming: 'It is not the Scripture, it is the Holy Spirit by which holy men of old gave forth the Scripture, by which religions . . . are to be tried.'[2] What matters, then, is inspiration, not a text: with slight exaggeration it could be said that their own word (because inspired) was more authoritative for these men than the so-called Word of God. 'I . . . lives only by faith in the sense of the love and power of the Lord and reades in the Revelation much, and often that is the book that I preach out of,' Richard Farnsworth said of himself. 'I am as a white paper book without any line or sentence; but as it is revealed and written by the Spirit, the Revealer of secrets, so I administer.' Indeed, not only is the Bible set aside by men of this conviction, it is demoted, often even reviled, by them. A Bristol Baptist, Dennis Hollister by name and a grocer by profession, went over to the Quakers, and his erstwhile fellow-Baptists tell of him that 'he did blasphemously say, the Bible was the plague of England'. In great disgust, the *Broadmead Baptist Records* add: 'Thus smoke out of the bottomless pit arose, and the locust doctrine came forth, as it is written,

[1] Knox, loc. cit., pp. 170, 169, 172, 173.

[2] Ibid., p. 152, note 3.

Revelation IX, 2, 3, 4.'[1] The Baptists' distress is understandable, but they, too, were a sect, and they, too, would not accept any authoritative Bible interpretation. Even for them, as their historian formulates it, 'the supreme qualification for the interpretation of Scripture was spiritual illumination'.[2] Nor was the grocer the most outspoken enemy of the Bibliolators. 'The Bible is described as a "nonsense thing",' by some Moravians, and it is asserted that '"when anyone gives himself to meditating on the Bible, it is a sure sign that he never had the least spark of grace in his heart"'; all he had was a head '"full of devout and biblish lumber"'.[3] It is by such ideas that we can discern how deep the rift was which, with amazing rapidity, developed between the authoritarian and the anti-authoritarian wings of Protestantism, the Protestantism of the palace and the Protestantism of the hovel.

But not only do we see at this point particularly clearly, how far established and dissenting religions were from each other in the West, we also see how near Western and Eastern non-conformity were to each other. The attitude of the Khlysty and Dukhobortsy to the Bible is near-identical, in its basic aspects, with that of the Quakers and Moravians. For the Khlysty, Scripture is a kind of chain in which a man can get entangled; he who reads it, is likely to become mentally unhinged. While the books of the Bible are thus demoted, there is much enthusiastic talk about a so-called 'Book of the Dove'. But this book is no book; the word 'book' in this context is merely an allegorical description of the indwelling Spirit. The great leader of the Khlysty, Phillipov, threw all his (real) books into the Volga and forbade reading altogether. Only ecstasy can bring forth the 'word of God', and the only medium through which it can be voiced is the mouth of a spirit-possessed Khlyst. If the Bible is to be used at all (as it was sometimes in an attempt to make converts), it must be freely interpreted out of the 'living spirit' and not understood 'according to the ink'. From what we know of the propaganda of the Khlysty, we can see that their use of the Bible story was so allegorical that no tie whatever remained to what Luther or what the Orthodox thought the Bible meant. The Garden of Eden is simply a communion of Khlysty; the sufferings of Jesus are the life of the Khlysty in the hostile

[1] Braithwaite, loc. cit., pp. 198, 199, 170. Cf. also pp. 288–90 concerning Samuel Fisher's *Rusticus ad Academicos,* 1660.

[2] Underwood, loc. cit., p. 21.

[3] Knox, loc. cit., p. 416.

world; the suicide of Judas was no physical self-destruction, but marriage on his part, or carnal intercourse with a woman, which destroys purity and hence the soul. Clearly, the Bible is abolished here: for the Khlysty it need never have existed. In a discussion between the Orthodox Hegumen Paul and the Dissenter Hermit Gerasimov, the latter called the former a 'necromancer' because of his addiction to 'the book'![1]

So hostile is the true sect to the authority of the Bible that a turning to the Bible appears as a half-return to the world. The Dukhobortsy and the Molokane were sister sects. Yet the Molokane, mild men, used the scriptures freely to prove their doctrines, and this was sufficient to judge them and describe them as backsliders: it was not only asserted by the Dukhobortsy, but agreed on all hands, that the sub-sect of this name was heading back into the mainstream, the maelstrom, of the world.

THE CONCEPT OF A GATHERED CHURCH

The sectarians, then, apply to themselves the words of Psalm LXXXI which the kings had claimed before them: 'You are gods, and all of you the sons of the Most High.' But this individual self-characterization of each implies of necessity also a collective self-characterization of all, one could almost say, a religious sociology of the sect as an entity and totality. The basic idea of it is the concept of a 'gathered' church, i.e. a church gathered out of the world. If there are sheep among the goats, if there is gold among the dross, it is better to separate the former from the latter. As Henry Burton expressed it in *The Protestation Protested*, 1641: 'Christ's voice must first be heard to call forth his sheep and to gather them into their flocks and folds. For the Church is properly a Congregation of Believers called out from the rest of the world . . . Surely God's people must be separatists from the world and from false churches, to become a pure and holy people unto the Lord.' In the same vein Richard Baxter wrote in *A Christian Directory*, 1673: 'The Church's separation from the unbelieving world is a necessary duty; for what is a church but a society dedicated or sanctified to God, by separation from the rest of the world.'[2]

[1] Cf. Grass, loc, cit., vol. I, pp. 298, et seq. Cf. also Conybeare, loc. cit. pp. 174, 175, 186.
[2] Cit. Wilkinson, p. 207.

Once again, we see the heavy value-contrast which is at the root of all sectarianism: the negative attitude to the out-group, the positive estimation of the in-group. And, once again, Eastern sects and Western agree. This, clearly, is no case of diffusion: it is rather a case of convergence. Parallel situations produce, on the basis of the same inherent logic, parallel, not to say identical, phenomena.

A Russian expert has made the following statement about the Dukhobortsy: 'Their church is the gathering together of those whom God himself separates from the people of the world.'[1] He could hardly have expressed himself better, and his words are applicable to all sectarianism rather than merely to one specific sect. In Russia itself, the thinking of the Skoptsy was perhaps the clearest and most radical on this point. They regarded themselves as the 'sealed' ones, the virginal attendants of the Lamb, referred to in the Apocalypse XIV, 1–5, and VII, 2–4. As their number is given in Scripture as twelve times twelve thousand, the Skoptsy conceived the conviction that this number would have to be collected together before this wicked world could be brought to heel. In 1876, the Neo-Skopets Kartamyshev made the following deposition before the district court at Simferopol: 'When 144,000 Skoptsy are once accumulated, the kingdom of heaven and judgement day will arrive, the [heavenly] tsar will give unto his believing children their will and freedom and they will rejoice, but the unbelievers will be decapitated.' A most alluring prospect for the Skoptsy, both in its positive and its negative implications! Understandably, their propaganda became frantic – as frantic as it could become under the eye of a police force that was a sworn enemy of the sect. To find the saints, to gather and garner them was their main obsession. If they succeeded, they would, as it were, force God's hand to do without delay what they wanted most, finally to divide them from the rest of humanity, as one divides wheat from chaff.[2]

In terms of history and geography, in general cultural terms, there is a great distance between the Russia of 1876 and the England of 1652, but the pure sect type can be found here and there, and the Muggletonians were filled with ideas very close – surprisingly close – to those which dominated the Skoptsy. Lodowick Muggleton 'and his cousin John Reeve began to have

[1] Conybeare, loc. cit., p. 286.

[2] Grass, loc. cit., vol. II, pp. 682, 683, 693, 872.

revelations of their own, and . . . announced themselves as the two witnesses of Revelation XI, sent, they said, to seal the elect and the reprobate with the eternal seals of life and death, after which Jesus would visibly appear in power and great glory. They add, with an earnestness insensible to humour, that "if any of the elect desire to speak with us . . . they may hear of us in Great Trinity Lane, at a Chandler's shop, against one Mr. Millis, a Brown Baker, near the lower end of Bow Lane"'.[1]

The Quaker historian who gives us this example of religious naïvety cannot help falling into a semi-facetious tone, but he would have done well to remember that his own Friends were not very far from this kind of conception, even if they were not addicted to the mystical number 12 × 12 × 1,000. He himself says on another page[2] that 'the first tentative beginnings of a Friends' meeting' consisted 'in gathering together a separated and convinced people' – the self-same idea. All the early Quakers based themselves on the Skopets-Muggletonian conception that their group was the gathering in, the separating out, by God, of His elect. When Camm and Howgill got to London and found few who would greet them as brothers, they exclaimed: 'O the rich and boundless love of God unto us, the people of the North [of England], who has separated us from the world, and from the pollutions of it, and has gathered us together into the unity of the Spirit.' James Parnell, whose missionary work was destined to end in a martyr's death, declared that he was in search of a people 'whom the Lord was a-gathering out of the dark world, to sit down together and wait upon His name'. Similarly, Margaret Fell announced that God 'is visiting and sending forth His messengers . . . to gather His elect from the four winds of the heavens. . . .'[3]

The appearance and reappearance, time and time again, of this mode of thought and even expression, proves that we behold here the core-conception of the sectarians' sect-sociology. The clearest formulation of it which we have found is in the deeds by which two early Friends, Thomas Hodgson and Elizabeth Hodgson, conveyed a plot of land which they meant to serve as a burial ground. Similar declarations occur in parallel documents of the period so that, in J. Wilhelm Rowntree's and William C. Braithwaite's opinion, we have here 'evidently an accepted formula'. The

[1] Braithwaite, loc. cit., p. 20. [2] Ibid., p. 71. [3] Ibid., pp. 156, 188, 189, 319.

land is to be dedicated 'to and for the only and proper use and behoof of the People of God who are gathered in the light and Spirit of Jesus Christ off from the outward temple made with hands in the time of apostasy (which ignorantly is called a church) and from the will-worship and superstition that attends it, to the Church in God (I Thess. I, I) . . . .'[1]

All this is clear enough. Only one fundamental point needs stressing. We must not think of the 'gathered ones' (whatever they themselves may be saying) as those who have definitely and irrevocably turned their backs upon the world: they are and remain in a sense turned *to* the world. 'Before one of you that is in the resurrection and life in Christ,' wrote William Dewsbury, another Quaker, to his fellow-believers, 'shall a thousand flee, and five put ten thousand to flight, for you in the life are the host of heaven.'[2] The fighting accent is unmistakable. No sect ever completely overcomes its entanglement in and preoccupation with the parent society, even though the relationship is merely a negative one – a relation of condemnation, damnation, and hate.

A special problem arose for those sects which based themselves on the Calvinistic theology of election. According to Calvin, it was impossible to say who was elect and who not, for this was part of the knowledge which the Father 'had locked up in His bosom'. But this would not do for a typical sect. They had to have the assurance that they were the lambs and their neighbours were the goats – everything in them cried out for this supremely comforting conviction. And so they began to reinterpret the doctrine. The Strict (i.e. Calvinistic) Baptists soon taught 'that Calvinists must offer the Gospel to all on the principle that preaching elicits who are the elect, as a magnet plunged into a mixture of sawdust and iron filings separates them and draws out the latter'.[3] This was no longer good Calvinism; but it was good, even essential, sectarianism. The idea which we have tried to elicit in this chapter travelled with non-conformity down the decades and centuries into our own day. Even the contemporary Elimite asks the question: has not the outpouring of the Holy Ghost in the pentecostal movement been sent 'for the specific purpose of gathering out a company of choice and chaste souls who in turn should be prepared for the imminent advent of the Bridegroom?'[4] And even he

[1] Ibid., p. 308. [2] Ibid., p. 362. [3] Underwood, loc. cit., p. 247.
[4] Wilson, loc. cit., p. 33. Cf. p. 374.

answers joyously: Yes! We are the gathered ones, the choice and chaste souls, the beloved of the Father, the brethren of the Son, the tabernacles of the Spirit.

THE INNER STRUCTURE OF SECTARIAN GROUPS: ANTI-AUTHORITARIANISM AND DEMOCRACY

The saints are gathered, the sect is formed. By what inner principles shall its common life be shaped? It is entirely in keeping with the nature of non-conformity that these principles turn out, on closer inspection, to be predominantly negative. Chief among them is anti-authoritarianism. A gathering of the saints must be a gathering of the free. The Scripture passage which is most often quoted is taken from II Corinthians III, 17: 'Now the Lord is a Spirit. And where the Spirit of the Lord is, there is liberty.'

Two important questions arise in this context. Is it not unfair, first of all, to characterize the inner life of a sect negatively, by saying that it rejects authority, instead of positively, by saying that it replaces authoritarian ordering by spontaneity and love? It cannot be denied that most sects are based on fellowship, on sympathy, on strongly emotional ties. Yet, here again, there is a certain logic at work, and its premises lie outside the dissenting group. What happens inside the sect depends once more on its attitude to the wider, abandoned society, the society 'out of' which the sectarians are 'gathered'. As this outside world is ruled by laws and functionaries who are adjudged wicked, a general principle of anarchy is formed, and this is then transferred to the inside world, the domestic world, of the dissenting community. The spirit of anti-authoritarianism washes in, if we may so express it, across the walls, and therefore it *is* allowable, in fact necessary, to characterize the inner condition by negative terms, by calling it *anti*-authoritarian, rather than by positive terms, by speaking of mutuality or the like. When an Irish homesteader in Canada killed a Dukhobor child and the Mounties were expected to arrive on the scene, the Dukhobors were doubly distressed – not only because the child was dead, but also because the State was going into action:[1] to call in authority was wrong in any case; all authority is wrong; all authority is of the devil. Men who feel like that will not easily accept guidance, even if it be at the hands of their own.

[1] Wright, loc. cit., p. 180.

Yet, the last sentence is not really quite true, even though there is every justification for letting it stand. There is a contradiction here, but it is the kind of contradiction which life itself is constantly producing and reproducing. Is a community life possible for any length of time without some principle of subordination, some principle even of discipline and disciplining? This is our second question, and the answer to it must be in the negative. We see here one of the deepest reasons for the transitory nature of sects. Having rejected the laws of the others, they fall victims of a law of their own, and this is a fated, an inescapable development. The very same Dukhobors who would not hand over even their persecutor to the State because authority is bad; the very same Dukhobors who exert no pressure on man and wife to stay together and who claim and exercise no authority even over their children[1] because they cannot abide coercion; these very men developed a theocratic government which did away with their freedom. And they submitted not only to Peter Verigin the Elder, a true charismatic type, but also to Peter Verigin the Younger, a type that was anything but charismatic.

While sects are still young, while sects are still sects, their inner life must be described by words like spontaneity, egalitarianism and democracy. The Khlysty, for instance, have no clearly developed hierarchy. The number of indiscriminate terms which describe members who stand out from the rest and fulfil certain functions is characteristic: nothing is settled in this respect. They speak of helmsmen, leaders, elders, presbyters, senior brethren, archangels, seraphim, cherubim, benefactors and more of this kind. Still more significant than this semantic multiplicity is the multiplicity of principles on the basis of which personal prestige is acquired. A man or woman can be respected, either because he or she has a special aptitude for ecstatic experiences, or alternatively because he or she inflicts on himself a particularly severe ascetic regimen. Cutting across this is the high valuation of sexual abstinence which gives virgins the highest rank, young men the next, married men the third, and married women, especially mothers, the last, the idea being that proven or provable virginity is most honorific, disproven most humiliating. If a Khlyst obeys another, it is not obedience to a person, it is always obedience to a message from God pronounced by a person. Only

[1] Conybeare, loc. cit., pp. 270, 281, 282.

God is above men; men among themselves are much of a muchness. Witness also the following Khlyst prayer:

> 'The teachers say: Give us, O Lord,
> The leaders say: Give to us, Jesus Christ,
> The virgin members say: Give us the Son of God,
> The just ones say: Give us the Holy Spirit.'[1]

The invocation itself does not distinguish different ranks.

Even more radically egalitarian are the smaller, but interesting sects of the Self-Baptizers, the Prayerless, and the Sighers. The very name of the Self-Baptizers reveals their anti-hierarchical attitude. They immerse themselves and say: I, a child of God, baptize myself; they marry themselves by saying: I betrothe myself, etc. Everyone is his own priest. But the whole logic of this attitude comes out in the Prayerless and Sighers. If we are Christ's because the Spirit is within us, then even an outer organ like the tongue should not be used; then, *a fortiori*, outer organs like ecclesiastics are meaningless or worse. These groups have doctrines reminiscent of those of Joachim of Fiore. In the past, in the ages of the Father and the Son, things may have been different. But now the age of the Holy Ghost has arrived and God is only in the heart. 'In their abrogation of ecclesiastical orders the Prayerless have reached . . . the conception of a single spiritual grade of election by the spirit . . . We are back in a stage of the development of Christian speculation and practice earlier than any priesthood at all.'[2] It was quite consistent on the part of these men that they all demanded to be jailed, when some of them were sent to prison.

Democratic convictions of this kind are also expressed in outer demeanour. The Dukhobortsy did not take off their hats to anyone; they used Christian names even in conversations with Grand Dukes. Indeed, they extended their principles to animals as well, for they, too, are God's creatures. When their North Sasketchewan River Colony was plagued by gophers, they caught them and let them run free on the other side of the water, for how could they kill their brothers? (The distress caused to the recipients of these pests, a Mennonite community, was conveniently forgotten.)[3] One thing which shocked contemporaries as much or more than

[1] Grass, loc. cit., vol. I, pp. 492–6.
[2] Conybeare, loc. cit., pp. 165–70.
[3] Wright, loc. cit., p. 186.

anything else about this sect was the mode in which parents and children dealt with each other. Not only was all correction out of the question, but there was no suggestion that the children were in *any* way different from the grown-ups. 'At first you have no idea of the degrees of kinship in which the members of families stand to each other,' a scandalized visitor reported in 1878. 'Imagine an old man of eighty and a boy of ten calling one another by diminutives or pet names. . . !'[1] This, certainly, was not the way of the world in Victorian days.

What we have just said of the Dukhobortsy, could, with little adjustment, have been written of the Quakers as well. Fox would not take off his hat even to the king and thee'd and thou'd all and sundry. He claimed a special divine instruction on this point: 'When the Lord sent me forth into the world,' he says in his *Journal*, 'He forbade me to put off my hat to any, high or low, and I was required to Thee and Thou all men and women, without any respect to rich or poor, great or small.' But Fox not only refused to honour anybody else, he also refused to *be* honoured by anybody else. Here truly was a consistent egalitarian, as the following incident shows. 'At Staithes the Ranters were greatly stirred by Fox's visit. Their leader, Bushel, pretended to have had a vision of his coming, and was to doff his hat and bow down to the ground before him as he sat in his great chair. When he proceeded to put his flattery into practice, Fox checked him roughly with the words, "Repent, thou swine and beast!"'[2]

Fox's pantheistic leanings are well known and led to the conviction that all creation is in equal measure God's creation, an attitude which implied respect even for gophers, no doubt. As for the intercourse between Quaker parents and children, the use of first names by the latter to the former is frequently the custom. This has shocked many in the West (including this writer), as the parallel Dukhobor practice did in the East. The consequences are the same where the antecedents are the same, and here the antecedent, the root of all that follows, is the doctrine of the inner light. 'This Spirit,' wrote Winstanley, the Digger, to whom the Quakers owed much, 'is not without a man, but within every man; hence he need not run after others to tell him or teach him.'[3] This, surely, is the acme of egalitarianism: not to need even a

[1] Conybeare, loc. cit., p. 281. [2] Braithwaite, loc. cit., pp. 47 and 70.
[3] Cit. Niebuhr, p. 49.

teacher. But the habit of treating children as if they were grown-ups proves that the sectarians really meant what they said.

We may admit that this is extremism even among extremists. But less extreme sects, too, are anti-authoritarian and show tendencies towards the democratization of religious life. The Old Believers, as the name indicates, wanted to preserve the medieval, pre-Nikonian church, the product of feudal society with its gradations and ranks. Yet one of their earliest leaders, Neronov by name, urged on the tsar that 'the priestly grade is one and the same in all . . . All priests are on a level . . . Among themselves they are all brethren, servants of one Lord'. The council which he wished to have called for the settlement of ecclesiastical questions was to include, in principle, not only all clerics down to, and including, deacons, but 'also those who inhabit the village communes and who, no matter what their rank, lead good lives'. This was the beginning of a long road which ended with the concept of the priesthood of all believers. 'Jesus Christ alone, the inner agent, is our true High Priest and Sanctifier,' so Novitsky summed up the common sectarian attitude, 'and therefore we need no outward clergy; in whomsoever Christ himself works, he is His successor, and of himself he becomes a priest.'[1]

In the West, the anti-clericalism of the Quakers has been so strong that it has survived through centuries. But even where it has not survived, it has lasted a very long time. The English Baptist William Steadman did much to wear down the tough prejudice of his denomination against an educated ministry, but 'even at the end of his life [in 1837] he was regarded with suspicion by some who disliked "man-made" ministers'. To speak of a man-made ministry is pungent enough, but the Particular Baptists expressed themselves still more sharply. They inveighed against a 'hireling ministry', obviously taking the term from the Gospel according to St. John x, 11–15, where the good and the bad shepherd are contrasted – hardly a fair application of the parable. Of the Particular Baptist Abraham Booth it is even asserted that he regarded it as a 'species of profaneness' to be denominated 'Reverend'.[2]

The positive side of this hostility against a special clergy was

[1] Conybeare, loc. cit., pp. 22 and 280; cf. also pp. 179, 180, 182–4, 279, 300, 301, 309.

[2] Underwood, loc. cit., pp. 175, and 166. Braithwaite, loc. cit., p. 12.

the use of lay-preachers, one of the high-marks and hallmarks of all sectarianism. The contrast between the Lutheran and Calvinist Reformation on the one hand and the Radical Reformation on the the other is once again easy to perceive at this point. Luther and Calvin were close enough to humanism to see learning as a value: to the left of them, it was often, not to say regularly, seen as an unvalue. When a Puritan divine at Henley-in-Arden argued against preaching without a call, he was opposed by five 'private preachers' – a weaver, a nailer, a baker's boy, a baker and a ploughwright.[1] John Wesley, though he was an Oxford man and a Fellow of Lincoln College, realized after some initial hesitation that in a movement such as that which he was leading, the use of laymen in the pulpit was essential: only the voice of the people could reach the people, and too few academics could speak in that voice. The great role played in early Methodism by the untutored is part and parcel of its revolutionary syndrome. 'One thing in your conduct I could never account for,' said the Anglican Archbishop of Armagh to Charles Wesley, 'your employing laymen . . . unlearned men.' Tartly, Wesley replied: 'The dumb ass rebukes the prophet.' We cannot be surprised to hear that, after this, the Archbishop said no more.

Recent sects show the same anti-clericalism as the classical sects. In his up-to-date report Bryan Wilson has found the attitude still alive in both Elimites and Christadelphians. 'All experience shows that a system of paid officialship in divine things tends to corruption by drawing to it idle minds,' wrote the Christadelphian leader Jannaway. Indeed, he asserted, it leads to 'hideous fossïlism' or to 'invertebrate flaccidity'. 'The officials of the Christadelphian movement . . . remain amateur,' Wilson confirms, and of Elim he writes: 'Pentecostalism as an inspirational movement was . . . committed not only to the priesthood of all believers, but virtually to the prophetship of all believers as well . . . By 1920 . . . workers was still the term used [for all functionaries] . . . It was usual for churches to have male or female lay-pastors.'[2]

CONTRACTUALISM AND CONGREGATIONALISM

The central principle of anti-authoritarianism is flanked by two corollaries: contractualism and congregationalism. Sects have a

[1] Cf. Braithwaite, loc. cit., p. 17. [2] Wilson, loc. cit., pp. 280, 35, 36.

voluntary membership; they must be contracted into; they are covenantal. This feature is easy to understand. No man can commit another to revolutionary action: either he feels revolutionary and is willing to accept the burden of a revolutionary attitude, or he simply cannot be part of an organization of this kind. Speaking of the 'primary distinction' between church and sect, Niebuhr puts the salient point well: 'Members are born into the church while they must join the sect . . . The former is a natural group akin to the family or the nation while the latter is a voluntary association . . . Membership in a church is socially obligatory, the necessary consequence of birth into a family or nation, and no special requirements condition its privileges; the sect, on the other hand, is likely to demand some definite type of religious experience as a prerequisite of membership.'[1] (The sociologist will have to add that this religious experience will regularly grow out of a total human and social experience: the experience of alienation from the surrounding world; contracting into the sect follows contracting out of general society.) Here, indeed, is a principle both vital and mortal. Vital, because the strength of sects lies in the underpinning personal commitment, in the dedication of its members to the cause; mortal, because the weakness of sects lies in the restriction of this commitment to individual lives, in the fact that a sectarian's children can hardly be expected to feel as he does. Birthright membership is really a contradiction in terms, and though, like other contradictions, it endures for a while, it weakens the dissenting spirit until shadow takes the place of substance, and the sect turns into a denomination – a sect without sectarianism.

The covenantal principle has often been consciously recognized by the sectarians themselves. Thus William Erbury, a Seeker and forerunner of Quakerism, wrote in *The Welsh Curate* (1652): 'Admission [in the "formal" churches] intimates the Church of Christ to be a corporation . . . whereas the Church is a free company or society of friends who come together, not as called by an outward, but freely chosing by the inward, spirit.'[2] In social theory, sectarians are definitely nominalists, as this quotation proves, and as it is also proved by the statement of Robert Roberts that a Christadelphian ecclesia is 'only a collection of like-minded individuals, drawn together in the confidence of the same hope'.[3]

[1] Niebuhr, loc. cit., pp. 17 and 18. Cf. also Underwood, loc. cit., pp. 15–18.
[2] Braithwaite, Appendix, p. 570. [3] Wilson, loc. cit., p. 293.

In passando, we may emphasize here that the individualistic-contractual-mechanistic-nominalistic social theory which Jean-Jacques Rousseau so impressively developed, had its historical roots in such *de facto* social contracts as the one concluded by the Separatists of Gainsborough and the Anabaptists of Schlatten am Randen in the sixteenth century.[1]

To the covenantal principle corresponds the congregational principle: the one characterizes the origin of the sect in time, the other its dispersal in space. If sects are the products of mutual covenanting, then each covenanting group (or 'congregation') must logically be an independent entity, for you cannot well covenant with people whom you do not know. True, we often voluntarily join, i.e. contract into, entirely impersonal and nation-wide organizations such as Trade Unions, but such a voluntary act is very different (apart from the formal, definitional aspect) from the voluntary act which leads a man into a dissenting group. It is easiest to bring out this difference by using an argument taken from Georg Simmel's sociology: into a Trade Union one brings little of one's personality, into a sect much. The common denominator which links fellow-unionists is nearly nil, that which links fellow-sectarians very large. The sect, in other words, absorbs those who enter it: well-nigh their whole existence is merged with, submerged in, this community. And therefore sects have a tendency to be local face-to-face groupings. This, of course, does not prevent them from having fraternal feelings for other local groupings and their members: but it does make them impatient with that remote control which is inseparable from all far-flung organizations. This face-to-face character is often of short duration. But, then, so is every sect. When impersonal replace personal ties, when a vast organization swallows up the small conventicles which have formed in the beginning, the kernel of dissent is dead and only the shell of denominationalism remains.

In Quaker history, there was a time when the whole heartland, the whole north of England, held General Meetings, such as that at Skipton in 1657. Yet Braithwaite speaks of 'the subordinate and almost accidental place of these meetings in the life of the Quaker community': 'They in no sense superseded the individual or the particular congregation. They did not assume any

[1] Underwood, loc. cit., p. 34, and Burrage, Ch., *The Church Covenant Idea: Its Origin and Development*, Philadelphia 1904, pp. 16 and 17.

control . . . They did not attempt to exercise authority.' What is most indicative of the sect's character is that when Fox was released from Scarborough jail in 1666 and tried to put the Friends' house in order, he did not remember these wider gatherings, and, to this day, a Quaker 'meeting' is a strongly local group.[1]

Wilson's research into more recent conditions has also highlighted the importance of the congregational principle in sect-life. Though he speaks of Elim at a time when some centralization, and indeed general routinization, had already taken place, he still has to report as follows: 'The local church appears as a community, and although its relation to the movement is known, its own operations appear essentially local, and almost personal . . . There is a marked family spirit. . . .' Even clearer is the case of Christadelphianism: 'The Christadelphian ecclesias are entirely independent and autonomous; they remain in the wider fellowship, but they evolve their own rules and formulate their own constitution; they may even independently draw up their statement of faith. . . . In practice most of the ecclesias . . . have adopted the Birmingham Statement of Faith . . . but the independence of each ecclesia has always been jealously guarded.'[2]

At a superficial glance it might appear that Methodism was, from its inception, a broadly based national movement, yet closer inspection shows that appearances are somewhat deceptive. True, the movement *was* nation-wide in scope and relatively integrated, but this does not mean that the congregational principle was weak or absent. For a good deal of the decisive religious life of Wesley's followers went on in the so-called classes, circles of twelve each, true face-to-face groups, indeed, quasi-families. Even the apparent monolith of the Jehovah's Witnesses is less monolithic than it looks. Before a congregation reaches the strength of two hundred members, it is invariably split, so that the local unit may not become too impersonal and anonymous.[3]

The importance of the principle of local autonomy in true sects can also be seen from the fact that it usually dies a very hard death. The history of the Salvation Army is a proof of this. The General had strong centralist leanings (as generals will have), but these

[1] Braithwaite, loc. cit., pp. 338 and 339.
[2] Wilson, loc. cit., pp. 69 and 273. Cf. also pp. 267, 268, 275.
[3] Cameron, loc. cit., pp. 37–9; Whalen, loc. cit., p. 116.

evoked passionate resistance – as we should say here, insubordination and mutiny. On June 18, 1880, the day of his Silver Wedding, Booth gave an address in which he lashed out at the opponents of unification. 'There is a growing spirit around us in favour of no government at all,' he thundered. 'All masters and no servants is the motto . . . The children don't want any authority; the work-people don't want any authority; sinners don't want any authority; saints don't want any authority. "*There ought to be no submitting of one Corps to another*," says one. A step further and there will be no submission of one man to another, and you will have, with individual independence, weakness, confusion, disorder, and destruction.' The words which we have italicized were the ones for the sake of which all the others were spoken. We feel, almost physically, the resistance of the anti-authoritarians to the authoritarian leader. Booth's biographer admits that schism threatened. He speaks of the 'position of power occupied by leading officers' as 'causing jealousy and ill-feeling' and records that the re-establishment of harmony in the ranks was 'a long and difficult task'.[1]

The Salvation Army in the end remained one, but centralization, however mild, may also lead to a parting of ways. 'Even after the regularization of government in 1934, local [Elim] churches retained the full appearance of local autonomy, bound in family-type association. . . .' Yet what little integration there was, had already had decisive consequences. 'Thomas Myerscough and J. Nelson Parr founded the Assemblies of God [in 1925], eschewing the idea of a centralized administration of the type existing in Elim. They adopted a loose constitution [and] stressed local autonomy.'[2] Even a little was too much for these men.

Research into Russian religious dissent has presented a somewhat ambiguous picture, in so far as congregationalism is concerned. Following the majority of local students, Conybeare has asserted that the Khlysty 'naves' or 'ships' were relatively independent and formed only loose congeries. Grass, on the other hand, has come to a different conclusion, first with regard to the Khlysty themselves, and then even more determinately with regard to the Skoptsy, an offshoot from, and opponent of, the Khlysty. In judging the situation, two points must be taken into account here. The one is the consistent and cruel persecution of

[1] Coates, loc. cit., pp. 133 and 150. [2] Wilson, loc. cit., pp. 39, 40, 37.

these sects which made any kind of central organization virtually impossible. How much influence *could* headquarters exert on distant groups, given the fact that they could not use the postal system? While this would seem to support Conybeare's assertion of local independence, the second and related feature pleads more on the side of Karl Konrad Grass. Where pressure is severe, the spirit of brotherhood among the outlaws is bound to be intense; and where that pressure comes from a nation-wide, well-integrated police force, there the persecuted will also tend to feel a nation-wide unity in suffering and fear. A careful reading of Grass's own exposition would seem to bear out this conclusion. What he proves are intense common loyalties rather than organizational ties.[1]

WEAKNESS AND STRENGTH OF SECTARIAN INTEGRATION

The point to which this discussion of the ideal-typical anti-authoritarianism of the sect must lead back is also the point from which it started out: the all-important fact that the sect is a group of rebels. But rebelliousness, if it can freely follow its own momentum, can have no end other than radical individualism. In view of the fundamental position which the doctrines of original sin and vicarious satisfaction – two strongly anti-individualistic dogmas, since they assume the solidarity of all mankind in guilt and merit – have occupied in the Christian tradition, it is not surprising that most sects have reinterpreted rather than abandoned them. But the most radical, and hence most typical, sects, have given them up and replaced them by teachings which see both fall and redemption in purely personal terms. For the Dukhobortsy, Adam's sin is merely an allegory of sinning as such. What he did, did not involve his descendants. Everyone falls, i.e. sins, for himself. Everyone returns to God, i.e. is saved, by himself. It was in this spirit, too, that the Quakers approached the basic Christian thought-patterns. There is no room, in their theology, for original sin. There is no room for Adam as the condemner, nor for Christ as the redeemer, of all – certainly no room for the historical Christ, as Christ is ever alive in the believer's heart, and works there. What happened in Jerusalem on

[1] Conybeare, loc. cit., p. 342. Grass, loc. cit., vol. I, pp. 491, 492; vol. II, pp. 852, 859, 861, 862.

the first Easter Sunday is not decisive: the Resurrection is within us – within each of us, not collectively, but individually.

It is for this reason, too, that truly radical sects have nothing that can properly be called common or collective worship. Their worshipping is always personal, at the most parallel, even if it is going on in a public place. In a letter of advice written in 1660, the Quaker Alexander Parker has this to say: 'The first that enters into the place of your meeting, be not careless, nor wander up and down either in body or mind, but innocently sit down in some place and turn in thy mind to the light and wait upon God singly, as if none were present but the Lord . . . and so all the rest coming in . . . A few that are thus gathered by the arm of the Lord into the unity of the Spirit, this is a sweet and precious meeting, where all meet with the Lord.' The word 'all' is ambiguous here: it is clear, however, in spite of the reference to unity, that it means 'every one' and not 'all together', for this alone lies in the true Quaker spirit. William Dewsbury, writing in the same year, puts the matter even more decisively: 'When you meet, let your hearts in the light be single unto God, wait to receive His gift in the inspiring of His Spirit, that there be no eye one towards another . . . but all single to God . . .'[1]

'It was not the magic of the crowd which had cast a spell over them,' Church assures us in his study of *The Early Methodist People*. 'Rather, as C. H. Crookshank says in reference to a revival while Conference was in session in Dublin in 1790, "One man, though surrounded with many, seemed as much alone with God as if he were in a desert". That was an essential in the Methodist experience. Whenever and however conversion took place, it was, in the last analysis, an affair between the individual and God.'[2]

This is the famous *solus cum solo* doctrine which is perhaps the most important spiritual conviction of modern, i.e. Protestant, religiosity, in contradistinction to medieval, i.e. Catholic, especially pre-Tridentine, religiosity which sees the human race as one – so much so that there is really never one man praying, but in the prayer of one there is always prayer of all. The sectarians drive it forward to a logical conclusion, as they do all things. They reduce institutionalism to the minimum and increase individualism to the maximum. And because of this, they are, one might almost say, the anarchists of religious life.

[1] Braithwaite, loc. cit., pp. 509 and 511. [2] Church, loc. cit., p. 123.

It is no contradiction to add, that sectarians as a rule regard the sect as their true family, a place of free and full fellowship, for men, especially strong-profiled men, will be happiest where they can be most themselves. There are many testimonies to the warmth which permeates the sectarian circle. Swarthmore, the home of Margaret Fell, was to William Caton a hearth where he 'always found refreshment in the fullness of the Father's love, which abounded much among us in that blessed family'. Wilson, in his participant observation, found in similar manner that among the Elimites of today 'the family spirit prevails within the church community', though he emphasizes that family-like bickering is as characteristic as family-like devotion. The Christadelphian ecclesia, too, proved a focus of friendship, indeed, a framework of friendships. Russian sects showed, if possible, even greater internal solidarity. The Communism which was the basis of some of their settlements was possible only, and worked so well, because it had this firm psychological foundation. Perhaps the most convincing proof of the coherence of dissenting groups, however, is the case of a colony which contained both employers and workmen. The village of Kimry, in the Korchevsky province of Tver, was inhabited by Old Believers. It was a boot-manufacturing place with the usual capitalist set-up. An eye-witness account of the year 1865 proves that class antagonism had no place in this class society.[1]

So close is the friendship and the fellowship inside the sect that a typical sectarian like William Dell could write: 'Nature of one makes many, for we were all but one in Adam . . . Grace of many makes one, for the Holy Spirit, which is a fire, melts all the faithful into one mass or lump.'[2] Sect solidarity found its fullest expression in the readiness of many sectarians to suffer with, and even for, their brethren. On April 15 and 16, 1659, for instance, one hundred and sixty-four Quakers presented a paper to Richard Cromwell's parliament which pleaded as follows: 'We, in love to our brethren that lie in prisons and houses of correction and dungeons, and many in fetters and irons . . . do offer up our bodies and selves to you . . . and do stand ready a sacrifice for to go into their places . . . that they may go forth and that they may not die in

[1] Braithwaite, loc. cit., p. 371; Wilson, loc. cit., pp. 78 and 283; Conybeare, loc. cit., pp. 215, 216, 223, 224.

[2] Cit. Huehns, p. 113.

prison as many of the brethren are dead already. For we are willing to lay down our lives for our brethren, and to take their sufferings upon us . . . We, whose names are thereunto subscribed, being a sufficient number . . . for the present sufferers, are waiting in Westminster Hall for an answer from you to us, to answer our tenders . . .' The document is moving, and it is possible to sympathize with the Quaker historian when, in printing it, he speaks of a 'spirit of devotion which entitles the action to rank among the golden deeds of history – those deeds which glow with the flame of a pure and unselfish love'.[1] It is the hard but inescapable duty of the sociologist of religion to reduce such statements to their proper dimension. The love was unselfish, no doubt, and it is to be admired for that; but it was not pure. Indeed, it was merely the reverse side of the antagonism which the Friends felt for the world which persecuted them. Here, as everywhere in the study of sectarianism, scholarly analysis is constrained by the facts to trace that which is positive to that which is negative – the mutual amity among the dissenters to their common enmity against the wider society. The dramatic solidarity displayed by the Friends of 1659 is, for all its glory, merely one instance of the typical fervour of all fighting groups, be they religious or not, and the Quakers shared it with Carbonari and Communists and many other groupings who were revolutionaries like them – groups alienated from, and linked in a life-and-death battle with, the established powers in Church and State.

THE SECT AS A CONTRACULTURE

In a particularly penetrating article,[2] J. Milton Yinger has insisted that it is imperative for the sociologist to distinguish 'contracultures' from subcultures. Subcultures are merely variants of the dominant culture, but contracultures are more than that: they are inversions of it. 'The values of most subcultures probably conflict in some measure with the larger culture. In a contraculture, however, the conflict element is central; many of the values, indeed, are specifically contradictions of the values of the dominant culture.'[3]

[1] Braithwaite, loc. cit., pp. 454 and 455.
[2] 'Contraculture and Subculture', *American Sociological Review,* October 1960, pp. 625 et seq.
[3] Ibid., p. 629.

This suggested conceptual refinement is of the highest realism and value, and there can hardly be a better illustration of the newly introduced concept and term than the sect. The sect is typically a contraculture.

The creation of a contraculture by and in the sect is merely a logical development from the fact that the sect is a conflict society. It is not, however, this objective fact itself so much as the subjective feeling connected with it which drives the dissenters so far forward on their road that they say 'nay' to everything that is valued around them. The Quakeress Ann Audland appears to have been a very simple soul, but just for that reason she shows the sectarian spirit of extreme and consistent negation with particular clarity. 'Ann Audland . . . cried out to the Banbury vicar, "Man, here see the fruits of thy ministry", and was asked what he had said which was untrue. She replied that when men were out of the doctrine of Christ, all they spoke was untruth, and though they should say "the Lord liveth", they would swear falsely.'[1] Other early Quakers would not express themselves in these terms of hysterical exaggeration, but their underlying sentiments were similar. Isaac Pennington was, by comparison with Ann Audland, an intellectual, even a staid one, but yet he could write: 'Our work in the world is to hold forth the virtues of Him that has called us . . . to forget our country, our kindred, our father's house, and to live like persons of another country, of another kindred, of another family.' The Christadelphians of today still feel as Ann Audland did: 'What the world does may not be intrinsically evil,' so Wilson sums up their philosophy. 'That the world does it, makes it indisputably evil.' When George Fox, on 9 September 1643, left his home to obey the command 'be as a stranger unto all', he not only did what he personally felt to be necessary, but symbolized the common sectarian attitude.[2]

That the sect develops a contraculture rather than a subculture, that it brings a transvaluation of values in which the first become the last and the last first, can be seen most dramatically in the attitude to learning. All settled societies value knowledge highly, and there is no need to explain why; but religious societies value it doubly, because in the great social division of labour it usually falls to the lot of the churches, as the guardians of the sacred

[1] Braithwaite, loc. cit., p. 199.

[2] Ibid., pp. 508 and 31; Wilson, loc. cit., p. 281.

traditions, to help in the development and transmission of the secular traditions as well: the clergy has everywhere been active in the intellectual and educational field. There was no difference, in this respect, between Catholicism and non-sectarian Protestantism. Luther and Calvin, for instance, were highly competent in, even masters of, the classical languages, and though they may have rejected some learning, they certainly valued learning as such. Indeed, the last clause may be something of an understatement: they were enthusiasts for learning. Against this, the sectarians, from the very beginning, asserted that revelation comes only to the simple and childlike, that the inner light cannot be lit in the mind that is taken up with the dead lumber of bookishness. The Anabaptists of Münster burnt the books they could find on the market place:[1] to them the 'new learning' was simply vanity, whether it was Erasmus or Zwingli, whether it was taught at Rotterdam and at Rome, or at Zürich and Wittenberg and Geneva.

There is nothing at all surprising in this condemnation of knowledge on the part of typical non-conformist groups. Recruited from the lower social strata, they are composed, not only of the socially and economically, but also of the culturally and educationally, underprivileged. A sect leader could never hope to hold his own in a debate with a trained theologian, though they often enough engaged in such disputations: he could not hope to hold his own, if the argument turned around the meaning of a Hebrew verb or a Greek noun. He could meet the onslaught only in the arena of inspiration, for as far as that was concerned, he was not disadvantaged. Inspiration is not a discerner of persons: the spirit bloweth where it listeth. This prejudged the issue for the sectarians: out of a philosophy of sour grapes, they devalued all formal education and its results. A psychological analysis of their attitude could take much material from Max Scheler's book on *Resentment*.[2]

So far as the Russian sects are concerned, we have already reported about their demotion and even destruction of the sacred scriptures.[3] But the matter went much deeper. The whole schism was really an outbreak of anti-humanism. It was because the

[1] Tumbült, loc. cit., p. 74; Cohn, loc. cit., p. 290.
[2] Cf. also the apposite remarks of Huehns, loc. cit., pp. 104 and 105.
[3] Cf. above, p. 110.

Patriarch Nikon wished to emend the liturgical Greek of the Orthodox Church which had become sadly corrupted in the course of the centuries, because he wanted to substitute the correct form *kyrie eleison* (O Lord, have mercy) for the incorrect and indeed ridiculous form *kyrios eleison* (the Lord, have mercy), that the Old Believers rose up against him and called him a heathen, a hound from hell. Of course, it was not a matter of grammar alone, or even essentially. It was innovation that these men fought, not good Greek. But the fact remains that they anathematized education as inherently impious, a work of wickedness.

So strong was this tradition that it survived even in radically altered circumstances. The Dukhobor leader Verigin rejected all education, even literacy. School-burning became one of the main pastimes of the sect after it had settled in Canada and drifted into a head-on collision with the Canadian government. And it was by no means only official schools which they condemned; they would not accept Quaker schools either after the Friends, with the kind intention of easing the situation, had moved in and offered private instruction to those whom they felt to be men not entirely unlike themselves.[1]

In the West, the self-same anti-intellectualism held sway among the dissenting groups. In the Thomason Collection of Pamphlets from the Civil War years, there is one called *The Sufficiency of the Spirit's Teaching without Learning*. A more revealing title could hardly have been chosen for it. It will surprise nobody to hear that its author was a cobbler named How. The description, by an extreme Puritan, of learning as 'smoke from the bottomless pit' has also been recorded.[2]

Once again, the Quakers stand out as highly characteristic. This was James Nayler's advice to Rebecca Travers: 'Feed not on knowledge . . . it is good to look upon, but not to feed on, for who feeds on knowledge, dies to the innocent life.' Nor was Fox's attitude different. When Cromwell wished, in 1657, to found a university in Durham, protests came not only from Oxford and Cambridge, but from the Quaker leader also. He met one of the Protector's emissaries and 'let him see that was not the way to make [men] Christ's ministers, by Hebrew, Greek and Latin and the seven arts, which all was but the teachings of the natural

[1] Wright, loc. cit., pp. 226, 238, 274, 282, 283, 311, 330, 331, 333, 422.

[2] Cf. Gooch, loc. cit., p. 110, note 3; Selbie, loc. cit., p. 112.

man . . . for Peter and John that could not read letters preached the Word, Christ Jesus, which was in the beginning before Babel was'. Even genuine intellectuals like Samuel Fisher, M.A. Cantab., shared the attitude when they became Friends, as his tract *Rusticus ad Academicos*, already mentioned, sufficiently shows.[1]

We have spoken above of a philosophy of sour grapes. We can see here very clearly that the expression is apt and deserved. Just as the fox of Aesop's fable really wanted the sweet fruit, though he pretended he did not, so too the Fox of Quaker history. 'A certain parade of learning was indeed one of his weaknesses,' Braithwaite admits. 'He regarded himself as possessing a spiritual counterpart to human knowledge which qualified him to meet experts on their own ground. He probably picked up a smattering of several languages, including Hebrew, Greek, and Welsh. His curious linguistic tastes are shown with respect to Hebrew by his strange interjection at the Lancaster trial in 1664, when he amazed the court by calling out "Lo-tishshab'un bekol-dabar" ("ye shall not swear by anything"), and by the Hebrew alphabet attached to a page of notes on the Old Testament, part of which is in his handwriting.'[2] The reported incident opens a deep insight into the non-conformist psyche. Fox remained preoccupied with that which he condemned, as the Communist remains preoccupied with the capital which he does not possess and endeavours to wrest from others. The sectarian remains in the clutches of the world which, on the conscious level, he has abandoned, as the Marxist does, who, while maligning bourgeois materialism, is a materialist himself. Hate, as every psychologist knows, is really an inverted and perverted kind of love.

Methodists, Christadelphians, Elimites, Jehovah's Witnesses, and all the rest: the denigration of academic – 'profane' – learning is common to them all. There is no room and no need to pile testimony on testimony, but one further example nearer our own day shows that these attitudes persist. When a Christadelphian, Robert Ashcroft, made mild use of biblical criticism, Robert Roberts attacked him with heavy heart and heavy hand: 'Brother Ashcroft . . . ought to know that very few learned men and women ever embraced the faith of the "poor and needy man" . . .

[1] Braithwaite, loc. cit., pp. 242 and 294; Knox, loc. cit., p. 152.
[2] Braithwaite, loc. cit., pp. 301 and 302.

Has brother Ashcroft forgot, or did he ever know, that it's the poor and simple-minded (and therefore unlearned) that God has chosen in every age in the working out of his plans?' Already the founder of the movement, John Thomas, had, in his *Elpis Israel* (1849), called the serpent in the garden of Eden an 'intellectualizer', and F. G. Jannaway, a twentieth-century leader, still asserted in *My New Bible* (1915) that theological training unfits, rather than fits, a man for the task of expounding biblical truth.[1]

While 'mere head knowledge'[2] is thus downgraded, pure heart knowledge is usually upgraded. A high valuation of the emotions is normally the counterpart and complement to the low valuation of the intellect, and this, too, is a typical contracultural feature. Since the end of the Middle Ages, the main intellectual trend in Christendom has been towards rationality and rationalism. Strongly emotional tendencies, like romanticism, appear as hardly more than interruptions of that overall trend. Champion of underdog ideas as well as human underdogs, the sect has ever regarded experience as the key to sanctification, leaving ratiocination, without regrets, to established religiosity.

We must be careful, here, however, not to give a wrong impression. Sects have differed greatly with regard to the element of emotionalism which they have allowed into their culture. The reason is that a second tendency has sometimes cut across the tendency towards the emotional. Fighting groups have always wished to produce disciplined men, and sentiment is apt to lead the other way, towards *abandon*. In the West, many dissenting groups have sported a crypto-Calvinism which drove them away from the open display of sentiment – witness especially the Calvinistic types of Baptism. Where this intellectual heritage is absent, where the sect conceives of itself as a suffering rather than a fighting servant, there, indeed, what in common parlance is called sentimentality can flourish. For examples we may consider Pietism in Germany and its English offspring, Methodism. Often enough enemies of these movements have used the pejorative word 'maudlin' to describe their religiousness. What has developed is at times a combination, an alternation, of soberness and sentiment. The Quakers were stern, even dour, in their everyday

[1] Cit. Wilson, pp. 248 and 290. Cf. also pp. 34 and 87 (*re* Elim).

[2] Ibid., p. 305.

demeanour. But when the 'trembles' were upon them, they were different altogether. It was possession by overpowering emotion that made the Quakers quake and the Shakers shake.

No doubt, many sectarians drew their strength for everyday living from discontinuous, but extremely potent, religious experiences, Sunday experiences as it were, or even better Whitsunday experiences, which 'recharged the spiritual batteries'. Now, these experiences had to be induced: the holy spirit had to be forced to come down on to its votaries, into its vessels. Many sects have developed elaborate techniques that propelled them into exaltation; typical are once again the Khlysty in the East and the Quakers in the West. But anybody who knows what is commonly meant by a revivalistic atmosphere will also know what we are speaking about here.

The Khlysty technique centred on a round dance called *radenie*, the very hub and heart-piece of their religious life – indeed, their whole life. Grass has provided copious information on this remarkable rite, the end of which is, in sectarian language, the descent of the Holy Ghost (pictured, characteristically, not as a hovering gentle dove, but as a swooping, fierce falcon), in scholarly language, however, trance, a near-hypnotic state. Clad in white, flowing garments, the Khlysty engage in a circular movement, waving white handkerchiefs and singing rhythmical hymns. Then the dancing becomes faster, the waving of handkerchiefs gives way to flagellation, often with sticks or rods, the hymns are replaced by frenzied, ever repeated shouts: *Oi Yegá! Oi Dukh!* Oh Jesus, oh Spirit! Panting, sweating, beside themselves, the dancers begin to jump into the air, to spin around, to break into tongues, to behave like maniacs, until, completely exhausted, they sink to the ground. There is remarkable unanimity on the experience which the frenzy produces in those whom it gets hold of: profound, unspeakable exaltation and joy. Sometimes, to this ecstasy is added a further – visual – element. The *radenie* may be around a tub, and – perhaps under suggestion originating with some brother especially prone to visionary states – the dancers see rising from the bubbling waters in a vapour the Christ-Child visiting His people, His other selves, or the Holy Mother with the bambino on her arm, or sometimes a bird, symbol of the Holy Trinity's Third Person. Experientially, the Khlysty are out of this world: they have visited their heavenly home.[1] What is miserable book-learning compared to this experience?

The far-reaching parallel between the Russian Khlysty and the American Shakers is immediately obvious. Though both had historical examples to go by, such as the Dionysian cults of the Greeks and the Dervish dancing of the Moslems, it is surely not likely that they were influenced by them or that they influenced each other. Once again, our material would seem to support the theory of culture-convergence, not of culture-diffusion. The Shakers, however, can hardly be regarded as a major sect. More significant are the Quakers from whom they derived, being originally often described as Shaking Quakers. The Quaker technique was different from the Shaker and Khlyst technique: David who danced before the Ark of the Covenant was not their model and patron. But this does not mean that they are not a parallel case. Probably, the parallelism was greater in reality than it now appears, for the sobered children are not likely to enlarge upon the extravaganzas of their less sober forebears. 'Quaking and trembling we own,' Fox said, 'though they in scorn call us so.' It would have been difficult to deny the fact for two reasons: firstly, because it was too often observed, even by outsiders; and secondly, because denying it would have meant denying the descent of the Holy Spirit. It was, in their conviction, by 'the mighty power of the Lord God' that the Quakers quaked.[2]

A petition to the Council of State drawn up by some Lancashire justices and clergymen who had seen Fox and Nayler work warned that they 'have drawn much people after them: many whereof (men, women and little children) at their meetings are strangely wrought upon in their bodies, and brought to fall, foam at the mouth, roar and swell in their bellies'. (The last-named phenomenon is repeatedly attested.) If this is hostile report, many Friends themselves have recorded their extraordinary states. Thomas Aldam states: 'I was taken with the power in a great trembling in my head and all of the one side all the while I was speaking to them, which was a great amazement to the people, and they was silent.' So too John Audland states: 'All my limbs smote together and I was like a drunken man because of the Lord and

[1] Grass, loc. cit., vol. I, pp. 119, 125, 150, 208, 272, 275, 278, 383–9; Conybeare, loc. cit., pp. 346–8 and 355, 356.

[2] Cf. Braithwaite, loc. cit., p. 57, note 2.

because of the word of His holiness, and I was made to cry like a woman in travail.' The influence on Audland's audience was electric. Charles Marshall was there and he writes: 'Ah! the seizings of souls and prickings of heart which attended that season: some fell on the ground, others crying out under the sense of opening their states, which indeed gave experimental knowledge of what is recorded (Acts II, 37).'[1]

So far as the Methodist movement is concerned, the wild scenes of emotionalism which accompanied it are well known and have evoked a copious literature. Books like John S. Simon's *John Wesley and the Religious Societies* (1921), F. M. Davenport's *Primitive Traits in Religious Revivals* (1905) and Charles A. Johnson's *The Frontier Camp Meeting: Religious Harvest Time* (1955) have given graphic detail *ad lib.*[2] Long before them, the Anglican Bishop George Lavington had pilloried Wesleyanism in his work, *The Enthusiasms of the Methodists and Papists Compared* (1749–51). Upon the quakes and shakes followed the jumps and jerks. The Welsh *hwyl* also deserves to be mentioned. But, once again, complete documentation is utterly out of the question. And, once again, this is a phenomenon which endures. The London *Daily Express*, in a report of an Elim convention in 1928, spoke of 'swinging arms and resonantly clapping hands', of the unceasing repetition of the same verse and similar goings on. 'It was a species of trance creation. Hysteria seemed at hand. They were lashed and urged by mass melody into an unearthly joy.'[3] Here, too, the swoop of the falcon was expected, nay, engineered. Wilson confirms that the 'intensely emotional part of the Elim meeting' brings 'tears, heavy breathing, groans, utterances of joy and rapture, and, of course, tongues'.[4]

This speaking with tongues, or glossolalia, a frequent accompaniment of the ecstatic condition, shows again what the essence of all these phenomena is: like dadaism, it is a rejection of the world and its rationality. Transcriptions of Khlyst glossolalia show a preference for the nasal n which is unknown, and for the combination of consonants *nt*, as in *umilisintru* or *nasophont*, which is rare, in Russian speech. The desire to be different is clear. Yet close study reveals that underneath these revolutionary utterances, there is still real Russian. The cadences, even the syntax, are still

[1] Cit. ibid., pp. 108, 73, 167.
[2] Cf. also Knox, loc. cit., pp. 520 et seq.
[3] Cit. Wilson, loc. cit., p. 38.
[4] Ibid., p. 103.

determined by the linguistic norm. The sectarians remain tied to those whom they abhor. They are to society what a negative in photography is to the positive: different, yet not so different at the same time.[1]

One final remark is needed on the subject of emotion. Niebuhr, following certain utterances of Ernst Troeltsch, has asserted that all lower-class religiosity will assume an emotional character. 'The religion of the untutored and economically disfranchised classes has distinct . . . psychological characteristics', he writes. 'Emotional fervor is one common mark. Where the power of abstract thought has not been highly developed and where inhibitions on emotional expression have not been set up by a system of polite conventions, religion must and will express itself in emotional terms.'[2] This assertion is misleading. Lower-class religion will become centred on sentiment only where upper-class religion is centred on reason. A proof of that is the comparative rationality of the Christadelphians whose case we have discussed above (cf. p. 37). 'Christadelphianism does not offer the emotional release supposedly characteristic of religious expressions of the poor,'[3] Wilson writes, and he is correct. Opposed to middle-class religion as well as to upper-class religion, it assumed definite anti-emotional, near-rationalistic, forms because middle-class religion, in contemporary England, was shot through with sentiment, not to say sentimentality. It is always the desire to be different which determines a sect's character and outlook. Christadelphianism was the answer to Methodism, when Methodism had become the creed of an aristocracy of labour, a foremen's religion. To the degree to which the latter developed a religion of the heart, the former preached and propagated a religion of the head.

Comparable in importance to the devaluation of knowledge by the typical sects is their devaluation of beauty – clearly another contracultural trait. When some General Baptist churches introduced psalm-singing on the sol-fa method, the Assembly of the denomination was horrified. It declared in 1689 'that it was not conceived anyways safe of the churches to admit to such carnal formalities'. Carnal formalities – the term is pungent twice over, a blast from a double-barrelled gun. At about the same time, one Benjamin Keach introduced hymn-singing in his congregation,

[1] Grass, loc. cit., vol. I, pp. 123, note 2. [2] Niebuhr, loc. cir., p. 30.
[3] Wilson, loc. cit., p. 324. Cf. also ibid., pp. 294, 299, 306, 311.

and his son-in-law, Thomas Crosby, relates what happened. 'Though he had very great success therein, yet it brought upon him much trouble and ill-will.' At first only two opposed him, but they 'drew over some others in the Church to join with them, and wrought up their uneasiness to that pitch that at last a separation ensued; and thereupon another church was founded on the same principles, singing only excepted'. A curious schism, it would appear to some of us, that happens because of so harmless a thing as hymnody. Yet the matter touched a sore point: beauty was heathen to many sectarians, one of the blandishments of the fallen angels, a net spread out by the powers of hell. Like the General Baptists, the Particular Baptists, too, suffered for years from a dispute about congregational singing.[1]

The Methodists, a hundred years later, felt very much the same way about beauty. An entry in John Wesley's *Journal* showed their attitude to sculpture: 'Thursday, 15 April 1669, I went to Halifax, where a little thing had lately occasioned great disturbance. An angel blowing a trumpet was placed on the sounding-board over the pulpit. Many were vehemently against this; others as vehemently for it: but a total end was soon put to the contest, for the angel vanished away.' The last phrase is rather metaphorical: the thing was in fact broken and the pieces burnt to ashes. Music fared little better. When there was talk of hiring a chapel at Manchester for a performance of Handel's *Samson* (not exactly a profane work!), John Valton noted: '14 June 1781 . . . So Sampson will be called in to make them sport. I am afraid if it does not bring the house about their ears, it will, however, do much harm to the Society. The people murmur and my soul grieves.' Of architecture, the Methodist historian Church writes: 'The early efforts of the chapel-builders were either pathetically crude and unlovely in appearance, or sometimes florid and much more repellent . . . Often they yielded to some strange inhibition that beauty was dangerous . . .'[2]

A particular *pièce de résistance* for the Methodists was the stage – Whitefield called the playhouse a house of the devil – and this is understandable, for in the eighteenth century the stage was not exactly what one could call a moralizing influence. But it is here, where we can see, from a most amazing incident, how deep the

[1] Underwood, loc. cit., pp. 124, 125, 132, 133, 128.
[2] Church, loc. cit., pp. 74, 75, 209, 210, 56, 57.

dislike of traditional culture went even with these comparatively mild men. Among John Wesley's effects was found, after his death, a copy of Shakespeare's works with notes from Wesley's hand. John Pawson discovered it and was upset. Should a good man, a godly man, take an interest in *any* stage work of *any* kind? Obviously, Pawson's conviction was that he should not. *All* plays were evil. So, out of anxiety for Wesley's reputation, he destroyed the book.[1]

This looks like a barbarian, Hun-like, act, but we must be anxious to remain realistic and fair. The term contraculture which we have been using all along has two ingredients, one negative, one positive, and this is a good point at which to bring up the latter. A *contra*culture is a contra*culture*. It contains, at least in outline, a system of values which, though opposed to the prevailing preferences, are, in principle, alternatives, possible substitutes, if not indeed equivalents. This truth can best be understood by thinking of architecture here. The rococo style which appealed to the 'best taste' of the day (which, to the sociologist, means no more than that it appealed to the aristocratic taste) repelled the Methodists, and, in opposition to it, they built particularly unadorned and plain chapels. But these chapels soon exhibited a beauty of their own – the beauty of simplicity, of right proportion, of what a later age was to call functional design. Church's derogatory remark, quoted above, is less than fair. Indeed, art historians have come to speak of a 'non-conformist' style, and this was no less a style than that of Versailles. Soon it was to become dominant in Europe in what the Viennese call *Biedermeier*. Sectarian groups which had a chance to develop it, like the Shakers, in fact created much beauty, as their remaining relics, especially their buildings, impressively testify.[2] Theirs was a contraculture, certainly, but yet a culture, if one entirely devoid of sophistication.

If this was a culture, then soberness was its keynote. But sectarian soberness was shown less in the development of an architectural or artistic style (apart from everything else, there were not the necessary means) than in a style of life. And this style of life had cleanliness as one of its main principles. Cleanliness was sometimes no less than an obsession, and the 'house-proud' middle class English housewife is a characteristic heir, a surviving

[1] Cameron, loc. cit., p. 58.

[2] Cf. Melcher, loc. cit., chapters XI and XII (pp. 191–226).

witness, to the sectarian – 'puritan' – tradition of her country and her class. Now, cleanliness can hardly be called a *contra*cultural value (though perhaps exaggerated cleanliness can). But there is another element at work here, that of symbolism. The sectarian wanted to be free of the dirt of this world, and though the preoccupation was metaphysical, it could be externalized and abreacted by physical actions as well.[1] Thus even the washing of hands and house can be part and parcel of a protest mentality.

In Russia, the Theodosians were well known to be overparticular about their cleanliness, but this character-trait was common to the whole tribe of sectarians. Speaking from experience, Conybeare says of the Khlysty that 'they are clean in person and in dress, and the inns or rest-houses which they keep, especially in the Caucasus, are models of tidiness and sobriety'. This is invariably confirmed.[2] When cholera epidemics raged in Russia, the Dukhobors escaped, for personal hygiene was their *forte*; and when they emigrated to Canada and became a public menace there, it was yet acknowledged that they had at least one virtue, that of cleanliness.[3]

In the West, sectarian neatness has become so proverbial that there is no need to parade passages in illustration of the fact. Descriptions of Shaker life provide many such illustrations.[4] The average New Yorker has no love of the Jehovah's Witnesses whose headquarters are in his city, but he feels about them the way Canadians feel about the Dukhobors. The *New York Times* wrote, after a great Witnesses' convention, on 1 August 1958: 'Whatever New Yorkers may think about the Witnesses' theology, they are unanimous in agreeing that the Witnesses' conduct has been exemplary . . . Their cleanliness is almost legendary. A week ago a corps of volunteer Witnesses washed down every seat in the Yankee stadium. When they leave on Sunday the ball park will be spotless. Three years ago Yankee maintenance men testified that when the Witnesses departed, the arena had never been cleaner.'

For many sectarians, the canons of cleanliness also included

[1] See the figure of Jaggers in Dickens's *Great Expectations*. Cf. chapter XXVI, Appleton ed., as quoted, p. 80.

[2] Conybeare, loc. cit., p. 360; Grass, loc. cit. vol. I, 504, note.

[3] Wright, loc. cit., pp. 128, 135, 252, 262, 263.

[4] Cf. Melcher, loc. cit., pp. 156, 201, 202, 222, 248.

certain principles (the big word is entirely justified) concerning hairdress. The Roundheads were or wore round-heads because they closely cropped their hair, while the Cavaliers sported flowing locks down to their shoulders. Lodowick Muggleton confessed: 'If a man with long hair had gone into the pulpit to preach, I would have gone out of the church again, though he might preach better than the other.'[1] In the same spirit the Assembly of Particular Baptists declared in 1689: 'It is a shame for men to wear long hair or long periwigs.'[2] But the negativity of sectarian attitudes becomes particularly clear at this point, for all the sectarians want is to be different, and if the world wears short hair, they will have it long. To the Quakers, the Roundheads were 'the world'; *ergo* they had to have unclipped locks like the Cavaliers or the *reges criniti.* In Sedbergh, George Fox had some encounter with the Roundheads early in his career, and already his outer appearance betokened difference: 'He stood on the bench under the yew tree in his leather dress with its alchemy buttons and his hair hanging in ringlets, contrary to the Puritan fashion.' Nayler, too, had 'long, low-hanging brown hair'. The matter was not regarded lightly. Leslie, in his *Defence of the Snake*, wrote with venom: 'George Fox had a mind to be a Nazirite like Samson and wore long strait hair like rats' tails' – perhaps a descriptive, but not a kindly, comparison. 'At Wrexham . . . one lady in her lightness asked Fox whether she could cut his hair for him, and afterwards boasted "in her frothy mind" that she came behind him and cut off a lock of his hair, "which [we are told] was a lie".'[3] Clearly, this was not a laughing matter to the Quaker worthy.

It was not, however, in England, it was in Russia, that the question of hairdress loomed largest. Peter the Devil brought clippers and razor with him from the West, and in an edict promulgated in 1700 ordered his subjects to use them: the Old Believers at once desperately resisted what they considered the desecration of the image of God, and they readily paid the fines inflicted on them for disobedience. 'The[se] Russians,' writes Perry, 'dedicated a kind of religious respect to their beards. They allowed them to grow down to their chests; they combed them and smoothed them, striving not to lose a single hair.'[4] It was

[1] Cit. Braithwaite, p. 19.
[2] Underwood, loc. cit., p. 130.
[3] Braithwaite, loc. cit., pp. 83, 243, 550, 349.
[4] Cit. de Grunwald, *Peter the Great,* p. 99.

doubted, nay denied, that a shaven man could go to heaven. Even a beard may have importance in time and eternity.

A concomitant feature of the sectarian contraculture is differentiation in dress, sometimes given biblical justification by quoting I Timothy II, 9, a verse enjoining women to be 'in decent apparel: adorning themselves with modesty and sobriety, not with plaited hair, or gold, or pearls, or costly attire'. The onset of Quakerism was also an outbreak of ribbon-burning. 'I met with none that could justly accuse them of any crime,' Thomas Thompson says, in *An Encouragement early to Seek the Lord*, of the Friends at Malton, 'only they said they were a fantastical and conceited people, and burnt their lace and ribbons and other superfluous things which formerly they used to wear, and that they fell into strange fits of quaking and trembling.' Enthusing about the 'glorious morning' of the sect in Bristol, Charles Marshall breaks into lyrical language: 'Oh! the strippings of all needless apparel . . .', and Camm reports from the same place about the effects of his preaching: 'They have, many of them, cast off their beautiful garments which was without.' Some of them, indeed, cast off more than outer garments in the process. Gilbert Latey was a court-tailor 'in great business in the world and concerned by reason thereof with persons of considerable rank and quality, who would have their apparel set off with much cost and superfluities of lace and ribbons'. The Quaker conscience was very active in this man: should he, could he, minister to pride? He found he could not. He lost both his customers and his hands and sank down into straightened circumstances. Braithwaite calls this 'cross-bearing', and, from the Quaker point of view, it was.[1]

The earnestness with which the Friends regarded men's outer appearance is matched, a hundred years later, by that of the Methodists. John Wesley preached a sermon on dress,[2] and it is reported of him that he 'had sometimes thought of suggesting a uniform style for all the women of Methodism'. Many of these women, for instance, Mary Lyth, wore Quaker dress, as portraits still extant prove.[3] The subject came up repeatedly at early Conferences. The minutes of one of them record the following exhortation: 'This is no time to give any encouragement to

[1] Braithwaite, loc. cit., pp. 72, 170, 166, 378.
[2] Cf. Sermon XCIII, in *Works*, as quoted, vol. II, pp. 258–65.
[3] Church, loc. cit., pp. 202 and 201; cf. also pp. 197 and 199.

superfluity of apparel. Therefore, give no tickets to any, till they have left off superfluous ornaments . . . high heads, enormous bonnets, ruffles, or rings.' The phrase 'give no tickets' sounds harmless, but it meant in effect: excommunicate! 'To deprive a Methodist of his ticket as a class-member was . . . to exclude him from the society . . .'[1]

The tendency to wear a distinguishing garb, to demonstrate otherness even in the outward appearance, was basically as strong in Russia as it was in the West, but it was arrested in midstream. Persecuted by the police, the Russian non-conformist could not advertise his non-conformity in the street, and so all he (or she) could do was to avoid ornaments. Khlyst women wore their headsquares in a particular way – deep over the eyes, so as to give the impression of great modesty. Skopets women did likewise and avoided all vivid colours. The general get-up had a remote resemblance to nuns' habits – or rather as near a resemblance as fear of recognition allowed. To cover the body's curves was a particular preoccupation, and the Khlyst women were said to ruin their figures by too close compression.[2] For the Skopets women, the problem did not exist, for reasons which we have yet to encounter.[3]

The Old Believers, who were not classed as a criminal sect and therefore had more freedom, were helped by their very enemy to show their otherness in their clothes. Peter the Great ordered them to wear a red square of cloth bordered with yellow on their clothing, or the lettering H.R.A. – meaning heretic, raskolnik (i.e. schismatic), apostate.[4] Needless to say – and here we see once more, as in a flash of light, the contracultural nature of sectarian attitudes – the mark of shame became in their eyes a mark of honour. Few regulations of 'Anti-Christ' were accepted with so much willingness as this one.

While the English Quakers had even more freedom than the Russian Old Believers, they shared some of the dangers incurred by Khlysty and Skoptsy. We have already pointed out that persecution was more official in Russia, being persecution by the

[1] Cit. Cameron, p. 105. Concerning Shaker fashions, cf. Melcher, loc. cit., pp. 68, 153, 154, 194.

[2] Grass, loc. cit., vol. I, pp. 176, 320, note 1, vol. II, pp. 751, 752.

[3] Cf. below, p. 167.

[4] de Grunwald, *Peter the Great*, p. 147; Conybeare, loc. cit., p. 227.

police, and more unorganized in England, being persecution by the mob. Wearing Quaker garb was therefore risky, as the following (lucky) incident shows. 'When [Thomas] Ellwood first went to a meeting in London, in the Restoration year, the mob were very abusive and mishandled Friends as they came out of the meeting. But they left Ellwood alone, as being [to all appearances] no Quaker, because he wore a large montero-cap of black velvet, the skirt of which was turned up in folds, beyond Quaker simplicity . . .'[1] The early Quakers were fighters – like the Jehovah's Witnesses of this century, they positively courted attack. The thirst for martyrdom was for a while rampant in them. They did not mind being recognized for what they were.

In his curious literary production, *Sartor Resartus*, Thomas Carlyle discusses George Fox's famous leather suit, and he interprets it, entirely in the spirit of the present book, as an externalization of an inner revolutionary urge. He speaks of the prophet on the day when he ceased to make shoes in order to mend souls instead: 'Let some living Angelo or Rosa, with seeing eye and understanding heart,' he writes, 'picture George Fox on that morning, when he spreads out his cutting-board for the last time and cuts cowhides by unwonted patterns and stitches them together into one continuous all-including case.' What did this sartorial effort mean? It meant a stroke on behalf of liberty! 'Stitch away, thou noble Fox!' Carlyle exclaims: 'Every prick of that little instrument is pricking into the heart of slavery, and world-worship, and the Mammon-god . . . Every stroke is bearing thee across the prison-ditch within which vanity holds her workhouse and ragfair, into lands of true liberty . . . Thus from the lowest depth there is a path to the loftiest height; and for the poor also a gospel has been published.' The last words may sound like a *non-sequitur*, but the reference to the poor is meant to indicate that Fox not only strove for liberty, but also for equality: his clothes were meant, not only for his own use, but as a pattern for all, and thus they were part and parcel of the 'mad day-dream . . . of levelling society and so attaining the political effects of nudity without its frigorific or other consequences'.[2] It is truly difficult to

[1] Braithwaite, loc. cit., p. 499.

[2] Carlyle, Th., *Sartor Resartus*, ed. Mac Mechan, A., Boston and London 1896, pp. 191, 192, 193.

decide whether one should admire Carlyle more for the depth of his insight or for his felicity in presenting it!

In matters of attire, as in matters of art, there was a certain stylishness about the dissenters which proves that even they had style, though it was not the fashionable one of the day. Quaker dress was by no means entirely unbecoming, and this goes for many kinds of sectarian dress, for instance the Salvationists', or the clothing of the Dunker women which, to this day, is a common sight in some mid-western towns. The Shakers especially showed remarkable taste in this particular, as they did in so much else.

One of the sectarian techniques for the challenging of the world, or, as we can also say, one of the sectarian outlets for their aggressiveness, was the rejection of accepted manners, their plain rudeness, as it appeared to respectable society. The Thomas Ellwood whom we encountered a page or two back, would not consent to sit down at his father's table without his hat on – without the 'hive' on his head, as Mr. Ellwood senior expressed it in his annoyance, for Quaker hats were high-crowned, shaped like bee-hives – and when asked to do as the rest of the company did, demonstratively removed to the kitchen to eat with the domestics. Braithwaite qualifies even this behaviour as part of 'taking up the cross' and seriously quotes Matthew x, 35 and 36: 'I came to set a man at variance against his father . . . and a man's enemies shall be they of his own household.' (Fox's own justifying quotation was Daniel III, 21, according to which Sidrach, Misach and Abdenago 'were cast into the furnace of burning fire with their coats *and their caps*'.) On other points of early Quaker conduct, Braithwaite is almost apologetic, calling them extravagances, whimseys, etc.[1] But here he takes his stand: 'The witness of Friends on points of speech and dress . . . touched some of the greatest issues of life, and is not to be treated as an excrescence on their main message . . . The witness of Friends was a standing rebuke to the world and to Christians for their emphasis on those differences in rank and position which amount to nothing in the sight of God.'[2] In this contracultural feature the basic fact of Quakerism and all sectarianism comes to the surface once again – the fact that it is from beginning to end a social-revolutionary phenomenon.

[1] Cf. Braithwaite, loc. cit., pp. 392, 398, 408.

[2] Ibid., pp. 492, 493, 232, 233, 196 note 3, 495.

Braithwaite mentions speech along with dress, and he is thinking of the 'thee' and 'thou' of the early Quakers which, unavoidably, has already cropped up in these pages. In the sixteenth century, a superior might say 'thou' to an inferior, for instance, a master to his servant; but an inferior could not use this form, and in a servant it was literally the height of insolence, an unheard-of affront – 'a gross affront and an act of insubordinatïon', as Braithwaite admits.[1] Richard Farnsworth defended the usage in *The Pure Language of the Spirit of Truth* (1655). This isolated instance of linguistic differentiation between sect and society is well known, but it should not obscure the fact that the phenomenon is of far more general distribution and of far deeper importance than might be suspected.

All sects have their particularities of speech. To the Quakers' 'convincement' and 'disownment' (for entrance into, and exclusion from, the Society of Friends) correspond peculiar Christian Science usages, e.g. 'claim' for 'illness' and 'demonstration' for 'healing' – not to mention the Salvation Army to which a speech is a 'bombshell', an unbeliever an 'enemy', and so on. The Jehovah's Witnesses, too, have some words of their own, and Father Divine is famous for what a reporter recently called 'flights of unorthodox rhetoric'.[2] But an odd term here and there means very little. What is much more significant is the spontaneous production of a new sectarian variant of the old common language, for instance, by a different manner of pronunciation. Robert Graves, who is as fine a historian as he is a novelist, says of the Calvinist predicant who replaces the Anglican vicar in Marie Powell's village: 'He pronounced words strangely in the new Presbyterial manner, with "Aymen" for "Amen" and "glaurious" for "glorious" and "the Laud's murcy" for "the Lord's mercy".'[3] The matter had world-historical importance for the English language, for the pulpit tone of the New England chapels, of sectarian origin, has deeply influenced what has become everyday American speech. 'Even the intonation can mark a Witness,' an acute observer has written about more recent developments, 'just as the long *a* pronunciation of Mary Baker Eddy usually identifies a member of the Christian Science church'.[4] This whole complex appears to be severely under-documented and under-researched, and would present a

[1] Ibid., p. 494.
[2] *The New York Times*, 10 May 1964.
[3] *Wife to Mr Milton*, Penguin ed., p. 100.
[4] Whalen, loc. cit., p. 202.

most promising field of joint endeavour for sociologists and linguistic experts.

Much though we may regret it, it does not seem possible to construct a sensible scheme which would realistically measure the degree of alienation on the part of a sect. On most tests, the Methodists would appear only as mild non-conformists, as people relatively close to the mainstream of national life. Yet when we consider what Methodism did to the English language, we find that its punch, its power of thrust, was considerable. Grimshaw has described Methodist speech as market English,[1] and the expression is not ill-chosen. It was the people's language that the Wesleyan preachers used, the language of the hovels, not the academics' language, the language of Oxford Common Rooms.[2] And they transformed this spoken idiom into a written one as well. Their popular literature, especially their penny pamphlets, transposed the audible into visible signs, made the preachers' lingo into a printable medium. If a perusal of their eighteenth-century literature does not give us the impression that here is a revolutionary achievement, this is simply due to the success of the revolution which has accustomed us to what, six generations ago, was a crude and strange – a contracultural – mode of expression. Popular journalism, in particular, owes much to Wesleyan pioneering.

But these are all comparatively mild demonstrations of sectarian alienation from the inclusive society. We come to a far more serious subject when we consider their refusal to bear arms, to defend their country, and similar acts irreconcilable with the basic civic duties. Mankind, wincing ever anew under the lash of war, has given high honour to, for instance, the Dukhobors and the Quakers for being so determined pacifists, and there is in fact an element of fine idealism in their non-combatancy. Narrowly and soberly considered, however, we find even here a negative rather than a positive attitude at work. The Dukhobors were – at least originally – not opposed to killing *per se* so much as to killing on behalf of the tsar, and in the case of the Quakers it was originally insubordination, inability to accept the structure of command, which drove them out of the army, rather than the ideal of pacifism. This fact is interestingly reflected in the following letter of Colonel Daniels to General Monck about a Captain Davenport:

[1] Lecky, loc. cit., p. 678.

[2] Cf. Church, loc. cit., pp. 12 and 13.

'My captain lieutenant is much confirmed in his principles of quaking, making all the soldiers his equals, according to the Levellers' strain . . . He has been under my command almost fourteen years, and hitherto demeaned himself in good order, and many of these whimseys I have kept him from, but now there's no speaking to him, and I do profess I am afraid lest by the spreading of these humours the public suffer, for they [who are like Davenport] are a very uncertain generation to execute commands, and liberty with equality is so pleasing to ignorance that proselytes will be daily brought in . . . and when I think of the Levelling design that had like to have torn the army to pieces, it makes me more bold to give my opinion that these things be curbed in time.'[1]

Conscientious objection to army service is in this way not necessarily an outcome of pacifist convictions as can also be seen from the case of the Jehovah's Witnesses. They maintain that they are enrolled in Jehovah's host and cannot therefore enroll in the U.S. forces as well, especially as the latter are no allies, but rather adversaries, of the former. Pacifism does not appear to enter into their considerations.[2] Similarly, the Christadelphians do not oppose war as such; indeed, some of them have tended towards acceptance of war as a divine institution; what is condemned is merely 'service of the sin-powers of the world'.[3]

In Russia, the Molokane put refusal to serve in fighting units very high on their list of duties and went to great lengths to find substitutes, buy themselves free, or get into medical or transportation corps. One practice of theirs which was very annoying to the authorities, was the hiding of army deserters, whether their desertion was religiously motivated or not. But their twin sect, the Dukhobortsy, went much farther still. As early as the Russo-Turkish war of 1806–12, the Dukhobor conscripts threw away their arms, but matters only came to a head when general conscription was introduced, in 1887, in the Caucasus region where the bulk of them was then domiciled. One Semyon Osachov turned conscientious objector and was whipped; others were imprisoned or sent to penal battalions. The crisis point was reached on 29 June 1895, still a great day in the Dukhobor calendar: all weapons were burned and all army passes demonstratively returned to the authorities. This brought the cossacks on to the

[1] Cit. Braithwaite, p. 520. [2] Cf. Whalen, loc. cit., pp. 18 and 19.
[3] Cf. Wilson, loc. cit., pp. 288 and 239.

scene, and there followed a horrible massacre which found its echo in all parts of the globe. The transfer of the sect to Canada was the direct, if delayed, consequence. The Canadians thought – accepting Tolstoy's estimate of these men – that they were accepting paragons of mildness and meekness into their country. They were soon to be painfully disabused.[1]

In Britain and America, conscientious objection to military service has, with reservations and safeguards, become a recognized and legally protected right, and not only the Quakers, but also the newer sects, like the Christadelphians and the Jehovah's Witnesses, have availed themselves of it, or tried to. This is too well known to deserve discussion here. But what is less well known is that even the Methodists showed, early in their history, tendencies towards conscientious objection. In England, John Nelson, stonemason turned preacher, thus addressed a court-martial at York in the days of the Stuart Rebellion under Bonnie Prince Charlie: 'I shall not fight; for I cannot bow my knee before the Lord to pray for a man and get up and kill him when I have done; for I know God both hears me speak and sees me act; and I should expect the lot of the hypocrite, if my actions contradict my prayers.' In America, Jesse Lee, author of *A Short History of the Methodists in the United States* (1810), expressed himself even more straightforwardly during the War of Independence: 'As a Christian and as a preacher of the Gospel I could not fight. I could not reconcile it to myself to bear arms or to kill one of my fellow-creatures.'[2] Unlike the Quakers, however, the Methodists did not make conscientious objection an abiding element in their tradition.

Hand in hand with the refusal of military service has sometimes gone a refusal to join the civil service, the argument being that the acceptance of office is irreconcilable with the Christian principles of equality and brotherhood. John Smyth, the Se-Baptist, standing at the beginning of all English Baptism, put a sentence to this effect into his Declaration of Faith.[3] This issue, however, was a purely academic one and has not churned up much mud in the stream of history. Sectarians never sought places in the bureaucracy, and establishmentarians would never have granted them anyway.

[1] Wright, loc. cit., pp. 17, 34, 57, 70, 71, 79–88.
[2] Cit. Cameron, loc. cit., pp. 54, 55, 90, 91.
[3] Cf. Underwood, loc. cit., pp. 23 and 42.

Far more crucial has been the non-conformists' refusal to use the official law-courts. They have ever been mindful of St. Paul's injunctions to the Corinthians in this respect (I, VI, 1–8): only a brother should adjudicate between brethren. Almost every sect has revived this principle. Smyth had it in his Declaration. The Quakers took it for granted. The English Methodists were sharply recalled to it by John Wesley, when occasion arose.[1] The American Methodists formulated it clearly and did much to develop substitute courts, indeed, one could almost say a substitute law of procedure. Christadelphians do not engage in litigation, and the stricter among them, the followers of F. G. Jannaway called Bereans, were characterized by 'the insistence . . . that to go to law before the unbeliever was unscriptural in all cases'.[2] The Old Believers, like the Methodists, tended to evolve their own courts and procedures, and so did the Khlysty. There was not only arbitration in what lawyers call civil cases, but also prosecution and punishment for misdemeanours and for crimes.[3]

One particular reason that official law courts were, or rather had to be, avoided is the ban on oaths which is a very widespread characteristic of sects (in accordance with St. Matthew, V, 33–7). When the General Baptists Ives and Denne defended the lawfulness of oaths, Henry Adis, a stronger personality, 'issued from prison an answer, written in a passion of indignation'. The oath of allegiance was a particularly sore point. In 1663, London's Newgate Prison held no fewer than 214 Anabaptists and Quakers for their obstinate refusal to swear it. 'No Quaker, or hardly any Anabaptist, will take those oaths,' a report from Bristol ran, 'so that the said oaths are refused by many hundreds . . . being persons of very dangerous principles . . . I had almost said, monsters of men . . .' Christadelphians still take no oaths, and the Dukhobortsy and kindred groups did not do so either.[4]

It goes without saying that a sect cannot agree to pay taxes which contribute to the support of the State Church, such as the old English tithe. But as the sects condemn, not only the State

[1] Cf. Church, loc. cit., pp. 192 and 193.

[2] Cf. Underwood, loc. cit., p. 42; Cameron, loc. cit., pp. 105 and 129–31; Wilson, loc. cit., pp. 289 and 265.

[3] Conybeare, loc. cit., p. 222; Grass, loc. cit., vol. I, p. 498.

[4] Cf. Underwood, pp. 91 and 92; Wilson, loc. cit., p. 289; Braithwaite, loc. cit., pp. 478 and 479, see also index, *sub verbo* 'oaths, testimony against'; Conybeare, loc. cit., pp. 283 and 171.

Church, but the whole State, the State as such, they have sometimes shown a disinclination to pay any imposts at all. The Molokane, for instance, asserted that 'they are under no moral obligation to pay taxes. They do not belong to Caesar, but to God, and can recognize no overlordship of Caesar'. It looks, however, as if they had gone too far. We are told that they refused to pay taxes in 1826, and that from 1827 on they paid them punctually.[1] A sect can only go so far in its challenge to the authorities. There is a limit, and when that is reached, either the sect must stop, or it must leave the parent society, or it will be rooted out. The Molokane seem to have recognized that the time had come for them to call a halt.

Sometimes, indeed, the limit is reached without an open challenge to the state, for purely technical reasons, as it were. The Stranniky asked themselves whether it was allowable for them to use coins, in view of the fact that they bore the imprint of Antichrist, and a subsect called the Moneyless arose which gave a negative answer to this question. 'They got over the practical inconvenience by getting novices to carry money for them and make their disbursements, just as the Manichaean elect ones carried their scruple against taking life so far as to make their novices cut their salads for them, shriving them afterwards for the sin they had committed.' Common sense seems very soon to have taken care of this impossible extravaganza.[2]

One of the chief purposes of the official registers of births, marriages and deaths was, in every country, to serve as bases for taxation, especially for poll taxes, and as Peter the Great made non-conformists pay double what their Orthodox neighbours paid, it is understandable that they developed a strong distaste – a desperate resistance, even – to these registers. It was estimated that 29,431 Raskolnik marriages were contracted between 1889 and 1903, but only 1,840 were reported to the authorities, and that 131,730 babies were born, but only 552 births were entered in the books. It would be entirely wrong, however, to assume that it was mainly economic considerations which prompted this opposition. We see, on the contrary, very clearly here that the struggle between state and sect is conceived and fought out in religious terms. II Kings XXIV was regarded as conclusive proof that God condemned the numbering of a people, indeed, considered it an

[1] Conybeare, loc. cit., pp. 312 and 313. [2] Ibid., p. 163.

impiety and a crime. The poll tax was interpreted as a payment to the devil. 'Verily we see fulfilled the mystery of the Apocalypse,' the Old Believers argued. 'The reign of the ... Beast is established among us, and the earth and all that live thereon are made to bow the knee to Satan and say: "Settle our account, we beg you humbly to grant us passports". He will answer: "Out with your poll-tax . . . pay up, for you live on my earth". There,' the Old Believers concluded, 'there you have a deep pit for the destruction of the human race.'[1]

What made registration particularly repulsive in Russia, was the fact that the technical unit was not 'one person', but 'one soul' (*dusha*, cf. Gogol's *Dead Souls*), and this supported and quasi-justified the conviction that the entry of a name placed its bearer in the power of Antichrist. But the Dukhobors took their hatred of the census with them to the new world, and though it again found some kind of justification there (e.g. in the fact that the register books had embossed on their covers the English crown), the whole attitude was independent of fortuitous local circumstances and stemmed from the very deepest essence of sectarianism. If this had not been so, the conflict between the Dukhobors and the Canadian people (the uncomprehending Canadian people) would not have centred on this apparently so petty matter,[2] nor would the Quakers have gone out of their way to develop their own civil records to which, in fact, they devoted much time, energy, and money.[3] To be different from the world – that was the overriding aim and wish of both. How could there be *one* register for *two* so dissimilar species – sheep and goats, accepted and rejected, God's companions and the Devil's? To be registered was to be thrust down into the dirt, and the dissenters, ever anxious to be clean in the sight of their Maker, recoiled from it as one recoils from some nauseous mire, from the pit of fire and brimstone, or worse.

Only one major point remains now to be touched upon under the heading 'The Sect as a Contraculture', and though it is very important in itself, it is somewhat marginal to the sociologist's area of interest. What influence did the underlying social conflict

[1] The source is quoted by Conybeare, loc. cit., p. 92. For the statistics, cf. ibid., pp. 237 and 238.

[2] Cf. Wright, loc. cit., pp. 185, 210, 254, 259, 304, 331.

[3] Cf. Braithwaite, loc. cit., pp. 144 and 340.

have on the sectarians' religious thinking? The answer is: a great, indeed determining and decisive, influence. Even in the field of dogma, the dissenters said 'nay' whenever and wherever the conformists said 'yea' – and *vice versa*. The contraculture contained in itself a contratheology. Its positions can almost be predicted in advance because they are in all typical cases simply inversions of the assertions characteristic of orthodoxy.

We have seen, when studying the sect as a system of action, that it is explicable as much as a protest against Wittenberg and Geneva as against Canterbury and Rome. Exactly the same is the case here, in the sect considered as a system of ideas. We gladly give, once again, the word to the Quaker historian Braithwaite for he puts the facts very clearly: 'The great affirmation that every man had received from the Lord a measure of light which, if followed, would lead him to the Light of Life, was in conflict with the current Puritan conceptions of . . . God and of human nature. One-sided doctrines of election and reprobation had obscured the Fatherhood of God and had magnified His sovereignty at the cost of veiling His love. And, on the other hand, the line was drawn sharply between the human and the Divine. The natural man belonged to an undivine order of life, marred by the Fall and under the dominion of Satan . . . These ideas of the age were part of Fox's mental environment and had their influence . . . on Quaker thought.' They had their influence, Braithwaite means, as a source of countersuggestions. Calvin's doctrine of the immeasurable gulf between the Creator and the creature was turned upside down and inside out by Fox's assertion of 'unity with the creation'.[1] We have pointed out already that this anti-Calvinism was the fore-runner of the anti-Calvinism of Mary Baker Eddy. Between the two sect-leaders divided by two hundred and fifty years, there is a historical and philosophical filiation, and the anti-Calvinism of both was basically also a common anti-capitalism, a common resistance to, and rejection of, the theological thinking of established society.

An intermediate station on this road was the appearance of Methodism, and the main stream of it was also an anti-Calvinist and an anti-capitalist current. Decaying Calvinism and developing capitalism had, between them, produced a strongly rationalistic temper in the eighteenth century, and it was against this that John Wesley took the field. No Lockean *Reasonableness of Christianity* for

[1] Ibid., pp. 36 and 37, and Appendix, p. 553, *sub* 'unity with the creation'.

him: his God was a mysterious God who spoke more to the heart of men than to their intellect. Above all, He was a God of love, and because He loved, He could not have condemned generations upon generations before they were ever born: against the Calvinist doctrine of predestination, so close to the doctrine of predetermination characteristic of a crude scientism, Wesley set his belief in free will: he was an Arminian with every fibre of his being. A close study of Wesley's thinking, which cannot be undertaken here, would show that even his technical theology was essentially a negative reflection of the prevalent theological ideas of the day. It was the effort to stem the tide of Arianism, Eusebianism, Socinianism, Latitudinarianism and similar rationalizing tendencies which determined, not only his polemics, but even his positive positions. True, Methodism had a Calvinistic as well as an Arminian wing, and one must not forget Whitefield over Wesley. However, even Whitefield's theology, though within the Calvinist ambit, was different from, and diametrically opposed to, Calvinistic rationalism. And, what is more, Calvinism, in its original, germinal, form, bore in itself truly revolutionary seeds, as we shall see in later chapters, and it was these which were developed by Whitefield, and not its rationalizing implications which rather led to such semi-respectable rational world-views as the Unitarian theology, an intellectual and intellectuals' creed, if not indeed to Humean and Voltairean unbelief. Compared to them, compared above all to their soul-enslaving iciness, Wesley's wild enthusiasm was a truly revolutionary stance, a true call to liberation. His whole philosophy, and even more that of his followers, in so far as they had one, was a pre-romanticism rather than a post-rationalism, and as such at least as different from established philosophizing as the philosophy of that great negator, Rousseau.[1]

As the Wesleyan Methodists were so determined contemnors of Calvinism and all its works, the idea gained ground that they were crypto-Catholics, and one of Hogarth's caricatures of a Methodist preacher shows his wig falling aside and revealing underneath a

[1] While any move towards pantheism was excluded by Wesley's highly personalistic conception of the deity (a counterblast to the rationalistic tendency to make god into a principle), he did have a characteristically vivid attitude to, and love of, nature, and to that extent at times recalls Fox's 'unity with the creation'. Cf. *The New Cambridge Modern History*, vol. VIII, pp. 69 and 70 (in the contribution of the present writer).

friar's *corona* or large tonsure.[1] The negation of a negation, people seem to have argued, brings you back to the original position, and though this estimate is marred by an inability to see how much genuine Protestantism there was in Wesley, it is yet not entirely without justification. Wesley was an intense admirer of St. François de Sales, and Wesleyanism as a whole is, without a doubt, a distant offspring of Franciscanism, an offshoot of it, as it were, that has sprung up beyond the garden wall.[2] But while it is not unreasonable to connect Catholicism with Wesleyanism, it is hardly reasonable even to compare Catholicism and Quakerism. Yet the Quakers, too, as negators of a negation, were suspected of Catholic tendencies. In 1660, at Dorchester, they took off Fox's hat and examined his hair, expecting to find a Jesuit's shaven head, and at Torrington in Devonshire, Dewsbury had been formally charged before mayor and justices with being a Jesuit as early as 1657. There appeared even quite a literature which embodied these suspicions. William Prynne published in 1655 a pamphlet entitled *The Quakers Unmasked and clearly detected to be but the Spawn of Romish Frogs, Jesuits and Franciscan Friars, sent from Rome to seduce the intoxicated, giddy-headed English nation*, and both Ralph Farmer's *Great Mysteries of Godliness and Ungodliness* (1655) and Richard Baxter's *Quakers' Catechism* (also of the same year) are similar in tendency.[3] In so far as there is a slight leaning in Franciscanism towards panentheism, and Quakerism had a similar bent, there was perhaps just a shadow of justification to these invectives; but no more than a shadow, for the distance between St. Francis and Fox in fundamentals is tremendous – much greater certainly than the difference between St. Francis and John Wesley.

As a general rule, the sects have attacked the established orthodoxies not by turning backward, towards medieval conceptions, but by moving forward, towards ultra-modern ideas, and this is fully in accord with their general revolutionary animus. The Jehovah's Witnesses and the Christadelphians have gone so far as to develop a kind of semi-materialism. The former, for instance,

[1] Cf. *The Works of William Hogarth,* London 1821, vol. I, not paginated. The engraving is called 'Credulity, Superstition and Fanaticism'.

[2] Significant, in this context, is the book of a Franciscan friar, Fr. Maximin Piette, *John Wesley in the Evolution of Protestantism,* trans. Howard, J. B., New York 1937. Both a Catholic bishop and a Methodist minister wrote introductions to it.

[3] Cf. Braithwaite, loc. cit., pp. 356, 362, 172, 173, 193.

deny that there is an essential difference between men and animals, men's superiority being due merely to his finer physical outfit and organization; the soul is located by them in the blood (hence their ban on blood-transfusion),[1] and is said to die along with the body; even of the deity they have a largely material conception as they assign to him a definite spatial habitat (the constellation called Pleiades); and the resurrection was not a reanimation of Jesus's body, but merely a reappearance in the form of a phantasm.[2] Similarly, 'the kingdom of God, as understood by Christadelphians . . . relates to a post-adventual dispensation to be established *on earth*, and not to a heavenly after-life . . . Christadelphians do not believe in an immortal soul which is regarded as a pagan accretion of Christianity . . . Biblical references to the soul are understood to refer to the individual's life or breath . . . .'[3]

These elements of rationalism in the two doctrinal complexes are significant, for they show the linkage of the sects with the intellectual leftists in secular society. But, on the whole, the sectarians make their protest against the orthodox, not by rational, but, on the contrary, by highly irrational means, for two reasons. Firstly, sectarian thinking arises from an irrational root, a feeling of alienation, resentment and hate, and such as the root is, so will the flower be; and secondly, the world against which the sectarians protest is, taken all in all, a basically rational world, the world of capitalism, science and technology, and if it is rejected, then irrational beliefs satisfy the rejector more than rational ones ever could. Consequently, we find in the philosophy of the Jehovah's Witnesses amazing evidence of a high flight of imagination. This, for instance, is how Russell explained the rise of the trinitarian conception of the deity (which he ridiculed): 'Nimrod married his mother Semiramis, so that in a sense he was his own father and his own son. Here was the origin of the Trinity doctrine.' It will be observed that the attempted 'debunking' of a supposedly irrational idea is inherently much more irrational than the idea meant to be debunked. And there are many more examples of this sort.[4] The thickest layer of irrationality, however, surrounds the Witnesses'

[1] On this curious tenet, cf. Whalen, loc. cit., pp. 197–9. The biblical reference used is Genesis IX, 4.

[2] Cf. Hébert, loc. cit., esp. pp. 164, 170, 137, 162.

[3] Wilson, loc. cit., p. 226, cf. also pp. 229, 230, 233, 237, 238. Our italics.

[4] Cf. Whalen. loc. cit., p. 83. Cf. also pp. 82, 83, 85.

prophecies concerning Armageddon, Judgement and Annihilation of the Wicked. Suffice it to record that Rutherford expected the physical return of the Old Testament patriarchs to the earth and prepared a mansion for them at San Diego, the *Beth-Sarim* or House of Princes, complete with palm and olive trees so that they – originally Palestinians – would feel at home.[1] The Christadelphians, as a sect dissenting from dissenters, were far more restrained in their thinking than Russell and Rutherford and their retinue. But even they had a fantastic view and vision of the Second Coming, and all religious non-conformists have experienced an irresistible fascination by the Book of Revelations, one of the greatest mysteries of all the world.

The Quaker Fox's doctrine of 'unity with the creation', in other words, the Quaker turn towards pantheism, is paralleled in Russia in the doctrines of the Khlyst leader Ivan Churkin: 'It is a great sin to kill beast or bird or fish – as great a sin as the murder of a man because in beasts, just as in birds and fishes, there is just such a soul as in human beings, only that animals do not speak – but all that breathes lauds the Lord, and for every animal that he kills, a man will have to account before God.'[2] The Jehovah's Witnesses' overall tendency towards rationalism can be traced in Russia, too. Uzov speaks in the following terms of the Raskolniks of the nineteenth century: 'Marching under the banner of Holy Scripture, at the same time admitting a "higher" or spiritual interpretation, they are . . . drawing ever nearer and nearer to religious rationalism,' and Kelsiev confirms this: 'Almost all the Bezpopovtsy [i.e. radical sects] allow, like the Protestants, complete liberty of research, and base their teaching not upon tradition, but upon logic and reasoning.' The end-point of these developments can be seen in the Dukhobortsy. While they have no clear-cut and consistent theology, one observer could assert: 'For them, paradise and hell exist not, and the former is lived here on earth . . . They reject the life beyond the tomb.' This may not, in fact, be the settled belief of the twentieth-century Dukhobortsy, but there seems little doubt that a certain drift towards ideas of this kind did exist among them. At the same time, they tentatively adopted a certain faith in metempsychosis. 'Men's souls, they say, after severance from the flesh, migrate, not into some other world, but into the bodies of other men.' The transfer is said to occur while

[1] Ibid., p. 56; Hébert, loc. cit., p. 58.

[2] Cit. Grass, vol. I, p. 137.

the recipient is between six and fifteen years of age – i.e. when he first is likely to experience the inner light. Comparable, from afar, to certain ideas of the Jehovah's Witnesses and Christadelphians is also the assumption that 'the end of the world can only be defined as an extinction of sinners; yet the world does not end, but persists for ever as we see it now'.[1] Here again, we have a curious mixture of semi-rationality and overwhelming irrationality, and both elements are, each in its own way, proofs of the contracultural nature of sectarian speculation.

THE PSYCHOLOGY OF SECTARIANISM

A deeper understanding of the social character of sectarianism would be impossible without at least a sideglance at the psychology of the individual sectarian. A sect, as we have seen, is not a social institution into which one is born, like a state church or a state, but an association which one must join, to which one must commit oneself, like a political, and especially a revolutionary, party. Why, then, do people join it? In Alfred Vierkandt's terminology: what is the inner furtherance which they expect from joining? what is the motive which induces them to seek re-baptism, and sometimes, as we shall see, to submit to greatly more unpleasant initiation ceremonies?

The scholar, even more than the ordinary man, should at all times shun the glib phrase worn threadbare by everyday use and abuse, for it is rare that it will do justice to the facts. Yet it can happen that such a phrase does do justice to the facts, and perhaps better than many a lengthy explanation. It seems true to us to say – in a term much bandied about in popular discussions – that the sectarian seeks in and through the sect an *overcompensation of an inferiority complex*. In his *Millhands and Preachers*,[2] Liston Pope has put his finger on the decisive point when he maintains that 'the sects substitute religious status for social status'. In a slight improvement on this formulation we would say that the sects substitute *high* religious status for *low* social status, for this is precisely what happens. One day, the impending and intending sectarian belongs to the lowest of the low: he is poor and despised, a pariah; the next day, he is the highest of the high, one of God's

[1] Conybeare, loc. cit., pp. 185, 186, 274, 275.
[2] New Haven 1942, p. 137.

saints. The last will indeed have become the first. Nothing will be changed, and everything will be changed. The social revolution which the objective class situation would appear to demand, and yet to make impossible, will have taken place in the individual mind of the new believer and those like him. The sectarians are, in their own specific way, men who have overcome the world.

Before going on to show, with the help of a few express confessions, how true this interpretation of the psychology of sectarianism is, let us pause to consider what the motive impelling men towards the sect means for the sociology of religion. It brings out, once again, the diametrical opposition between state church and sect. The language of functionalism can best serve to make this matter clear. A state church fulfils a fully and strictly social function: it gives stability to established society. A sect, on the other hand, fulfils a function, not so much in public as in private life: it substitutes exaltation for depression, self-confidence for self-doubt and self-despair. Naturally, this statement is an over-simplification of the case. A state religion may, and often does, help an individual, or an indefinite number of individuals, to develop a happier state of mind; mass conversions to sectarianism may, and often do, have highly positive consequences for social life, for instance (to give but one illustration) by substituting – at times throughout a whole class – a better work ethos for a worse one. But these are merely secondary or side effects. The point to be retained is that conversion to a dissenting group is an individual act with a personality-based motive and a personality-centred consequence.

Sectarians are not, by and large, highly introspective or articulate men, and for this reason literary testimonies to the overcompensation of the original inferiority complex are not too numerous. This is especially true because the sectarian may, in harmony with his whole mental condition, put the emphasis on the psychological change from the consciousness of sin, rejection and damnation, to the consciousness of grace, acceptance and salvation, rather than on the change from inferiority to superiority feelings: witness Bunyan's *Grace Abounding*. Yet every now and then we are permitted to look into the soul of a man who, by joining a sect, has got himself out of the slough of despond. This is, for instance, how Menno Simons contrasts his low social position with his high religious status, and thereby indicates what the passage from the former to the latter must mean in terms of self-assurance: 'Am I not as a lost sheep in the wilderness of this world, chased, pursued and sought unto death by ravenous wolves? My flesh had almost said, I am deceived, because I find the unrighteous . . . living in great quietness and peace, in riches and prosperity, while the godly must endure so much hunger, thirst, persecution and affliction. Their habitation is insecure; with difficulty they earn their bread; they are accursed, defamed, persecuted and despised of all men; they are hated of all men as the filth of the world, and as an abomination [but] I am assured and certain that . . . in the day of the revelation of Christ, I shall judge not only the world but also the angels.'[1] Here we can almost physically touch the psychological revolution of which we are speaking: from as low as filth to higher than the angels – can there be any better illustration of the mental process, or rather the mental jump, which is vulgarly called the overcompensation of an inferiority complex?

About a century after Menno Simons, William Dell's sermon *The Building, Beauty, Teaching and Establishment of the Church* (1646) betrayed the same psychological condition: 'A poor mean Christian that earns his bread by his hard labour,' he writes, 'is a thousand times more precious and excellent than he [the gentleman] according to the judgement of God and His Word,' and a contemporary, Francis Rous, in a passage of his *Mystical Marriage* (1653), reveals yet a further facet of the mental consequences of sectarian conversions. 'Fulness is glorified most by filling the greatest emptiness, and majesty by succouring the greatest infirmity,' he says. 'There is a peculiar height and abundance of consolations, which none can attain unto but those that have a special height and abundance of tribulations.' In other words: the deeper the antecedent depression, the greater the ensuing exaltation; the greater the initial despair, the greater also the final assurance.[2] But perhaps the most transparent statement has come from the pen of a Quaker, Francis Howgill. Looking back, somewhat nostalgically, to the early days of Fox's preaching, he recalls his own mood and that of his brethren in the following words: 'The Kingdom of Heaven did gather us, and catch us all, as in a net . . . and the Lord appeared daily to us, to our astonishment, amazement, and great admiration, in so much that we often said one to another, with great joy of heart, "What? . . . Shall we, that were

[1] Horsch, loc. cit., pp. 208 and 209.
[2] Cit. Huehns, pp. 84, 85, 14, 67.

reckoned as the outcasts of Israel, have this honour of glory communicated amongst us, which were but men of small parts . . ." ?'[1]

These are a few characteristic self-revelations from the past, spontaneously made. In more recent times, privacy has waned, prodding and prying have waxed strong, and so we have a more plentiful, artificially elicited supply of statements which show how a social inferiority complex comes to be transmuted, through sect membership, into a religious, and indeed total, superiority complex. Miss Harris's book on *Father Divine* is full of convincing examples, one of which is the founder himself. Says Miss Harris: 'Father Divine is barely five feet tall. He is squat. He is African of feature, completely bald . . . One who looks less like a divine being would be hard to imagine. [But] Father Divine has turned his liabilities into assets. He asks rhetorically: "Why is it that God comes in the most insignificant, the most illiterate, the most downtrodden among the children of men? He comes among them that He might lift them and bring down the loftiness of the mighty, the self-exalted . . ."'[2] It is not difficult to imagine how exalted Father Divine, or rather George Baker, must have felt when he discovered that his physical ugliness as well as his black skin and his poverty could be written off as totally irrelevant in the face of the spiritual beauty, the shining whiteness, and the promise of wealth which would spring up for him from the assumption of a religious-sectarian role.

But Father Divine not only had the great liberating experience himself, he also knew how to evoke it in others, and it is for this reason that he became a great sect-leader. 'He talked about racial equality, stating that he had come from another world to achieve it. It was a new kind of chauvinism the Messenger preached to his early New York followers and friends. He went a step beyond what even Marcus Garvey, the most aggressive Negro chauvinist of recent years, had ever dared to say. Where Garvey had said that black was basically superior and white was basically inferior, the Messenger exemplified that statement. He said, I am a Negro and God dwells in me. You are a Negro and you are like unto me. Therefore, you are superior to white.'[3] The transformations which such preaching worked can almost be called magic. The testimonies to them which Miss Harris has collected are certainly

[1] Cit. Braithwaite, pp. 95 and 96.
[2] Harris, loc. cit., pp. 10 and 11.
[3] Ibid., p. 21.

moving. '"It is wonderful," Thunder Territo, domestic worker, says, "truly wonderful. Before I came to Father, I used to be laid out like a floor so's people I worked for could step all over me. Now I ain't laid that way no more because now I knows me to be good. . . ."' Another inhabitant of 'heaven' whom Miss Harris interviewed was a 'Miss Holy Grace', ninety-seven years old at the time, a former slave child from Kentucky. '"Used to be I thought me to be dumb,"' she recalls, but '"Father put the wonderful spirit in this old temple and showed me, You ain't dumb, Holy Grace, but you is smarter than them light-complected people, Massa John [her erstwhile owner and employer on a cotton plantation] 'n all them, because you is one of my chosen, sure enough."'[1] These are just two examples, simple yet supremely significant, of that *valorisation personelle* of which Gérard Hébert is speaking when he discusses parallel phenomena among the Jehovah's Witnesses.[2]

We have claimed above that even Christian Science is a sect, though certainly a sect with a difference, and we see here once again how justified this classification is. Even the man or woman who becomes a follower of Mary Baker Eddy experiences a specific overcompensation of an inferiority complex. 'There we have Mrs. Eddy as her followers see her,' Mark Twain has written in his *Christian Science*. 'She has lifted them out of grief and care and doubt and fear and made their lives beautiful . . . She has delivered to them a religion which has revolutionized their lives, banished the glooms that shadowed them and filled them and flooded them with sunshine and gladness and peace.'[3] The alternative which the prophetess put before her would-be followers was neatly expressed in the formula: suffering or science. Suffering – a state of underprivilege and depression; science – a state of over-privilege and joy. The transition from a consciousness of inferior health to a consciousness of superior health, and also of superior knowledge, is an experience which can as legitimately be described as the overcompensation of an inferiority complex as any psychological renewal that starts from purely social or socio-economic depression.

The superiority which sectarians claim and, more important

[1] Ibid., pp. 141, 196, 202. [2] Hébert, loc. cit., p. 128.
[3] Turpin, M., *Christian Science,* New York 1907, pp. 287 and 286. Cf. also Wilson, loc. cit., p. 200.

still, experience, is often expressed in the very name of the sect. Sect names fall into two categories: those given to the group by the wider society, and those given to the group by itself. The former are, as a rule, not very complimentary. Methodist – which originally meant: pedant – is merely a mild example. The latter are, as a rule, highly complimentary, and more than that. 'God's people' is a frequently encountered sobriquet. The convert becomes one of God's sheep, God's friends, God's brethren. How could he feel anything but elation when he joins this truly elected, truly elated, group?

It is imperative to understand, so far as the psychology of sectarianism is concerned, not only the *nature* of the basic experience, which we have, somewhat colourlessly, summed up as the overcompensation of an inferiority complex, but also the *intensity* of that experience, and this is not easily appreciated. Only he who has gone through it himself will fully know what it means. The cool scientific observer will only know it, or come near to knowing it, if he can summon up a sufficient *effort de sympathie*, and this is given only to very few. But even he who is incapable of entering into the inner experience itself, of re-living it in imagination, will be able to form an idea of the magnitude of the psychological revolution concerned by studying certain outward effects of it. They alone can prove that after conversion there is indeed – as the converts themselves invariably claim – a new man, a man re-made.

When John Nelson made a Methodist out of William Clarke, a great speech impediment, which had plagued Clarke from early years, disappeared without leaving a trace.[1] Stammering, as everybody knows, is a prime proof of excessive self-depreciation. It was this self-depreciation which dropped away from him and was replaced by self-appreciation: the physical healing was merely a consequence. With the root of the trouble gone, the trouble itself had to vanish as there was no longer any mental malaise to feed and perpetuate it.

While more such cases could, no doubt, be found if one were to look for them, there is ample evidence from a kindred sphere: the conquest of drink and drug addiction by neo-converts, which is often reported. 'At one of the early [U.S. Salvation Army] meetings an emancipated slave rose, with tears running down his

[1] Church, loc. cit., p. 65.

furrowed cheeks, and said, "Everybody in dis city knows what I was. I was de worst drunkard in de city ob Frederics Town – a poor, miserable, bare-footed, gutter drunkard. Now I hab got out ob de gutter, out ob de ditch. I am changed from de dirty grub to a beautiful butterfly, and I suck de sweets ob Hebben!"'[1] Far from being an isolated case, this is one in a million, and far from being exaggerated, the poetical language used expresses a sober fact. When, in the first years of this century, alcoholism among the factory population of the great Russian cities increased so much in extent and intensity as to constitute a threat to survival, life reacted in a most characteristic manner: it produced a new sect, commonly known as the Abstainers, which was on the theological side not very different from dissent in general, but made soberness into a must for its members. 'E. P. Kovalevsky testified that he had visited the factory region of St. Petersburg, where thousands of people had attended the temperance meetings of the Abstainers, and had found the results to be excellent.' Nevertheless, the State and the State Church did their best to repress the movement, for the Abstainers were a sect and a sect is always a focus of revolt, whatever else it may be besides![2]

In so far as drugs hold their victims in an even tighter grip than drink, the astounding successes of some sects in breaking this vise and vice are still more noteworthy. Americans in general have no love for the Black Muslims, a radical, aggressive, and near-criminal group of dissenting, alienated Negroes, yet they have had to admit that this community with all its crudeness and naïvety has conquered where society at large, aided by medicine, psychiatry and refined police methods, has utterly failed. 'The claims of the Black Muslim movement of phenomenal successes in rehabilitating narcotics addicts and alcoholics are beginning to attract professional attention,' the *New York Times* reported on 10 January 1964. 'Malcolm X, the New York Black Muslim leader, has been invited to explain the movement's therapy to the Negro Probation Officers' society . . . Psychiatric social workers of Harlem Hospital . . . have also approached Malcolm X in the last year.' They could not have turned to a more knowledgeable man, for this leader (later divorced from the Muslims and before his assassination in charge of an independent, even more extreme grouping) was himself once subject to, and then cured of, the evil. 'Malcolm said that

[1] Coates, loc. cit., p. 164.

[2] Curtiss, loc. cit., p. 334. Cf. also p. 335.

he used marijuana, opium, cocaine, and heroin before his conversion, and that he broke his addiction within twenty-four hours, without the attendant withdrawal symptoms of convulsions.' How is this semi-miracle accomplished? It is accomplished by the creation of 'a new identity' for the patient, by producing a new psyche filled with pride in his 'negritude'. In the case of other sects, we must substitute different words for this last term, but for the rest the situation is always the same. What a shot in the arm does for the body, entry into a sect does for the soul: it provides prodigious new strength – precisely what is needed in the fight of a man against his worst enemy, weakness in the face of his own ingrained weaknesses. It is much to be feared that the Black Muslims' recipe is of little practical value to the official probation personnel: for how are they to evoke the cathartic experience which exchanges a man's personality for a new one?

The marvellous, often near-miraculous, renewal of a man through conversion to a sect also explains the amazing faithfulness of the sectarians, their steadfastness under attack. A Khlyst or a Skopets who fell into the hands of the police could not expect an easy time, but few of them ever wavered, even under the knout. What they defended, what they suffered for, was not a specious theology full of abstruse dogmas – although they may have believed that they did – but their strength came from their subconscious rather than from their conscious selves. What they in fact stood up for was their own self-respect. Their conversion had lifted them from humiliation into glory; would their betrayal not thrust them down again from glory into humiliation? Nothing can prove better *how* deep the conversion experience is in all successful cases than the often evinced willingness of the converts to accept martyrdom, to have their bones broken and their flesh mangled – how deep it is, and how deeply personal.

From all that has gone before, it is amply clear that the entry into a sect – which is in fact the birth of a new man, the beginning of a new life – is an event of supreme importance for the personality, and for this reason it must be suitably marked, as Caesar's point of no return was marked by his crossing of the Rubicon. Two types of marks can be distinguished here, even though admittedly they shade into each other. One group of sects marks, and, as it were, fixes, the conversion by an external ritual, in many cases by the baptism or re-baptism of the new believer. Another group relies more upon an inner turning from sin to salvation, on convincement, as the Quakers have it. Baptism by water is thus contrasted to baptism of the spirit. Even the latter, however, is an act and not a process. To John Wesley, for instance, it came at 8.45 p.m. on 24 May 1738.

No great purpose would be served here by enumerating the groups who have preferred one form over the other. Nor is it our task to enter more deeply into the variants of external rite and internal experience, even though they are significant – for instance, the difference between symbolical washing, partial immersion, total immersion, the use of 'living' water (a lake or pond or river) rather than tap water, etc., etc. All this belongs to a phenomenology rather than to a sociology or even psychology of religion. It is only important to ask how effective each of the two alternatives is, and the answer is that both have their characteristic strengths and weaknesses.

An external rite has all the definiteness of an historical event. When the waters close over an immersed body, the old life is over and the new has begun, and nobody can shed any doubt on what has happened. For this reason, re-baptism is highly satisfying to seekers of assurance. But there is a difficulty. Why should an outer cleansing cleanse the inner man? The vast majority of sects in both East and West cannot have a concept of efficacy *ex opere operato*, as does Catholicism, for their whole outlook is averse to that philosophical realism in which the Catholic view of the sacraments is rooted. Not having an outer *opus operatum*, convincement escapes the difficulty. But it has its own cross to bear. You can know (and 'you' here means the man himself as well as his fellows) that a man has been immersed; you cannot know whether he has been truly converted. The nagging question is apt to remain: has it really happened? have I really been reborn? am I a new creature? And these difficulties have prompted developments in either camp, some of which are of considerable sociological importance. In the ritualist fold, there have appeared new rites; in the other, new supporting theories; and there has also been considerable borrowing from each other.

With crude and cruel logic, the Russian Skoptsy concluded that the running of water over a human body would not change that body: something more decisive had to be done. Now, the downfall of man had been his indulgence of the sex urge: so, a real transformation would be worked if that urge were totally abolished. It *could* be totally abolished in one way, and one way only: by the removal of the sex organs. The sacrifice demanded would appear to normal people too great for almost any gain. But these Skoptsy were not normal people, they were people in the lower depths of humiliation, and they did *not* think castration too high a price to pay for the load of glory which awaited them. So castration became the dreadful entrance rite of this fierce sect. It was practised on men and women alike. It is characteristic, however, that even these *castrati* and *castratae* were still at times a little uncertain for they could yet – however unavailingly – sin in thought. Therefore the Skoptsy finished up with the theory that 'the royal seal' (i.e. excision of the sex organs) was effective, with final effectivity, *ex opere operato*.[1] This, indeed, is one journey's end.

On the other side of the fence, the Russian Khlysty rejected formal rites such as water baptism – for who could guarantee that such a ceremony would bring the descent of the Holy Ghost? Their logic led, not to a more telling outer act, but to a more convincing inner experience. This, of course, had to be somehow induced in the neophyte, and for this purpose the trance-producing round dance (*radenie*) was developed. We baptize ourselves in sweat (through swirling round until exhaustion) and blood (through flagellation), they proudly said. But the aim was neither the flowing of sweat nor that of blood: it was ecstasy, ecstasy so deep that it could not be doubted afterwards. Whatever the Khlysty felt when the climax of the exercise was reached – the present writer and his readers will never know – one thing is certain, namely that they emerged from it with the conviction that 'the falcon had swooped down on them', that 'they had seen the heavens open', or however else they expressed themselves – the conviction, more soberly formulated, that they had in truth had an all-renewing mental experience.[2] Still, this experience was not a unique one: it was repeated again and again. Did it need to be

[1] Cf. Grass, op. cit., vol. II, *passim*, but esp. pp. 694–9. It was the belief in efficacy *ex opere operato*, without experience of conversion, which led to castrations of unwilling and unsuspecting persons through force and fraud (e.g. under drugs). Cf. ibid., pp. 65, 66, 327, 343, 344, 700–6, 868.

[2] Cf. ibid., vol. I, *passim*, but esp. pp. 122, 123, 264–6, 269, 369–78, 410–12.

repeated to still remaining, perhaps repeated, doubts? However this may be, clearly we have here, in orgiastic rapture, the most intense of all inner states, the end of the other journey.

The psychological plight of the sectarians in the West was no different from that of their brethren in the East. We can take John Wesley as our typical case here. 'Converted' (in the technical sense of the word) on 24 May 1738, he found, only a brief month later, that 'God hid his face', as his *Journal* reports on 29 June. All through that fall and winter he worried, and Zinzendorf regarded him as a *homo perturbatus*. Was he, in fact and in truth, a new creation, or did it only seem to him that he was for a fleeting moment? Indeed, had that moment really occurred? Where, oh where, was assurance *quantum satis*?

It is a fact of truly far-reaching importance that the avenues pursued by Skoptsy and Khlysty were blocked for the sectarians of the Anglo-Saxon world. For reasons which are deep and devious and cannot be adequately discussed here, but the chief of which was the total movement of society towards a more rationalistic mode of life and thought, the sects of the West distrusted extremism and emotionalism. Therefore neither an extreme physical act like removal of the sex organs nor an emotional frenzy like the one engineered by ecstatic dancing was thinkable for them. True, the revival meetings in which many Westerners underwent the experience of conversion were to all appearances highly emotional, but they appear so only when they are seen against the background of ordinary, everyday Western soberness. The same is true even of the Pentecostal Sects which add the fire-baptism of the Holy Ghost (speaking in tongues) to the water-baptism and to the conversion which precedes it, and thus generate a deal of excitement in their conventicles. Compared to the goings-on in a Khlyst 'ship', they pale. The well-known fact that in a revival meeting a great many put up their hands when asked whether they 'accept Christ', and that only very few join the religious grouping concerned afterwards, is a clear enough proof that the personality is rarely shaken to the depths.

The search for assurance had to go very different ways here. Among comparative rationalists, an appropriate theological dogma can be of some assistance, especially if that dogma itself is comparatively rationalistic. Thus there arose the doctrine of the 'perseverance of the saints'. The Quaker Edward Burrough tersely formulated it by saying: 'Whom God loves once, He loves for ever.'[1] The god of such men was above all a consistent god, a god who would not capriciously (i.e. unpredictably, irrationally) change his mind. 'God loved them before the world began so as to choose them,' Samuel Richardson wrote in *Justification by Christ Alone* (1647), meaning by 'them' those who felt themselves accepted. 'Is He so changeable as now to hate their persons when they sin, and afterwards to love them again when they believe?'[2] No, 'the enrolled names are never obliterated'.[3] Discussing the attraction which Spurgeon's Calvinism had in the 'damp low-lying, thickly peopled, struggling regions of South London', in other words, in the slums, Robertson Nicoll puts this very doctrine into the foreground, as the magnet of magnets: 'Mr. Spurgeon's hearers had, many of them, missed all the prizes of life; but God did not choose them for reasons that move man's preference. . . . Their election was of grace. And as He chose them, He would keep them. The perseverance of the saints is a doctrine without meaning to the majority of Christians. But many a poor girl with the love of Christ and goodness in her heart, working her fingers to the bone for a pittance that just keeps her alive, with the temptations of the streets around her, and the river beside her, listened with all her soul when she heard that Christ's sheep could never perish. Many a struggling tradesman tempted to dishonesty, many a widow with penury and loneliness before her, were lifted above all [and] taught . . . to anticipate a place in the church triumphant'[4] – a *secure* place, a place reserved, regardless of what may befall them. Psychologically, this doctrine meant that anyone who had ever felt that he was one of God's chosen, however quickly his conviction may have vanished afterwards, was in fact entitled to a lasting certainty and peace. His flash of insight, it was implied, was the revelation of an eternal truth. Teachings of this kind were sometimes flanked by the assertion, kindred in inspiration and tendency, that excessive feelings of uncertainty were of diabolical origin, one of the Wicked One's tricks for the torturing of God's dearest children. Clearly, such articles of belief were

[1] Cit. Braithwaite, p. 90.

[2] Cit. Huehns, p. 110.

[3] Thomas Adams, cit. Weber, M., *The Protestant Ethic and the Spirit of Capitalism,* trans. Parsons, T., New York 1930, p. 237, note 90.

[4] Cit. Underwood, p. 220.

something to fall back on and to hold on to when the evil moment of doubt arrived.

But the true solution (if it can be called a solution) came in the West not through a religious dogma, nor through a religious experience: it came through the headlong plunge into a feverishly active life, religious or otherwise. Arnold Lunn, in his book on *John Wesley*,[1] has suggested that Wesley ceased worrying over his own salvation as soon as he began his never-ending, physically exhausting campaign of field-preaching, and the facts bear him out. The medicine which cured him, cured many others as well. The fire-and-spirit-baptism of the Pentecostalists, for instance, the coming of the gift of tongues, is not only regarded as an experience which cannot be doubted because it is observed and confirmed by others, but also, and essentially, as an 'impartation of power' for service.[2] Thus, there was born a supremely activistic, supremely dynamic type of man.

The first aim of this activity, of this dynamis, was what Wesley called 'entire sanctification' and Whitefield called (not without criticism, indeed, not without sarcasm) 'sinless perfection'. Men ought to regard conversion not as a point of arrival, but as a point of departure, and as a rule they have a long way still to go. By starting them on this career, Wesley gave his followers something to do, and in doing it, they forgot their doubts – for doers rarely doubt; they have too little time for doubting. We see the effects of this policy most dramatically in the Salvation Army. Not only is there heavy emphasis on the possibility of entire sanctification and sinless perfection – 'holiness to the Lord is to us a fundamental truth; it stands to the forefront of our doctrines; we write it on our banners; it is in no shape or form an open debatable question,' Booth declared[3] – but the definition of the sectarian-saints as a *soldiery*, a fighting force, was a master-stroke which perfected what Wesley had merely begun. Though other religious movements did not go in exactly the same direction, nor drive forward with the same energy and consistency towards the same consummation, the conquest of doubt through activity was the specifically Western technique of securing and perfecting the psychological liberation which conversion to a sectarian grouping usually brings or begins.

The first aim of this activity, of this dynamis, is not as a rule the

[1] London 1929, p. 118. [2] Cf. Wilson, loc. cit., p. 22. [3] Cit. Sandall, p. 209.

only one, nor – more importantly – is it the last. According to Wesley, Richard M. Cameron tells us, 'this quest for Christian perfection should be pursued, not in retirement, but in the midst of society, and while following one's ordinary business'. Through working on this stage, it would generate 'a pervasive sense of social responsibility',[1] and finally, of course, a certain measure of social reform.

As the knowing reader will be clearly aware, we have, in the last paragraphs, drawn close to Max Weber's famous thesis about the connection of capitalism and Calvinism. Weber is basically right: an activist society presupposes an activist type of man, and the rise of modern activism is due, in part at least, to the decay of medieval assuredness, not to say smugness, where salvation is concerned. What was there to worry about, medieval man might have asked his unhappier successors? The Church holds the means of salvation, including the sacrament of penance, which allows the greatest sinner to crawl back into the light of God's love. By fulfilling the basic ethico-religious duties – the general precepts – it was easy to keep the doors of heaven open; and even when a general precept had been broken, the damage could easily be repaired, provided only that there was contrition or attrition, a suitable sorrow for one's past sins and an honest desire for future amendment. When and where Catholicism lost, an open question took the place of the old Church's assured answers to the greatest query which the believing person can and must raise – the twin query: what his fate will be in eternity? and what he can do to make it favourable? And as purposeful activity is a splendid antidote to purposeless brooding, many non-Catholics, Calvinists as well as others, chose an active and eventful life as the most promising escape-route from a state of unrelieved uncertainty, thereby helping to replace a static by a dynamic, a repetitive by a progressive, society.

Weber's basic intuition would therefore – within limitations – appear to be valid. Religion *did* have something to do with the rise of capitalism. But the way in which he elaborated his insight in *The Protestant Ethic and the Spirit of Capitalism* calls for corrections. First of all, religion may lead to a stilling as well as to a stirring up of doubts, and in so far as it gives contentment, it will produce, not activity, but quietude. The person who said to Wesley at

[1] Cameron, loc. cit., pp. 34 and 35.

Wednesbury: 'I never find any cloud between God and me; I walk in the light continually,'[1] is not likely to have suffered from inner tensions which needed to be relieved by outer activities, by bustling from job to job. True, Calvinists rarely felt like that, indeed, rarely could feel like that, for the conviction that God's eternal decree was absolutely unknowable was too basic to their theology. That is why Cromwell, even in his most dramatic fighting days, which left hardly a minute for contemplation, still frequently felt the pangs of doubt and fear. But even among Calvinists, an inner conviction that one's name *was* written in the book of grace could at times appear, and it is recalled by Weber himself[2] that Calvin personally belonged to the lucky ones who achieved it. Calvin, of course, was a typical man of action, but not for the reason which Weber has taught us to regard as causal for Calvinist activism in general – doubt of one's election, of one's place among the sheep. There may have been many minor Calvinists who were complacent about their eternal destiny, all preaching about the closedness of the book of knowledge notwithstanding, and they were hardly co-authors of the capitalist mode of production.

But quite apart from the fact that religion could lead to quietism, Weber's thesis is too narrow in two respects. Doubts could assail not only Predestinarians like the Calvinists, but also Arminians like the Wesleyans, and this parallel cause would have a parallel effect – escape into activism. The uncertainty then stemmed, not from the inscrutability of God's will, but from the inscrutability of one's own experience – the impossibility of knowing whether an experience, the experience of conversion, was in fact what it seemed to be. And the activism thus engendered was not necessarily worked out in one's private life, for instance one's business life, it could also find its proper field in the pursuit of public concerns. What did the Booths mean when they asserted, time and again, that the Salvationist 'must be about his Father's business'? Perhaps the prohibition of alcohol; perhaps the eradication of prostitution; perhaps even the abolition of sweating in industry and the achievement of higher wages. The religious life of modern, i.e. Protestant, man – man bereft of the assurance-giving influence of the Catholic sacraments – could therefore make for the reform

[1] Cit. Knox, loc. cit., p. 541.

[2] The *Protestant Ethic*, etc., as quoted, p. 110.

and final emaciation, as well as for the rise and first formation, of capitalist society. The sects in particular were as much factors in its decline, as they were in its ascent and establishment.

TYPES OF SECTS

Unlike established religion, which stands before us incarnated in a few comprehensive and enduring culture-complexes, sectarianism has produced numerous, not to say innumerable, little groupings and grouplets. There are two main reasons for this; one of them we have already discussed, the other still remains to be considered. The former is the principle of congregationalism, of the primacy of the face-to-face group. It is the essence of sectarianism, for the withdrawal from the world into the sect, which is the core of all socio-religious dissent and alienation, is among other things a withdrawal from the impersonality of the wider society into the personal closeness and warmth of a 'set-aside' group. The second reason is the extreme transitoriness of sectarian formations. Twenty years, fifty years at the most, and the red-hot fervour of the sect is lost, replaced by the semi-conservatism of a denomination which is often even a little ashamed of its youthful enthusiasms. Such 'sects' which are sects no longer, cannot offer a live outlet for the rebelliousness of new oncoming generations. These must form for themselves fresh vehicles of the revolutionary spirit, new sects in the full and firm and proper sense of the word. History has been a graveyard of sects, but also an ever fruitful womb of sectarianism.

Because sectarianism has appeared in so many different shapes, there has been an understandable desire on the part of scholars to make multiplicity more manageable by developing an appropriate typology. Several leading men in the field have tried their hands at this task.[1] Their taxonomies are by no means mutually exclusive, for a wide field can be divided up in many ways. All depends on the main direction of the student's interest, and one such direction, one such interest, is in principle as legitimate as any other. There is

[1] I mention particularly J. M. Yinger, *Religion, Society and the Individual,* New York 1957, pp. 144 et seq.; P. L. Berger, 'The Sociological Study of Sectarianism', in *Social Research*, 1954, pp. 467 et seq.; B. Johnson, 'On Church and Sect', in *American Sociological Review,* 1963, pp. 539 et seq.; B. R. Wilson, 'Typologie des Sectes dans une Perspective Dynamique et Comparative', in *Archives de Sociologie des Religions*, 1963, pp. 49 et seq.

therefore no need here to engage in long summations, comparisons, polemics, but there is a need to bring forward a scheme of division which will fit neatly into the total framework of the present book. Without it, our study of sectarianism would be but partial and patchy.

A sect, according to our basic definition of it, is a religious conflict society, a grouping in deviance from established religiosity, using 'deviance' here in an entirely neutral, value-free sense. But deviation from a central position can tend in two different directions: it can be deviation to the right or deviation to the left. For instance: a sectarian contraculture can be – as we shall presently perceive – progressive or retrogressive, desire a revolutionary thrust into the future, or a counter-revolutionary return to the past. Thus we propose to base our typology of sectarianism on the principle of duality, and we hope to show, with the help of several bisections, that this principle is useful in the field. But not only do we believe it to be useful: we also suggest that it is consistent with the total picture of the sociology of religion which we are painting in these pages. As we have seen all along, unity is the keyword of established religiosity, and opposition the keyword of religious dissent. But opposition and duality are sister concepts, and there is a deep inner connection between them. The next pages, it is hoped, will show how, out of a common rejection of established society, there develop regularly two sectarian tendencies which both complement and contradict each other. In addition to retrogressive and progressive sectarianism, we shall compare and confront the rigoristic and the antinomian sect, as well as the groupings which in principle accept, and those which in principle reject, the use of violence in the pursuit of their ends.

THE RETROGRESSIVE VERSUS THE PROGRESSIVE SECT

The first broad distinction which seems relevant, not to say important, is that between backward-looking and forward-looking or forward-striving dissent groups. The Russian Raskol typifies the former possibility, the Western Reformation the latter.

Because it will be our task to show the contrast in all its colours, it is essential to emphasize at the outset that both retrogressiveness and progressiveness are forms of opposition to existing society. Whether a man prefers yesterday to today, or whether he prefers tomorrow to it, in either case he rejects the given situation, the contemporary state. Our linguistic habits induce us to think of the reactionary and the revolutionary as irreconcilable types, opposed to each other in the manner of $+a$ and $-a$, but in reality the reactionary is a revolutionary, just like the revolutionary commonly so called, for he, too, would overthrow the ruling powers, if only he could. Summing up the unanimous opinion of leading historians, Conybeare has insisted, and rightly, that 'the events of 1667 [i.e. the Raskol] laid the foundations of liberty and revolution in Russia'.[1] The Raskolniky fought for already lost, rather than for yet-to-be gained, rights, but the essential point is that they fought for rights, indeed, that they *fought* at all, and he who fights is, whether he likes it or not, the foe of that which is. Thus even Communism owes a historical debt to the Raskol, Lenin to Avvakum, 1917 to 1667.

The reasons that the spirit of religious revolt, smouldering among the lower classes of Russia after the merger of Church and State, turned into retrogressive rather than into progressive channels, are easily found in the history, and especially the social and economic history, of the Empire. In the Middle Ages, the position of the peasantry had varied greatly from place to place, from estate to estate. There was a whole gamut of conditions, reaching from downright slavery at the one extreme to full freedom at the other. Everywhere, however, there was stability, and stability meant, as it always does, adjustment, if not indeed relative contentment. From the time of Ivan the Terrible (1462–1505) on, things began to change, and in retrospect the medieval period appeared to the peasants like a lost paradise. The development of the two centuries from 1500 to 1700 brought the reduction of all villagers to one low level, the level of serfdom, a process in which the old freemen, for instance the so-called ownlanders, lost a good deal more than was gained by the erstwhile slaves. *Glebae adscriptio* was introduced by ukases issued in 1597 and 1601. But what was most serious was the subjection of the peasantry to the local lords who now emerged as the absolute masters of the individual, even private, lives of their subjects. They became the official tax-collectors (while themselves exempted from all taxation); they became the governmental recruiting officers (after 1762 only serfs had to join up); they became the district judges and the police

[1] Conybeare, loc. cit., p. 68. Cf. also pp. 76 and 77.

chiefs of their territories. The local lords acquired the right to flog their peasants, to send them to hard labour in Siberia, to permit or to forbid their marriages, and so on, and so forth. The State, in a word, set them up as petty tyrants, and many of them acted as powerful men will act when they know that there is nobody to control them. The serfs became their chattels, indeed, their playthings, as can be seen from the fact that they could sell them, pawn them, and even gamble them away, as every lover of great Russian literature, and especially every reader of Gogol's masterpiece, *The Dead Souls*, knows. This downright abandonment of the peasantry to the landlords was the indirect, but unavoidable, consequence of the power politics of the Russian rulers. Russia could become strong only if she organized her State; but that State could only be organized through the one and only class capable of carrying it – the gentry; there was no other on which the tsars could have relied; in particular, there was no budding bourgeoisie that would have helped, and that did help so much in the West, especially in France. The subjection of the serfs, the misery of the rural masses, was the price which Peter and Catherine paid for such inner modernization and outer prestige as they managed to achieve. To the land-working classes it meant catastrophe – if the term be permitted, it meant lasting catastrophe, a gloom for centuries.

Not surprisingly, the peasants took their fate very hard. The hundred years between 1550 and 1650 formed a century of runaway serfs, but the cruel code of 1649 made even this mode of escape impossible. The revolt of Stenka Razin (1670–1) was led by the so-called barebacks, i.e. runaway serfs who had turned into desperadoes. During the rebellion known as *Khovanshchina*, the rebels tore up writs and ordinances relating to serfdom and declared the serfs to be free. Ninety years later, Pugachov's rebellion (1773–5) had at its core the peasants who had been 'ascribed' to the mines and metal industries, men who would rather die than exchange God's clear sky for the gloom of subterranean regions or the stench of factories. It is estimated that Pugachov's gangs killed about 1,500 gentry; certainly, the fear of his name remained with the upper classes for many a long day. Between 1835 and 1854, two hundred and thirty serf-owners or their bailiffs were murdered in the country, and between 1845 and 1855 no fewer than four hundred peasants' risings were counted.

Such was the background of Russian revolutionary non-conformity.[1]

There was, in the circumstances, only one way in which the rebelliousness of the masses could find adequate expression: the formation of radical sects. A practical-political movement was out of the question: it did not become a possibility before the second decade of the twentieth century, and even then it took extraordinary developments, especially the loss of a world war, to bring it to maturity. Neither Razin's nor Pugachov's, neither Bolotnikov's nor Bulavin's revolts were more than still-born acts of desperation. Scattered over immense spaces, with next to no communication with each other, not supported, as the French peasants were in 1789, by a vigorous town population, divided also by linguistic and cultural barriers, the Russian peasants could protest only in terms of the spirit. But that spiritual protest was a social protest as well. As always, sectarianism was above all a vehicle for the venting of the revolutionary feelings of a downtrodden class. Nothing could be more characteristic than the proclamation which Pugachov issued when it looked for a moment as if he would be able to march on Moscow; the religious and the social concern are jumbled together in one sentence: 'We grant to all hitherto in serfdom and subjection to the land-owners . . . the old cross and prayers, heads and beards, liberty and freedom . . . without recruiting levies, poll taxes or other money taxes, with possession of the land, the woods, the hay meadows, the fishing grounds, the salt meadows, without payment and without rent, and we free all those hitherto oppressed by the malefactor land-owners. . . .'[2]

It is remarkable that this manifesto of a revolutionary leader should not only contain, but actually start with, the promise to bring back the old cross – remarkable, but understandable. For this and similar ancient forms had become the symbols of the happier days which the Russian people had lost and could not forget. As the old, medieval ways were destroyed in social life, so were they also destroyed in religious life, and the peasants cannot be blamed if they regarded the two processes as one, for so they were. Both were manifestations of the same phenomenon – the

[1] Sumner, B. H., *Survey of Russian History,* ed. London, 1944, pp. 167 and 141.

[2] Ibid., p. 166.

coming of the power and police state. As soon as the unification of Russia under the rulers of Muscovy began, there was interference with traditional religion. All the holy ikons and relics were transferred to the capital; new saints were canonized at the behest of Ivan the Terrible; later Maximus and Nikon remodelled the liturgy. Soon the flame of revolt started to burn high. Nil of Sorsk, Vassyan and Arfemy refused to acknowledge the 'new saints'; they condemned the stripping of the provinces of their religious treasures; and the defeat of their conservatism at the Council of 1503 did little to mute the echo which their voices had evoked among the masses. But it was a hundred and fifty years later that the Raskol or Schism openly erupted, although subterraneously it had existed since that ill-starred Council. In 1666 the opponents of the Nikonian reforms were condemned; in 1667 an anathema was pronounced against them.[1] The Archpriest Avvakum, burnt at the stake in 1681, made himself a champion of the cause of conservatism; his followers finally broke with the new ecclesiasticism which the tsars had ushered in; and characteristically the label of the Old Believers or Old Ritualists was pinned upon them. Revolutionary in relation to the State, they were reactionary in matters of religion, and the two attitudes were in fact but one – one great rejection of the new social realities which were appearing in the interval between Ivan the Terrible and Catherine the Great.

Unless the symbolism, i.e. the deep socio-economic and socio-political meaning of the religious traditions, in defence of which the Old Believers took their stand and often died, is fully appreciated and constantly remembered, their whole conduct must appear quaint and even ridiculous. In the Middle Ages, Russians had made the sign of the cross with two fingers; now they were expected to make it with three. In the Middle Ages, they had sung halleluja twice, now it was to be three times; their processions had walked with the sun, now they were to walk against its course, and so on. Even the Image of God was to be disfigured: the tsar demanded that men go clean-shaven, though it was God who let the beards grow! Avvakum was quite willing to suffer any torture rather than abandon the old time-hallowed traditions.

[1] Though Nikon was deposed in 1666–7 for having tried to make the patriarchate independent of the tsardom, his reform, especially his revision of the liturgy, remained and was backed and enforced by the State.

'Basil Petrovich Sheremetev, who was sailing up the Volga to Kazan to take over the Governorship, took me on board,' he recalls in his *Life*. 'He sternly . . . ordered me to bless his son who had a shaven face. And when I saw that image of shame I would not bless him . . . So my Lord waxed terribly wrath and ordered that I should be flung into the Volga, and having inflicted on me many hurts, they cast me aside . . .'[1] To bless a shaven man may be but a little thing, but to Avvakum it was not. So it was with the other minutiae of ritual. 'Come, True Believer!' he shouts, 'name thou the name of Christ standing in the midst of Moscow [*Isus* in the old manner, not *Jisus* in the new!], cross thyself with . . . two fingers . . . Glory to God! Suffer tortures for the placing of thy fingers . . . I with thee am ready to die for this . . . It behoves every man to endure for this, even unto death.'[2] These were no vain words: Avvakum accepted martyrdom as he said he would, only it was not martyrdom for a few formal gestures, but martyrdom for a whole real world that had been loved and lost.

However irrational an attitude like Avvakum's may appear, it was in fact fully rational, or at least logical. For in fighting religious innovation, he fought innovation in general,[3] and the figure who was responsible for it all – the tsar. But the tsar's authority, the authority on the basis of which he allowed the peasants' happiness and freedom to be destroyed, was in essence a religious authority. Hence by attacking the ruler's right to change the ritual, he attacked the citadel of his position, the palladium of all autocracy. (Not that he was clearly aware of this: still, his was a total rebelliousness which merely used the specific forms of religion in order to express itself.) 'The Schismatics . . . ceased to believe in the sanctity of the hierarchical power of the Russian Tsardom,' says Berdyaev in *The Russian Idea*.[4] 'The Schism was a way out of history because the Prince of this World had reached the summit of power in Church and State and dominated history . . . In the person of the Tsar Alexis, Avvakum saw the servant of Anti-christ.'

[1] *The Life of the Archpriest Avvakum, by Himself.* Trans. J. Harrison and H. Mirrless, Hamden 1963, p. 48. Cf. also pp. 39, 53, 54 (and *passim*).

[2] Ibid., pp. 131–3.

[3] For Avvakum's passionate resistance to modern (more realistic) painting, cf. his *Life*, as quoted, pp. 22–4; for the Sectarians' resistance to the introduction of tobacco and of the potato, 'the Devil's herb' and 'the Devil's apple', cf. Grass, loc. cit., vol. I, pp. 311 and 313.

[4] London 1947, pp. 12 and 13.

But it was less Alexey than Peter the Great who became, in the eyes of later generations, the Devil's Stadthouder. When he returned from abroad on 25 August 1698, the *Streltsy* tried to prevent his entry into Moscow – tried in vain, for his foreign-recruited *Reiters* were stronger. There immediately followed a whole series of impious acts – Peter did not worship in the Kremlin (he was afraid, it was said, that the holy relics would unmask him); he changed the calendar (to confuse the people who had calculated and found out when the reign of Antichrist would begin); he did not ask the Patriarch's benediction; he systematically cut the boyars' beards – all sins against religion, and religion only, it would seem. But even Peter's condemnation by his people was basically social, and sometimes this fact comes to the surface. In his book, *The Flower Garden*, one of the most important later sect-leaders, the 'Wanderer' Evfemy accused Peter of having separated the nation into different classes. By allotting to some much land, to others little, and to yet others none at all, he had introduced private property and social inequality and from this there had resulted the struggle between rich and poor, a condition utterly unacceptable to the true Christian, for Christianity condemned the very words 'mine' and 'thine'. In such statements we must certainly see harbingers of a social revolution as yet far in the future. But even Evfemy was a man of retrogression, for he taught that little had been amiss before Nikon and Peter.[1] The Russian Raskol thus was, and remained, a movement of men who wanted to turn the clocks of history, not forward, but back.

In this essential respect, the Western Reformation was quite unlike the Eastern Raskol, and the last explanation of the contrast lies without a doubt in the fundamental differences in socio-economic conditions and developmental tendencies between the two culture areas. The East had but one revolution, and it was a revolution from above: the transition from the feudal to the modern state. The West had two revolutions, one a revolution from above and similar, if not identical, with that in Russia, but the other a revolution from below, not political but social and economic, not initiated by a power-hungry ruler but carried by a newly emerged class, the bourgeoisie. Briefly expressed, the East brought to birth a new type of state, the West a new type of society, and therein lies the key to the fact that the sectarianism of

[1] Cf. Milyukov, P., *Outlines of Russian Culture*, vol. I, Philadelphia 1948, p. 72.

the West was progressive, pressing for the full realization of the new forms of life, and not retrogressive, not hankering after old forms of life which history had already overcome.

In so far as the transformation of England and the transformations in Germany were parallel to the transformation of Russia, the end-results were also comparable: the fusion of Church and State, caesaropapism. What the tsars from Ivan the Terrible to Catherine the Great achieved in Moscow, Henry VIII and Elizabeth I achieved in London, and princes or princelings like Friedrich III of Saxony achieved in their German territories. But underneath the surface, there is a difference already noticeable here, in the first act of the Western Reformation drama. The main actors are not courtiers and bureaucrats, they are townspeople like their great archetype Martin Luther, son of a Saxon miner. But the townspeople had from the beginning been inclined towards democracy, and their impetus towards some sort of egalitarianism showed itself at once. Its chief manifestation was the important Lutheran doctrine of the priesthood of all believers, which, negatively expressed, was his repudiation of class division so far as the Church was concerned. A hundred years before, the Hussites of Bohemia, the Empire's economically most advanced region, had raised this issue and made it a central concern. Even their more moderate wing was known as the Utraquists or Calixtines – Utraquists because they demanded holy communion *sub utraque specie*, by wine as well as bread, i.e. because they rejected the priests' privilege of the wine, and Calixtines because they demanded to be served from the chalice as well as from the paten, as the priests had hitherto served themselves. The only thing common to these men and the Raskolniky was their attention to ritual; their direction was, not back to the Middle Ages, but forward to modernity.

Surveying the history of the cities, especially the progressive democratization of their government and administration, one of the foremost recent students of the Reform, André Biéler, in his *Pensée Economique et Sociale de Calvin*,[1] has spoken of an '*étrange parallélisme entre cette émancipation démocratique et l'adoption de la Réforme*'.[2] The parallelism is a well-proven, if not indeed an obvious fact, but there is nothing strange about it. Does not M. Biéler, shortly afterwards,[3] quote a sixteenth-century source to the effect that the state of the old Church was particularly obnoxious to

[1] Geneva 1959. [2] Loc. cit., p. 4. [3] Ibid., p. 9.

laboureurs, marchands et mécaniques, the three elements which, taken together, composed the budding bourgeois class? In the West it was not only a new type of ruler, it was also a new type of man, who condemned and destroyed the medieval Church.

In Germany, however, the burgher was too feeble to finish what he had begun. If the princes had not stepped in and substituted their strength for the weakness of the towns, all Luther's effort would have ended in a little smoke and no fire. The princes rescued the Reformation. Luther's sojourn on the *Wartburg* meant his preservation, but it also meant his enslavement. The princes had no interest in democracy; their interest in fact was for the contrary. Thus it happened that what had started as a movement in favour of freedom, ended as a movement in support of authority. The change is reflected in Luther's own mental development. He himself became ever more authoritarian in outlook, and the doctrine that it was everybody's duty to accept society as it was, and especially the station in which he found himself, was the final upshot of his socio-political philosophy, in so far as he had one. Thus was born the German citizen of latter days who saw his king or Kaiser or *Führer* suffused in a supernal light; the German citizen of whom Bismarck once said that he had no 'civil courage'; the German citizen whose submissiveness to established power was pilloried in Heinrich Mann's great novel, *Der Untertan*; the German who said *amen* to all the deeds of a tyrant between 1934 and 1945. But all this does not mean that the Reformation, even the Lutheran Reformation, was not originally a forward-looking movement. It merely means that it became captive to other (to some extent also forward-looking, but narrowly power-political) energies.

Far different was the development where the bourgeois was, not weak, but relatively strong, as in the cities of Switzerland. Drawing strength from their surrounding mountain fastnesses, from an aboriginal peasant democracy which was still in full force and vigour, but above all from an economic efflorescence due mainly to their key position along the great trade routes, the men of Zürich and of Geneva did not allow their revolutionary effort to be arrested in mid-passage. They found spokesmen in Ulrich Zwingli and Jehan Calvin who, in the form and under the guise of a philosophy and theology, presented to the world an all-comprehensive blueprint of a new society, a new order that would be a full and true alternative to the feudal system which they and their backers wished, once and for all, to wipe from the face of the earth. Zwinglianism and especially Calvinism were not aiming at the establishment of a state religion, as did Anglicanism and Lutheranism; nor were they, in original intention at least, sectarian movements, for their aim was a new godliness for a new society embracing all classes; they were a *tertium quid*, like Catholicism, and will therefore have to be analysed in the third volume of this work. Here it is essential only to emphasize that it was the leftish, democratic, popular element that led these heresiarchs to victory. The very calendar of events proves it. In February 1536, the radical element gains an election victory in Geneva; in May, the Reformation is formally and finally adopted; in July, Calvin arrives, to be henceforth the head of the city which he endeavours to turn into a new Protestant Rome. While the Bishop's party, the so-called *Mamelous*, is characterized, in Michel Roset's chronicle, as composed of *gens riches et apparents*, all sources go to show that the Reformers' party consisted of merchants and artisans, in other words, the champions of democracy.[1] What is true of Geneva is true also of other, similarly placed cities, notably Zürich and Berne.

It was not, however, within the narrow walls of Geneva; it was on the wide stage of England (and, to some extent, on that of New England, Holland and Scotland) that Calvinism proved itself a forward-looking and forward-leading movement. The Civil War was a struggle between the forces of conservatism and the forces of modernization, between the remnants of feudalism and the rising bourgeois class. But England also shows – as does Zürich for that matter – that even the Calvinist push into the future did not fully and finally succeed. Cromwell, for all his victories, was defeated, if we look upon him, not as the figure of two decades (the decades of the Civil War and the Protectorate), but as a figure of world history. The attempt of the bourgeoisie to build a social and religious order that suited it was only partially successful because it was caught between two fires: the world of yesteryear, of royalty especially, which refused to die, and the world of tomorrow, of the proletariat, of the fourth estate, which was slowly

[1] Biéler, loc. cit., passim, esp. p. 56. Cf. also p. 51 *re* Lyons: 'The *Evangile* can be seen to gain ground particularly among the shopkeepers (*marchands*) and the petty people who will not hesitate to go over to revolutionary acts in 1529.'

standing up against the bourgeoisie, the third estate, and proved as invincible as the old power – indeed, much more so.

Hardly had Zwingli climbed into the saddle, when the Anabaptists raised their heads in the city; hardly had Cromwell established himself in the seat of power, when a host of radical sects appeared in England, notably the Levellers, who were not only consistent formal democrats, but in tendency social democrats as well, Communists in the egg-shell. The phenomenon which dominated the nineteenth century, the break-up of the bourgeoisie into a capitalist and a proletarian class, was anticipated in the seventeenth century by the parting of the ways between Cromwellians (some landed gentry and the big city merchants) and the Levellers (whose leader, John Lilburne, described himself as the spokesman of the 'poor and men of middle quality', i.e. small traders and artisans).[1] With the Levellers, however, the forerunners not only of the Quakers (who were still largely petty bourgeois), but also of the Methodists (who were already largely proletarian), we have reached the end of the story. Every phase of it has proved what we undertook to demonstrate, that the Western Reformation, in the widest sense of the word, was, unlike the Eastern Raskol, a movement of the progressive forces of society, an active pursuit of things to come, and not a regretful remembrance of things past.

THE RIGORISTIC VERSUS THE ANTINOMIAN SECT

A second significant dividing-line which runs across the field of sectarianism concerns the various groups' attitude towards the moral code. The dos and don'ts of respectable society are always rejected, but the spirits divide when it comes to the question as to what is to be substituted for them. Some sects have called for sterner and stricter principles of conduct; others, however, have gone in the opposite direction and have experimented with far-reaching freedom, if not indeed with the abandonment of moral restraint. Once again the sheep and the goats separate, but this time they are innocent sheep and lascivious goats.

When discussing, in the last section, the contrast between the retrogressive and the progressive tendencies, we strongly em-

[1] Cf. Zagorin, P., *A History of Political Thought in the English Revolution*, London 1954, p. 10.

phasized that both are variants of one and the same attitude, the attitude of revolutionism. Here we find the same fact, only that it is more obvious and more intriguing. Sometimes a rigoristic sect brings to birth a sect that is anything but rigoristic so that we cannot say: like father, like son, and yet we must say that the latter is descended from the former. The Calvinists were surely highly disciplined people, but their progeny (albeit illegitimate) was, at times, not so; for instance the Rev. David Crosley (1669–1744), a drunkard and womanizer, excommunicated, but not with finality expelled, by the English Baptists in 1709. Underwood remarks in connection with this case: 'Antinomianism has always been the dark shadow cast by the more extreme forms of Calvinism . . . By making man's depravity total and divine grace irresistible, it denies the freedom of the human will . . . By its doctrine of their final perseverance it teaches that the elect can never forfeit divine grace, however great and grievous the sins into which they fall.'[1] No doubt, Mr. Crosley felt that he was neither responsible for, nor endangered by, his 'free' mode of life. This road to moral ruination[2] has inspired one of the most arresting books in the English language: James Hogg's *Confessions of a Justified Sinner* (1824), a story with a truly bloodcurdling climax that would have been worthy of the pen of an Edgar Allan Poe.

Corruptio optimi pessima, one might say. But it is not always a case of corruption, i.e. transition, in time, from a state generally adjudged moral to 'demoralization'. Sometimes rigorism and licence coexist. From the point of view of textbook logic, it might appear impossible for a group not to be either more or less 'moral' than society in general, not to be either comparatively ascetic or comparatively lax. But in life contradictions often dwell close together and even take up an ambiguous position. This ambiguity can be observed best at the time when a sect forms. Only one thing is clear then, namely that the morality of the new group will be different from the morality which dominates the old world around it. But it is, and remains, an open question wherein

[1] Underwood, loc. cit., pp. 136, 133, 134.

[2] This mode of expression must not be taken to imply condemnation of the sectarians by the present writer who is, in accordance with the canons of scholarship, withholding all personal judgement. It only means that there is deviation from the standards prevalent at the time, a falling away from what is the generally accepted code – a purely empirical statement, not an ethical judgement.

precisely the difference will consist. The sect can go in either of two directions, towards a repressive or towards an indulgent morality. Naturally, as it develops, as it gains a face, it will have to prefer one possibility to the other. But in the depths, the original ambiguity is apt to survive and to show itself on occasions. The reproach often levelled against rigoristic sects, namely that underneath their exceptional purity there hides an exceptional impurity, is not without substance, as an unprejudiced analysis can prove.

The Baptists, for instance, as we know them from English history (the Anabaptists of Germany were a different case!), were a decidedly rigoristic group which condemned all pruriency in no uncertain manner. Yet A. C. Underwood, in his *History of the English Baptists*, has this to report about F. B. Meyer, a leading member of the denomination: 'Meyer had an alarming habit of speaking with great frankness about his own temptations which sometimes embarrassed his audiences. They never knew when he would suddenly draw aside the veil of reticence and embark on one of these embarrassing confessions which contrasted so strongly with the austere lines of his refined ascetic face.'[1] The case is by no means an isolated one. Meyer had a great predecessor in the Pietist Zinzendorf whose sermons on marriage 'dwelt on its implications with a revolting circumstantiality of detail'.[2] This lends colour to Pareto's assertion that those who buy pornographic literature are not so different in character as it might seem from those who campaign day and night for its suppression.

The ambiguity characteristic of the Rev. F. B. Meyer can be seen on a larger scale among the Shakers. On the surface they were great contemners of sex and all its implications. Basing themselves on St. Matthew XXII, 30 – 'for in the resurrection they shall neither marry nor be married, but shall be as angels of God in heaven' – they claimed that they were leading, here and now, the 'virgin life of the resurrection order'. Men and women were allowed to talk to each other, but no more. Their settlements had, for instance, curious contraptions which would allow females to alight from their horses without having to accept the helping hand of a male person. When two young girls were discovered to watch two flies who were chasing each other, the community was appalled by so much wickedness and the culprits were made, in

[1] Loc cit., p. 257. [2] Knox, loc. cit., p. 413.

punishment, to whip each other. Even their shaking, i.e. their ecstatic dancing, stood in the service of the de-sexing of their lives, for it was meant to exhaust the animal spirits to the uttermost. Thomas Brown, in his *Account of the People called Shakers* (1812) writes as follows: 'They often danced with vehemence through the greater part of the night, and then, instead of reposing their wearied bodies upon a bed, they would, by way of further penance, lay down upon the floor in chains, ropes, sticks, in every humiliating posture they could devise.'[1] No, the flesh did not have it all its own way among these people.

Yet, it was precisely Thomas Brown's book which threw a great deal of doubt on the purity of the 'people called Shakers', and his assertions have never been officially repudiated by the sect. 'The Shakers of the early days were a wild crowd, among whom passion, when it broke loose, assumed violent forms,' a student of the communities, M. Holloway, has written. And he adds: 'It is odd that such enthusiastic celibates should have lived together in the same buildings . . . One must presume that this proximity of the sexes, united yet scrupulously divided under one roof, was another delicious thorn in the hated flesh, a minor barb of mortification, a constant reminder that lust must be subdued.'[2] This was, to say the least, a dangerous play with the fire which the truly moral man will shun as a wile of the devil. The Shakers have had many friends and admirers, and it is possible that this discussion of them may arouse resentment here or there. But one of their greatest friends and admirers, Marguerite Melcher, bowing to the truth, has finely expressed herself on this issue as follows: 'Celibacy was a cornerstone of their spiritual life . . . yet the believers were probably farthest from the essence of celibacy when they were most fervently worshipping. For the more devout and inspired the ritual, the more emotional its effect. Shakers who held themselves rigidly repressed in all their workaday human relationships gave way to such emotional excesses in their worship that they were even suspected . . . of breaking all their workaday rules of conduct on the Sabbath day.' And, as if fearing that these sentences were not clear enough, Miss Melcher adds: 'This spiritual abandon had in it, of course, some of the elements of sex excitation . . .'[3]

[1] Cit. Holloway, M., *Heavens on Earth*, New York 1951, p. 66.
[2] Ibid., p. 67. [3] Melcher, loc. cit., p. 254.

This ambiguity of sexual mores in sect-like groupings, the tendency either to demand an over-exacting discipline or to accept an under-disciplined mode of behaviour, can be observed in the early Christian communities, typical dissenting bodies standing over against the ruler-deifying state religion of their Roman masters. St. Paul's first epistle to the Corinthians is highly revealing. In the sixth chapter, the Apostle is at grips with those who argued that purity was merely a Mosaic principle which could not be regarded as binding on the converted who had left the Mosaic law behind them. 'The body is not for fornication, but for the Lord,' he has to remind them. But in the seventh chapter, he fights a different foe. They were the people who doubted whether even marriage, or the normal conduct of it, was permissible. 'It is better to marry than to be burnt,' he answers them. Were there two parties, then, at Corinth, one immoral and the other over-moral? Knox believes that it is 'quite possible that the libertines of Chapter VI were actually the rigorists of Chapter VII. The same ultrasupernaturalist point of view which looks upon bodily impurity as a mere imperfection among the elect because it is only something carnal, will, in other moods, condemn the whole institution of marriage as a carnal institution'.[1] The history of sectarianism is clearly on Knox's side on this point.

This initial facing-both-ways cannot, however, last for ever. Life demands some kind of decision, and early Christianity soon came down on the side of a moderate rigorism with occasional deviations in either direction. But not always will all the members of a religious movement agree on this point. There may come, there often does come, a parting of the flock. An example are the Ranters and the Quakers. Close to each other, not to say identical, in other respects, they split on the issue of practical morality, and especially sex mores. 'The Quakers were but the Ranters turned from horrid profaneness and blasphemy to a life of extreme austerity on the other side,' wrote Baxter. 'Their doctrines were mostly the same with the Ranters.'

Braithwaite who quotes this passage[2] accepts the burden of it, but asserts that the charges of moral laxity brought against the Ranters were exaggerated. Hereby hangs a special problem of historical research. We can hardly see the Ranters and similar

[1] Knox, loc. cit., pp. 14–16.

[2] Braithwaite, loc. cit., p. 22. Cf. also pp. 277 and 278.

groups as they really were. The sources come either from detractors or from apologists. In either case the truth is heavily overlaid by legends. Norman Cohn has recently gone over the material with great care and come to the conclusion that the Ranters were indeed an a-moral sect.[1] It was hardly for nought, we gather from his investigation, that Parliament appointed, on 14 June 1650, a committee 'to consider of a way for suppressing of the obscene, licentious and impious practices used by persons under pretence of liberty, religion or otherwise', especially 'the several abominable practices of a sect called Ranters', and that, on 9 August, after due deliberation, it passed a law for the punishment of what to them (and probably to most) appeared as shameless immorality.

If, however, some doubts may remain about the justification of calling the Ranters an a-moral sect, there can be none about the justification of calling the Quakers a rigoristic group. Only one example shall be given here, but it is truly convincing. The core of a developing Quaker meeting in Cardiff was one Thomas Holme who married a Quakeress called Elizabeth Leavens. When, in due course, a baby appeared to be on the way, Margaret Fell was greatly annoyed and expostulated with the couple. How could they dare to put the charge of a child upon the cause? Holme wrote a letter of apology 'with tears upon his cheeks', and promised to behave better in the future. 'If our going together be the ground of what is against us, the ground shall be removed,' he humbly says to Margaret Fell. 'We had both of us determined long before thy letter came to keep asunder.'[2] This demand of intra-marital continence was fairly widespread among the early Quakers, especially in New England. It goes to show, not only that they were a rigoristic group in the fullest sense of the word, but also that the sect's much vaunted anti-authoritarianism, the respect for the self-determination of the individual and his private judgement, proclaimed as a basic principle to the outer world, had its painful limitations.

Once again, however, it is not the West, but the East, which has produced the most colourful illustration of the contrast between the rigoristic and the antinomian sect, namely those Khlysty and Skoptsy to whom we have repeatedly referred before because

[1] Cf. Cohn, loc. cit., esp. pp. 322–7 and 335–56.

[2] Cit. Braithwaite, p. 236.

there are hardly any dissenting groups anywhere which show the characteristics of extreme sectarianism with equal clarity. Theologically very much akin, akin also for a stretch of the way in their principles of conduct, they ultimately went very different ways and stand before us now as contradictory models: the Khlysty as an orgiastic and dionysiac sect, the Skoptsy as self-torturers and self-destroyers. Neither the principle of moral *abandon* nor that of moral control could possibly be driven further than it was by these hostile twins.

The Khlysty were at first a rigoristic sect, like the Skoptsy after them. As we have seen, they were flagellants, and shed not only sweat but even blood in abundance. They kept the strict Orthodox fast not only during Lent, but all the year round. They condemned not only the consumption of alcoholic drinks, tobacco and potatoes, but also that of fleshmeats, onions and garlic, some indeed of fish also. Many went barefoot even during the winter months. On entering the sect, people had to take a solemn oath of sexual continence: married couples had to promise to live like brothers and sisters. Children brought into the group were taught to call their parents 'uncle' and 'aunt'; they, on their part, were often referred to as 'little sins'. No talk of sex was permitted, not even a single word, and both the attendance at weddings and christenings were forbidden as they were regarded, in their different ways, as proofs that the original sin of Adam and Eve was still being re-enacted among men. One of their propaganda pamphlets showed a woman in hell, serpents gnawing at her head and breasts, fire breaking from her mouth, arrows of flame protruding from her ears, dogs biting her hands – all in punishment of the fact that she had been a wife to her husband in the way in which the world understands the relationship. It was a widespread Khlyst custom to take a spiritual sister or a spiritual wife (the same thing to the Khlysty) to replace the carnal wife in the house: sometimes carnal wives were exchanged for each other and thereby transmuted into spiritual wives – pure spouses for pure men.[1]

But, in spite of this, the Khlysty ended up as one of the most licentious sects the world has ever known – in spite of this, or perhaps because of this, for what is too much is too much and is apt to lead, by a sort of dialectical development, to its own oppo-

[1] Grass, loc. cit., vol. I, *passim*, but cf. esp. pp. 164, 171, 235, 313–17, 359.

site. Curious phenomena were appearing in the group: 'In the district of Kostroma,' one informant reported, 'the following custom is part of the entrance ritual: the local mother of god clad in a white shift, lies down, face upward, on the floor, and the entrant must crawl between her body and shirt from the head to the feet: this is being called rebirth.'[1] The symbolical meaning of the act need not be doubted, but its moral implications could not very well have been uplifting. Similar reports are by no means rare.[2] This is the same playing with fire which we have already observed among the Shakers, another dancing sect many thousands of miles away. But what remained a game, however dangerous and doubtful in wisdom and morality, among the Shakers, became a real debauch among the Khlysty.

Khlyst dancing was dancing in shirts only, and the rhythmic character of it could have led only to physical excitement, even if its original aim was possibly physical exhaustion. Shouting *evoé* (as did the Bacchantes of antiquity), the dancers danced themselves into a state of frenzy in which rational self-control was utterly out of the question. The truth is that the Khlyst meetings led to an orgiastic climax, the main ingredient of which was promiscuous intercourse. This was sometimes called the 'common sin', but from the point of view of the Khlysty themselves, this word was of course a misnomer. Man was not responsible for all that went on, rather the Spirit was, and it was supposed to have swooped down on the dancers like a fire or a falcon. It was the Spirit which led the believers to what they did and in what they did; it was the Spirit which led the couples together irrespective of age and family relationship; it was the Spirit which engendered any children that might come to be born nine months afterwards – the Spirit whose bidding is not to be resisted and which in fact cannot be resisted without grievous sin. Hence it is hardly surprising that what the world called a common sin, the sectarians themselves described as 'Christ's love'.[3]

[1] Ibid., vol. I, p. 380.

[2] Cf. ibid., pp. 209, 221–4, 243–4, 296; vol. II, p. 765.

[3] Cf. esp. ibid., vol. I, pp. 119, 120, 434, 435, 439, 441, 442, but the whole from p. 434 to p. 447 is relevant. The matter causes Grass much distress and he tries to mitigate the facts as much as he can. Particularly amusing is his insistence that the orgy is not part of the sect's worship but only happens after it, and that it is not something prescribed, but 'merely' something permitted!

In putting all the blame on the Spirit, the swooping fire or the swooping falcon, the Khlysty used an apologia which was roughly identical with the self-defence on which their cousins in the West also relied. 'The free-man of Christ has this freedom,' Tobias Crispe asserted in *Christ Alone Exalted* (1643), 'that Christ does all his work for him as well as in him.'[1] 'There is no act whatsoever that is impure in God, or sinful with or before God,' Laurence Clarkson declared in his tract, *A Single Eye all Light, no Darkness, or Light and Darkness one* (1650), putting the emphasis on 'whatsoever'. 'As all powers are of God, so all acts, of what nature soever, are produced by this power, yea this power of God . . . Therefore what act soever I do, is acted by that Majesty in me . . . All acts that be are from God, yea as pure as God.'[2] 'When God comes to dwell in a man,' the Grindletonian Familists argued, 'he so fills the soul that there is no more sinful lusting.'[3] This statement is ambiguous, as ambiguous as all sectarianism is where sex morality is concerned. It may either mean: when God comes to dwell in a man, his sinful lusting ceases, or it may mean his lusting ceases to be sinful. It is the latter interpretation that was very often preferred, not only because it allowed the sectarians to do what they desired, but also because it fits better with the whole logic of sectarianism. Ephraim Paget, in his *Heresiography* (1645) accused the 'unpure Familist' of pretending 'to be godified like God', and, as we have seen, some such claim to exceptional metaphysical status is characteristic of, and essential to, all true sect movements. But a god-like or angel-like or reborn creature cannot sin, for what he does is, by definition, not under the law, but rather above the law. Hence the term antinomianism is preferred, in the title of this section, to such words as lax, libertine or licentious. Not only is it more neutral and thus better for scholarly use, but it is also more descriptive, for the core of the whole attitude is that the 'free-man of Christ' is free even of the *nomoi*, free of the laws which apply to lesser people.

Formidably supported by this argument, antinomianism has played a larger part in the religious history of the West than many would like or care to admit. Of course, it always shunned the light of day and so the evidence is often shadowy, yet there is plenty of evidence at our disposal. Few sect movements have been

[1] Cit. Huehns, p. 91.
[2] Cit. Cohn, pp. 349, 348, 350.
[3] Cit. Braithwaite, p. 24.

entirely free from it, to the embarrassment of their latterday historians. Even the Quakers, otherwise paragons of decorum, did not think it sinful to appear naked in public if a brother or sister was 'moved' to do so. The English and Scots Baptists (or Sandemanians) also played with fire, and so did the Moravians and the Methodists. What has lifted the curtain for us is the habit of sect-leaders to expose and accuse each others' communities. There is, on the one hand, for instance, the book of the Moravian Andrew Frey about Herrenhut and Herrnhaag, claiming that Count Zinzendorf's birthday celebrations were marred by 'many filthy, gross indecencies'; there is, on the other hand, the Mennonite pastor Stinstra's *Essay on Fanaticism* on the Moravians and Methodists which carried a number of detailed *pièces justificatives* at the end, and did not precisely belong to John Wesley's most beloved books.[1] Even the nineteenth century still showed phenomena of this kind to be rampant in the West,[2] both in England and in America, and also in Protestant Germany.[3] But perhaps there is no need to go further into this matter.

In any case, it would be wrong to believe that the victory of antinomianism over rigorism, of *ecstasis* over *ascesis*, was easily won. Even a group such as the Khlysty put up a good fight on behalf of purity, with icy cold baths, blood-lettings, etc.[4] Some of their dietary rules aimed at elimination of supposed aphrodisiacs rather than at a reduction of food intake as such[5] – in Bentham's language, aimed at the pleasures of the venereal appetite rather than at the pleasures of the palate. These tendencies towards a consistent, even uncompromising, self-control, towards a total sanctification in the sense of total self-conquest, were probably strengthened every time a group slipped from rigorism into antinomianism, when its members – to use an often-employed phrase – stained the wedding garment, the shining white raiment in which the redeemed soul should appear before its Master. To the degree to which the Khlysty became dionysiac, they also evoked and evolved a counter-movement, that of the Skoptsy,

[1] Cf. Knox, loc. cit., pp. 415, 390, 451. Concerning the antinomian undercurrent of Methodism, cf. Lecky, loc. cit., pp. 648–50.

[2] Knox, loc. cit., p. 566 et seq.

[3] Algermissen, loc. cit., p. 71.

[4] Cf. Grass, loc. cit., vol. I, pp. 320 and 321.

[5] Ibid., pp. 309; vol. II, pp. 160 and 742 et seq.

who, in the fullness of time, became their absolute antitype, men and women who 'whited' themselves for good so that they simply could no longer fall into the filth of sexual sin.

If it can be said of the Khlysty that they were obsessed with sex, the same is no less true of the Skoptsy, though the last consequences of this obsession were very different. Every physical contact between male and female, however innocent, was regarded with abhorrence. Their, founder, Andrey Selivanov,[1] appealed to the brothers and sisters to avoid indulgence in idle talk and laughter with each other; to avoid looking at each other; indeed, to avoid even sitting down near to each other.[2] This, however, was merely the starting point of their folkways. How far they could develop in some areas becomes clear from the following report of a Siberian Skopets 'prophet': 'With us it is the custom that a Skopets woman, who, as his mother, has washed a shirt for her son, must put it on a chair or table if she wants to give it to him. She must not hand it to him directly in order not to defile him . . . Woman is sin, and sin one must not touch.'[3] This division of the sexes is enforced even after death. Only men carry the coffins of men, only women those of women.[4]

Appalled by the 'common sin' of the Khlysty, Andrey Selivanov strove to separate himself and his followers as radically as is humanly possible from this fallen, and ever-anew falling, sect. It did not take him long to discover how this could best be achieved with absolute finality. 'The [early] preaching of Selivanov,' so Protopopov has recorded, 'concentrated mainly on one point, the wish to preserve his disciples from the lechery so common in the Khlyst naves [= local groups]; when all means to this end were exhausted . . . when they all had failed to lead to the desired end, the living god [= Selivanov] began to preach castration and accepted it as the first to the fullest possible extent.'[5] From that moment onward, the life of the man bears both success and suffering – mainly perhaps the latter. The Khlysty kill his friend and companion Martin; they try to kill him; they betray him to the authorities, for much as they hate the authorities, they hate Selivanov more; he is knouted and sent to Siberia, and though a

[1] There is some uncertainty about his real name; other forms are given, e.g. Kondraty and Ivanov, but this is irrelevant for our purposes.

[2] Grass, loc. cit., vol. II, p. 735.

[3] Ibid., p. 737.

[4] Ibid., p. 844.

[5] Ibid., p. 37.

later Tsar is more kindly to him and allows him to return to the capital, he has to end his days in the monastery-prison of Suzdal. It is not easy to read this super-ascetic's autobiography – his *Sufferings*[1] – with indifference.

Most of the detail contained in Grass's 1,016 pages is of little consequence in our context, but one point should perhaps be mentioned, be it only in passing: the considerable intellectual sophistication of this sect. They developed a whole mystical theology, including a step-for-step reinterpretation of the Scriptures. Numerous are the passages with the aid of which they seek to justify their peculiar method of salvation (especially Matthew XIX, 12, in conjunction with V, 29, 30, and XVIII, 9, 10; Isaias LVI, 3–5; Hebrews IX, 22; and much of the Apocalypse). Numerous also are the passages to which they ascribe a new meaning. For instance: it was Noah's castration (i.e. physically ensured sanctity) which Ham discovered; Abraham castrated his son Isaac (thus sanctifying him for ever); Mary's visit to the Temple was for the purpose of desexing, as was Jesus' visit to the Baptist; and so on, and so forth. Most characteristic is the sect's version of the story of the fall. At first, Adam and Eve had no sex organs; these began to sprout after the eating of the forbidden fruit; hence their removal would also remove the consequences of original sin.[2]

In taking leave of this truly extreme sect, it is well for us to remind ourselves that it has had more influence on world literature than any other. Tolstoy's country seat was in the Tula district, and that district was the very cradle of the Skopets movement. Tolstoy, needless to say, rejected the surgical solution to the problem of sexual morality which the Skoptsy advocated. But he caught something of the blazing hatred of the very fact of sex which animated these obsessed men. The best illustration of his more than puritanical attitude can be found in his novel, *The Kreutzersonata*, especially in Chapter XI, but also in some of the shorter stories, notably *The Devil*.

In the East, the Dukhobors (who, collectively, abstained from sex satisfactions, even in marriage, for six years around 1895, so that their birthrate dwindled to next to nothing) would provide another example of rigorism. As for the West, it does not appear

[1] Cf. *Die Geheime Heilige Schrift der Skopzen*, translated and edited by K. K. Grass, Leipzig 1904.

[2] Cf. Grass, loc. cit., pp. 645–62.

to have produced sects of comparable radicalism. But if self-mutilation has not been resorted to, some of the spirit which produced it among Selivanov's followers was by no means absent. Indeed, most of the Anglo-American dissent groups, sprung up as they are from Puritanism, fall into the category of asceticism. The harmless custom established in the United States for men to shake hands with men, but not with women (in sharp contrast to the French, Austrian and Hungarian habit of kissing the ladies' hands) is descended from the one time more vital and vigorous idea that all physical contact between the sexes is to be avoided, and has a close parallel in a Skopets principle. Evidence is not lacking either in documentation of the fact that self-control inside marriage is still a live tradition in certain classes of English society, especially the lower middle class.

The Massachusetts law which forbade the display of male and female undergarments in close proximity, for instance on the same clothes line, can fairly be said to have been characteristic of the older puritanical tradition. But even such relatively recent movements as Christian Science, the Jehovah's Witnesses, and Father Divine's Peace Mission, show a considerable, if often submerged, bias against freedom in sexual behaviour. Mrs. Eddy, as we have seen, was successor to Mrs. Lee, of Shaker fame, and so Luke xx, 34–5, if not indeed Matthew xix, 10–12, meant more to her than many other Gospel passages. 'These words of Saint Matthew have special application to Christian Scientists, namely, "it is good not to marry"', she wrote; and though she doubted that this precept would be widely accepted today, she would have liked to confine intercourse to the business of procreation. Man 'pledged to innocence, purity and perfection' was her ideal. The definition of children as 'sensual and mortal beliefs; counterfeits of creation' recalls certain Russian formulations. Mrs. Stetson was even more determined in this respect than was Mrs. Eddy, and if time has washed away much of this attitude, the interesting fact remains that Christian Science knows no solemnization of weddings.[1] 'For a period, the cult actively discouraged marriage,' Whalen tells us of the Jehovah's Witnesses. 'Rutherford's book *Children* released in 1941 relates the story of two young Witnesses who decided to wait until after Armageddon to get married.' Cohn even asserts that 'an

[1] Cf. Wilson, loc. cit., pp. 186–9; cf. also Dakin, loc. cit., pp. 307 and 308. Cf. also p. 18.

attempt is made to banish sexual activity completely from the lives of Witnesses'.[1] If this is true of the Witnesses, it is much more true of Father Divine's flock. 'He proclaimed any sex expression, even between husbands and wives, a glaring black sin.'[2] His own (second) marriage to white, blonde and much-younger-than-himself Edna Roe Ritchings appears to be what it pretends to be – a purely formal and symbolical relationship. But Father Divine works not only through example. As he claims to be the Almighty, he obviously feels that he may put asunder what God has joined together. Married couples are housed in separate rooms in separate wings of his hotel-havens, for so it is demanded by the Peace Mission's 'International Modesty Code'.[3] In the case of Father Divine, the repression of sex is due, in part, to his jealous desire to be the one and only object of all his followers' affection.[4] Nevertheless, the basis is the same in his case as in that of the Shakers or the Skoptsy – the fact that his sect movement has opted for the ascetic, as against the antinomian, form of sectarianism.

In speaking of antinomianism, we mentioned that it is still alive in twentieth-century Protestant Germany. We had in mind mainly the so-called 'Evangelical–Johannine Church' of Herr Joseph Weissenberg (who has been in prison for alleged offences against minors), his illegitimate wife Gretchen Müller, and their illegitimate daughter Frieda Müller (born in 1911).[5] The picture is completed and balanced by a reference to the highly ascetic sect, now sadly reduced to a mere conventicle, called the Nazarenes. 'In the Nazarene community are gathered,' according to its tenets, 'the perfect saints, in whom justification has reached the stage of sanctification and transformation into divine light . . . The perfectionism is expressed above all in complete abstention from anything to do with sex; unmarried members are not allowed to marry and married members must abstain from sexual intercourse.'[6] And so we see, once again, the antitypes of asceticism and antinomianism in contrast and juxtaposition.

1 Cf. Whalen, loc. cit., pp. 63, 200, 21; also p. 200 (Cohn quotation).

2 Harris, loc. cit., p. 20.

3 Cf. a report in The *New York Times*, 10 May 1964.

4 Cf. Harris, loc. cit., p. 97.

5 Cf. Algermissen, loc. cit, p. 71.

6 Ibid., p. 116. This page and the next also give a summary of the Nazarenes' very curious re-writing of the story of the fall which yields nothing to the Skopets version, so far as imaginativeness is concerned.

THE VIOLENT VERSUS THE NON-VIOLENT SECT

To the inclusive society within which a sect is established, it is a matter of comparative indifference whether this sect develops along progressive or retrogressive lines: in either case there is opposition to the *status quo*. It is more the degree of opposition that is of practical importance here than the direction of it. The case of the dichotomy between asceticism and antinomianism is not the same. It is relatively easy to live with people whose moral principles are stricter than your own: true, the holier-than-thou attitude which they are apt to assume may act as an irritant, but if so, it is as a rule not causing a very painful irritation. It is only if and when these ascetics try to force their way of life on their neighbours, and especially if and when, in doing so, they fall afoul of the criminal code, that there is real trouble: such was the situation with regard to the Skoptsy when they started to castrate children and unsuspecting, unwilling strangers. But such extremism is rare. On the whole, society at large looks with a mixture of pity and amusement on a minority which makes itself miserable by semi-starvation or sex-continence. It is not so easy, however, to live with people whose moral principles are laxer than your own, even if they carry on their orgies behind closed doors. An outcry against the corruption of youth will soon be heard, and, indeed, it will rarely be entirely unjustified. Moreover, in these cases the criminal code is very likely to be infringed, not to speak of the informal moral code which is regularly infringed by antinomian sects – which, one might say, is almost infringed by definition. If history has left many more records of rigoristic than of licentious sects, the main reason is that the life-expectation of the latter has always been low. Their removal was regularly a simple police job, with the wider population looking on in approval.

The case of a third essential dichotomy is different again. It is the distinction between violent and non-violent sects, between those who say that they had come to bring, not peace, but the sword, and those who remember that he who lives by the sword, will also perish by it. There can be no Canadian who does not prefer the Mennonites or the Hutterites of his country, who follow their principles in meekness, to the Dukhobors who have from time to time shown fierce aggressiveness. It is possible, perhaps, to laugh about their nude parades, but it is not possible to be amused by the arson and murders they have committed. The subsect called the Sons of Freedom has been a special thorn in the side of Canada, a wound which has tended to fester, and no effort has been spared to remove it by a surgical operation.

Yet, even the difference between violent and non-violent sectarianism is only relative. As before, we find that the two contrasting attitudes are merely surface variants of an underlying common trait. The fact is that the contrast of which we are speaking – a contrast real enough if looked upon from a practical, one might even say, from a police, point of view – lies less in the sect itself, less in the sect spirit, than in the outer circumstances, notably the relation of power between the dissenting minority and the conforming majority. If the minority is very small, and if it sees no prospect of becoming strong enough to defeat the majority, it will develop in the direction of passivity and pacificity. If, on the other hand, it is considerable in size, and, in particular, if it can hope that it will be able in the end to impose its will on the rest of the society, it will not be averse to a trial of strength, and long before the test actually comes, it will fall into modes of thinking of an activist and aggressive character. In this way, non-violence is the policy of the weak, violence that of the strong; indeed, it is no contradiction in terms to say that non-violence is the violence of the weak. Let us explain what we mean.

Perhaps we can do our explaining best with the help of an example of major historical significance which is merely parallel to what we are discussing here, though a religious aspect is by no means missing. When the people of India had made up their minds to get rid of the British raj, their leaders decided, not to engage in open fighting, but to drive the foreigners out through passive resistance. Whatever the ethico-religious cloak that has been woven for, and wrapped around, Gandhi, his was a realistic policy, for an open confrontation with the colonial power would not have been successful. True, the English were outnumbered 99:1 or worse, but they had all the arms, the Hindus none, and they were one of the most warlike races of history, the Hindus one of the least. In this situation, a slow wearing down of the adversary's desire to remain in the land was better than a quick uprising, followed by an equally quick defeat. Besides, in a conflict of this kind, the attitude of the outside world is important,

important not only in a vague and general, but even in a narrow, i.e. practical-political, sense of the word. If you do not co-operate with your government, for instance, if you refuse to pay taxes, the authorities will be forced to attempt coercion. That will bring odium down upon their heads, and, in case of extreme measures, general execration. But once you have managed to appear as innocence outraged, you have gained an important victory. At first, it will perhaps be no more than a moral victory, but in the end it may well mature into a material victory also, as was the case in the Indian struggle for liberation.

The policy of many sects was very much like the procedure of the Indian Congress Party. Once again, as so often before, the Quakers provide an instructive illustration. In 1655, Ann Audland, whom we have met before, had accused the Vicar of Banbury (probably in church and during a service) of lying. She was thereupon, not without cause, accused of blasphemy. Both judge and jury, however, were unwilling to convict her. All that they required was that she gave bond for good behaviour in the future – not an unreasonable request. But, characteristically, she refused. She would not make things so easy for the ungodly. So there was nothing for it: she had to be sent to prison. To the world it looked as if intolerance had victimized innocence. In fact, the case was far different. There would be few fair-thinking men who, when informed of the facts, would not place the blame for any cruelty committed on the Quakers who forced him to act as he did, rather than on the Deputy-Recorder who sentenced her. But the public is as a rule neither fair-thinking nor informed. Mistress Audland no doubt felt that she had landed a good blow in a godly fight: she clearly knew what propaganda was, and used it cleverly like any politician. Hers is not an isolated case. Friends (the word sounds a little strange here –), Quakers, rather, regularly refused to secure their liberty by giving bond for good behaviour. This policy came up for open criticism in the polemical literature of the day. When Thomas Goodaire behaved (in the same year) at Kidderminster very much the way in which Ann Audland had behaved at Banbury, Richard Baxter wrote in *The Quakers' Catechism*: 'It pleased the magistrate to bind one of you to the good behaviour for the public disturbance and railing . . . And upon this you send another paper with an outcry against us as persecutors . . . Alas, what impatient souls are you to cry out so much of persecution, when many a poor scold is ducked in the Gumblestool for words more incomparably sweet and lamb-like than yours?'[1]

The considerable success of this non-violent strategy of the Quakers is confirmed by no less a witness than their own Robert Barclay. In his famous *Apology for the True Christian Divinity* (1775), he speaks in these terms of his brethren and their relationship to their adversaries: 'When they came to break up a meeting, they were obliged to take every individual by force, they not . . . dissolving at their command; and when they were haled out, unless they were kept forth by violence, they presently returned peaceably to their place. Yea, when sometimes the magistrates have pulled down their meeting-houses, they have met the next day openly upon the rubbish and so by innocency kept their possession and ground. . . . When the malice of their oppressors stirred them to take shovels and throw the rubbish upon them, there they stood unmoved. . . . As this patient but yet courageous way of suffering made the persecutors' work very heavy and wearisome unto them, so the courage and patience of the sufferers, using no resistance, nor bringing any weapons to defend themselves, nor seeking any ways revenge upon such occasions, did secretly smite the hearts of the persecutors, and made their chariot wheels go heavily.'[2] In other words, not fighting was an efficient way of fighting.

Even if a sect (which still deserves to be called a sect, which has not yet turned into a mere denomination) is on the surface non-violent, it often harbours, not too deep beneath the surface, a very different animus. To outward appearance, all Russian sects were non-violent. Although the Russian Empire was not very different from the Austria which Viktor Adler described as despotism mitigated by inefficiency, its police-forces were strong enough to take care of any would-be aggressive dissenters so that these were reduced to a few clandestine murders or acts of arson. But while law-abiding behaviour was, for most of them, a necessity rather than a virtue, the Stundists regarded themselves as the Quakers of Russia, as men who truly believed that all violence, nay all assertion of power, is inherently evil. Yet even they did, on occasions, break the peace, to put it mildly. 'In 1901, the Governor of the Province of Kharkov reported that in the village of Pavlovka

[1] Braithwaite, loc. cit., pp. 199, 175, 194. Cf. also p. 220.

[2] Cit. Wilkinson, pp. 93 and 94.

some Stundists, "being in a condition of religious frenzy . . .", broke the windows of the church and the sacred vessels, ripped the hangings from the altar, tore apart the Gospel . . . Several even trampled on the altar . . . and the women tore off the ceremonial coverings with their teeth. When the mounted constable appeared, they attempted to pull him from his horse, so that he had to seek safety in flight.'[1] These were no lambs, rather they were lambs who had for a moment turned into wolves – with no miracle involved.

We have seen a short while ago that the Quakers were in part descended from the Ranters, a sect which claimed that the whole concept of sin was absurd and the whole fact of sin was non-existent from a religious point of view. Fox himself 'speaks of an abundance of Ranters and professors in Sussex and the adjoining counties – men who "had been so loose in their lives that they began to be weary of it", and he says that the Lord's truth caught them all and they became good Friends'.[2] But it was not only the antinomian Ranters, it was also the violent Fifth Monarchy Men whose remnants swelled the ranks of the Quaker movement; and as the former Ranters turned from licentiousness to asceticism, so the Fifth Monarchy Men turned from violence to peacefulness. The contrast between Ranters and Quakers illustrated for us the distinction between ascetic and antinomian sects; the parallel conflict between Fifth Monarchy Men and Quakers can exemplify the distinction between the violent and the non-violent groups.

In the crucial year 1655, John Thurloe wrote to Henry Cromwell: ''Tis certain that the Fifth Monarchy Men, some of them I mean, have designs of putting us into blood,'[3] and Henry Cromwell agreed: 'These incendiaries are very dangerous and of an inveterate temper.'[4] Two years later it became quite clear that these were not groundless apprehensions, for a 'Book of Characters' was discovered, containing the names of those to be dispatched. It should not be thought, however, that these wild men were overanxious to keep their plans under cover. 'Wicked kings and tyrants ought to be put to death,' a pamphlet of the day openly declared, 'and if the judges and inferior magistrates will not do their office, the power of the sword devolves to the people.'[5] Christ's enemies, Cary asserted in *The Little Horn's Doom and*

[1] Curtiss, loc. cit, pp. 166 and 167. [2] Braithwaite, loc. cit., p. 397.
[3] Gooch, loc. cit., p. 261. [4] Ibid., p. 266. [5] Zagorin, loc. cit., p. 3.

Downfall, may be combated by the material sword, and he only put into words opinions widely current on the left wing of the Barebones' Parliament.[1]

The Quakers of later days rejected such sentiments with unfeigned horror; but not only the Fifth Monarchy Men, i.e. ancestors of their grouping, even Friends in the proper sense of the word, founders of the Society, were originally violent. 'The earlier phase of the movement,' so one outstanding student of the period has written, was 'no more like the generation which succeeded it than is the mountain torrent swollen with melting snows and turbid debris like the stream which lazily trickles over the pebbles in summer.'[2] When William Dewsbury stood before Judge Wyndham at Nottingham in March 1655, the magistrate told the Quaker: 'If thou and Fox had it in your power, you would soon have your hands imbrued in blood.'[3] This is, of course, merely an accusation, but not entirely a groundless one. Indeed, the Judge's words are well chosen. For it is lack of power, more than anything else, that turns a sect to peaceful ways.

So long as a hope of power lasted, or even lingered, violence, to say the least, was not foresworn by the Friends. A publication directed against them, Leslie's *Snake in the Grass*, presented a number of eulogies on Charles I's execution, culled from various Quaker sources.[4] 'Though they were never seen with a weapon in their hands, several had been found carrying pistols under their cloaks. A Quaker took up his position at the doors of Parliament and drew his sword on a group of members. When questioned, he replied that he was inspired by the Holy Spirit to kill every man that sat in the House.'[5] Thus the Paraclete was made the excuse of intended murder as he had been the excuse of fornication. In view of the fact that later on refusal to do military service became one of the hallmarks of the sect, it should be mentioned that around 1655 many of them infiltrated into the army of the Commonwealth – so much so that Henry Cromwell, fearing for the discipline necessary in the field, could declare: 'Our most considerable enemies are the Quakers.'[6] When Richard Farnsworth informed Margaret Fell about the methods used by Friends to spread their message – 'the priests is all on fire', he assures her with glee – he also mentioned

[1] Gooch, loc. cit., p. 261.
[2] Ibid., p. 281.
[3] Braithwite, loc. cit., p. 175.
[4] Gooch, loc. cit., p. 275.
[5] Ibid., p. 277.
[6] Ibid.

to her that they take troopers as their escorts: 'Some soldiers is made to go along with them and stand by them whilst they are reading.'[1]

Two attempted revolts by the Fifth Monarchy Men were quickly defeated: their belief that each of them would be able to subdue a thousand proved illusory.[2] This bitter experience created an entirely new mental condition, not only among them, but also among all who belonged to the religious left, including the Quakers in the narrower sense of the word. Henceforth the sword is condemned as the tool of the heathens. The time had arrived when all could use, with a good conscience, the words which George Fox had employed at Exeter: 'You speak of the Quakers spreading seditious books and papers. I answer, we have no seditious books or papers. Our books are against sedition and seditious men and seditious books and seditious teachers and seditious ways.'[3] And thus it was that the fermenting leaven was purged from the sectarian paste.

For the reason which we have adduced, Russia, otherwise so rich a quarry for the student of sectarianism, yields little that is of use in the investigation of the contrast between violent and non-violent groupings. But where Eastern Europe fails, Central Europe provides all the more material. Twice in history did it show the dichotomy of which we are speaking here: once when the Hussites gave way to the Bohemian and Moravian Brethren, and then again when the Anabaptists gave way to the Mennonites. We shall speak of the latter, i.e. the later, instance first because it is on a somewhat smaller scale than the former, earlier, development.

In the twenties of the sixteenth century, the territories now known as Germany were in a state of complete unrest. It was clear that the old (feudal) order of things was on the way out; it was not so clear what would take its place. The mood was millenarian; anything seemed possible. The possibility that a small group of 'saints' would gain supreme power certainly seemed far from fantastic. The sect-leaders of the day, Thomas Müntzer, Johannes Hut, Melchior Hoffmann, Bernhard Rothmann, Jan Bockelson, and all the rest, were consequently of the violent variety. Johannes Hut saw a significant parallel between the Hebrews of old and the Anabaptists of his time: as the former were allowed to wipe out

[1] Braithwaite, loc. cit., Appendix, p. 569. Cf. also p. 358.
[2] Gooch, loc. cit., p. 324. Cf. also pp. 263–6.
[3] Ibid., p. 274.

the Canaanites, so the latter were called and commissioned to wipe out the 'heathens'. 'The day' loomed large in his thought and preaching. 'The day' was 'the day of the Lord's vengeance'. On reading him one is reminded of 'the night of the long knives' which played a great part in Hitlerite speeches before 1934 (alas, after 1934, too, only that the one night became twelve long years). Melchior Hoffmann counselled non-violence until 'the day', then, however, the forcible destruction of the 'mystery of iniquity' would have to take place. All the apocalyptic plagues, he asserted, had already come upon the world, bar the vengeance of the Seventh Angel. Bernhard Rothmann can best be characterized by a quotation of *The Little Book of Vengeance* which he put out in 1534: 'Dear brethren, the time of vengeance has come upon us. God has raised up the promised David and armed him to vengeance and punishment on Babylon with its people. Therefore, dear brethren, arm yourselves to the battle, not alone with the apostle's weapon of patience in suffering, but also with the glorious armour of David, to the end that you may, with God's power and help, utterly root out the might of Babylon and all the godless world.'[1]

In the hubbub of those days, the little town of Nikolsburg in Moravia attracted international attention because it was one of the hotbeds of bloodthirsty sectarianism. It is interesting in our context because a division soon showed itself between the 'men of the staff' (*Stäbler*) and the 'men of the sword'; the former were forced to leave the city. But the crisis came, not in Nikolsburg, nor in Strassburg, where, at one time, it seemed to come, but in Münster. This holy city of Anabaptism became also a hard city of the armed fist. However many allowances we may make for the fact that the revolutionary rulers of this New Jerusalem were defeated and are consequently known only by the reports, often distorted, of their enemies and vanquishers, there can be no doubt whatsoever that their regiment, while it lasted, was cruel in the extreme.

When the extremists had got the upper hand in the city, a smith by the name of Hubert Rüscher voiced opposition to their policy. He was taken to the cathedral square where demands for an ordinary process of law were set aside, and Jan Bockelson stabbed him twice from the front while Jan Matthisson fired a bullet into

[1] Bax, loc. cit., p. 263. Tumbült (loc. cit., p. 89) quotes a different, far longer title for Rothmann's pamphlet.

him from the back. This done, a historian tells us, 'the multitude sang some hymns to the honour of God and dispersed'.[1] Later, another smith, Heinrich Mollenhecke, organized some resistance. He and his friends – about two hundred of them – were taken, and 'the great majority of them were shot dead or decapitated'.[2] On 3 June 1535, no fewer than fifty-two executions are said to have taken place; on 12 June, the 'King of Zion', Jan Bockelson, in person publicly executed his wife, Elisabeth Wandscherer, who had asked for permission to leave the doomed city.[3] There is one word which recurs in Dr. Tumbült's historical account: the word 'terrorism', and it is usually connected with some strong adjective such as 'unheard of' or the like.

In January 1536, this whole experiment in violent sectarianism came to a sorry end with the death of Jan Bockelson at the hands of his victorious enemies, and half a year later the Anabaptists assembled at Bockholt in order to see what could be rescued from the shambles. Two parties stood against each other: the Batenburgers, followers of Jan of Batenburg, still bent on violence; and the Obbenites, followers of one Obbe Philips, genuine non-violent men. As might be expected, the Obbenites won the day. The sect had learnt the lesson that the sword is a two-edged tool, that armed aggression does not pay and that cruelty recoils on the head of him who has had recourse to it. No good society is to be expected in this life, Philips taught, and so existing conditions must be meekly accepted. The day will come, David Joris predicted, when the kings themselves would divest themselves of their crowns; until then, their rule had to be suffered. Once again, a pack of wolves turned into a herd of lambs.

The Obbenite who was destined to lead the renewed and reformed movement was Menno Simons, from whom the Mennonites have taken their name. His own words show how anxious he was to prove that his was a non-violent sect. 'We consider the Münsterite doctrine, cause and life, namely concerning king, sword, uproar, striking back, vengeance, plurality of wives and the outward kingdom of Christ upon earth a new Judaism, a deceptive error, an abomination, radically at variance with the spirit, word and example of Christ,' he says in one passage.[4] In another[5] he writes: 'Our dear brethren . . . have formerly transgressed a

[1] Tumbült, loc. cit., p. 74. [2] Ibid., pp. 78 and 79. [3] Ibid., p. 93.
[4] Cit. Horsch, pp. 165 and 166. [5] Ibid., p. 164.

little against the Lord in so far as they undertook to protect their faith with the sword . . . in which respect it behoves us not to follow them.'[1] The Christian's weapons can only be: the Bible and patient endurance. With Menno's doctrine, the transformation of Anabaptism is complete. The Mennonites are sometimes described as a mixture of Anabaptist and Quaker elements, and though this is but half true, they certainly stand in the same relation to the Men of Münster as the Friends stood to the Fifth Monarchy Men.

While the 'war' of Münster was merely an incident in history, the Hussite Wars were wars in the proper sense of the word, and they deeply affected the whole Empire. If, in the definition of sect, great emphasis were put on the habitual face-to-face-ness of the groups, the Hussites would not qualify for inclusion, for theirs was a broad national movement, and the same is true if only socio-religious tendencies were comprised under the term, for theirs was a nationalistic, anti-German, movement. But we have not defined sect in this way. Both the broadness of the Hussite appeal and the politico-cultural aim of their effort rooted in a socio-religious rebellion against the established masters of Bohemia and Moravia: the people of these two countries were socially different from those of the Empire at large; they were already well on the way to modern capitalism, while the surrounding imperial territories were still substantially feudal; the presence and importance of the great mineworkers' contingent among the Hussites alone is characteristic. It was largely for social reasons that the Bohemians and Moravians became aware of their linguistic and cultural peculiarities, at a time when nationalism in general was still asleep; it was largely for social reasons that they became heretical and tended to become schismatical. We can therefore justifiably discuss Hussitism here. In the present sub-section at any rate its deviating features are of no consequence: and it offers an excellent illustration of the contrast between the non-violent and violent variants of sectarianism.

The Hussites, and especially their more extreme part, the Taborites, were a typically violent religious grouping. They felt

[1] Horsch (loc. cit.) insists that the 'dear brethren who have formerly transgressed a little' were, not the Münsterites, but the Oldcloisterites, a smaller and less extreme group. But Menno himself calls the Oldcloisterites 'poor straying sheep who . . . *through the ungodly doctrines of Münster* (our italics) . . . drew the sword in self-defence . . . .' Horsch himself quotes this sentence on p. 25.

thoroughly at home on the field of battle, so much so indeed that they loom larger in the annals of war than in the history of religion. What exactly their contribution to the art of warfare has been, is a moot point among historians. Not all accept Lynn Montross's judgement: 'A peasant army of eastern Europe discarded its flails and led the entire continent in the creation of a tactical system based upon weapons of gunpowder. This system not only overcame every foe without a single check; it proved fully two hundred years ahead of its own day, teaching lessons that were never understood by soldiers again until the seventeenth century. A greater miracle has not been recorded in the annals of war.'[1]

It may be that these words are exaggerated.[2] But the sociologist can subject the historical material to his own tests, and if this is done, the Hussites do emerge as true pioneers of the modern methods of mass destruction. Two points are decisive: firstly, that their commander, Jan Žižka, rationalized, and, secondly, that he mechanized, warfare. 'In an age of sorcery, Žižka's approach was that of the military scientist basing his formula on precise analysis and experiment,' Montross asserts.[3] If this is still an exaggeration, it is at least relatively true, for the feudal hosts with whom the Hussites had to contend were as yet quite untouched by the modern tendency towards systematic rationalization of even this sorry business. As for the mechanization of fighting, Oman himself, who otherwise minimizes the role of the Taborites, ascribes to them revolutionary innovations: 'Žižka was the first general in Europe who specialized in the smaller firearms as weapons for large bodies of infantry . . . The Bohemians also took to employing a great number of bombards. These were . . . real cannon, and we may almost call them field-guns . . .'[4], but their

[1] Montross, L , *War through the Ages,* New York 1960, p. 187.

[2] Cf. Oman, C., *A History of the Art of War in the Middle Ages,* New York 1924, pp. 361–70, esp. pp. 368 and 370.

[3] Loc. cit., p. 189.

[4] Loc. cit., pp. 365 and 366. Cf. also the more technical details given in Denis, E., *Huss et la Guerre des Hussites*, Paris 1878, esp. pp. 224–8. Denis compares the soldiery of Žižka with that of Cromwell and shows that there was a specific style of warfare common to both. His information could have been utilized by Max Weber when he wrote *The Protestant Ethic and the Spirit of Capitalism*, for discipline and rationality were the leading principles of these armies. The English word *howitzer* is derived from the Czech *haufnice, via* the German *Haubitze.*

day was only just dawning around 1420, when the Hussite Wars began.

The Hussites, then, and particularly the Taborites, were a fierce, aggressive movement which had no objection whatsoever against the shedding of blood. Indeed, great cruelty characterized their conduct. For many years, the classical study of their intervention in world history was a tome called *Huss et la Guerre des Hussites* by Ernest Denis (1878). A Frenchman in the age of Sédan, and a Jew in the days when the French were developing the anti-semitic tendencies soon to produce the Dreyfus scandal, Denis hated both Austria and Catholicism, on the principle: *les ennemis de mes ennemis sont mes amis*. A more fervent defender of the Hussite hordes has never existed! Yet the facts about their atrocities continue to show through all the whitewash. Even he has to show us – right at the beginning of the troubles (19 July 1419) – a predicant standing calmly by, a chalice in his hands raised towards heaven, while a mob murders a whole town council and so mutilates their bodies as to make them unrecognizable;[1] even he has to speak about fierce vandalism, devastations, the burning of convents in large numbers, the wholesale massacre of monks and nuns, and especially the pillage of the hapless peasants who in the end abandoned their villages in utter despair. 'The Taborites,' he writes, 'during a long time, strove to mitigate the evils which they inflicted . . . Unfortunately, mind and soul got gradually accustomed to carnage and incendiarism; all pity disappeared, drowned [as it were] in floods of blood, and no dam henceforth contained the torrent of devastation which had been let loose.'[2] Denis's defence is conceived in the same spirit which also pervaded the manifesto which the Hussites nailed to the doors of the Minster at Basle where the Council was in session (November 1431): 'It is a great and gross lie if it is said that all we wish to do is to kill men, women and children. We do it only if violence is used against us . . .'[3] What a use of the little word 'only'! It is not so that Mennonites or Quakers feel or speak.

But the day came, as it was bound to come, when force was met by greater force: the battle of Lipany (16 June 1434) annihilated Hussitism. At once non-violence took the place of violence in the

1 Denis, loc. cit., p. 206.
2 Ibid., p. 384. Cf. also pp. 240, 276, 403, and, indeed, *passim*.
3 Cit. ibid., p. 396.

thought of the defeated sectarians: indeed, it was raised to the height of a sacred principle. The place of the fierce, battle-scarred, one-eyed Žižka was soon occupied by the gentle, soft-spoken, ever-smiling Komensky (or Comenius), the children's friend, the protagonist of peace. Denis has well described the mood out of which the *Unitas Fratrum* or Bohemian Brethren (better known in the Anglo-Saxon world as the Moravians) was born: 'The souls had fallen victim to a profound discouragement. What good had the exploits and victories of . . . Žižka's associates done? . . . How should any man succeed where the fighting bodies had failed? A general reaction made itself felt against brutal force, violence and war.'[1] In 1450, Petr Chelčicky wrote his *Network of Faith* in which he condemned, in the most decided manner, all violence. Why had Christendom fallen from its high estate? Only because the Church had become linked to the secular arm. But Christ had rejected physical force in all its forms. The Christian had to forego and to foreswear the sword, to live in meekness, as the Master had done.

Thus the waning of their power turned these religious groupings in the fifties from violence to non-violence, as the waxing of their power had turned them, thirty years earlier, from non-violence to violence:[2] ideology here appears to be almost a simple function of strength. But one argument at this point is likely to come up against considerable resistance on the part of the pacific groups. We have implied that these groups are merely revised versions of the earlier bellicose sects, but that Quakers and Mennonites and Moravians have never admitted and will in all probability never be willing to admit. On the contrary, their apologists and even their scholars have gone out of their way to prove that the Quakers had nothing to do with the Ranters and Fifth Monarchists, or the Mennonites with the Münsterites, or the Moravians with the Taborites. Their religions, they have invariably asserted, have come from a purer source than that.

The Quakers, for instance, have insisted that they have sprung

[1] Ibid., pp. 462, et seq.

[2] On the latter point, cf. ibid., pp. 204–206, esp. p. 204: 'In the measure in which their ranks swelled, they became conscious of their strength and grew gradually used to the idea of defending their . . . faith by force of arms.'

up from the kindly and good-living Seekers,[1] not from the wild Fifth Monarchy mob or the licentious Ranter rabble. But for once the hostile, hate-filled, Paget is not so wrong when he asserts that Ranters and Quakers were 'much of the same puddle'.[2] While the neutral observer must reject the word puddle because it has a pejorative meaning, he may rightly speak of the Society of Friends as a pool in which many little streamlets came together, one of them certainly being the quiet Seekers or Waiters, but others no less certainly the turbulent Ranters, Fifth Monarchy Men, Diggers and still other groups. Even the pool which thus collected was not, at first, showing a smooth surface to the world. Fox complained that 'Ranters and loose persons' disturbed the gatherings in the capital, two females, Mildred and Judy, being particularly obnoxious. 'Persons of a loose ranting spirit got up,' George Whitehead reported, 'and frequently disturbed our Friends' meeting in London by their ranting.'[3] Thus it is not true to suggest that there were two rivers coming from two sources, one muddy and the other clean, the muddy disappearing and the clean remaining: there was much rather a copious influx from many directions into the same reservoir which was at first churned up by unruly passions and only finally gained stability, composure and lasting form.

It is the same with the question as to whether or not the later Baptists have had anything to do with the earlier Anabaptists. The Mennonites were so closely connected with the latter that it would be vain for them to deny the relationship, embarrassing though it must be. But even the English Baptists will vainly repudiate their Münsterite origin, if the case be pleaded before an unprejudiced tribunal. For if they assert that they have sprung from the Mennonites, not the Münsterites, they merely make the parentage a little more remote, for what they are saying then is that it was their grandfather, and not their father, who covered himself in blood.[4]

The case of the Moravians is again the same. The *Unitas Fratrum* has maintained in its *Confessio* of 1572 that it did not come into existence before the middle of the fifteenth century. Thus there would be about twenty-three years between the end of Taborism

[1] Braithwaite, loc. cit., pp. 26 and 27.

[2] Gooch, loc. cit., p. 271.

[3] Braithwaite, loc. cit., pp. 269 and 270.

[4] Cf. Gooch, loc. cit., pp. 73–5.

in 1434 and their alleged foundation in 1457 – a kind of *cordon sanitaire* between violence and non-violence. Yet Knox is entirely justified when he calls the argument – 'that the Brethren cannot have been Taborites since there were no Taborites left in the world at the date when their movement was founded' – 'somewhat disingenuous'. Hussitism did not disappear after the battle of Lipany, it merely changed one plank – admittedly a most important one – in its platform. The butterfly looks different from the caterpillar, but it is the same insect. Incidentally, Rudiger, the Brethren's own historian, does not attempt to deny their descent from the men of Tabor.[1]

It is in this fashion vain to try to draw neat dividing lines between the three pairs of sects which we have studied: the Quakers remain Ranters, the Baptists Anabaptists, the Moravians Taborites *minus* only violence. The best proof that the later pacific groups had come from, and still carried within them something of the spirit of, the earlier militant ones is the fact that they showed a tendency to revert to the original form as soon as circumstances appeared to change in their favour and they could hope, once again, to have the better of any open struggle that might ensue. Let us grant, for a moment, that the English Baptists who organized themselves in 1611, when Helwys founded his church in London, were children of Menno Simons and not of Jan Bockelson. How did they behave in the Civil War period when their ranks filled up and those of respectable royalist religion thinned? The same Gooch who, on pp. 73–5, had denied their connection with the fanatics of Münster, writes on p. 129: in 1645, 'they were described as the most numerous of the sects. The character of the movement was undergoing a corresponding change . . . Lord Brooke . . . testified to the existence of a radical wing, and Baillie was soon after offended by their "insolencies intolerable" . . . Charges of a more definite character are met with. "In all sects, especially the Anabaptists," wrote Baillie, "there is a declared averseness from all obedience to the present magistrates and laws . . ."' While Gooch tries to minimize the aggressive temper rising among the Baptists in these years, he has to admit that their 'connection with the Fifth Monarchy Men was very close,'[2] and

[1] Cf. Knox, loc. cit., pp. 392 and 393.

[2] Gooch, loc. cit., p. 268. Cf. also p. 267. Cf. further Underwood, loc. cit., pp. 82–4, 92–5. On pp. 92 and 93, Underwood writes: 'There were a few Bap-

the same assertion is made by Braithwaite[1] who thus shifts the firebrands from the history of his own sect into that of another. 'The Fifth Monarchy movement,' he blandly declares, 'originated among the Baptists.' If this was so, to where then had the spirit of Menno Simons disappeared?

Did it perhaps migrate to the Quakers, Mr. Braithwaite's Friends? Alas! What had happened to the Baptists in the mid-forties, tended to happen to the Quakers in the late fifties: a renewal of the solemnly foresworn spirit of aggressiveness. In 1660, Fox sharply had to remind his followers straining on the leash: 'Our weapons are spiritual and not carnal.' Braithwaite's editors add to this quotation a revealing note: Fox, they say, was 'forbidding the plans of rash spirits among Friends to take up arms. . . .'[2] No doubt, Fox himself never wavered in his conviction that all recourse to the sword is inherently evil: but, surely, he was also wise enough to foresee that physical opposition to the Restoration would be simple madness. He realized that, for the weak, passive resistance is a more politic, as well as a more moral, tool of aggression than active intervention. Let us not go so far as to say that he made a virtue out of a necessity; that would be unfair; yet virtue and necessity are inextricably intermixed and interfused in the pacific attitudes of the typical non-violent sects.

Our whole analysis has shown, then, that, appearances notwithstanding, sect movements are often at first violent and embrace non-violence only later, in a second phase. The formal fact that they regularly change their names when they cross that borderline is too superficial to cover up the substantial concatenation of the two stages underneath. Hence, in contrasting non-violent and violent groupings, we are not only distinguishing two possible types of sectarianism, we are also uncovering a developmental tendency inherent in it. If we may for once indulge in a little play upon words, we may say that a non-violent sect is a little less

[1] Braithwaite, loc, cit., p. 19.

[2] Ibid., pp. 462 and 581.

---

tists who were far from adopting the attitude of passive resistance . . . These men were only a handful . . .', but on p. 94 he says: 'The authorities . . . knew that not a few Baptists were Fifth Monarchists.' In any case, three Baptists were prominent in the Rye House Plot of 1683, as Underwood has to record (pp. 107 and 108). Clearly, militancy died a hard death, all admiration for Menno Simons notwithstanding.

sectarian than a violent one. A sect is a conflict society: here the conflict is already a little muted, a little reduced. But this leads us to the next and final aspect of the phenomenon of religious anti-establishmentarianism which we have to investigate: the decay of sects, their decline into mere denominations.

3 · THE DECAY OF SECTS

One of the most subtle, yet at the same time most decisive, dividing-lines which separate conservative from revolutionary religion, state church from sect, is the very different attitude towards the flow of time which they entertain. For the conservatives, all is settled, and they do not see why the present form of society should not continue into an indefinite, if not infinite, future. God has accepted or even inspired the constitution of the State; He rules in and through the King whom He Himself has raised to the throne; the people at large are His arms and His hands – what, then, could be amiss? why, then, should He shorten the days and bring on the end of the world? For the revolutionaries, all is unsettled, and they cannot see how the present form of society can possibly endure much longer. All that happens in the world is an outrage to Almighty God; a devil incarnate or a devilish creature sits at the controls; the few saints that are left, Jehovah's faithful remnant, sadly reduced in number, are the prey of daily persecutions at the hands of an ungodly majority. Surely, the Lord will not delay much longer? History, so the sectarians have always felt, has not much longer to run; the hour of reckoning is near. The mood of the conventicles has ever been: *gladius domini supra terram, cito et velociter* . . . Not only those officially called Adventists, but all sectarians in the proper sense of the word have been adventists, believers in the imminent second advent or coming. The gentle Jesus will return in the guise of the fearful Judge to separate the saved and the damned – that is to say, to establish the sectarians in the glory which is theirs, and to hand over the rest of the world to the infernal powers to whom they belong and always have belonged.

A game which sociologists enjoy very much is the arrangement of the phenomena which they study along a simple linear continuum. It is assumed that there must be a gradual transition from the one extreme (total acceptance of the world as it is) to the other (total rejection of the world as it is), and that any given group must have a place somewhere along the line. The trouble with this pattern of thought is that it translates what is qualitative into purely quantitative terms and thereby sheds a good deal of realism and truth. The acceptance of the world by Roman Catholicism and by Calvinism is qualitatively, not quantitatively, different from the acceptance of the world by a state church like the Anglican; their rejection of the world is again qualitatively, not quantitatively, different from the rejection of the world by a sect like the Jehovah's Witnesses or the original Quakers or Skoptsy. A philosophy, an attitude, cannot be compressed into an index figure. But for those who enjoy the pastime, here would be a golden opportunity, for conservative and revolutionary religion are distinguished above all by their belief or disbelief in the nearness or remoteness of judgement day. The more revolutionary the sect, the larger it looms in their thought, the more conservative, the further away it appears. When a sect cools down and turns into a denomination – a process which we have to study in the subsequent chapters – the historical horizon of the group concerned becomes wider and wider, until the end of the world disappears into a hazy distance where the eye cannot focus on it and the mind cannot feel it any more.

A relatively good and easily grasped indication of the animus of a sect in this respect is its attitude – the attitude of its theologians – towards the Book of Revelation, the Apocalypse of St. John the Apostle. Whatever the truth about the exact date at which this extraordinary document was written, one thing is amply clear, namely that it originated at a time when the persecution of the Christians by the State was at its height. Only men who know that tomorrow they may, nay will, be thrown to the lions or turned into flaming torches or skinned alive or broken on the wheel, can feel that way. Sectarian thought has usually been preoccupied (to put it mildly) with the detail of this tail-piece of the biblical canon, and few parts of Holy Writ have evoked more acute and yet more abstruse exegesis than this. Nothing, indeed, could be less surprising. The situation which the Christians of those days faced is identical with – hence archetypal for – the situation in which all truly revolutionaty sectarians find themselves. When, on 15 September 1775, Andrey Selivanov was knouted at Sosnovka until his shirt was drenched with blood, he could feel that seventeen centuries were as nothing; the same fiend who had martyred God's friends in Nero's or Domitian's or Diocletian's day, had struck again, and that was all. Selivanov's people, and almost all other true sectarians, could therefore slip into the mood of the Apocalypse as one slips into a ready-made suit. Every acute sect persecution has sent the sectarians back to the cryptic numbers of St. John: would they not yield, if rationally interpreted, a key to the moment when the trumpet was to sound, all suffering end, and supreme happiness begin?

To the Christians of Constantine's age, the Revelation was no longer the book which it had been to their forefathers two hundred, or even one hundred, years before. What did it mean? what were they to make of it? Increasingly satisfied with the given state of affairs, they felt no burning desire for the end of the world. Like the proletarians, or rather ex-proletarians, of another century, they knew that they had a good deal more to lose than their chains. The subconscious stream of ideas which feeds, as it were, the thought of the sectarian brooder was not for them: the world as it is should not be allowed to go on; the world as it is cannot be allowed to go on; the world as it is will not be allowed to go on. The Apocalypse is quietly handed over to librarians and antiquarians; the *dies irae* undergoes a *prorogatio sine die*: the sect then has become a denomination. This process of transmutation from alienation to adjustment, from rebelliousness to acquiescence, and ultimately acceptance, of established society was characteristic of Christianity in the first centuries or so of its existence. The same process inspired Max Weber's doctrine of the routinization of charisma, and was repeated over and over again in the history of sectarianism. A flame, however high it may burn at first, which cannot engulf all that is around it and cause a general conflagration, must slowly undergo the influence of its environment, which is dark, cold and damp; it must burn ever lower until it becomes a mere flicker in the end.

THE MILLENARIAN PHASE

For the normal man it is difficult at any time to enter into an alienated mentality such as that of the typical sectarian, but it is doubly and trebly difficult for him to do so while that mentality passes through an acute crisis like the daily expectation of the last hour. The theme has, understandably, attracted novelists who felt themselves endowed with a particularly wide human sympathy and a particularly fertile psychological imagination: witness, Hugh Walpole's *The Captives* or Joyce Cary's *Except the Lord.* The scholar can learn something from Walpole and Cary, for they have succeeded in conveying an impression of the atmosphere of expectancy which pervades a sect while the millenarian hope is yet alive. In spite of the poetic licence which they enjoy and rightly claim, even their work is ultimately based on observation. But the scholar is much more narrowly confined to the facts: he needs descriptive materials in the sober meaning of the term, and such are woefully scanty. The man who feels certain that tomorrow the sun will set for the last time is not likely to write an essay of introspection analysing his mental condition for the benefit of a posterity which he thinks will never exist. But where revelations are lacking which would make understanding *ab intra* a little easier, records *ab extra* of sectarian behaviour in the adventist phase have, here and there, been transmitted to the historians. These enable us to draw conclusions from the visible about the invisible, to deduce an inner state from the description of its surface manifestations.

A good example is afforded by the Old Believers in the second half of the seventeenth century, the period when the birth-pangs of their movement were still upon them. In 1649 there was printed in Moscow a book, usually called *The Book of Faith*, whose author, Stepan Vonifatev, had been the candidate for the patriarchate whom Nikon had defeated. This book is pervaded by a spirit of deep pessimism: dark days were soon to descend on once holy, but now unholy, Russia. The gloomy prophecy, once pronounced, spawned a whole host of dire predictions. The Apocalypse mentioned two figures: the figure 1,000, standing for the millenial kingdom, the beginning of a new aeon, and the figure 666, standing for the Beast and therefore also for the end of the old doomed world. 1,000 + 666 = 1666; it was in the year 1666, therefore, that the final chapter of human history would commence. The chapter would not be long, for the Apocalypse allotted to Antichrist merely a brief earthly reign: two and a half years. Hence the trumpet would sound in 1669: 'The sun would be eclipsed, the stars fall from the sky, the earth be burned up.' 'In anticipation of these calamities,' the historian Milyukov writes in his *Outlines of Russian Culture*, 'there appeared many phenomena, of which we have only [concrete] information concerning the region of Nizhny Novgorod. In the autumn of 1668 the fields were neglected, no one ploughed or sowed, and at the beginning of the fateful year 1669 the huts, too, were abandoned. Assembling in crowds, people prayed, fasted, confessed their sins to each other, partook of the holy sacrament, and, being prepared, awaited with awe the archangel's trumpet call. According to an ancient superstition, the end of the world was to come at midnight; and so at nightfall the zealots of ancient piety, arraying themselves in white shirts and shrouds, lay down in coffins hollowed from the trunks of trees, and awaited the trumpet call.'[1]

When the year 1669 passed and sun and stars still calmly wandered across the firmament, a most significant development took place among the Old Believers– the movement divided into two halves: those who asserted that Antichrist *had* come, namely spiritually, and that the spirit of evil, or rather of the Evil One, had appeared on earth, therefore fulfilling the prophecy; and those who continued to assert that Antichrist had *not yet* come, at least not come in visible form, and that therefore his incarnation had still to be expected. We call this disagreement most significant, for it is by splitting into a more radical and a more moderate wing that sects – as we shall see in more detail – usually react to their disappointments. The moderate wing which reinterprets its apocalypse in symbolical terms is really already less than a full sect: it has taken a step, however short, towards denominationalism. Not so the radical wing: it stands its ground; it continues to believe in the impending downfall of the wicked and elevation of the godly; it perpetuates the twin character of the full sect: its hate and its hope.

What gave colour to the idea that Antichrist had come to Russia 'spiritually' in 1666 was the fact that the Council of that year had consummated the great Schism or Raskol. The godly had been driven from the House of God – what more could anyone want? While moderates reasoned in this manner, radicals recalled that the Book of Revelations predicted a visible, tangible, physical Antichrist. Their theologian Avram went back to the *Book of Faith* and recalculated Vonifatev's calculations. His considerations and speculations are interesting, but a sociology of religion cannot dwell on the vagaries of a cabalistic mind; suffice it to say that he

[1] Milyukov, loc. cit., vol. I, p. 43.

predicted the final catastrophe for 1699, a date which could be understood to mean 1691, as there were eight years difference between nature and the calendar then in force. 'In 1691, there was a terrific paroxysm in anticipation of the end of the world.'[1] Again nothing happened. But everything happened in 1699. Antichrist appeared. He appeared under the cover-name of Peter and has entered into history as Peter the Great. Avram was vindicated. 'The "Liers in Coffins" once more spent their nights in hollowed tree trunks, singing mournful hymns.'[2]

But sleeping shrouded in wooden caskets was not the supreme expression of the state of mind which we are trying to delineate with the aid of its external manifestations. Let us hear our historian further: 'In exultant natures the fervent anticipation of the second advent produced an epidemic of religious ecstasy, when the most zealous . . . lost patience and strove to expedite the end. As the Kingdom of God was not coming to them, they would hasten to meet it, and, having settled all accounts with the world, they decided to be free of it through suicide, should they not succeed in attaining the same end by martyrdom.'[3] Avvakum, before his death, encouraged this trend; after his death he was reported to have appeared to visionaries to encourage it some more. The way of escape, it was said, lay through water or fire – i.e. through drowning or burning. Either route appears to have been taken by multitudes. Surprising though it may seem, we are face to face here with a mass phenomenon. 'A modern student figures that from the beginning of the Schism to the nineties of the seventeenth century, no less than 20,000 people had committed suicide.'[4]

Max Weber, in urging us to make the *understanding* of human action the great aim of sociology, has emphasized that there are extremes of conduct – running amok, for example – which may be impossible to understand, so that we must be satisfied in their case with mere description; there they are concerned, we must, as it were, be behaviourists, Watsonians, *malgré nous*. The self-immolation of the early Raskolniky is perhaps a case in point – yet not entirely so, for there was a factor in the situation which makes their suicidal mania a good deal more comprehensible than it first appears to be. This factor was the cruel persecution of the dis-

[1] Ibid., p. 44.
[2] Ibid., p. 46.
[3] Ibid., pp. 56 and 57.
[4] Ibid., p. 59.

senters initiated by the Tsarevna Sophia in 1684.[1] A decree of hers threatened every impenitent Old Believer with the stake, and the government was in dead earnest. Of the 20,000 suicides estimated, only 3,800 are said to have occurred before 1684 – an eye-opening fact. When whole communes refused to turn from the old ritual – which would have meant symbolically to accept, to approve of, the new order of things, including their own enserfment – troops were sent, and it was then that the villagers would lock themselves up in some large house and lay the torch to it. Better to die voluntarily at home, with one's dear ones around, than to be killed – after suffering the excruciating 'threefold' torture prescribed by Sophia – in some distant prison yard alone. Seen in this light, the suicides, and even their number, appear much more understandable. Fear and desperation are mental conditions which a normally sensitive onlooker should be able to comprehend, though the hysteria which accompanied them may remain impenetrable – incapable of experience at second hand – even for the most determined *effort de sympathie*. Once again we see that a socio-economic interpretation of sectarianism makes more sense than a purely religious one – makes more sense even so far as the apocalyptic mood and its consequences are concerned.

Already in 1694, a Council of Old Believers had officially endorsed the 'spiritual' interpretation of the doctrine concerning the appearance of Antichrist, and after 1702, this version had perforce to be accepted by all as the true one, since the Beast's rule was prolonged beyond the two-and-a-half year span foretold in Scripture. From this moment onward, the Old Believers (or at any rate the majority of them, known as Popovtsy) drifted to the right, and to the left of them there arose more radical sects, many of whom we have already encountered, each with an adventist element in its make-up. New clues were sought, new calculations carried out. The spiritual interpretation was broadened along the lines followed in the West by Joachim of Flora, or, nearer to these sects in space and time, by August Cieszkowski. History was divided into four periods (spring, summer, fall and winter) or into three (the age of the Father, the Son, the Holy Ghost): the year 1666 A.D. of the Julian Calendar or the year 7000 or 8000 from the day of creation was declared to be the onset of the kingdom of God, the invisible fulfilment of the prophecies. Other eyes

[1] Conybeare (p. 87) gives the date as 1685.

remained fixed on the future but with an expectation more elastic, not to say more vague. Some, for instance, taught that the key to the secret lay where it had not been suspected before, in Revelations IV, 4: judgement could not take place ere the twenty-four 'ancients' mentioned there had been assembled, whereas there had been so far only twenty-two.[1] But we cannot hope to study all these variants in detail.

One development, however, must be recorded because it is of the utmost importance. Needless to say, the Skoptsy were fervent adventists, and they, too, had to face the great adventist problem of 'the Day' or date. Incapable, because of police persecution, of using the printing press and the postal system to any significant extent, a large number of local traditions grew up, observers' accounts of which are rather confusing.[2] But two potentially clear-cut theories are contained, dissolved, as it were, in the discussions of which we have any knowledge. One was conceived along realistic, not to say materialistic lines. The Saviour Selivanov would leave his present hide-out, appear in the capital city, ascend the tsaric throne, subdue the kings of the earth and mete out justice to the quick and the dead, whereupon a paradise on earth would be established. Tell-tale details were sometimes added: the assertion, for instance, that Selivanov (in reality identical with Peter III, the rightful tsar) would 'pierce the heart' of the reigning monarch (in reality an interloper and usurper, a satanic figure); or the prediction that regiment after regiment will join him, and that ships freighted with gold and jewels will arrive for his faithful children (an interesting anticipation of the main tenet of the present-day cargo-cults so widespread in underdeveloped countries). Here are the makings of a doctrine characteristically this-worldly: all the salient events will take place within the framework of space and time. Even hell would be in a concrete location somewhere on this globe. It was in line with this this-worldliness that Selivanov was declared immortal. He was still among men, just biding his time. Even in 1842 his presence in the flesh was asserted, although by then his age would have been over a hundred. But other Skoptsy thought in metaphysical rather than physical terms. Selivanov had died: he had ascended, returned to his home above the clouds, but not to bide there for long; he

[1] Conybeare, loc. cit., pp. 165–70; Grass, loc. cit., vol. I, p. 193.

[2] Cf. Grass, vol. II, p. 662 et seq.; Conybeare, loc. cit., pp. 366 and 367.

would descend again, come in glory to fetch his children to the seventh heaven where they would be immeasurably happy for ever and evermore. This other-worldly version is clearly less revolutionary than the first: the revolutionist wants to see a transformation of the workaday world, not some consummation, however happiness-laden, in the beyond. Thus we can discern, in the fog of Skopets speculations, a threatening split of the movement. The parallel to the division of the Old Believers into moderates and radicals, 'spiritual' ones and non-spirituals, is obvious. Yet while the Old Believers did break up, and very soon, the Skoptsy did not. It is interesting to search for the reason of their continued unity.

The answer lies in the activist twist which this interesting group managed to give to its eschatology. Their speculations spontaneously concentrated on Revelations VII, 4: 'An hundred forty-four thousand were signed . . .' Here was the key: the kingdom would come once 144,000 men or women had been castrated 'for the kingdom's sake'. There was something to *do* now: to fill up the ranks of the virginal ones, to complete the holy number. Henceforth, the theoretical differences were swallowed up by practical action. We see again that activity is the great specific against brooding. Not that the Skoptsy ultimately escaped the fate of all sects: the day was to come when the Neo-Skoptsy would appear for whom 'whiting' meant, not the divorce of a sinning member from the body, but a freeing of the mind from sinning thoughts. But these spiritual castrates and castrators were a new grouping rather than a fragment broken off from the old; and even if they can be described as an offshoot of the Skopets movement in the wider sense of the word, it was not a difference in eschatology that induced them to go their own way.

This activism showed itself in other forms as well. One, of which we shall have to study the wider manifestations and implications before long, was mass migration. The tradition according to which paradise was located somewhere near Mount Ararat was fairly alive among the Russian peasants, and whenever the apocalyptic mood was upon them, they were apt to cast their eyes – and even to move their feet! – in this direction. In 1830, Conybeare tells us, 'the Russian sectaries . . . greedily welcomed the idea [put to them] that Christ would ere long inaugurate the Millennium in the basin of Ararat . . . the thousand years of glory were to begin in 1836, according to Niketas Ivanov, a Molokan prophet of Melitopol, and others like him. The result was a considerable movement of peasants towards the new Jerusalem, and they began to flock from various districts to the Caucasus'. Conybeare adds the following story which will seem tragic to some and funny to others, but which will prove to all that the millenarian mentality can really take hold. 'An Elias appeared among them in 1833 in the person of [one] Byelozorov of Melitopol, who even foretold the very day on which, at the expiration of two and a half years [he] Elias would, as . . . required, reascend to heaven. Crowds duly collected to witness the miracle, and the prophet, with desperate leapings and wavings of his arms, attempted . . . to take to the air. But earth chained his specific gravity, and . . . officials his further freedom . . .' Instead of heaven, jail became his destination. Movements like that inaugurated by Ivanov had been led by one Sidor Andreev before and were to be repeated under one Lukian Petrov afterwards.[1]

The last-named outbreaks were purely psychological in origin. They sprang from the frustrations of the social strata from which the Molokane were recruited. There was little in the historical situation to evoke them, for contemporary Russia was a rather stable state. In this respect there is a difference from the earlier Old Believers' crises. In the second half of the seventeenth century, it was easy to develop end-of-the-world feelings, for a whole world was in fact coming to an end – the Middle Ages: hence in addition to the subjective, there existed also objective roots to millenarianism. But what is true of Russia around 1700, is still more true of Germany around 1500: the vague impression that a great turning-point, if not an end-point, of history had been reached, was general. And how could it be otherwise? A great turning-point had indeed been reached, an end-point, not of history as such, but of a great historical epoch. Thus the *fin-de-siècle* mood incarnated in such works of art as Albrecht Dürer's *The Mysterious Revelation of John* (1498) and Hans Holbein's *The Dance of Death* (a little later)[2] – characteristically produced as woodcuts, i.e. for wide distribution – was widespread, something

[1] Conybeare, loc. cit., pp. 322 and 323.

[2] A little known, but very powerful, expression of the apocalypticism rampant around this time are the windows of the Church of All Hallows, North Street, York, England, depicting the last two weeks of the world.

like a mist covering a whole landscape. Still, it was in sectarian circles that it concentrated, so to speak, to produce more tangible phenomena, and it was in Münster that it found its most striking *éclat*.

An anonymous author, writing just after the year 1500, predicted that the Emperor Frederick would return to rule the world as Davidic king for a thousand years: but before he would appear in his white resplendent robes to occupy his fiery throne, there would be a universal judgement which the author fixed, first for the year 1509, then for 1511, and finally for 1515. In 1521 the weaver-prophet Nikolaus Storch presaged the end of the world in five to seven years. Then Hans Hut appeared and declared the date to be Whitsunday, 1528. Hardly had this feast passed without catastrophe, that Augustin Bader produced a new version of the scare and hope – the mood was thickening. Melchior Hoffman at Strassburg and Bernhard Rothmann at Münster were the next to blow that horn. Both expected 1533 to be the year when the wrath would break loose. From Rothmann it was only a short step to Jan Matthisson, and from Jan Matthisson to Jan Bockelson. But the latter two were not just preachers, not just speakers of the prologue: they were actors of the apocalyptic drama itself. Matthisson claimed to be Enoch *Redivivus*, the precursor of *Rex Davidicus*, and Bockelson was proclaimed to be *Rex Davidicus* in person, foretold by Jeremias and Ezechiel, though it was at first only a local predicant called Dusentschur who saw the marks of royalty in him. Soon the whole town fell in with these ideas – the whole town with a few remarkable exceptions. For example, when the nuns of the convent of Überwasser were told by Rothmann that their house would presently collapse, the doughty Abbess Ida von Mervelt quietly went to bed.[1] But what to her still appeared as a rather bad joke, turned out to be deadly earnest when the new King began to wield the sword of justice. The violence at Münster which we studied in the last chapter would not have been possible without the apocalyptic mentality to back it up.

When the Mennonites succeeded the Münsterites and non-violence took the place of violence in the Baptist camp, much was changed, but the apocalyptic expectation still continued for a while. The following passage from the pen of Menno Simons himself reflects that expectation; it also allows us to see the social

[1] Cf. Tumbült, loc. cit., pp. 6, 9, 29, 30, 61, 32, 33, 79, 80, 81, 71.

as well as the psychological background of it: 'However lamentably we may here be persecuted, oppressed, smitten, robbed, burned at the stake, drowned in the water by the hellish Pharaoh and his cruel unmerciful servants, yet soon shall come the day of our refreshing and all the tears shall be wiped from our eyes and we shall be arrayed in the white silken robes of righteousness, follow the Lamb, and with Abraham, Isaac and Jacob sit down in the kingdom of God and possess the precious, pleasant land of eternal, imperishable joy. Praise God and lift up your heads, ye who suffer . . . The time is near when ye shall . . . rejoice . . . for evermore.'[1]

About a century after Simon's death, Dr. John Pell wrote to Secretary Thurloe, with a remarkable insight into the sectarian-millenarian mentality: 'Men impoverished by long troubles must needs have great propensions to hearken to those that proclaim a golden age at hand, under the name of Christ and the saints . . .' He knew what he was talking about, for the apocalyptic horsemen who had not been in evidence since the forties of the sixteenth century were on the rampage again since the forties of the seventeenth. 'Many prophecies are applied to these times,' Pell adds. 'The end of paganism was in 395, to which they add 1260. Others pitch on 1656, because the lives of the patriarchs in Genesis make this number. Therefore Christ will come this year or next.'[2] But 1655 marked the height of the new outbreak rather than its beginning. 'In November 1652, the infant [Quaker] community in Furness was seriously compromised by James Milner, a tailor, who, after a fourteen-days' fast, prophesied, amongst other wild fancies, that Wednesday the 1st December would be the Day of Judgement, and Thursday the 2nd December would be the first day of the new creation, when a four-cornered sheet would come down from heaven with a sheep in it. He and another Friend of a like "airy" spirit drew some after them . . .', Braithwaite reports.[3] A slight tendency to play down the whole phenomenon is noticeable in the last words. It is not easy for the grandchildren to speak about their grandfathers' extravagances. G. P. Gooch, a more

[1] Cit. Horsch, p. 65.

[2] Cit. Gooch, pp. 263 and 264. (Gooch's text is shorter and otherwise slightly different from that given by Robert Vaughan in *The Protectorate of Oliver Cromwell*, London 1838, vol. I, p. 156.)

[3] Braithwaite, loc. cit., p. 147.

independent historian, corrects Braithwaite on this point: 'At the basis of the creed of every religious body of the time, except the Presbyterians, lay the millenarian idea,' he asserts.[1] 'The abilities and the high position of Joseph Mede [author of *Clavis Apocalyptica*, published in 1627 and often reprinted] had given currency to millenarian notions as far back as the twenties. But not till the outbreak of the crisis in 1640 did the doctrine cease to be the property of professors. It then appeared in an extravagant form in a tract by a lady [*The Lady Eleanor's Appeal*] and in the following year was championed by [Henry] Archer in a lengthy pamphlet [*The Personal Reign of Christ upon Earth*] . . . So popular did the teaching become that Bishop Hall thought it necessary to compose a refutation [*The Revelation Unrevealed*]. But the idea was too much in harmony with the age to yield to argument, and its spread was exceedingly rapid.'[2]

The close connection, nay total fusion, of the social and religious moments and movements, to the exploration of which the present book is devoted, is nowhere more easy to grasp than in the millenarianism of the Ranters and the Fifth Monarchy Men. In 1649, Abiezer Coppe published *A Fiery Flying Roll: a Word from the Lord to all the Great Ones of the Earth . . . being the last Warning Piece at the dreadful Day of Judgment*. The scriptural passage to which this visionary likes to turn and to return is Isaias XXIII, 9: 'The Lord of hosts hath designed it, to pull down the pride of all glory and bring to disgrace all the glorious ones of the earth.' Wealth and wickedness are one for Coppe, and there is no distinction for him between the divine wrath and the wrath of the lower classes. The pamphlet is too long to give all the passages that are relevant here,[3] but the following lines are a fair example. 'Thus says the Lord . . . who is putting down the mighty from their seats and exalting them of low degree . . . Behold, I, the eternal God, the Lord of Hosts . . . am coming to level in good earnest . . . Your gold and silver, though you can't see it, is cankered, the rust of them is a witness against you, and suddenly, because of the eternal God, my self, it is the dreadful day of judgment, says the Lord . . .'[4] Coppe tucks on to this last passage a reference to the Epistle of St. James the Apostle, v, 1–7 (or rather 1–8): 'Go to

[1] In this sense also Underwood, loc. cit., p. 83.

[2] Gooch, loc. cit., p. 127.

[3] Cohn, loc. cit., pp. 357 et seq.

[4] Ibid., pp. 360, 361, 365.

now, ye rich men . . . You have stored up to yourselves wrath against the last days . . . The coming of the Lord is at hand.'

It is not so much the interpenetration of the social and the religious elements, however, which concerns us here – we have seen that at every step which we have taken – as the focusing of expectations on one point of time, and that a point of time in the immediate future. The 'Men-Levellers', i.e. the Sectaries, Coppe says, are but shadows of 'that mighty Leveller . . . the eternal God . . .', 'shadows of most terrible, yet great and glorious good things to come'[1] – the shadows to which he refers are those which the events are already casting before them. While the word 'Ranter' has no millenarian implication, the name 'Fifth Monarchy Man' has. It is a reference to the Prophecy of Daniel (especially II, 36–44): there will, in all, be five kingdoms, the last being the Kingdom of God. The four earlier ones – symbolized by gold, silver, brass and a mixture of iron and clay respectively – have crumbled already. This is especially true of the last, the colossus with feet of clay, the rule and realm of Charles I. Therefore, the day of fulfilment is dawning . . . Just as the interlude at Münster would not have been possible without its adventist background, so the two rebellions of Harrison and Venner had as their indispensable historical precondition, their releasing element, the mood summed up in the title of John Rogers's pamphlet of 1653–4, *Domesday Drawing Nigh*.

While Coppe's *Fiery Flying Roll* and the attempted *coup d'état* of the Fifth Monarchy Men show us a mixture of social rebelliousness and religious exaltation in which the former ingredient clearly predominates, the case of the Quaker leader James Nayler presents the two elements in a different combination, with the religious form covering and all but hiding the social content. Yet even Nayler's conduct – culminating with his entry into Bristol riding on an ass, with his followers running ahead, waving boughs, spreading garments and shouting hosanna – sprang from the same root, the same mood. When all was over and Nayler had to defend himself before the Puritan authorities, horrified at what they could not but regard as rank blasphemy, he said: 'I do abhor that any of that honour which is due to God should be given to me as I am a creature. But it pleased the Lord to set me up as a sign of the coming of the righteous One.' This, too, was revolutionary

[1] Ibid., p. 360.

propaganda clad in adventist clothes, or rather conceived and expressed in adventist terms. This, too, was aggressiveness inspired by the idea that the end of the world was imminent. And we need not doubt that the gruesome punishment meted out to the unhappy man – standing at the pillory, branding at the forehead, and, worst of all, boring through the tongue – was meant as much to hit Nayler the enemy of law and order, the enemy at least of that political pacification which Cromwell had achieved with so much difficulty, as Nayler the adjudged enemy of God. It was part and parcel of that same sullen but undaunted apocalyptic rebelliousness when another Quaker, Robert Rich, stepped forward and fixed above James Nayler's head a sign with the legend: 'This is the King of the Jews.'[1] (The sorry scene is preserved for posterity by the pencil of a supreme master draughtsman, Wenceslaus Hollar.)[2] Rich, like Nayler, felt that Cromwell - according to Cary's pamphlet of 1651 the 'little horn' of the beast of the Revelation, whose 'doom and downfall' was impending – would soon, perhaps tomorrow, perhaps today! be dead and done, while they and their Friends would presently be exalted by the power of the Almighty, their brother in righteousness, and it was this conviction, this eternal delusion of the millenarian mind, which induced them to demonstrate defiance as they did. The difference and distance between Harrison and Venner on the one hand, Nayler and Rich on the other, was not so great at the time as would appear in retrospect.

A short sideglance at Russia is in order here. We have seen that the Molokane were a sect particularly given to millenarian ideas. Their founder Semyon Uklein re-enacted Palm Sunday at Tambov under Catherine II as James Nayler had done at Bristol in the days of the Commonwealth.[3] Like produces like, and logic is everywhere the same. Christ is in me, or I am Christ, said both the Russian and the Englishman. Christ is sure to descend again, they reasoned, His Second Coming is due; hence if I come, He comes. The syllogism will not, of course, stand up to critical examination; both the major and the minor premises of it are muddy, so to

[1] Braithwaite, loc. cit., pp. 244, et seq., esp. pp. 251, 252, 256, 266.

[2] Cf. Parthey, G., *Wenzel Hollar, Beschreibendes Verzeichnis seiner Kupferstiche*, Berlin 1853, pp. 119 and 120, number 568. (Hollar's authorship is not accepted by all experts.)

[3] Cf. Conybeare, loc. cit., p. 318.

speak. But our formulation may help to explain what went on in these men's minds, and why they acted as they did.

What sped, or perhaps even started, James Nayler on his road to disaster was his acquaintance with a number of overwrought women, notably Martha Simmonds, more millenarian still than her husband Thomas and her brother Giles Calvert. This woman saw herself in the role of the Sunamitess who befriended Eliseus and was in turn befriended by him (IV Kings IV, 8 et seq.): 'And she came and fell at his feet and worshipped upon the ground . . .' (verse 37). Martha tried her adoration on both Fox and Nayler, but while Nayler accepted it (not as James Nayler, to be sure, but as Christ, or a Christ, or a harbinger of Christ, or as host to Christ in his soul: poor man, he never could make up his mind what it was),[1] Fox rebuffed her in his usual forthright but bluff, blunt and brutal manner.[2] This has led to the assertion that in the two leading Quakers we behold above all two contrasting psychological types: in Nayler the enthusiast, the fanatic, if not indeed a psychopath; in Fox the man of reason, the man of self-control, a sound and sober leader. There is no need to quarrel with this assessment, but in our present context another facet of the contrast should be moved into the foreground: Nayler represented an earlier, Fox a later phase of the sect movement. True, they were contemporaries rather than members of succeeding generations: but the difference lies not in the dates; it lies in the attitudes; and Nayler was still filled with that millenarianism which is a feature of the first stages of sect development, whereas Fox was already to some extent reconciled to the necessity of living permanently in a hostile world.

Since the days of Fox and Nayler, society in general has become a great deal more rationalistic, but the irrationality of millenarianism has remained a distinguishing mark of sectarian groups in the narrower, the narrowest, sense of the word. Such contemporary movements as the Christadelphians, the Pentecostalists, the Elimites and the Jehovah's Witnesses (not to speak of the Adventists in the official sense of the word) show it in full bloom. *Who are the Christadelphians?* the founder, Dr. John Thomas, asked; and he answered that they are 'a people prepared for the Lord' and 'living in the period of the sixth vial in which Christ will appear again'. 'From the evidences of the Scriptures and from the signs of the times, it is believed that the second advent of Jesus is now

[1] Cf. Knox, loc. cit., pp. 164–6.

[2] Braithwaite, loc. cit., pp. 244–7.

imminent, and that his return will precede the establishment of God's kingdom on earth,' so Wilson has summed up the doctrine for us. 'As a preliminary to this development the Jews will be gathered to their traditional homeland and Jerusalem will be rebuilt to become the throne of Jesus and capital city of the earth.' It is easy to see what strength a hope of this kind would draw from the establishment of the State of Israel, its successes and even its perils: things were shaping as they should. Nevertheless, even here a second phase which abandons, to all intents and purposes, the millenarian attitude, can be seen alongside the first which upholds it: 'Some shift of emphasis has occurred on this subject in recent years among Christadelphians,' Dr. Wilson has to report. 'Some have recognized a more "devotional" tendency in the movement.'[1] There is more patient prayer than concentration on an immediate prospect. 'Watch the coffin lids fly open,' an Elimite exclaimed in 1925; and another declared in 1944 that that year might be 'the year of the great out-calling and up-taking', when Christ would appear in the upper air and his saints would be caught up to him. 'How long?' the writer asked, and he answered: 'Perhaps today . . . Are we prepared for the skyward summons?'[2]

Among the Jehovah's Witnesses, the focus on the *finis* of history is so intense that, through the sect's propaganda, its apocalypticism has become common knowledge. There is no need to follow Russel or Rutherford into the mazes of their Bible mathematics. Suffice it to say that the years 1914, 1918 and 1925 wese successively declared to be the dates of the end. *Millions of People now Living will never Die*, was the title of a book by Rutherford published in 1920, and in it he asserted: 'In 1925 we can expect to witness the return of Abraham, Isaac, Jacob and other stalwarts of the Old Testament.' What is particularly interesting in this case is the persistence of the millenarian condition of mind even after 1925: like Lévy-Bruhl's *mentalité primitive*, the millenarian mentality, too, is obviously *imperméable à l'expérience*. In *Hell*, his last book, Rutherford had indeed to assume, as already Russell had done, that the Second Coming had already taken place and had been spiritual, i.e. invisible. Yet he could write: 'All things are fulfilled in our day, testifying that the Lord Jesus is present and that his kingdom has come. The resurrection of the dead will

[1] Wilson, loc. cit., pp. 219, 226, 227; cf. also 230–5.

[2] Ibid., pp. 25–7, 114: cf. also p. 107.

soon begin.'[1] Theologically, there may be a great difference between those who look forward to the apocalyptic day and those who claim that it is over and that they are looking back upon it; sociologically, the difference is not so great. Few groups have emphasized more clearly and consistently than the Shakers that 'they were living in the beginning of the millenium'; or that that 'to which people had so long looked forward had already taken place'; yet even they had the belief 'that they would soon leave behind this world of the flesh'.[2]

Far more pertinent for the sociologist is the question as to whether we can find sects in which the millenarian element is totally absent, and while no assured general answer can be given, one or two cases of major groupings in which it is said to be underdeveloped may be tried and tested. What about Christian Science, supposedly a movement of those who merely wish to enjoy the good things of this earth and thus will hardly clamour to see it come to a close? The answer is given by Mrs. Eddy herself: 'It is authentically said that one expositor of Daniel's dates fixed the year 1866 or 1867 for the return of Christ . . . It is a marked coincidence that those dates were the first two years of my discovery of Christian Science,' she writes in one context, and in another context she remarks: 'some modern exegesis on the prophetic Scriptures cites 1875 as the year of the second coming of Christ. In that year the Christian Science textbook, *Science and Health with Key to the Scriptures*, was first published.'[3] Shades of James Nayler! shades of Ann Lee, the self-styled She-Jesus! Augusta Stetson, we are told, 'took Mrs. Eddy wholly seriously and literally,' when she made her veiled claims,[4] and so, no doubt, did countless other adherents.

The crucial case, however, is not Christian Science, but Methodism, and Niebuhr has asserted that it 'was far removed in its moral temper from the churches of the disinherited in the sixteenth and seventeenth century . . . The difference lay in the substitution of individual ethics and philanthropism for social ethics and millenarianism'.[5] The statement, as it stands, is difficult to accept. True, Methodism – a mass movement, not a petty conventicle; a movement whose perscution was relatively mild; a

[1] Cf. Algermissen, loc. cit., pp. 78, 79, 83, 84, 87, 88.

[2] Melcher, loc. cit., p. 155.

[3] Dakin, loc. cit., p. 334.

[4] Ibid. Cf. also Wlson, loc. cit., p. 331.

[5] Niebuhr, loc. cit., p. 65.

movement, too, with many master-craftsmen in it who might yet hope to make good – was not on the extreme left, so far as millenarianism was concerned. Yet it *was* millenarian all the same, Niebuhr's assertion and authority notwithstanding. Niebuhr can hardly have heard of what Knox has called 'the ravings of poor George Bell'. This Bell, characterized by the Wesleyan historian J. S. Simon as 'a man of piety, of deep communion with God, and of extraordinary zeal', was yet something of a thorn in John Wesley's side. He showed all the hallmarks of a typical fanatic and vividly recalls some of the early Quaker extremists. The perfect, he taught, were holier than Adam before his fall, and, unlike him, they were not in danger of falling; they were not in need of self-examination nor yet of instruction by others; and so on. Wesley was dismayed even by Bell's outward conduct in prayer: his and his friends' 'postures and gestures were highly indecent', Wesley told his *Journal*. 'When Bell tried, unsuccessfully, to cure a woman of blindness, no special publicity attached to the incident,' Knox relates. But 'it was otherwise when he confidently announced the end of the world for 28 February 1763'. An outbreak of millenarianism was thus initiated.

The outbreak was not of minor proportions as can be seen from the fact that the Methodist leaders immediately intervened to contain the craze. Lady Huntingdon hurried post-haste to London 'to endeavour to stop the plague by every means in her power'; Wesley preached on the critical day a sermon on the text: Prepare to meet thy God, and showed how absurd it was to expect the end of the world in twenty-four hours. But for once his words did not find their mark. 'Notwithstanding all I could say,' Wesley admits, 'many were afraid to go to bed, and some wandered about in the fields, being persuaded that, if the world did not end, at least London would be swallowed up by an earthquake.' Bell and not Wesley determined, on this occasion, the mood of the crowd, as is evident from the action of the authorities: they locked Bell up, for he was too dangerous an influence to be at large.

The last lines might conceivably suggest that millenarianism only touched the fringe of the Methodist movement, while its core was not affected by it. But this was not in fact so. Discussing the hubbub of 28 February 1763, Knox expresses himself as follows, and we would accept his judgement: 'It is fair to say, though the fact has been generally overlooked, that for this development Wesley himself may have been remotely to blame. All enthusiastic movements, in their effort to detach people from worldliness, are apt to talk the language of chiliasm; and there must have been some ground for the charge, even made by so unreliable a critic as Bishop Lavington, that Wesley in early days was heard to speak as if the coming of Christ was now at hand.'[1] Even this comparative rationalist was irrational enough to fancy that the end of everything was near; what then should we think of his followers, enthusiasts of the purest water? Bell was a symptom, not a freak, a typical figure of the movement's – any sect movement's – first days.

In the important book to which we alluded a little while ago, *The Social Sources of Denominationalism*, Niebuhr has suggested that the decay of sects, their loss of revolutionary tension, is due mainly to the inevitable succession of the generations. 'The sociological character of sectarianism,' he writes, 'is almost always modified in the course of time by the natural processes of birth and death, and on this change in structure [or rather in membership] changes in doctrine and ethics inevitably follow. By its very nature the sectarian type of organization is valid only for one generation. The children born to the voluntary members of the first generation make the sect a church long before they have arrived at the years of discretion . . . Rarely does a second generation hold the convictions it has inherited with a fervour equal to that of its fathers, who fashioned these convictions in the heat of conflict and at the risk of martyrdom.'[2] There is much truth in this assertion. It is very difficult for parents to infect their children with the enthusiasms which they feel, and many a religious man's or woman's life has become unhappy because of the lukewarmness, if not indifference or even hostility, of a son or daughter to their dear-won and dearly-held faith. Nevertheless, Niebuhr has not put his finger on the prime reason for the invariably downward development of the typical sect.

That reason lies in the very nature of the phenomenon of sectarianism, not in a secondary feature like the change of the names on the membership roll. Cool words cannot convey the heat of the sectarian mentality, yet without realizing its intensity we cannot possibly hope to understand why it does not last. The tension simply cannot be continued for long: the conflict of the

[1] Knox, loc. cit., pp. 545 and 546.
[2] Niebuhr, loc. cit., pp. 19 and 20.

sect with society must be solved somehow, for it is an acute crisis which cannot be turned into a lasting state. Millenarianism, with restriction of the future to the few days or months ahead, is the credal expression of this underlying and overpowering impatience, of this conviction that either there is victory soon, or disappointment and defeat are inevitable. Once it is realized that victory is unattainable – and this means (as a dissenting group can hardly ever hope to prevail by its own strength), once it is obvious that divine intervention, the fulfilment of the apocalyptic prophecies, is not going to take place – the sect finds itself before an inescapable dilemma: it must either withdraw from society or learn to live with it. Differently expressed, this means that either the unbearable tension must further increase until the breaking point is reached, or it must decrease until the differences with established society are so mild as to make pacific co-existence possible. If the latter alternative is chosen, the end of the road is *de facto* integration; but then, by definition, we have no longer a dissenting group; we have instead a denomination, a religious body distinct in name rather than in fact from the mainstream of contemporary life.

ISSUES OF THE CONFLICT OF SECT AND SOCIETY

(A) ANNIHILATION

If a sect is to have a choice between withdrawal from the surrounding society or adjustment to it, it must, logically, first reach the point of decision, the crucial moment at which continuance of the prevailing tension in its unresolved state is unbearable and unthinkable. Most sects do reach this impasse, but a few do not: before they can do it, they are wiped out by the forces which they have challenged and cannot overcome. Such was the fate of the Fifth Monarchy Men in the seventeenth century; such, too, was the fate of the Adamites in the fifteenth and that of the Oneida Community in the nineteenth century. And, in Germany at least, the Jehovah's Witnesses escaped physical extinction in this century only through the defeat of their cruel enemies, Hitler's Gestapo, on the battlefields of the Second World War. If the system had been in the saddle much longer, none of the *Ernste Bibelforscher* (the German sobriquet of the sect) would have been left to tell the tale.

By annihilation, we do not, and need not, mean the murder of every member (or even of any member) of the sect: in the case of the Oneida Community, nobody was physically hurt and, indeed, formally the group still exists as those who look at silverware advertisements in America are sure to know. What is extinguished is the community, not its personnel. Perhaps forcible dissolution is the term which best fits the facts: when we say an army has been annihilated, we mean just this, we mean that it is dispersed and has ceased to count and to act as a collective unit. We have seen already that many Fifth Monarchy Men reappeared in the Quaker Meetings. What had been broken was merely the Fifth Monarchy movement, the little band of fighters that made a desperate stand on 6 January 1661 ('Venner's Insurrection') and was beaten once and for all. Yet, in this case there *was* mass destruction: no quarter was given during the street fighting and afterwards the leaders at least were all beheaded. The remnants that joined forces with George Fox were the marginal men of the Fifth Monarchy movement, not its core, which had been liquidated, as Himmler would have said – vaporized, as Orwell liked to express it.

Very similar was the end of the Adamites, and also of the Picards, of Bohemia. In 1420, a great wave of millenarianism went over the country. God, it was said, would presently send his heavenly hosts to help his own. The wicked world would be wiped out and only five cities, refuges of the saints, would be spared. When nothing happened, many returned to their normal mode of life, while the militants organized themselves for a protracted war against the national foe. A small group, however, developed along its own peculiar lines towards antinomianism. God *had* come, they asserted; His kingdom *had* been established; and those who had joined it were no longer under the law of sin. They were like the new Adam, Christ Himself, or like the old Adam before he fell – *perfecti*. The Taborite majority, Protestant and puritanical in outlook, was horrified and decided to make short work of the Adamites. Their general Žižka sent a force far outnumbering the hapless extremists: those who did not perish in battle were dispatched afterwards. It is unlikely that many or even any escaped with their lives. Žižka, no doubt, thought that he was merely cutting a cancerous growth from the body of his nation, and if only a tenth of the stories current about the conduct of these people was true, he had the right to take drastic action. But he dealt no more kindly with the contemporary Picards. This group is less easy to characterize than the Adamites. They seem to have been inclined towards rationalism rather than the irrationalism of the antinomians. Not dangerous men, to all appearances: but soon condemned men, in spite of it. The Picard leader Martinek Houska shared the fate of Hus: he was burnt at the stake – burnt, however, not by the Germans or Catholics, but by the Hussites, who clearly did not accept the saying of Marcus Aurelius that the best revenge one can take on one's enemies is not to become like them. Houska's martyrdom was merely the curtain-raiser to the martyrdom of his followers. There was a mass massacre of them at the behest of Jan Žižka, as there had been of the Adamites before.

The case of the Oneida Community, needless to say, was by comparison a comedy rather than a tragedy: it had more farce than force in it. But we should make no mistake: the outraged neighbours of the settlement were grimly determined that it should disappear from the face of the earth. For reasons which lie deep in history, three unconnected but parallel outbreaks of antinomianism–perfectionism occurred between 1830 and 1840: one in East Prussia led by Johann Wilhelm Ebel; one in Wales and England, led by Henry James Prince; one in America, near Lake Oneida, led by John Humphrey Noyes. Noyes, after his conversion which occurred in 1831 in the course of a revival campaign, attended the Andover Theological College where a Professor Moses Stuart propounded a curious interpretation of the seventh chapter of St. Paul's Epistle to the Romans. According to Stuart, the inner conflict of man revealed there – 'I with the mind serve the law of God, but with the flesh the law of sin' – was characteristic only of the unconverted, but not of the Christian. Noyes soon declared that he could discover in himself no feeling of guilt, no sense of sin – an attitude that was theologically underpinned by the doctrine that the Second Coming had taken place, unnoticed, in A.D. 70, so that the world, without realizing it, was in fact living in the Kingdom of God. A local movement along these lines formed in the village of Manlius in 1834. 'Spiritual unions' were established between males and females from whom the burden of evil had been lifted: chastity, so it was asserted, being preserved. On the latter point there existed (to say the least) grave misgivings on the part of those who still believed in the sinfulness of human nature, and one day two of the awakened were tarred and feathered. Noyes himself returned about this time to his childhood home at Putney in Vermont where he founded a community which, step by step, advanced in the direction of communism (in the widest sense of the word). After a while hostility began to thicken against the group and insiders as well as outsiders came to feel that the limit of toleration at Putney was reached, as it had been some time before at Manlius. The Perfectionists around Noyes then fled to another state, namely New York, where their prophet founded a settlement at Oneida Creek around 1848.

This settlement was soon rumoured to be the scene of extraordinary goings on. The least objectionable, to the community at large, was an experiment in eugenics: a superior generation was to be bred by the mating of older men with young girls. More objectionable was the practice of 'male continence', i.e. *coitus interruptus*, by those who did not feel like having offspring just then. Up-state New Yorkers did not like this policy at all, and liked propaganda for it even less. But what incensed them most was the system of 'complex marriage' which Noyes had instituted for the pure ones of his community. Already in 1837 a Philadelphia paper, *The Battle Axe*, had printed (without his permission) a private letter from his pen which revealed his idea on the proper sex relations in a circle of *perfecti*: it was a sort of sex communism. 'The marriage supper of the Lamb is a feast at which every dish is free to every guest. Exclusiveness, jealousy, quarrelling, have no place there . . . I call a certain woman my wife; she is yours, she . . . is the bride of all the saints.' At Oneida, this idea was made a reality (though there were some safeguards against extreme promiscuity).

This was more than the neighbours of the Oneida Community were prepared to allow. The Presbyterian Synod of Central New York mounted a major attack, but proved unable to bring the community to an end. Much had happened since the tarring and feathering in 1834: it was now 1874 or thereabouts; due process of law had replaced earlier, more direct methods of social control. Finally, a Professor Mears of Hamilton College organized a propaganda drive against the nest of free love and succeeded in convincing a fair proportion of the inmates that there were errors in their ways. Noyes fled to Canada and, on 20 August 1879, suggested 'that we give up the practice of complex marriage, not as renouncing belief in the principles and prospective finality of that institution, but in deference to the public sentiment which is evidently rising against it'. And so it was done. The industrial workshops which the movement had built up became the property of a joint-stock company called 'Oneida Community, Limited'. The communist duckling developed into a capitalist swan, or, as some might prefer to say, the communist swan developed into a capitalist duckling. Either way: the sect was dead; it had committed suicide, though a suicide remarkably free from pain. We have here a particularly gentle form of sect annihilation.[1]

If the winding-up of the Oneida Community shows democracy at its best, the treatment of the Jehovah's Witnesses in Germany during the Hitler years shows dictatorship at its worst. The very names given by the S.S. guards to these dissenters reveal something of the intense hatred with which they were regarded by their enemies: bible worms, sky comedians, heavenly dogs . . . 'The National Socialist régime set out from the start to exterminate the sect,' Algermissen recalls, 'and many of its members were arrested and murdered or thrown into concentration camps.'[2] By the end of 1937, Buchenwald alone had over 450 inmates from the ranks of the *Bibelforscher*. Algermissen's words must not be taken to mean that there was an essential difference between being thrown into concentration camps and being murdered. At Buchenwald, reprisals were taken against the Witnesses when they refused, on principle, to surrender clothing for use on the eastern front. They had to work in the open without underwear and wearing wooden clogs instead of shoes until after dark, the day being New Year's Day, 1942, when the temperature was well under freezing-point. The consequences can be imagined. At Sachsenhausen, a few selected Witnesses were asked to 'volunteer' for the fighting forces. They refused, and for every refusal ten Witnesses were shot.[3] Most of the *Bibelforscher* were from Lutheran Silesia and Saxony – states with a religious (caesaropapist) establishment and hence prone to the formation and proliferation of sects. When the Soviet forces occupied these territories, many Witnesses were driven out and had to seek refuge in the West. Victims of aggression in their old homes, they turned aggressors as soon as they arrived in their new ones. Numerous are the complaints of their

[1] Cf. Knox, loc. cit., p. 566 et seq., and Holloway, loc. cit., p. 178 et seq.

[2] Algermissen, loc. cit., p. 91.

[3] Whalen, loc. cit., pp. 141–3.

neighbours about their methods of proselytizing, and their own year-book of 1948 boasted that the 'Torchbearers of the Kingdom' had 'scared', and 'disturbed the slumbers of', the religious leaders in the 'districts where no ray of divine truth had penetrated within living memory'.[1] A sect is and remains a conflict society while it is and remains a sect.

(B) WITHDRAWAL

When a man who is used to systematic modes of thinking approaches the study of the developments which fall under this heading, he feels a spontaneous tendency to distinguish 'voluntary' from 'enforced' withdrawals. Such a distinction would be meaningless, however, an empty exercise in paper logic. If a case of emigration, for instance, looks at first sight like a purely voluntary action, a closer inspection of the circumstances will invariably reveal that it was prompted, at least in part, by gentle, or even not so gentle, social pressures. If, on the other hand, it seems that a dissenting group is loath to go, if it puts up some resistance to the attempts to drive it out, the final expulsion is usually greeted with relief. This is so not only because now all fears are at an end, but also because there has been, from the beginning, underneath the apparent unwillingness to abandon the host society, a true willingness to be rid of it, to contract out of its wickedness, filth and corruption. It is not a paradox to say that sect and society, antagonistic in all other respects, are agreed on one point, namely that their ways should part. This is, indeed, a necessary agreement: the dissenter is the alienated man *par excellence*. If he emigrates, he merely draws the last logical conclusion from his whole attitude. And if he is expelled, the case is in truth the same: the conclusion is then drawn, not by him, but for him. Society seems to be saying (though it says it often not in words, but in deeds, by tarring and feathering and throwing stones or burning houses and such demonstrations whose import it is impossible not to understand): you cannot live with us; all right, don't; go; this is what both of us really want.

The distinction between voluntary and enforced withdrawals is thus impossible to implement, and hence is unable to help us in our search for a more systematic view of the phenomena here to

[1] Algermissen, loc. cit., p. 92.

be considered. However, that between partial and total withdrawals is obviously more realistic, and hence also more easily applicable to the historical material. The Shakers put an ocean three thousand miles in width between themselves and their erstwhile neighbours; the early Quakers dug in their heels, stayed where they were, and fought out their battle for survival at home: the contrast seems to be clear, and something can be made of it. It is also possible to distinguish, within partial withdrawals such as that of the first generation Quakers, several sub-varieties: it is one thing to say, we shall not interdine with those outside our circle; it is another thing to say, we shall not intermarry with the world, however fair its daughters may be; it is yet a third thing to say, we shall not interchange goods and services with the devil's children and helpmates. The decision not to appeal to the law courts is less radical than the decision not even to use current coin and legal tender: the former form of withdrawal is more partial, the latter more total, and a scale of relative partiality and relative totality of withdrawal could perhaps be elaborated. But this would be an effort hardly worth the trouble, because in the end even this whole distinction proves problematical, as we shall see. There have been sects which have left their society and yet stayed within their country. Internal emigration is a contradiction in terms according to paper logic, but life has produced several instances of it, notably the Russian Stranniky (see page 258 et seq).

It is extremely difficult to draw a clear line of demarcation even between partial and total withdrawal as can be seen from the fact that what is in one sense the mildest and most partial form of it, is in another sense the most radical and total. We have in mind what might be called mental emigration, as instanced for example by the Jehovah's Witnesses. These people, truly alienated from the parent society, have – quite logically – claimed the status of aliens for themselves. 'Since Jehovah has chosen his witnesses out of the world to be ambassadors in behalf of his kingdom to the peoples of the earth, they are no part of this world,' they argue in *Let God be True* (1946). They continue: 'As their allegiance is to the Most High God and his kingdom, they do not take part in local, national or international elections or politics.' And: 'An ambassador of a foreign power is by the laws of this world exempted as an alien from giving allegiance to the government of the land in which he is resident. He is relieved of rendering political obligations of any sort. The nation where he resides is without authority to impose any regulation that burdens or abridges his performing duty as such.' As can be seen, the word 'ambassador' is not used in a metaphorical or metaphysical, but in a literal and legal meaning. Rightly does W. J. Whalen, who quotes these sentences, characterize Judge Rutherford's policy in another context as follows: 'In a sense, his role in the Witnesses paralleled that of Brigham Young in Mormonism. Answering inquirers as he pushed West, Young had only one explanation for the Mormon exodus: "To get away from the United States and the Christians". The frontier was gone. Judge Rutherford nevertheless led his followers into the wilderness of the Theocracy. They became strangers in the lands of their birth, men without a country, Philip Nolans.'[1]

The parallel here drawn between Brigham Young who withdrew into the wilderness and Joseph Rutherford who did not, might appear exaggerated, but it is substantially valid. 'Association in a social way with those outside the truth is dangerous,' the Witnesses are warned in *Make Sure of all Things*, and many acted accordingly. 'They withdrew from most secular contacts such as active Union membership, P.T.A.s, social clubs, lodges.' In a word, 'Witnesses try to isolate themselves and their families from all contamination by the world, Satan's world'.[2] It would be no good saying that these men emigrated 'merely' mentally: the word merely would be curiously misapplied in a statement of this kind.

The Christadelphians, as Bryan Wilson has so ably described them, were a proletarian group, whose standard of living was entirely dependent on the success of Trade Unionism. Yet, in their anxiety not to 'soil the wedding garment', abstention from this very movement was enjoined on the brethren: one must not be 'yoked with unbelievers', as a particularly striking formula expressed it. 'We do consider the brethren of Christ are on doubtful if not forbidden ground when they are identified with Trades Unions,' announced a resolution passed by a branch in the industrial north of England. 'We therefore advise brethren to stand aloof from these altogether.' Fraternal organizations like the Odd Fellows were also condemned; insurance plans, on the other hand, were not. The idea is obvious and the attitude consistent: human contacts are to be minimized, but a business deal is not a

[1] Whalen, loc. cit., pp. 165, 166, 67. [2] Ibid., pp. 195, 63, 20.

human contact. It does not commit the soul and therefore will not soil it.[1]

The Christadelphians are a particularly low-class sect: but what about the Christian Scientists, also studied in Dr. Wilson's volume, whom he regards as a particularly high-class sect? Do we observe any flight from the world in their case? Not according to Dr. Wilson; but Mrs. Eddy's biographer, E. F. Dakin, had a different idea. Mrs. Eddy, he writes, 'created for herself a unique universe . . . She created it after finding herself in complete conflict with the world in which her fellows moved by norms that were utterly at variance with her own nature . . . She . . . designed and built a little enclosure of her own . . . Had Mrs. Eddy taken ship from her own isolated island and returned to the world known to the majority of men, she might possibly have been classed as a paranoiac. But Mrs. Eddy never returned. She lived and moved and reigned in isolated state, building herself an empire and eventually attracting, from among passers-by, visitors who stopped off and remained to be ruled . . . Since she not only tamed her wilderness, but attracted to her novel empire many others willing to give her fealty, the world can well recognize her unique achievement . . . For few individuals who have found themselves utterly at variance with all other men, have ever succeeded in going forth and establishing, apart from the rest of humanity, a world of their own design'.[2] Dakin does not draw a parallel between Mary Ann Morse Baker and Brigham Young, as Whalen does between Brigham Young and Joseph Rutherford; but there is hardly any need to spell out the parallel – it is obvious from Dakin's subtle (and very true) observations. Christian Science, no less than Christadelphianism, no less than Rutherford's Watchtower, presents a case of mental emigration.

Mental emigration, of course, though it creates an encapsulated condition, is not itself an easily contained principle. On the contrary: it tends to break out in all directions and leads to various forms of physical separation. The two most important directions recall the walls of isolation which separate a caste from other castes: the bans on intermarriage and interdining.

The ban on intermarriage appears with great regularity whenever a sect in the true sense of the word has been formed. John Smyth told his Baptists that wedlock with an unbeliever could not

[1] Wilson, loc. cit., pp. 284–6. [2] Dakin, loc. cit., pp. 452 and 453.

be regarded as allowable.[1] Among the Quakers, it long led to disownment,[2] and it is estimated that in America alone this hard regulation may have halved the number of Friends which otherwise would have been collected. Up to 1804, the penalty among American Methodists for taking a spouse from the ranks of 'unawakened persons' was expulsion.[3] And so on down the long list of dissenting groups. Sects have invariably remembered the words of the Apostle (II Corinthians IV, 14): 'Bear not the yoke with unbelievers. For . . . what fellowship has light with darkness?' In 1961, Wilson found this sentiment still alive in the Elim movement, and also among the Christadelphians. Marriage with an outsider, declared a resolution of the important Birmingham branch of the latter movement, is 'an offence against the law of Christ' and 'those who maintain the contrary are unfit for fellowship'. This is apparently no dead letter: 'Christadelphians maintain the rule of endogamy well,' the contemporary observer remarks, 'and those who break it, are almost certain to be excommunicated'. Christadelphian 'disfellowshipping' is thus identical with Quaker 'disownment'.[4]

In the matter of interdining, it is important to remember, first of all, that the central rite of all Christian groupings, whether sectarian or not, is some form of a eucharistic meal, whatever the name by which it is known – Breaking the Bread, or Love Feast, or the Lord's Supper, etc. Any sharing of the table with unbelievers on these supremely sacred occasions is, of course, out of the question; it would be a desecration of the first order. But while Catholics or Anglicans or Russian Orthodox do not extend this restriction of commensality to ordinary meals, many sectarians have a desire to do so if it is at all possible. On 14 June 1962, the *Guardian* carried the following report: 'Members of a sect of Exclusive Brethren – an extremist group among the hundred thousand [Plymouth] Brethren in Britain – were said yesterday to be leaving the movement in thousands because of new decrees forbidding them to have any social contact with members of their own families or relatives who are not members . . . A Manchester family, members of the London Brethren, have sent a circular

[1] Underwood, loc. cit., p. 42. Cf. also p. 124.

[2] Hinshaw, D., *Rufus Jones; Master Quaker,* New York 1951, pp. 30 and 38.

[3] Cameron, loc. cit., p. 105.

[4] Wilson, loc. cit., p. 292. Cf. also pp. 293, 309, 310, 336 and (*re* Elim) 92.

letter to relatives asking them in the future not even to send greeting cards to them . . . Some members of the Exclusive Brethren have in the past relinquished official posts and membership of professional bodies because they felt unable to associate in any way with people who did not share their beliefs. The Close Brethren in Peterhead, Scotland, operate their own fishing boats, and will not dine with people of other faiths.'

The transition from a refusal to interdine ritually to a refusal to interdine in any shape or form is very easy, because all meals may, in the eyes of the sect, assume the character of sacredness. An example is the practice of Father Divine's hotel-heavens. Banquets have figured very prominently in this so-called Peace Mission movement. They are eating for the sake of sustenance, yet they are also eating in the presence of divinity. Outsiders are not necessarily excluded, nor need insiders take all their food at the common table. But the fact remains that the taking of ordinary nourishment is here suffused with the light of sacredness and thus a further step towards the division between in-group and out-group is effected.

The extremely interesting report from Peterhead in Scotland which we have just quoted shows how mental encapsulation may lead to economic encapsulation – encapsulation in consumption and production. But we need not go to a tiny sectlet in a small township in the remote north to observe the tendency, we can see it on a large and wide scale in the majestic Methodist movement (which shows, once again, how wrong it is to regard this movement as a particularly mild form of sectarianism). 'As the Moravians tried to preserve their own culture by banding together in local settlements,' Ronald Knox recalls, 'so Wesley would make a world of his own, but it should be decentralized in a thousand little towns all over England . . . Wesley was unashamedly a retailer; his societies formed a kind of co-operative movement . . . They were to deal for preference at one another's shops . . . It was all part of his scheme to make them not merely a church within the church, but a nation within the nation; a sort of enclave, not only in their piety, but in daily life.'[1] While this looked as if it were to become a case of isolation in consumption, the following quotation shows us an incipient instance of isolation in production: 'In 1901, Pobedonostsev [the Procurator of the Holy Synod] wrote to the Minister of Internal Affairs to complain of the activities of Ivan

[1] Knox, loc. cit., pp. 449 and 448.

Roslavlev, who, he said, was spreading Stundism. Pobedonostsev said that this man was steward on a large estate, and that he refused to rent land or to give employment to Orthodox peasants, while he helped his own people greatly. The governor of Kharkov reported that this was true . . .'[1]

The Stundists had a built-in tendency towards communism of production, and indeed communism in general; so much so that they are sometimes numbered among the precursors and path-breakers of the Soviet régime. But John Wesley, too, was playing with the idea of communism, and this proves once more how mental emigration tends to draw total emigration behind it. One of Wesley's *confidants* was Richard Viney who recorded in his diary, on 22 February 1744, this about his illustrious friend: 'He told me of an intention he and some few have of beginning a community of goods . . . Each is to bring what cash they have and put it together. If any owe small debts, they are first to be paid. Then each abiding in their dwellings and following their business as they do now, are to bring weekly what they earn and put into the common box, out of which they are again to receive weekly as much as is thought necessary to maintain their families, without reflecting whether they put much or little into the box.'[2]

Viney calls this 'a plan which I told him I doubted could not succeed'. What he meant was that it could not succeed without *total* withdrawal from contemporary life, without physical emigration, and he was right. When encapsulation is driven forward to the length of communism, the moment arrives when all perceive that it is better (to put it mildly) to pack up and go away. Wesley was soon weaned from day-dreams of communism or co-operation. As Cameron says in another context, if there was creeping socialism in the Methodist camp, it was creeping out rather than creeping in.[3] But other sects were determined to realize their desires for a communal life, and in the pursuit of it they abandoned their old homes in order to seek new ones, far away, for instance, in the wilderness of America.

This brings us to the subject of sect migration, but before we finally turn to it, we have yet to consider the cases in which the encapsulation process ended, not in recourse to open withdrawal, but in the organization of secret societies. Sects like the Khlysty and the Skoptsy could not even flee the country, for – being classed

[1] Curtiss, loc. cit., p. 170. [2] Cit. Cameron, p. 70. [3] Ibid., p. 101.

as criminal – they could not come out from under cover: yet, submerged as they were, they were yet hounded and hunted. Their only hope lay in efficient concealment, and this in turn presupposed close control of the membership. In this way we get something comparable to gangsters' organizations, to mafias, to freemasonries at the time when freemasonry was still a fraternity beyond the pale of the law.

Basically, the Khlysty and the Skoptsy used three techniques to effect their flight into obscurity which was their specific form of withdrawal from general society: strict oaths of secrecy and supervision to ensure obedience to these oaths (what German writers, in an excellent but untranslatable term, call *Arkandisziplin*); concealment of their meeting-places, and especially of the approaches and entrances to them; and finally the systematic cultivation of hypocritical conduct with the aim of creating the impression that they were entirely conforming, model, citizens.

The very solemn oaths which Khlysty had to take when they entered the sect were characterized, first of all, by the long lists of guarantors of the undertaking which were invoked. Not only was the 'Holy Lifegiving and Indivisible Trinity' asked to witness the promise, but so was a whole array of angels and saints and, indeed, 'the ocean, rivers, lakes and springs'. Equally significant are the contingencies in which the candidate bound himself not to waver: knouting, imprisonment, exile and bloodletting, to which burning and the threat of block and axe were sometimes added. Long, too, is the list of persons *vis-à-vis* whom silence is to be observed: father, mother, relatives, the confessor (even in the case of a death-bed confession), even the 'moist earth', i.e. the grave, is mentioned as a possible receiver of confidences to whom a man must not open up – in short, everybody without exception. The whole Khlyst faith is covered by the oath, including, of course, the place of assembly and the goings-on therein. The end of the ceremony usually consisted in a conditional self-condemnation in case of treason; for instance: 'If I, a sinner, do not prove true to God's cause and do not persevere in God's ways, then, O Lord, bring me to fall in this world and in the world to come!' Or: 'If I betray the secret, may the earth cease to carry me and the sun to shine upon me!'[1]

The Khlyst meeting-places were as a rule underneath the houses

[1] Grass, loc. cit., vol. I, pp. 120, 124, 160, 333, 334, 335; vol. II, pp. 798–800.

of sect-members and thus not easily identified. Care was taken that discovery by means of the ear was as impossible as discovery by the eye: the singing and shouting which was part and parcel of the Khlyst round dance had to be deadened sufficiently to be inaudible outside the house. From the subterranean prayer-room secret passages were dug which led into the open only at some distance, for instance in the forest or in some wasteland. This was comparatively easy because the tendency of the sectarians was to settle on the very outskirts of their villages. Writing in 1906 (!), Grass reported that, according to rumour, the Khlysty had two 'naves' in St. Petersburg, the whereabouts of which were vaguely known. One was near the Moscow Gate, the other in a villa suburb. 'Still, attempts to track down their houses of worship have so far been unsuccessful.' Sometimes careful watch was kept in the whole neighbourhood to warn worshippers of the approach of possible persecutors, e.g. policemen; passwords, too, were in use, as were passports for the use of Skopets travellers. The Imperial Post Office was either not employed at all or only after well-thought-out precautions had been taken (secret signs, completion of messages through oral communications, etc.).[1]

The Khlysty did not bid their members to avoid the Orthodox sacraments such as confession and communion; on the contrary, participation under *reservatio mentalis* was recommended. Only this, it was felt, would throw their enemies off their trail. In some cases the sectarians went so far as to make sizeable contributions to official church funds. Grass even speaks of 'grandiose liberality': better to lose money than to lose everything . . . Schools, too, were frequented, though play with other children was discouraged. It was not least this systematic hypocrisy which incensed the average Russian against the heretics. The heretics, for their part, developed ideologies which justified their slyness: Did not Rahab the harlot deceive the authorities when she hid and saved the spies sent to Jericho by Joshua? And did not one Apostle praise her for her good work and another for her faith?[2] Did not Judith lie to Holofernes for the Lord's sake? Did the shepherd who misled the persecutors of Barbara the Martyr not do the same?[3]

[1] Ibid., vol. I, pp. 206, 498–501; vol. II, pp. 207, 879, 880–2.

[2] Joshua II, 1–21; VI, 17, 23, 25; James II, 25; Hebrews, XI, 31.

[3] Grass, loc. cit., vol. I, pp. 120, 502; vol. II, pp. 160, 161, 773, 774, 777, 782.

In view of the almost desperate situation of the criminal sects in whose case discovery was tantamount to destruction, it is not surprising to find – indeed, it is understandable – that they should have closely supervised each other's conduct. What if a traitor was at work, a snake in the grass? The risk could not be taken. But where there is close supervision, there is also apt to arise a vehmic court with an assassins' organization to carry out its judgements. We are particularly well informed about the Dukhobors in this respect, for in 1834 an official investigation was carried out of their treatment of backsliders. It revealed twenty-one murders, some involving cruel mutilation, others live burial of the hapless victims. These unpleasant facts were confirmed by an outsider, the German Professor Haxthausen.[1]

Tolerated sects did not need to go so far, but it is amazing to see how far they did go. The Old Believers, for instance, had an underground hierarchy, which the authorities tried hard to bring out into the open. A detective was detailed to identify a certain Old Believer bishop. 'In this task he displayed a rare zeal. Petersburg was full of "secret" and "very secret" items of information about him, one bit of news came flying after another, and more than once the authorities entertained the . . . hope that the moment was approaching when they would catch him. It was destined never to be realized.'[2] It is also significant that the non-criminal sects trusted the Imperial Post Office as little as did the criminal ones. 'The Raskol communities,' Conybeare records, 'have their own post office. In their communications they employ a cipher and conventional language. They usually send their letters by confidential messengers . . . On how considerable a scale this correspondence goes on, one can judge from the fact that in the inquisition of the year 1852, the dissenters of Moscow, Grusia (Georgia) and Siberia were found to be communicating with one another. They . . . circulate necessary information all over the provinces in the course of a few days.'[3] Clearly, what we have before us is a state within the state; but this is precisely what a sect is.

The information we have just given has about it something of the nightmarish quality of Tsarist Russia; it smells, so to speak, of the dank casemates of the Peter-Paul Fortress, and sends shivers

[1] Wright, loc. cit., pp. 18 and 19.
[2] Conybeare, loc. cit., p. 223.
[3] Ibid.

down one's spine which are, in the last analysis, caused by the ice of the Siberian vastnesses in which so many sectarians vegetated in misery until the mercy of death released them. But what about the West? As the police incubus was absent, there was no necessity for sects – even radical ones – to don the cloak of secrecy. And yet, in its own way, the Western sect, too, was a state within the State, a self-enclosed community in the shadows. Hugh Walpole's novel, to which we have already referred, has a masterly, much-revealing title: *The Captives*. The Kingscote Brethren whose life this fine author describes bear no iron manacles, but they are prisoners none the less, for their whole existence is confined within the bounds of their sectarianism.

In the West, the incarceration of sectarians in the sect was practically everywhere purely psychological, and for this reason we have few of the external, hard and fast facts required by the historian and the sociologist to demonstrate it. But certain organizational safeguards did tend to appear. One example is afforded by the Methodist 'tickets' – a means of domination and discipline, even if a comparatively mild one. Any member of a Methodist 'class' who showed disloyalty to the movement – who did not meticulously fulfil the high demands of ethical conduct pressed on him – lost his ticket, meaning that he was excluded from chapel. Thereby, an admirer of the system has asserted, 'the difference between Methodists and "the world" was kept sharp and clear'.[1] Another observer, who was something less than an unqualified admirer, had, however, this to say: 'It is . . . doubtful whether, in the early Methodist societies, there was not too much emphasis on what Wesley himself called "watching over one another in love" . . . He did not, indeed, reproduce that rather questionable expedient of Moravian discipline which encouraged "secret monitors" to spy on the behaviour of their brethren. But the "classes", originally designed to ease the payment of subscriptions, developed into a system of close supervision.'[2] The Methodists did not control their brethren as closely as the Skoptsy did; they had no need to; but the hold of the movement on its members was strong and so there was at least the tendency to erect a state within the State, a society within society, an alien body in the body politic.

[1] Cameron, loc. cit., p. 39. Cf. Church, loc. cit., p. 198; 'Give no ticket to any that wear enormous bonnets' (Wesley's own instruction).
[2] Knox, loc. cit., p. 429.

In view of this tendency inherent in all typical dissenter groups to make themselves practically independent from society at large, there can have been few who did not, at one time or another, raise the question whether it would not be better to make a clean break – whether it would not be better to emigrate. To those who hesitated when face to face with this fateful question, the inclusive society and its organs sometimes gave very definite encouragement in an equally definite direction. In 1857, for instance, a Russian statute was introduced which ordained that Skoptsy, Molokane and Dukhobortsy, and other 'Judaizing' sects as well, were to be forbidden to receive into their families 'under any pretext whatever' persons of the Orthodox persuasion. Another law extended this principle from the non-conformists' families to their factories. The conditions were hard enough, but they were worsened by the fact that the Molokane and other similar sectarians for their part were prohibited from taking employment with Orthodox house fathers or factory owners.[1] This meant, in plain English, that all labour contracts between the radical sectarians and their neighbours were outlawed, that it was impossible for them either to be entrepreneurs or working men. If there were such a word as 'extegration', in contrast to integration, we should say that this was systematic economic extegration; but the term expulsion, though perhaps a little too strong, in view of the legal (non-violent) means employed, would almost also be appropriate. In any case – what could the sectarians do but withdraw completely? Rumania, for example, became the refuge of many Skoptsy. Just as after 1918 many Parisian taximen were émigré Russian aristocrats, so after 1857 many Bucharest cab-drivers were émigré Russian dissenters.[2]

This, finally, brings us to the great subject of sect migrations. Somebody has said (whoever he was, he was a wise man) that America is Europe's finest achievement. But this achievement would hardly have been possible – would, at the very least, have taken much, much longer than it did – if dissenters had not fled from their home states, especially caesaropapist England. What would New England have been without the Puritans or Pennsylvania without the Quakers? What would the West have become without the Mormon trek? Population pressure did much, but

[1] Conybeare, loc. cit., pp. 293 and 294.
[2] Ibid., p. 367.

religious pressure did as much or more, to bring about emigration to America.

In Russia, withdrawal was often a shift towards the frontiers, not beyond them, but the difference from emigration out of England was formal rather than real. When the Old Believers fled to the forest of Kirzhen or to Vetka in the Polish marshes, they removed themselves as definitely to a wilderness as did the Pilgrim Fathers or Penn's companions. In the folklore of the Raskolniky, a place called Belovody (or White Waters) played a great part. It was to them the blessed spot where they could live, work and worship in peace, secure against the ever-threatening knout. Belovody was more than a legend. It was a settlement among the Altai mountains where streams were in fact white (or icy) – a settlement of which the Ministry of the Interior had no knowledge for many years.[1] It was to the Raskolniky the image of Utopia, in pursuit of which so many English dissenters crossed the Atlantic to the Western shore.

In Conybeare's history of Russian dissent, the subject of migration and emigration comes to the surface again and again, and one central chapter is characteristically entitled 'The Dispersion'. We have already mentioned the Old Believer settlement in the forest of Kirzhen; it was founded by contemporaries of Nikon and Avvakum. Other, similar, in-Russia-but-out-of-Russia colonies were on the sea of Rostov and in the Bryn and Starodub forests, and, indeed, in many other remote spots. It is impossible to go into detail here. However, the general direction of the drift should be mentioned: the dissenters moved further and further away, and sometimes only came to rest in non-Christian territory. Thus 'in 1703, a rebel against the Tsar's government named Nekrasov . . . fled . . . to the river Kuban, where he made his submission to the Khan of the Crimea and founded the Raskol community known under his name which subsequently was settled in Turkish territory'. Siberia, too, was a *terminus ad quem* for Raskol flights, so much so that an ukase of 1722 attempted to arrest the movement thither.

When a period of relative toleration, or rather religious indifference, descended on Russia under the rationalist rulers, such as Catherine the Great, a drift back to Muscovy was possible, but it is characteristic that the sectarians settled inside in two com-

[1] Ibid., p. 225.

paratively isolated cemeteries, the Rogozhsky and the Preobrazhensky, each surrounded by a wall. The reactionary Nicholas I suppressed both communities. Emigration in the narrower sense of the word had to be resumed. In the end about 20,000 Old Believers had settled in Moldavia and Wallachia. Byelo-Krinits, Jassy and Braila became their centres; also Maenos in Asia Minor.[1] It was from there that some of them, in 1963, removed themselves to Rockland County in the State of New York.

What applies to the Old Believers, applies to the sectarians more to the left as well. Kapiton led his followers into the depths of the Viaznikov forests, Astomen to the banks of the Yenisey; many of the so-called Theodosians built new lives for themselves in Poland and Sweden. They were wise, for 1,700 of Astomen's movement are said to have burnt themselves alive to escape persecution and cruelty. Even more impressive (and depressing) is the fate of the men who sought safety on the island of Pal in Lake Onega. On one occasion 2,700 were reported to have perished in the flames, on another 500, on a third 800.[2] Four thousand is a large figure, and the reader of the historical record must be excused if he finds it difficult to accept. And yet – what are 4,000 compared to the millions hatred has destroyed in the twentieth century?

Later, many Molokane were exiled, or exiled themselves (it makes little difference), to Siberia, the Caucasus or the Tauric Khersonese. But the migratory sect *par excellence* were the Dukhobortsy. The origin of this group is obscure, but after 1792 they emerged from obscurity because the Tsarist bureaucracy of the Ekaterinoslav district started to harass them, a policy which seemed right to the Tsar Paul who objected to the anarchist element in Dukhobor doctrine. Paul's successor, however, the mild and understanding Alexander I, preferred to isolate these men, and they were allowed and encouraged to settle at a place called Molotchnaya Vody in the *gouvernement* of Taurida, to the north of the sea of Azov. A true state within the State developed in consequence of this concentration and isolation. A proper dynasty sprang up (the existence of which was, however, kept a strict secret covered by *Arkandisziplin*). The rulers Savely Kapustin, and Vassily and Ilarion Kalmikov claimed for themselves divine honours. They surrounded themselves with a governing body of

[1] Ibid., pp. 79, 80, 83, 84, 87, 101–4, 118, 119, 127, 141, 143.

[2] Ibid., pp. 151–4.

twelve apostles and tried to implement a theocratic *régime*. In 1841, Nicholas I had enough of this and ordered the removal of the villages to the Wet Mountains of Georgia. There, after a weak interregnum under Pyotr Kalmikov, his widow, a remarkable woman called Lukeriya, became the *de-facto* head of the tribe. She decided in favour of a policy of peaceful co-existence with the State: taxes were paid, the army provisioned; even military service was accepted, if with obvious reluctance. Though the setting in which the sect was forced to live now was poor and forbidding, it achieved rising material prosperity under this enlightened matriarchal despotism, and it looked as if the 'Spirit-wrestlers' would soon end their wrestling and become a pure denomination like so many other one-time revolutionary groups.

This, however, was not destined to happen. In 1881 a new leader emerged, Pyotr Verigin (the Elder), who tried to reverse the trend. Exiled for a while by the government, he returned and assumed the reins after Lukeriya's death in 1886, calling himself in secret tsar, prophet and Christ. In 1894, he refused the loyalty oath to the new emperor Nicholas II. The sect once again became a sect. Steps towards communism were taken (cancellation of debts, merging of flocks, re-distribution of clothes). In 1895, the Dukhobors burnt their army passes and their arms: they would never again fight in behalf of Antichrist. They also refused to pay taxes. The cossacks were brought in; a massacre followed. Only total emigration could now guarantee survival, and with the help of sympathetic friends abroad (mainly Count Tolstoy's friends) they fled the Russias, leaving Pyotr Verigin behind as a prisoner and condemned criminal.

After a stay in Cyprus, the Dukhobors moved in 1899 to the western prairie lands of Canada, settling near Yorkton. The good people who brought them there thought the sect's migrations (and troubles) would now be over, but they were in fact beginning rather than ending. To the surprise, dismay and resentment of Canadians, the strange new-comers declared the Canadian government oppressive. The Homestead Act, on the basis of which land was allotted, demanded a loyalty oath to the Crown – but how could a Son of God solemnly asseverate that he would be loyal to Caesar, or rather to Satan? How could he even comply with the demand to register births and deaths? A Son of God had no age; he was eternal; he had no name beside that of Christian; he had no need to be entered in a book for he was inscribed in the Father's book of life. Verigin was brought over from Siberia to smooth and steady his people. But all he achieved (he was by now rather more conservative than before) was to split the movement into a more moderate and more radical wing. The latter – the Sons of Freedom – promptly moved to British Columbia which was not under the Homestead Act. But they could not settle down there either. They wanted a land where there would be no government at all to annoy them, a land where you could live without enslaving animals (man's brothers), without using metals (to free the miners from toil), without houses (so as not to be divided from God's sky), and so on, and so forth – a revolutionary, utopian programme if ever there was one. When further emigration proved impossible – not only because of the wickedness of the world, but also because of the vagueness of the search; all the zealots knew was that their new Eden lay somewhere to the south – the subsect of the Sons of Freedom turned anarchist. School-burning and other forms of arson became rampant, creating a major problem for the authorities. Finally, in disgust, a sizeable group retreated to Krestova, about twenty miles north of Brilliant, there to enjoy at least relative security against 'satanical interference'. This was in 1932.[1]

Thirty years passed, and then – a new eruption. We can tell it in the words of the Vancouver correspondent of the *New York Times*, written when death removed the main figure in the new migration: 'Big Fanny Storgoff, who emerged from obscurity to lead the Sons of Freedom in a year-long trek, died here yesterday . . . Florence Storgoff was brought to Canada from her birthplace in Russia, near the Turkish border, when she was three years old . . . She came to Vancouver, where she was married. She and her husband moved to Krestova, Freedomite capital in the Kootenay. There Fanny served time in prison at Piers Island, near Victoria, and then at Kingston penitentiary for arson and parading in the nude . . . Mrs. Storgoff came to public attention as the leader of the Sons of Freedom in September 1962. At that time members of the sect burned their homes in the Kootenay Valley of British Columbia and started a march to the coast. The 1,000 Freedomites moved westward across the province, eventually arriving here and then moving to Agassiz, 70 miles to the east, where more than 70 of their number were jailed for acts of terrorism . . . Her death

[1] On all this, cf. esp. Wright, loc. cit., passim.

leaves the 400 Freedomites still living in shacks at Agassiz without a leader.'

Wistfully, the correspondent adds: 'Big Fanny, 240 pounds of dynamic personality, excited the admiration of friend and foe alike as she kept the trek going.' And he quotes an officer of the Mounties, a gallant man, in a just remark and apt epitaph: 'She might have been a great woman, if the circumstances had been different.'[1]

One detail in this stage-by-stage Odyssey is revealing: the selection of Krestova as a place of retreat – a bleak plateau where very little food can be grown. Why should a group of men in search of an earthly paradise come to rest (however temporarily) in an area which more resembles an earthly limbo? We cannot be sure about the answer, but we can guess, and those who know the sectarian mentality will agree that we are guessing aright. A more promising habitat, so the leaders of these wild men felt, might, and probably would, make their brethren slick and satisfied. Welfare would increase; the plates would become fuller, the beds softer, and the end would be a sect that would be a sect no longer, a collective Esau that had sold his birthright for a mess of pottage, a collective Jacob no longer capable or willing to wrestle on behalf of his God. No, better to be poor and godly than to become rich and ungodly as the 'bad Dukhobors', lost brethren of the 'mad Dukhobors', had done in Saskatchewan, the land that flowed with milk and honey. If the Sons of Freedom felt like that, and there is every evidence that they did, then their renewed *wanderlust* of 1962 is not surprising.

It is said of Brigham Young that he halted the trek of his Mormons near the Great Salt Lake for a similar reason. Here life would be hard and therefore healthful. Yet today Utah is prosperous and the Latter Day Saints have become Americans like other Americans. Migration was as prominent a feature in the history of Anglo-Saxon dissent as it was in that of Russian sectarianism. Anglican divines complained in the seventeenth century that their countrymen 'flew out of England as out of Babylon',[2] and it is estimated that between 1620 and 1640 'some twenty thousand of the finest English folk crossed the Atlantic in

[1] *New York Times*, 13 September 1964. The spelling 'Storgoff' is the correspondent's; we should have preferred Storgov.

[2] Gooch, loc. cit., p. 92.

the hope of finding religious freedom'.[1] Of these English (and other European) emigrants and American immigrants, a minority built up settlements in the wilderness such as the Shakers or the Rappites,[2] while the majority remained dispersed in the population at large. In either case the end of the story was adjustment to society, change of the sect into a denomination. What happened to religion in America in general, under the impact of these successive sectarian influxes and influences, will be investigated in a separate chapter.[3] Our next major task will be to discuss, in general terms, the process of adjustment broadly characteristic of the English-speaking world, which is the alternative to the process of separation better exemplified in the East; cisatlantic and transatlantic instances of it will not have to be distinguished, since they conform to a common pattern. But before we take up the subject of denominationalization, we have yet briefly to mention two further forms of withdrawal, namely religious suicide and religious vagrancy.

Religious suicide and religious vagrancy may be described as forms of withdrawal practised by those who could not otherwise withdraw. We have seen that self-destruction by means of the self-lit funeral pyre was a desperate way out on the part of the Old Believers when they were cornered and had not even the *flebile ius emigrationis*, but faced the terrible choice between torture with death following or death before torture could be inflicted. Even in the eighteenth century, this solution (if solution it can be called) was embraced by a number of sectarians. In 1735, General Samarin raided some communities which had established themselves in the far north, the so-called Pomor or seashore, for instance near Olonets on Lake Ladoga. In their terror, the majority promised henceforth to pray for the tsar; a minority of some fifty families demurred. 'Attacked by Samarin, thirty-eight of the community burned themselves alive, and in 1742 and 1765 . . . there were fresh burnings on a much larger scale. The sect [or rather subsect] for its rigour was singled out by the government for persecution and that explains why they came to be known *par excellence* as the Self-burners.'[4]

The case of these poor sufferers proved that even withdrawal to

[1] Wilkinson, loc. cit., p. 4.

[2] For a study of them, cf. Holloway, loc. cit.

[3] Cf. below. pp. 333 et seq.

[4] Conybeare, loc. cit., pp. 152 and 156; cf. also pp. 88, 89, 101, 105, 154.

the arctic wastes did not necessarily mean safety; complete safety lay only beyond the confines of the empire. Yet emigration was not easy to accomplish. It is difficult at any time and for anybody; it is doubly difficult for simple folk who may not even be able to name a country besides their own; and it is trebly difficult – even downright impossible – if it is to be carried out in defiance of a governmental ban backed by vigilant police and well-organized frontier-guards. Many sectarians, especially the poorest of them, were virtual prisoners of their fatherland; yet the desire to be out of it persisted. In this quandary some of them took to vagrancy as a possible, if painful, way of life. The tramp is in the country, but not of it: his enclosure in it is merely physical. From the human, social, political and religious point of view he is as free as the wind which bloweth where it listeth.

After the cruel decree of 1684 or 1685, some Old Believers took to the roads rather than to the forests. Disguised as beggars or as pedlars, they roamed the countryside, here today, gone tomorrow, collecting alms and distributing pamphlets – dangerous as broadcasters of a doctrine of rebellion, but difficult to catch and bring to book.[1] Their example was followed, two or three generations later, by the so-called Stranniky or Wanderers, a sect founded by an army deserter and hobo called Evfemy. Evfemy grew up at a time when the persecution of dissenters was comparatively mild, for Catherine the Great, half-Lutheran and half-deist, was not greatly concerned about religion. But Evfemy was, and he saw the semi-toleration of his day merely as a new wile of the devil, a temptation that would lure the righteous into the pit.

In his *Tsvetnik* or *Flower Garden*, Evfemy developed his grand idea: a community of wandering hermits, who – unlike sedentary hermits or settled sects – would be less exposed to persecution by the police. The Stranniky were to be Beguny, i.e. Fugitives – fugitives from the world. Had God not commanded His prophets to leave Babel? The lesson was meant, not only for the men of old, but for the present generation as well. Only those who have no home can hope to escape the nets of Antichrist. You cannot look to the sky with one eye and to the ground with the other, Evfemy insisted. You must make up your mind: if you wish to go to heaven, you must avoid growing roots in the soil.

Internally this tramping sect, as organized after Evfemy's

[1] Ibid., p. 88.

death, was divided into two sets: there were on the one hand the 'true wanderers', also called 'Christ's people'; there were on the other hand the 'domiciled Christians' or 'friends of the wanderers' or 'hospitallers'. The latter were predominantly the young, the former the older members of the movement. The charge laid on the hospitallers was, as the name implies, to provide wayside stations for the wanderers where they could rest a while and recuperate. These hide-outs were as deeply hidden and as carefully guarded as any Skopets nave. We have deliberately spoken of a charge laid on the hospitallers for, in the sect's thinking, their existence was less saintly than that of their tramping brethren. 'Domiciled Christian' was almost a contradiction in terms to the Stranniky. Should death come to a Strannik before he had time to turn into a 'true wanderer', he was taken to the highways and woods to meet his last hour there – for that is how he could hope to gain entrance to the Kingdom of Heaven.

In addition to the secret hide-outs which the Stranniky had strewn all over the country, they possessed a kind of centre at Sopelky near Yaroslav among the dense forests of that region. 'According to a rumour gathered on the spot by a member of an expedition sent out with a view to a persecution of [this variant of] the Raskol', an expert, Kelsiev, has reported, 'there existed . . . in the Poshekonsky Sykhotsky forest an inaccessible underground *skete* where the virgins of the sect repair for their confinements.' Conybeare adds that 'the existence of this skete was affirmed [or rather confirmed] in 1834 by a person brought up in it'. It was most certainly needed for the tramps had a tendency to tramp in pairs. Evfemy, for instance, had had his Irena Fedorovna. The couples were not officially married but united in free love, and, according to the antinomian tenets of this group, they did not for this reason commit sin through cohabitation. It was the officially married people who, according to their way of thinking, were guilty of fornication. The word 'virgin' used by Kelsiev in connection with the word 'confinement' is not a joke in bad taste. It is technically–theologically correct, for a male Strannik was by definition a true monk, a female Strannik, equally by definition, a true nun. Neither of them can sin; neither of them therefore can be anything but a virgin, a large number of offspring notwithstanding.[1]

[1] Conybeare, loc. cit., pp. 158–60 and 210–12; Milyukov, loc. cit., pp. 71–4.

Under the draconian Nicholas I (1825–55), the number of Wanderers greatly increased, but under the tolerant Alexander II (1855–81) a decay set in. Property and marriage, consistently and passionately rejected by the older generation, came to be increasingly accepted by the younger. It therefore looked for a while as if this truly extreme sect had gone the way of most Western dissent groups and become adjusted to the world. Yet the American Press carried the following amazing news item on Wednesday, 22 July 1964:[1] 'Soviet authorities have smashed an anti-Communist religious sect called the True Orthodox Wandering Christians, it was reported Tuesday. Leaders of the sect have been sent to Siberia for forced labor, the Communist newspaper *Literary Gazette* said. According to the *Gazette*, sect members lived by day in hidden basements and came out by night to worship Christ and spread anti-Communist literature. "They do not recognize Soviet power but call it the power of Anti-Christ . . . they do not have passports [which everyone in Russia must carry]," the newspaper said, "and they do not apply for welfare services". The *Gazette* did not give any figures for membership in the sect. But it said the religion had recruited dozens of young persons.' The source from which this information is taken, the *Literarnaya Gazeta*, is beyond suspicion. *Plus ça change, plus c'est la même chose.*

The Western world does not appear to have produced anything even faintly resembling the radicalism of the Stranniky, but the germs of a similar development were there, though they did not come to much in the end. A close student of Quakerism's early years, for instance, will discover a certain tendency towards religious vagrancy in this rather typical sect. We have already encountered more than once that great preacher of the inner light, William Dewsbury. What was the call that came to him in October 1652? 'To leave wife and children, and to run to and fro,' says Braithwaite, echoing his own words. 'Fox in a well-known passage says that by the spring of 1654 "a matter of seventy ministers did the Lord raise up and send abroad out of the north countries".' It is not for nought that Braithwaite sums up these men as 'Itinerating Publishers of Truth' – some emphasis lying on the word 'itinerating' (almost a technical term). It was, significantly, the 'itinerating' that gave the authorities a handle for dealing with

[1] Cf., e.g., the *Los Angeles Times*.

them: 'When the Publishers of Truth began their vigorous itinerating work,' our historian points out, 'they exposed themselves to a fresh form of oppression, the savage application of the Act of Elizabeth (St. 39 Eliz. cap. 4) "for punishment of rogues, vagabonds, and sturdy beggars". The brutal flogging of Mary Fisher and Elizabeth Williams at Cambridge in December 1653 was probably the earliest case of Friends suffering under the Act, but in 1654 and 1655 it became one of the readiest means of acting against the Quakers.' Stubbs and Caton were persecuted at Maidstone under the same statute. And, most significantly, it was again this same statute that was strengthened when Quakerism, and with it itinerancy, increased: 'Parliament... stiffened the law against vagrancy so as to include persons, whether actually begging or not, who were found wandering from their usual place of abode without a good cause that satisfied the magistrate before whom they were brought [Act 1656 cap. 21]. Under this law a persecuting justice clearly had the itinerating Quaker ministers at his mercy.'[1]

Why was this new act needed in 1656? Clearly because the Quakers, though vagrants, were not beggars. And why did they not have to fall back on begging for their daily bread? Because their friends in the various localities along their route provided them with whatever they needed. This was part and parcel of their religious duty. Surely, we have here, in a nutshell, something like the Strannik distinction between 'Christ's True Wanderers' and 'Domiciled Christians'. There are even some indications that tensions arose at times between the two groups – an infallible sign that the contrast and the division of functions it implied had become fairly well established. Farnsworth inveighed against those who went about in idleness, in whose case the tramping 'is nothing but flesh and deceit that would be at ease'. 'Let such be noted and cause that they abide at some place and labour,' he advised. He would accept religious vagrancy, but not vagrancy (at the Friends' cost) without religion. On 16 March 1656, three itinerant ministers, Howgill, Burrough and Audland, spoke at Birkhagg, near Kendal. 'After they had spoken, Robert Collinson, one of the first at Kendal to be convinced . . . denied all that had been said as only a form of words without the life and power, and bade them stay at home . . . and not go idling up and down.' Some sided with him, some against him; as for the three

[1] Braithwaite, loc. cit., pp. 73, 132, 141, 445, 187, 268.

'Publishers of Truth', they 'afterwards issued a testimony against him as a Friend without the wedding garment' and 'exhorted all the Children of Light to deny fellowship with him until he came to repentance'.[1] Thus the distinction between wanderers and stay-at-homes could bring on an occasional crisis.

It was not, however, this budding conflict which brought the tendency towards itinerancy among the Friends to an early close. There were two far more important reasons which amply account for the arrest of the trend. The one was the open frontier: Penn could lead those who wished to be out of England across the seas to Pennsylvania. The other was the passing of the heroic period of Quakerism, and this second reason interests us far more at the juncture which we have now reached. Quakerism, so characteristic of sectarianism in many respects, was characteristic of it also because it went the way of most dissenting groups in the West – the way of progressive accommodation to the world.

(C) ADJUSTMENT

Those who would like their sociology to be a kind of applied physics might be inclined to explain the ever-repeated process of sect decay with the help of the second law of thermodynamics: objects which are hotter than their environment tend to give off heat to that environment until an equalization of temperatures is brought about. Such a formulation, though rather awkward and unduly metaphorical, would contain a good deal of truth. A strain of consistency goes through every social order, as a tendency towards the mutual adjustment of the component elements goes through every biotic and physical system. Or, radically to change the metaphor, there is a stream of life in whose direction it is easy to swim: those who attempt to go against it – and this is precisely what the typical sectarians try to do – will find that their forces get exhausted, that their resistance grows fainter all the time. Rebelliousness, as we have seen, may be strong and passionate at the beginning, but it is difficult to preserve the sentiment intact. Do not all human enthusiasms wear thin in the end? Do not the humdrum habitudes of everyday existence make slaves of all of us after a while?

A theory of sect decay, of denominationalization – or, to be

[1] Ibid., pp. 136, 137, 344, 345.

exact, of the decay and denominationalization of those sects which remain within the parent society – would be easy to develop along these lines, but it would not contain or convey the whole truth. It would lay the main emphasis on the processual character of the adjustment: the equalization of temperatures of which the second law of thermodynamics speaks involves of necessity a stretch of time, a gradual narrowing of the distance in temperature. Not that the facts do not agree with this description; they most certainly do; but an analytical (in contrast to a purely descriptive) view of the matter reveals a different and deeper aspect. Sectarian attitudes do not, as a rule, fade and fail until years, perhaps decades, of live sectarianism have come and gone; the germ of death lies in the very act of birth. It is necessary to understand this, if a proper explanation of the involution of dissenting religious groups is to be achieved.

We must, at this point, cast our minds back to the subsection of this book which we have called 'The Psychology of Sectarianism'. We have learned there why sectarians join their sects: it is because they are plagued by an inferiority complex, due sometimes to more social, sometimes to more individual, circumstances, and often, of course, to a combination of the two. When 'convincement' or 'conversion' is achieved, or when the baptismal waters have closed above the immersed body, or when 'the snake', the offending organ, has been severed or excised, the cloud begins to lift and the sun to shine: depression is removed and its place is taken by exaltation. But the person who is no longer in the grip of an inferiority complex is no longer in need of that psychological support which the sect provides. He is, in the apt phrase invariably used, reborn – reborn unto success, not, as before, born unto failure. And so the whole basis of his negativism, of his alienation, is dissolved. Well might the sect, if it had a collective personality and could speak, use the words of bitterness which the poet puts into the mouth of one of his characters:

> 'The moor his duty has performed.
> The moor may go. . . .'[1]

The concrete development which, better than any other, shows that the entry into a sect destroys the mental condition on which that very entry was based, is the growing affluence which is often

[1] Schiller, F., *Die Verschwörung des Fiesko,* III, 4.

observed among those who have undergone some kind of conversion. We must be careful here not to exaggerate. Not every 'reborn' man has become rich; far from it. Nevertheless, the upward movement of sectarians in the scale of prosperity, and their correlated downward movement in the scale of rebelliousness, is so general that it may justly be called a mass phenomenon. We shall speak of it presently in some detail. Here we must complete our argument: if, and in so far as, a sectarian does not make good, but remains indigent where his companions grow affluent, he will certainly continue in his mood of rebelliousness. But then the sect which is partially changing to a more conservative outlook will no longer please him. He may change to a newer, younger, as yet hotter group; or – a more frequent case – he may wish to purge his group of those who have drifted away from its erstwhile fervour. This tendency, which has not so far received all the attention which it deserves, accounts for the splitting of dissent groups which is an event as often repeated as their birth and decay, their evolution and involution. We shall devote a whole subsection of this chapter to its study.

There is a danger, at this juncture, of a conflict between the present writer and two of the foremost workers in the field, Milton Yinger and Bryan Wilson. Yinger, in *Religion and the Struggle for Power*,[1] presented a concept very relevant in our context, and later developed it in a second treatise, *Religion, Society and the Individual*[2] – the concept of the 'established sect'. As this technical term implies, the established sect is not moving down an inclined plane, but along an even road, as it were: it is not caught up in a process of involution but has achieved relative stability, persistence over time. Wilson has taken over this definition. A sect, he points out in the very first pages of his book, 'can sometimes preserve the distinctive features of its protest, and transmit them from one generation to another'. There is no need to speak of a denomination. 'If a group continues to support rigid barriers of membership, remains exclusive and typically radical or reactionary, it appears useful to continue to designate it a sect.'[3]

Later in his work, Wilson gives his reasons for thinking along these lines, and his words gain weight from the fact that they are spoken in connection with the discussion of a concrete case, the

[1] Durham 1946, p. 18 et seq.
[2] New York 1957, p. 144 et seq.
[3] Wilson, loc. cit., p. 3.

Elim Foursquare Gospel Church: 'Men persist in their beliefs and behaviour long after the causative factors in their adoption of such systems have disappeared. They are often unaware of the causative forces conditioning their acceptance of certain systems of belief or behaviour, and do not react immediately to their disappearance. There is rather a persistence of behaviour- and belief-patterns which tend to be integrated into the *Weltanschauung* of the individual, and which are disrupted, not so much by the removal of genesaic conditions, but rather only by the emergence of circumstances which render such patterns disadvantageous to, or contradictory of, newer goals and aspirations. Thus the disappearance of the circumstances favourable to the conversion of men to particular attitudes and activities, may in no way affect the continuance and resilience of these orientations in those previously convinced . . .'[1]

Outwardly, Yinger and Wilson appear to have the facts on their side. The Elim Movement in the narrower sense of the word emerged shortly before World War I, but Wilson has no difficulty in tracing it further back, to the famous Keswick Convention of 1875. Even more striking is his other sect, the Christadelphians, who may not have gained much profile and consistency before the sixties, but go in the last analysis back to the early thirties of the nineteenth century. Wilson did his observational and descriptive work in the late fifties of this current century. Eighty-five years are a long, 130 years an even longer, time. A group which can endure for so considerable a period may surely (so many may feel) lay claim to the title 'established sect'.

In a sense, yes; in another sense, no. A sect is a little like an individual human being: his personal identity remains from the cradle to the grave, but there is no stopping on the life's journey: with every hour, a step away from the cradle towards the grave is taken. Invisible to the naked eye, these slow changes in vital tension are revealed to the trained observer. Even if it looks as if the sect were established in its ways, there is in truth a progressive, albeit often creeping, loss in vigour – if for no other reason than simply because an action repeated is an action less spontaneous and more mechanical, and a hope deferred is a hope diminished or even a hope destroyed. But even this comparison, apt though it is, does not completely convey the facts of the matter. Growth and

[1] Ibid., p. 42.

decay, though, as biologists tell us, not entirely gradual processes, are yet normally at least continuous: but the evolution-involution of a sect passes through acute crises which will leave it different from what it was before. 'It appears quite unjustified to deny the term sect to organizations like the Christadelphians and Jehovah's Witnesses simply because they have both outlived the generation from which they originally recruited,' Wilson asserts.[1] We may certainly continue to call them so; outwardly there is perhaps little change. But inwardly much is changed after a very brief period. Christadelphian mentality, as Wilson himself describes it to us, was originally all centred upon and concentrated around 'events *soon* to take place – the second advent of Jesus Christ':[2] the little word *soon* is surely psychologically of the greatest importance in this context. The outlook of the Jehovah's Witnesses was in like manner at first entirely dominated by the millenarian expectation. However we (or rather the sectarians) may interpret the word *soon*, even if it is taken to mean decades, it cannot be equated with an indefinite period. It cannot mean one hundred and thirty years. It cannot even mean eighty-five years. If the *dénouement* is postponed beyond the immediate future, sectarian and sect *must* change. It is one thing to live in feverish anticipation and quite another thing to live in quiet resignation: indeed, there is a great, nay essential, difference even between living in feverish and living in quiet expectation. The mentality of the one condition is not the same as that of the other. The term 'established sect' would therefore appear to be something of a *contradictio in adjecto*, which is justified only if the outer history of the group is all that is considered, the enduring of its forms, the repetition of its formulae, and so on. It is unjustified if the group's inner history is taken into account, the painful progression from the rosy hope of dawn into the sharp and increasingly discouraging light of a protracted day which is sure to bring in the end, sooner or later, the dusk of despair.

Wilson himself is by no means blind to the truth of what we are saying. The following passage concerns formally only a point of detail, but it is really of much wider bearing: 'The spontaneous sect, which, if it persists, generates the established sect, may ease psychological tensions by encouraging individuals uninhibitedly to express their feelings; but the established sect finds need . . . to

[1] Ibid., p. 3.

[2] Ibid., p. 220. Italics added.

discipline in some measure the spontaneous expressions of its members, and to pattern enthusiasm into institutionally approved channels.'[1] What else does this mean but that (to use a colloquialism) the fizz is going out of the group, that it is turning stale? And what else is a 'patterned enthusiasm' but the same sort of contradiction in terms as an 'established sect'? A revolutionary movement that becomes repetitive in its manifestations is a square circle, a black white, a runner who does not get beyond the spot. A sect that ceases to be an elementary expression of passionate protest is a sect no more, if the word be taken in its proper sense. It is in effect a denomination.

Hence while there is no doubt that sects do endure over time, and while Yinger and Wilson are entitled to emphasize this endurance, it is wrong to think of sects as in any sense static. Their life process is never at a stop, and it is in principle a process of waning life. 'When economic conditions improved,' Wilson says of Elim, immediately before the long passage which we have quoted, 'the revival message, and particularly the adventist appeal, appeared to have much less consequence.'[2] He is speaking here of the change from the early to the middle thirties of the twentieth century, of the passing of the great world crisis which plagued humanity after 1929. But what he is saying is universally true: to the extent that economic conditions improve, sectarian attitudes decay. And the improvement of economic conditions among the members of a sect is not an outer, accidental and adventitious process, as a reference to the thirties might suggest; it is an inner, essential and self-generated transformation which nearly all dissenting groups have evinced in remarkable independence of the economic history unfolding around them, in independence even of the gyration of the trade cycle. There is something in sectarianism itself which leads – *via* worldly success – to the decay of sectarianism.

How and why the lot of sectarians tends to improve has been explained in classical and convincing fashion by one of the greatest sect-leaders of all time – John Wesley. 'Wherever riches have increased, the essence of religion, the mind that was in Christ, has decreased in the same proportion,' he sadly says. 'Therefore,' he adds, 'do I not see how it is possible, in the nature of things, for any revival of true religion to continue long. For religion must

[1] Ibid., p. 10.
[2] Ibid., p. 42.

necessarily produce both industry and frugality; and these cannot but produce riches. But as riches increase, so will pride, anger, and love of the world in all its branches. How, then, is it possible that Methodism, that is, the religion of the heart, though it flourishes now as a green bay tree, should continue in this state? For the Methodists in every place grow diligent and frugal; consequently, they increase in goods. Hence they proportionably increase in pride, in anger, in the desire of the flesh, the desire of the eyes, and the pride of life. So, although the form of religion remains, the spirit is swiftly vanishing away.'[1]

It would perhaps be possible to expose the central fact – one might almost say, the central mechanism – of sect life and sect decay in more scientific and sophisticated language, but it would certainly be impossible to describe it more truthfully. Wesley has put his finger on the essential point. We must overlook the moralizing undertone of his statement for it detracts nothing from its truth. Indeed, it helps to bring it out. The words are genuine; the words are deeply moving. We have before us a man in a supreme moment of truth. Surely, he of all people would have wished things to be different, but he knew them and had the courage to see them and say them as they were.

Wesley was right; there is in every typical dissent group an upward movement in prosperity and an associated downward movement in rebelliousness, with the latter being a function (in the mathematician's terminology) of the former, as can be proved by broad and cumulative evidence. We need put forward no great effort in order to prove it: all we have to do is to hear what the historians have to say. They speak, as they must, of individual cases only. The sociologist who collects and collates their reports can easily draw from them a wider conclusion, a more general regularity.

First, then, for the Old Believers, with a history of three hundred years behind them, the form indeed has remained and is 'established', but the spirit, the substance, has vanished away. 'Under Catherine II, Paul, and Alexander I,' Curtiss tells us, 'they enjoyed a period of toleration, and many of them, especially those who had grown rich in the manufacture of cloth, in trade, and in money-lending, grew more moderate in their attitude towards the

[1] *The Works of the Rev. John Wesley*, ed. John Emory, New York 1853, vol. VII, p. 317.

government.' So great was the change that the official Church tried to bring the straying sheep back into the State fold, and though these efforts had no great success, they were intermittently continued right to the end of the Tsarist *régime*. Especially after 1905, there was new effort in this direction. The spokesman of the Old Believers, through whose mouth a new collective 'nay' was returned to the official wooings, was, significantly, a great Moscow industrialist, Morozov by name. And why did he say 'nay'? Was he still a revolutionary, as Avvakum and Avram had been? By no means. 'In 1912 . . . Morozov asked the Council of Ministers to have the State contribute to the building of parish schools for the Old Believers, as the children educated there would learn piety and patriotism and true loyalty to Tsar and Fatherland.'[1] It is not in these tones that a sectarian, who is still truly a sectarian, is wont to speak. Clearly it was more the form, not to say, merely the form – the form which had become hard and set – which prevented the merger. It was no longer the spirit which once had seen the Tsar as Anti-Christ, that was gone with the wind.

Even more characteristic than the Old Believers are the Molokane and the Dukhobortsy whom we have so often encountered in these pages. Originally red-hot revolutionaries, they had, by the year 1900, turned tame, even though their history – the time during which the second law of thermodynamics could assert itself – was much shorter than in the case of the Popovtsy. 'At the opening of the twentieth century,' Curtiss remarks, 'the Molokane and those Dukhobortsy who had not emigrated to Canada seemed to be losing much of their zeal for opposing the obligations imposed by the State; their place in the van of the sectarian movement was taken by the more aggressive Stundists.[2] In other words: the Stundists were now *a* living sect, or *the* living sect: the Molokane and Dukhobortsy were so no longer. Ossification had, by this time, reached and engulfed even the Khlysty. Grass's great work about them is purely descriptive. He does not ask the searching questions with which analytical theory approaches the factual material. And yet, so obvious is the matter, that even he is struck by the fact that in the Khlyst religion a process is to be observed which turns personal leadership based on ecstatic superiority into a mere matter of organization.[3] This is what Max Weber was soon

[1] Curtiss, loc. cit., pp. 131, 132, 319, 320, 322; cf. also pp. 334 and 394.
[2] Ibid., p. 155.
[3] Grass, loc. cit., vol. I, pp. 296 and 297.

to call the routinization of charisma – the killing of a revolutionary live content by a deadening, repetitive form.

In the West, observers and describers have substantially identical reports. Richard Niebuhr is a little like John Wesley: he talks about his own people; he does not like what he has to say about them; but, honest man that he is, he says it all the same. This is how he deals with the first phase of modern dissent: 'Brownists and Separatists in the waning sixteenth and early seventeenth centuries appeared . . . to represent the religious needs and ethical desires of the religiously disinherited . . . But Independency did not remain the people's church . . . By the early fifties it had lost its place as the dominant sect. "They had no great congregations of the common people," Clarendon now wrote of them, "but were followed by the most substantial citizens" . . . In a short time the sectarian branch of Puritanism was scarcely distinguishable in social character from its churchly brother, Presbyterianism.' Quakerism then arose. And what happened to Quakerism, the next phase in the history of modern dissent? 'In the second and third generations, with the aid of the prosperity prevailing in the days of Good Queen Anne, this church of the disinherited became a more or less respectable middle-class church that left the popular movement from which it originated far behind . . . Once more, therefore, the poor were without a gospel.' And the third phase? Only Niebuhr's words are different, their substance is the same: 'Methodism was adapted from its beginnings to become a church of the respectable middle class . . . Religious enthusiasm declined in later days because Methodist Christianity became more literate and rational, and because, with increasing wealth and culture, other escapes from the monotony and exhaustion of hard labour became available . . . Sooner than was the case with the other movements, this religion of the disinherited became a respectable church of respected classes . . . Once more a religious revolt, issuing in the formation of a sect, led finally to the establishment of a middle-class church, a yielding servant of the social order.'[1]

After this survey of the three classical sect movements, it is high time for us to stop adding example to example, lest we begin to bore our reader. Who wants to see the same play again and again, with only a change of attire on the part of the actors? Should further evidence be wanted, especially regarding the nineteenth

[1] Niebuhr, loc. cit., pp. 43, 44, 45, 55, 56, 69, 63, 71, 72.

century, it can easily be found in such books as K. S. Inglis, *Churches and the Working Classes in Victorian England*.[1] To finish, a brief side-glance at the Elimites will be interesting in view of what has gone before. The same author who has insisted that the change of time, the change of the generations, does not necessarily alter much in a sectarian grouping, has this to say where he is face to face with the hard facts: 'There is some reason to suppose that Elim has not met with very great success in the recruitment of the second generation.' On the next page, this statement is made a little stronger: 'Elim as a religious faith offers very definite satisfactions for the unprivileged and emotionally ill-adjusted, but how far it is adapted to the second generation is very difficult to say.' One further page on, a fact is adduced which makes the statement much, much stronger still: 'In a city where Elim has had a church for twenty years, there are no second-generation adherents.'[2] Wilson calls this 'perhaps not surprising'. It is even less surprising to us than to him, for we believe that, in its admittedly slow but inexorable decay, the sect proves a magnet with decreasing power of attraction, simply because its inner potency is on the wane.

Taking, then, the fact of sect involution for granted, or rather proven, let us look at the causes of it. These are not difficult to detect, and there is remarkable consensus about them. What Wesley so sadly said about the withering of the green bay tree in the eighteenth century, was repeated by Niebuhr in similar, if more sober and scientific terms in the twentieth: 'Wealth frequently increases when the sect subjects itself to the discipline of asceticism in work and expenditure; with the increase of wealth the possibilities for culture also become more numerous and involvement in the economic life of the nation as a whole can less easily be limited. Compromise begins . . . So regarded, one phase of the history of denominationalism reveals itself as the story of the religiously neglected poor . . . who rise in the economic scale under the influence of religious discipline, and who, in the midst of a freshly acquired cultural respectability, neglect the new poor succeeding them on the lower plane. This pattern recurs with remarkable regularity in the history of Christianity. Anabaptists, Quakers, Methodists, Salvation Army, and more recent sects of like type illustrate this rise and progress of the churches of the

[1] London 1963.

[2] Wilson, loc. cit., pp. 115, 116, 117.

disinherited.'[1] To rise and progress we must add – without moving an inch from the analysis of this distinguished author – regress and decay, decay into denominationalism. 'Restrictions on consumption accompanied by emphasis upon production,' he says on a later page,[2] 'have their inevitable result in an economic salvation which is far removed from the eternal blessedness sought by the enthusiastic founders of the Protestant sects.'

We have entered here an area which has become veritably commonplace among sociologists, partly because the facts themselves all point in one direction, and partly because Max Weber has provided an analysis of these facts in and for a restricted field which is now widely accepted in its basic idea, even if there is much criticism of its concrete detail. Our task is twofold: to show that Weber's thesis holds good in the East as well as the West; and to discuss whether it is as universally valid as Weber assumed.

Among the sworn enemies of the Old Believers was Liprandi, who was almost a modern Eastern equivalent to the medieval Western *malleus maleficorum*. Hate may have animated him, but it did not blind him, for this is what he wrote in 1853: 'The Orthodox envy the affluence of their Raskol neighbours. They do not reflect that they never spend a farthing at the grog shop, that they keep sober and work hard every day. The Raskolnik wife, when she goes to town, wastes no money on ribbons, whereas the Orthodox one purchases all she sees when she goes there or visits her friends, goes to weddings, baptisms or church, all of which the Raskolnik finds superfluous.' On the Molokane, Conybeare adduces three completely unanimous witnesses, and then, for good measure, confirms their findings by his own first-hand observations. The Molokane, one writer asserted in 1828, 'endeavour to banish from their lives anything that in their opinion can corrupt a man. Thus they condemn card-playing . . . Nothing is so pernicious as play and drink, they say . . . Both of these vices are equally to be shunned. Hard work, according to them, is as necessary to man as bread and breath of life . . . Consequently they look upon work as a religious duty'. In 1870 another writer estimated that the Molokane were on the average three to four times as rich as the Orthodox, and yet another authority asserted in the same year that these sectarians showed their soberness in everything: in their personal appearance, their mode of expression, their homesteads and

[1] Niebuhr, loc. cit., pp. 20 ad 28. Cf. also p. 54.

[2] Ibid., p. 55.

villages, and all the rest. Significantly he praises the Tauric Molokane especially for their great success in wool production. In the early years of this century, Frederick Conybeare visited the Caucasian Molokane and found that 'everywhere prevailed an air of sobriety and quiet industry'. It was a pleasure to behold these men and women at work.[1]

In the same style, the Dukhobortsy who were still in Russia are described as 'sober, hardworking and hospitable . . . distinguished by their comfortable circumstances . . .' 'Their superior morale marked them out among the surrounding population as ears of corn among tares.'[2] As for the Khlysty, Grass adduces a whole series of testimonies to their 'honesty, industry, intelligence, cleanliness' and self-control in food and drink. One of the witnesses, Abramov, mentions two character traits which are particularly interesting because they recall the typical Quaker virtues: the Caucasian Khlysty (or Shaloputy) will never take a penny more for their produce than the market price, and they will exact no payment for work done in the public interest.[3] Summing up the evidence about the Skoptsy, Grass uses these few words to describe them: love of labour, spirit of enterprise, industriousness, competence, reliability, and cleanliness. Of their Siberian settlements he writes: 'The Skoptsy are the best tillers of the soil, vegetable gardeners and artisans. By their economic well-being they stand in sharp contrast to the general condition of poverty all around them . . . They are for this reason the best part of the population . . .' High praise indeed for a criminal sect! Conybeare, who observed them in towns rather than villages, remarks: 'Being ascetics, thrifty and unencumbered with families, they have been able . . . to accumulate great wealth; and the mere fact that they cannot waste money on mistresses recommends them in so corrupt a society as Russia. Financial magnates who have important credit transactions to conduct, can trust them, just as a rich Turk trusts his harem with their Mohammedan analogues.' Their wealth also explains why the police do not extirpate them, even though it is not too difficult to identify them by their yellow skin colour and sparse beards: they can bribe those who are supposed to hunt them.[4] A Tsarist policeman's eye could easily be blinded.

[1] Conybeare, loc. cit., pp. 315, 316, 308.
[2] Ibid., p. 285.
[3] Grass, loc. cit., vol. I, pp. 503–5.
[4] Ibid., vol. II, pp. 886 and 581; Conybeare, loc. cit., p. 367.

It is, as these facts from Russia prove, sectarianism in general, and not only Calvinism, that leads to economic ascent. This is a different and much broader concept than Weber's, but this does not mean that Calvinism did not have a potent influence on the rise of capitalism, as he asserts. It merely means that we have two distinguishable religious factors before us, both supporting the growth of wealth: Calvinism and (potentially anti-Calvinist) sectarianism. It also means that we must expect decidedly Calvinistic sect movements to be particularly fertile breeding grounds of economic success, for in their case the two horses run in harness. This expectation is fully borne out by the study of English Baptism which had in its make-up a good deal of the Calvinist mentality. True, the General Baptists were less in the tradition of Calvin than the Particular Baptists, but even they can justly be called Calvinists without unduly stretching the term.

An almost archetypal figure which we encounter here is William Kiffin (1616–1701). Orphaned while yet rather young, he was made to learn the brewing trade – 'a very mean calling' according to his later opinions. He did not stick to it, but entered the woollen trade in which he became, before long, one of London's wealthiest merchants. His standing can be seen from the following incident: 'In 1663, a group of General Baptists in Buckinghamshire had been arrested and twelve of them condemned to death under the Elizabethan [Conventicle] Act . . . Their friends brought the matter to the knowledge of Kiffin who interceded for them with the king. Charles immediately issued a pardon. He . . . could hardly offend a man who could let him have £10,000. The story goes that Charles once asked Kiffin to lend him £40,000. The Baptist merchant replied that he could not possibly lend His Majesty so large a sum, but he would be pleased if he would accept £10,000 as a gift. When telling the story, Kiffin used to say that he had thereby saved £30,000 by his liberality.'[1] This is an excellent anecdote: it not only shows that Kiffin had become very rich in twenty-five years or so, but also that he had developed considerable business acumen. He realistically saw that a political debt would be practically irrecoverable. 'William Kiffin was one of the ablest of the Baptist leaders of his generation,' W. K. Jordan has judged. 'His career illustrates . . . the rising social and economic strength of the communion . . . during the period.'[2]

[1] Underwood, loc. cit., pp. 60, 61, 98, 99. [2] Cit. ibid., p. 110.

Other monied Baptists were John Collet and Thomas Guy, the former growing rich through dyeworks, the latter through his bookshop, or rather, to be exact, through the sale of bibles. As the founder of Guy's Hospital – 'endowed with £200,000 which he had made out of selling his South Sea stock at the right time' (splendid business acumen again!) – he set himself a lasting memorial. So, in a different, less public-spirited way, did Thomas or rather Thos. Cook, the originator of the world-famous firm of travel agents. Originally a wood-turner and an evangelist, he soon became a professional organizer of train excursions and thereby, riding on the crest of the railway boom, a man of substance and generosity.[1]

To these men, Max Weber's basic thesis seems entirely applicable. They wanted to grow rich, not because they cared about money as such, but because they valued economic success as a signal proof of divine favour, and indeed as the only sure proof of that favour available in the present life. But even more convincing than their cases is the striking difference in treatment meted out by the Baptists to two of their nineteenth century worthies, C. H. Spurgeon and Sir Samuel Morton Peto. Spurgeon was a great preacher who drew crowds, and through the crowds, money: the pulpit made him prosperous. 'He lived during the last twelve years of his life,' so the historian of Baptism reports, 'in the style of an affluent businessman, in a large house, with gardens, lawns, a lake and some fields beyond . . . That kind of thing was almost expected at a time when the evangelical world regarded a man's material success as evidence that the blessing of God was resting upon him. Spurgeon was as genuinely convinced as any of his supporters that the Lord had given him library, fernery, vinery, and rose-garden.'[2] We see the obverse side of the medal in the sorry life history of Sir Samuel Morton Peto. He had risen in the world through the railway boom of which he was one of the chief engineers and benefitees, but what raised him up also laid him low. 'The financial troubles of the years 1866–7 forced his firm into bankruptcy, with liabilities estimated at several million pounds. He started life afresh and built other railways. Though he had devoted a great deal of his energy and his once ample fortune to the work of Baptist extension, he never again occupied quite the same place among the Baptists owing to their attitude to one who

[1] Ibid., pp. 144–6 and 241. [2] Ibid., p. 223.

has once been bankrupt, even through circumstances beyond his control.'[1]

There are two points here which are apt to disturb, or even dismay, the non-Calvinistic Christian. He is likely to ask, concerning Spurgeon: is it right for a man to grow rich through his ministry of the Gospel? And concerning Peto: is it right for a community to turn away from a man who has generously, even unsparingly, given for the cause, just because he has fallen, temporarily, on evil days? Many would answer these queries with a resounding *no*, but the Calvinist reply must logically be a decided *yes*. Once the deity is defined, in Calvin-fashion, as 'the dispenser of all things', it follows that he who grows rich, no matter how, is the favoured son of the heavenly father, and he who goes broke, no matter why, is the rejected offspring, a Cain to his brother Abel. The distribution of property and income was to the Baptists clearly a distribution of praise and blame. No wonder that these men went all out to fill their barns and pockets, their pocket books and bank accounts.

The Quakers, too, became very rich. In Britain, for instance, it is common knowledge that they occupy a prime place in the upper echelons of economic society (the Rowntrees, the Frys, the Cadburys, etc.). Weber asserted that their ascent in the eighteenth and nineteenth centuries was due to the same reasons as the ascent of the Calvinists: he lumps the two groups together as 'ascetic sects', sects rationalizing all life and thereby laying a basis for great riches. But his argument is only half true. What drove the Calvinist into feverish economic activity was, on Weber's own showing, his inability to know whether he was accepted or rejected, saved or damned. If he grew rich, he was accepted and saved, for had God not shown His favour to Abraham, Isaac and Jacob by filling their granaries and increasing their kine? Such a mode of thinking presupposes a definite metaphysic, the conviction that God and man are deeply divided from each other, that God's eternal decree – especially concerning redemption and rejection – is withheld from men, that it is locked up in the Father's bosom, as it was at times expressed. The emphasis with the Calvinists lay heavily on the fact of the fall and its catastrophic consequences. But the theology of the Quakers stood (as we have seen) in diametrical opposition to this philosophy. There was

[1] Ibid., p. 240.

no chasm between God and man, they thought, for God was in man, or man was in God, or God and man were one. Fox's key passage, as Weber might have known, was the Gospel according to St. John, I, 9: '. . . the true light . . . enlighteneth every man that cometh into this world'. There was no need, for the Friend, to ask in anguish: am I fore-ordained to eternal glory or to eternal punishment? And because he did not have to ask this question, the great spring of action which Weber discovered in the Calvinist's mind was missing from the Quaker's mental mechanism.

There was, however, a similar spring of action there. The Quaker did not have to prove to himself that he was in God's favour, but he had to prove to other men that he was worthy of their acceptance, that he was a neighbour worth living with. We have seen how deeply the first Friends shocked the respectable part of society, for instance through their nudism. As the movement began to settle down into more quiet and abiding forms, it strove for a *modus vivendi* with the world around, and one (in our context most important) technique for bringing it about was fair dealing with all, especially fair dealing with customers and other contract partners. The matter is reflected with all desirable clarity in a passage of Fox's *Journal*: 'At the first convincement when Friends could not put off their hats to people, nor say you to a particular, but thee and thou; and could not bow nor use the world's salutations nor fashions nor customs – and many Friends being tradesmen of several sorts – they lost their custom at the first, for the people would not trade with them nor trust them. And for a time people that were tradesmen could hardly get money enough to buy bread; but afterwards, when people came to see Friends' honesty and truthfulness and yea and nay at a word in their dealing . . . and they knew and saw that they would not cozen and cheat them for conscience sake towards God; and that . . . they might send any child and be as well used as themselves at any of their shops; so then the things altered so that all the inquiry was where was a draper or shopkeeper or tailor or shoemaker or any other tradesman that was a Quaker: then that was all the cry, insomuch that Friends had double the trade beyond any of their neighbours, and if there was any trading, they had it. . . .'[1] 'If we let these people alone,' so the competitors soon

[1] Cit. Braithwaite, p. 152.

began to say, 'they will take the trading of the nation out of our hands.'[1]

The fears were exaggerated; it did not quite come to that; but it was true that business flowed in broad streams towards the Quaker traders and washed a torrent of money into their hands. It is no wonder that they rose in the world. The salient point in our analysis is that it was their sectarianism and not only their asceticism (and certainly not any Calvinism, for their whole philosophy was opposed to that of the grim Genevan) which made many of them into great capitalists.

We would urge, against Weber, then, that in the case of Quakerism, it was not a religious ethic but a social policy that built up their businesses and their opulence. Indeed, we can go further. The religious ethic of Fox and the early Friends was something of an inhibiting factor in the pursuit of wealth, though not one so strongly inhibiting as to prevent, or even perceptibly to delay, the end result. 'Ye can hardly do anything to the service of God,' Fox soon chided his followers, 'but there will be crying, "my business, my business", and your minds will go into the things, and not over the things.' The more fundamental convictions from which this reproach stemmed can be seen from an epistle of 1661, published under the title 'The Line of Righteousness and Justice stretched forth over all Merchants'. This paper lays a deeper basis for the prudential attitudes which the Quakers evinced in their day-to-day dealings: 'All Friends everywhere live in the seed of God [i.e., in Christ] which is the righteousness itself . . . and in the wisdom itself, with which wisdom ye may order, rule and govern all things which are under your hands,' including 'all exchangings, merchandizing [and] husbandry.' But living in the seed of God, Fox insists, means striving to be rich in the life and kingdom that is to come and has no end, rather than to covet the riches of this present and transitory world. 'Let him that buys or sells or possesses or uses this world be as if he did not,' says Fox, remotely echoing pre-Calvinistic, and evidencing post-Calvinistic, attitudes. The following passage is certainly prudential in inspiration; it condemns over-extension of business because it may lead to bankruptcy rather than because it would be wrong in itself. Yet there is no mistaking a certain petty-bourgeois philosophy of

[1] Ibid. Cf. also the strongly corroborating passages on pp. 211, 378, 379, 516, 517.

self-restriction which could not but militate against aggressive capitalist enterprising, or at the very least against boldness in risk-taking: 'Go not beyond your estates, lest you bring yourselves to trouble and cumber and a snare: keep low and down in all things ye act . . . Dwell every one of you under your own vine (that know redemption from the earth) and seek not to be great but in that, and dwell in the truth, justice, righteousness and holiness, and there is the blessing enlarged.'[1]

Such words were not spoken to the wind: to give but one example, 'William Edmondson, the apostle of Quakerism in Ireland, found himself prevented "by a secret hand" from accepting a tempting business opening in Dublin, and from an easy evasion of customs duties, and a little later left shopkeeping and took a farm in order to bear his testimony against tithes'.[2] The contrast with the Calvinists must not be exaggerated: the *guid man* of Calvinism would as little have swindled the customs collector as did William Edmondson. But the Quakers were over-scrupulous rather than scrupulous, and over-scrupulosity in and for itself is no help towards economic success – no direct help, that is; indirectly, it will pay in terms of confidence and enlargement of contracts and opportunities. In the case of the Quakers, certainly, the advantages of self-control clearly outweighed its disadvantages, and that is why they grew rich. That is also why they lost their sectarian impetus, why their green bay tree came to wither. 'What survived,' so Knox has said, and with some justification, 'was a religious coterie rather than a sect; a band of well-to-do reformers, distinguished by their wide influence and active benevolence, but numbering only a handful of adherents among the multitudes on whom they had compassion.'[3]

The case of Methodism is different again, and there is even less sense in bracketing it together with Calvinism and Baptism, under the heading of 'ascetic sects', than there is in the case of Quakerism. Methodism is, historically considered, a link in the long chain of lower-class movements which stretches from Medieval Franciscanism to the modern Labour Organizations. We must, *prima facie*, expect it to be anti-capitalist in theory (which does not, however, necessarily mean that it was not pro-capitalist in practice, i.e. in its – largely involuntary and unforeseen – effects). Max Weber's thesis is hardly applicable here. John Wesley was not

[1] Ibid, pp. 309, 516, 517. [2] Ibid. p. 517. [3] Knox, loc. cit., p. 168.

by nature a passionate man; but the proposition that God gave wealth to those whom he loved and who must therefore be presumed to be virtuous, and sent poverty to those whom he did not love and who must therefore be presumed not to be virtuous, drew from him a passionate protest. He calls it 'wickedly, devilishly false'[1] – strong words indeed for a quiet man.

Wesley's opposition to capitalism – or, to borrow a technical term of Karl Marx's here, to capitalist accumulation, the central process in the formation of the capitalist order – is not, however, evidenced merely in a stray remark. It formed the inspiration of a consistently carried out life policy. The sermon on the withering of the green bay tree which we have quoted ends in a most important passage which Weber has transcribed, but to the understanding of which he had no clue.[2] This is what Wesley says: 'Is there no way to prevent . . . this continual declension of pure religion? We ought not to forbid people to be diligent and frugal; we must exhort all Christians to gain all they can, and to save all they can; that is, in effect, to grow rich! What way then can we take, that our money may not sink us to the nethermost hell? There is one way, and there is no other under heaven. If those who gain all they can and save all they can, will likewise give all they can; then, the more they gain, the more they will grow in grace, and the more treasure they will lay up in heaven.'[3]

The salient question is, of course, what Wesley meant by *give all they can*? An answer is provided by the following passage in which he speaks of himself, although he uses the third person: 'One . . . had thirty pounds a year. He lived on twenty-eight and gave away forty shillings. The next year, receiving sixty pounds, he still lived on twenty-eight and gave away thirty-two. The third year he received ninety pounds and gave away sixty-two. The fourth year he received a hundred and twenty pounds; still he lived as before on twenty-eight and gave to the poor all the rest.' Clearly, this is what he regarded as right – accumulation he therefore regarded as wrong. 'I have kept my accounts exactly,' he asserted when the evening was closing in. 'I will not attempt it any longer, being satisfied with the continual conviction that I

[1] Cameron, loc. cit., p. 58.

[2] Cf. *The Protestant Ethic and the Spirit of Capitalism,* as quoted, pp. 175 and 176.

[3] Works, ed. Emory, as quoted, p. 317.

save all I can and give all I can; that is, all I have.' There is a way of checking up on this, and one who was in the know, who in fact had Wesley's account books at his disposal, has estimated that he gave away, in fifty years, considerably more than thirty thousand pounds – a truly staggering sum.[1] A generation of John Wesleys would not have produced a capitalist society, all asceticism notwithstanding!

A generation of John Wesleys. . . . The idea is intriguing. If such a thing could come to pass . . . But, clearly, it cannot. The common run of men will not 'give all they can, that is, all they have'. Wesley knew this. He recommended his followers to divest themselves of their surplus, but he did not press them to do so. His sermon on *The Good Steward* shows how far he was prepared to go. 'The Lord of all,' he told his listeners, 'will inquire: "How didst thou employ the worldly goods which I lodged in thy hands?"' Did you use it in 'first supplying thy own reasonable wants, together with those of thy family; then restoring the remainder to me, through the poor, whom I had appointed to receive it'? If a man could answer this question in the affirmative, he was a good steward; if not . . . 'Thus far, the Wesleyan doctrine sounds quite Franciscan', Cameron remarks on this passage.[2] But this passage was clearly no more than a counsel of perfection. It was a personal confession of faith; it was the propagation of a model; but it was not a universal precept. And even if it had been meant as such, it would not have made much difference. The strongest beam becomes refracted and dulled when it meets with an obscure and obtuse mass. If we can say that Wesley's followers reflected his light, we must mean, not only that they mirrored it to some extent, but also that they threw it back.

In practice, therefore, the anti-capitalist, neo-Franciscan element in Wesley's doctrine was countermanded and overpowered by the near-Calvinist tendencies which were also present within it. 'Gain all you can and save all you can' won over 'give all you can'. Methodism does not appear to have produced types like William Kiffin who grew rich in a very short time; the economic success stories which one meets in its history are all on a much smaller

[1] For the evidence cf., for convenience sake, Cameron, loc. cit., pp. 58–60, but the detail was provided by a most meritorious Columbia dissertation, North, E. M., *Early Methodist Philanthropy*, New York 1914.

[2] Cameron, loc. cit., pp. 66 and 67.

scale, and philanthropy acted with some power to retard them. Nevertheless, even typical Methodists had a way of rising in the world, at least to the status of comfort. There was, for instance, George Cussons, of Ampleforth in Yorkshire, an excellent cabinet-maker, whom friends urged to migrate to London, a better setting for a good craftsman than the narrow native vale. 'I felt no desire to be rich,' he recalled in later days. 'I was already worth near forty pounds, beside my furniture, and never thought of adding ten pounds more to my stock.' This is no capitalist animus: it is rather petty-bourgeois self-satisfaction, not a dynamic but rather a conservative mentality. Yet Cussons did go to London after all, and there he prospered. In spite of generosity to men and causes, Cussons became a person of substance. And why? He himself ascribed his success to the Methodist ethos. 'Our business was [at first] but small; but we were industrious and did our utmust to be punctual, and laid all our concerns daily before the Lord.'[1]

Thus it was self-confidence, hard work and reliability which raised this man in the scale of opulence; these are sectarian virtues, but not necessarily Calvinist ones. 'Use all possible diligence in your calling,' Wesley urged in his sermon *On the Use of Money*. 'Lose no time . . . Never leave anything till tomorrow which you can do today. And do it as well as possible . . . Let nothing in your business be left undone if it can be done by labour or patience.'[1] The duty of industriousness is thus directly inculcated; the duty of parsimony, on the other hand, is, characteristically, only indirectly inculcated. It was wasteful expenditure, pampering the lust of the flesh and of the eyes and the pride of life, that was banned, not economy that was imposed. The accumulation of capital was a by-product of this ethos – but whether a by-product or an intended product made little difference in the end. And so the Methodists' green bay tree withered after a time, as Wesley feared it would, even though ledger and balance sheet were not regarded, by these distant and illegitimate and well-nigh unrecognizable offspring of St. Francis, as pages on which the content of God's decree – acceptance or rejection – could be read and recognized, as Calvinists of William Kiffin's stamp had assumed.

John Wesley was by no means the only sect leader who realized that increasing wealth will bring – not to say, must bring – de-

[1] Church, loc. cit., pp. 226, 228, 229.
[2] Cameron, loc. cit., p. 67; cf. also pp. 68 and 69.

creasing religious fervour. Others recognized this fateful concatenation as well, and were even prepared to do something about it. Among the early General Baptists Matthew Caffyn was a man of considerable standing. He had in his congregation one Richard Haines (1633–85) at whom he began after a while to look askance. 'Farmer, inventor, manufacturer, a man of wealth and ability, he [Haines] wrote pamphlets on such topics as the prevention of poverty and unemployment and a new way of improving cider.' The mixture of interests is highly significant! 'In 1672, he was granted by licence a monopoly for the process he had invented of cleaning hop-clover. Caffyn classed all patentees as covetous, with idolaters and unclean persons (I Corinthians, v, 11) and excommunicated Haines who then appealed to the General Assembly where, after many years and much debate, the excommunication was rescinded.'[1]

It is difficult to see what else that General Assembly could have done but to rescind the excommunication. Growing rich is neither a sin nor a crime, especially not for a Calvinist. If Caffyn's over-strict principles had been applied, not only Haines would have had to go, but such *nouveaux riches* as Kiffin also. There would have been a proper decapitation of the movement. What Caffyn wanted simply could not be countenanced. And yet, Caffyn had an inkling of the truth: men like Haines, or Kiffin for that matter, would ruin the spirit of the sect, would make the refuge of the poor into a rallying point of the rich.

It was only very rarely that the effort to stem the tide of denominationalization took the direct and radical form which Matthew Caffyn gave to it. For the most part, there was merely a tinkering with the symptoms, not an attack on the core of the trouble. To stay with the Baptists, there was, for instance, a ban on the use of a set bible text. 'Smyth . . . thought that the person who was teaching should bring with him the original Hebrew and Greek and translate them by voice. It is important to grasp his reasons for this, which are not so finicky as one might suppose,' says Underwood in defence of his co-religionist. 'He was of opinion that to read the English translation savoured of formality: there would be less quenching of the Spirit if a free translation were made on the spot . . . Smyth also objected to sermons being read and to psalms being sung from a book.'[2] Among the Quakers

[1] Underwood, loc. cit., p. 122.

[2] Ibid., pp. 35 and 36.

it was originally a principle that only he should address a meeting whom the spirit moved to speak. Alas, the cooling-down process before long produced the embarrassing situation that there was much waiting for inspiration and little real response. An admonition addressed to the Skipton General Meeting of Northern Friends, held in early October 1659, and probably from the pen of Anthony Pearson, urges 'that we be not again led back into the errors of those that went before us and got into the form', i.e. set, prepared, pre-arranged preaching. William Britton published in 1660 a tract called *Silent Meeting. A Wonder to the World*, in which he uncompromisingly announced, 'he is no true minister of Jesus Christ but who is led forth by His Spirit', these words having the technical meaning: but who is inspired to speak. But Braithwaite admits, albeit *sub rosa*, that even at this early time all was not well. 'Many of the utterances,' he concedes, 'were deficient in positive teaching, and in this directon, as in some other, the Quaker meetings, with all their vitality, were already showing signs of the weaknesses which developed later.'[1]

Just as set bible texts and set sermons were condemned as routinizers of the original sectarian charisma, so were set prayers. Quite a number of groups condemned formulae and insisted on what is called 'ejaculatory prayer'. It is clear that even this will work only while the heart is overflowing; when quieter sentiments supervene, there may indeed be no repetition of words, where formulated supplications are forbidden, but there may well be repetition of sentiments, repetitions in substance, no less deadening than repetitions in expression. Insistence on ejaculatory prayer has not always had entirely happy results.

Some sect leaders were even more determined in their attempts to avoid the denominationalization of their group. They not only outlawed set texts and set sermons and set supplications, but tried to keep the original wildness of the sect going. 'I am convinced that we must stick to our concern, and also that we must keep up its so-called extravagances,' Bramwell Booth wrote to George Railton on 6 October 1874. 'They, and they only, will save it from drooping down into a sectarian nothing.'[2] Booth was right – but how does one keep up extravagances? We are face to face here with the inherent self-contradiction of the established, or merely enduring, sect. What Booth wanted was precisely what Trotsky

[1] Braithwaite, loc. cit., pp. 328, 329, 509, 510, 511.

[2] Cit. Coates, p. 98.

wanted: a permanent revolution. But that is a hot object that will not cool down in a cold atmosphere – an impossibility. Booth achieved it as little as did Trotsky.

In the last analysis, this self-contradiction is the self-contradiction implied in the word 'a well-to-do religious dissenter'. Shaw once said that one could make a revolutionary out of a conservative simply by giving him nothing to eat. But the opposite holds true as well, and it is amply illustrated in the history of sectarianism.

By representing the economic success which regularly follows upon conversion, i.e. a man's mental and moral renewal and reconstruction, as the main cause of sectarian involution, we do not wish to put forward a narrow mono-causal explanation. Nothing is quite so simple. An incidental remark of Braithwaite's brings out another concomitant factor. At the end of his great study of the beginnings of Quakerism, he asks why the preaching of repentance through the streets and markets, that witness-bearing which so often became a cross-bearing, ceased around 1660, and he answers with deep insight: 'With the development of a corporate consciousness on the part of the whole Quaker community there was inevitably a shifting in some degree of responsibility for witness-bearing in these pronounced ways from the individual to the group, and this no doubt tended to control and to limit these manifestations of an eager spiritual activity.'[1] The observation is universally true. Institutionalization itself is routinization, and nobody would agree more with this proposition than a first generation sectarian. Here again, the very founding of the sect is revealed as the cause of its ultimate undoing – the same mortal contradiction as before.

Finally, there is the change of the generations to which we would not ascribe as much efficacy as Richard Niebuhr does, but which is surely one of the factors making for sect decay. Where a group has withdrawn into the wilderness, and where consequently sect and society coincide, the guiding of the young generation into the paths pursued by the old may be comparatively easy. But giving the young the 'right' spirit is difficult where sect and society co-exist and consequently conflict, for here a painful dilemma confronts the boy or girl approaching adulthood: should they integrate themselves into the wider society which beckons to them, or should they merge themselves into the narrower sect which would

[1] Braithwaite, loc. cit., p. 525.

retain and control them? The outcome is bound to be different in different cases, much depending, not only on objective factors, such as the poverty of the family, but also on subjective ones, the pedagogical know-how, the persuasiveness, and so on, of the parents and their peers. Certain is only that the tensions generated in the children are apt to be painful ones, for if children – by dint of their whole psychology – hate one thing, it is to be different from other children, from children at large. Many sectarians' lives have been darkened by the fact that a son or a daughter was unwilling to don the wedding garment, to walk in the way of truth. Often, of course, head-on collisions which would destroy families are avoided, but then there frequently is – there frequently must be – a desire on the part of the young to sidestep the issue, to be at peace both with the parents and with the people outside, in the wider world. This desire, then, this willingness or even anxiety to compromise, will constitute one of the most potent causes for sect decay, for the denominationalization of the dissentient group.

The life-process of the sects is therefore at the same time also a death-process, in the sense that the spirit of revolution, characteristic and constitutive of the sect in the proper sense of the word, dries off and dies off, and this can also be seen from the simple fact that they have all gone the same way.[1] There could be no better

[1] By 'all' we mean all those who have remained within secular society; those who have withdrawn completely and founded communities of their own, e.g. communist colonies, are a special case and cannot be considered here. But we can say this much: a consideration of their histories would not force us to modify our general impression. Even sectarian settlements are under the law of involution. If they are economically not a success, hunger forces them to disperse (e.g. the Icarians); if they are economically a success and grow rich, prosperity undermines their sectarian spirit as it does that of their brethren 'in the world' (e.g. Bishop Hill). Sometimes, indeed, a happy medium is struck; there develops a life of comfort without apparent damage to religious convictions. The Shakers are the best example: they have lasted for a long time. The first communities were established in 1787; the last are now coming to a close. This looks very much like an 'established sect'. But appearances are deceptive. Even in the case of the Shakers, only the body has endured; the spirit has not. Marguerite Melcher, in her extremely favourable report on *The Shaker Adventure*, has given plenty of proof that very soon a process of routinization set in. Cf. pp. 40, 41, 56, 82, 87, 88, 100–4, 106, 110, 111, 148, 149, 218, 219, 254, 255, 283, 284. Most characteristic was the growing routinization of the Shaker dance, concerning which cf. Knox, loc. cit., pp. 562–4. Knox's words, though a little flippant, are just: 'Enthusiasm does not maintain itself at fever heat; dance as you will, flap your hands as you will, you

witness to the truth of this assertion than W. B. Selbie, for his book *English Sects* (a summary of summaries) sees things very much from the left wing point of view. We therefore give the word to him and allow him to close this section of our book. 'The gradual abandonment of the names Non-conformist and Dissenter, and the substitution for them of "Free Church" is significant . . . When every allowance has been made . . . it still remains true that the great masses of the wage-earning population are altogether alienated from the churches, whether Nonconformist or Anglican. The reasons for this are predominantly social. In the large towns working men realize that the churches belong rather to the order of the employers than of the employed. They are democratic only in name, and both their government and finance are so arranged as to suit the haves rather than the have-nots.'[1] Such a statement is perhaps a little too extreme; there are religious groups which still attract and subserve the poorest of the poor, but there is no reason to believe that they will be better able to resist the relentless grinding of the mill of time, the slow but sure process of attrition, than their many predecessors whom Selbie has in mind.

THE SPLITTING OF SECTS

Among the phenomena which accompany and characterize the decline of sects into denominations is the appearance of a definite fissiparous tendency. Part of the group shows itself prepared to accept the cooling-down process as inevitable, if not indeed as desirable, but another part is appalled by it and resists it as much as it possibly can. This split-up of the sects into a right and a left has nothing surprising in it if we remember, as we always should, that a sect is a conflict society, a revolutionary movement. All

[1] Selbie, loc. cit., pp. 225 and 240. Cf. also Wilkinson, loc. cit., p. 211 (in exactly the same sense).

---

cannot conjure up the old days when people rolled on the floor in agonies of convincement and talked in strange sounds which might, for all they knew, be the language of the Hotmatots' (p. 565). It would be quite misleading to speak of the Shakers as a *sect* which has survived for upward of a hundred and fifty years. They, too, changed before long from a sectarian to a denominational character. By 1826, at the latest, the transition was accomplished. Even this successful community was therefore truly sectarian for only one generation or so, thirty to forty years.

revolutionary movements have, after a while, evinced the same tensions and tendencies: *la Montagne* confronted *la Gironde* shortly after 1789; Trotskyism collided with the official party line shortly after 1917; the Spartacus League broke from the German Social Democrats in 1918, a month or so after their joint triumph over the Kaiser; and so on, and so forth. If anything is apt to amaze the student of religious dissent, it is merely the regularity with which this break-up of sectarian unity occurs: it appears as inevitably at the end of the first, heroic period, as amen does at the end of a prayer.

Where the recruiting ground of a sect takes in two different classes, the coming split is inherent from the very beginning, for it is unlikely that historical development will not produce discrepancies between them, will not – for instance – allow one of them to rise in the scale of wealth, while keeping the other down, at least relatively. A good example are, once more, the Old Believers. The merchants and the townspeople generally became well-to-do and consequently lukewarm in religion; the country-folk, on the other hand, remained for a long time in their erstwhile condition, both objectively and subjectively, both in standard of living and in sentiment. It is revealing that by 1909 the complaints of the bourgeois against Tsarism had become muted, while the peasantry continued loudly to complain.[1]

The conflict between left and right in the Old Believers' movement had, however, erupted long before 1909 when the existence of a *de facto* split became obvious to the nation at large by the holding of a special Old Believer Peasant Congress. Half a century before it had been an accomplished, though not perhaps an admitted, fact. By 1847, the denomination had acquired a hierarchy of its own with the help of a foreign metropolitan, and with its centre in a foreign land (Austria); yet Alexander II, in contrast and reaction to his strict and aggressive father, turned a blind eye to this evolution, unpatriotic though it necessarily appeared. 'This very mildness of Alexander caused a split in the ranks of the [so-called] Austrian denomination,' Curtiss reports. 'The wealthy leaders of this group living in Moscow were so pleased with the new order of things that in 1861 they induced the council of [their] bishops to send forth a "diocesan message" saying that it was time to discard some of their old beliefs. It was no longer

[1] Cf. Curtiss, loc. cit., pp. 321 and 322.

fitting, they said, to believe in the imminent end of the world and the coming of Anti-Christ. The Tsar was to be recognized as a holy person protected by God and worthy of the prayers of true believers. Of course, they were not ready to recognize the official Church as the true church, but they should no longer regard it as the handiwork of the devil and should admit that the Christ whom it worshipped was the Saviour. But . . . many of the rank and file of the Austrian group, especially those living along the Volga and in the forests of the north, were not willing to make their peace with the Tsar and his government . . . Consequently the ranks of the Austrian group were cleft into two sections – those conservative Old Believers, some of them wealthy, who were concentrated in Moscow, together with most of their hierarchy; and at odds with them the mass of peasant Old Believers . . . in the provinces. This split continued to plague the Old Believers for decades.'[1]

It may be permissible, and will be useful, at this point, to interrupt our normal routine and cast a first quick glance at the West because we have a chance here to show, how the complexity and multiplicity of the descriptive facts yields, on analysis, to the comparative simplicity and uniformity of typological characterization. In 1827, there came to the Quakers of America the 'great separation': Elias Hicks and his (liberal) party were disowned and driven out by the conservative-orthodox majority. As among the Old Believers, one cause of the schism was the social contrast between city and country, between the city which had enriched some Friends, and the country where others still lived in their erstwhile condition. 'The situation was . . . complicated,' a historian writes (we should almost say: caused), 'by the conservatism of city dweller Quakers, many of whom had acquired considerable wealth, whereas their less prosperous rural brethren . . . had caught a breath of the progress that was in the air. The latter group urged changes, while the former clung tenaciously to the *status quo* . . . Their opposition helped to make [Hicks] the champion of the popular dissatisfaction with the authority of the city leaders.'[2] As can be seen, the American sect split for the same reason as the Russian. In either case, there was a differential rate of readjustment to the world, one sub-group pulling ahead and the other holding back. In these circumstances inner tensions arise

[1] Ibid., pp. 134 and 135.

[2] Hinshaw, loc. cit., pp. 34 and 35.

which will, if not relieved, lead to cracks in the structure and ultimately to a bursting asunder of the frame.

In the crucial period around 1905, when it looked for a moment as if the frozen forms of Russian political life would be liquified and reforms would become possible, another inner conflict among the Old Believers was revealed – that between the older and the younger members. Some of the capitalists were in sympathy with the parties of the right; the bulk of the Old Believers adhered to the Cadets and their programme; some of the rank and file, however, were in sympathy with the parties of the left. It is said that the older men were Cadets, i.e. occupied a position near the centre of the political spectrum, whereas the younger men were pre-and pro-Communists, assuming a place on the extremist wing.[1] This radicalization, which might seem *prima facie* to run against our thesis of the progressive cooling-down of the sects, in reality confirms it, for what the younger people did was simply to get into line with secular society, and especially the non-religious youth of the country, which at this juncture happened to be revolutionary.

Lest it be thought that the Old Believers were particularly apt to split because they were comparatively numerous and had a comparatively long history, let us quickly look at the Stranniky, a truly compact and crisis-born group. Very early in their collective pilgrimage through history no fewer than four crossroads were reached. The first concerned marriage: some would allow it, others condemned it. The second concerned money: some would allow its use, even though every kopek had the image of the Tsar-Antichrist on it, others condemned it for that reason. The third concerned printed books: was it lawful to use one which had the imprimatur of the authorities in it, or was it not? On this point a compromise seems to have been reached by means of the tearing out of the offending page. Yet the fissiparous tendency is clearly observable, even if it did not lead to fission in this case: those who were prepared to use the same books as the other Christians were the right, those who would not touch them were the left, of the movement. Finally, there were attempts to organize the group by appointing office-bearers of some sort. Semenov, who broached the idea, was immediately branded by some of his fellow-sectarians as a new Nikon. Here was another parting of the paths.[2]

[1] Curtiss, loc. cit., p. 234.

[2] Conybeare, loc. cit., pp. 162–4.

As with the Stranniky, so with the Dukhobortsy. There is a whole complicated history of dissensions and dispersions. The Molokane, whom we have treated as a separate sect in these pages, were originally an offshoot of them. But part of them developed into a denomination, introducing rites, if not indeed sacraments, elders, if not indeed priests, permitting army service, and, with certain safeguards, the swearing of oaths, and so on. Others, understandably, did not follow the example of this so-called 'Don Sect' and remained Molokane in the older, or even in the original, sense of the name. The Dukhobortsy, for their part, broke in two when some followed Pyotr Verigin in his more radical policies, while others stuck to the milder ways of Lukeriya Kalmikov. As we noted in another context, the two sub-sects were, not inaptly, described as the Mad Dukhobors and the Bad Dukhobors. When the Mad Dukhobors shifted to Canada, a tripartite development took place. Some became to all intents and purposes Canadians, settling in homesteads of their own (the so-called Independent Dukhobors); others adjusted to Canadian life, but not entirely, remaining, as they did, in isolated, self-enclosed settlements (the Community Dukhobors); yet others refused to adjust (the Sons of Freedom) and were seen by Canadians in the same light as the Russians of Tsarist days saw their criminal sects.[1]

Turning now to the great sect movements of the West, we find the very self-same fissiparous tendency at work. The Mennonites were founded, as we have seen, in the mid-thirties of the sixteenth century; by the mid-fifties they had already split. There were the Waterlanders in the north of Holland, and the Flemish and Frisian Mennonites more to the south and east. The Waterlanders (like the Molokane of the Don) steered into ways which, to their erstwhile brethren, appeared to be backsliding. The Flemish–Frisian sub-group was characterized by the uncompromising, fierce, practice of excommunication by which they tried to keep their community clean. Compared to them, the Waterlanders were liberals. This conflict was connected with, and reflected in, the split of the English General Baptists into followers of John Smyth and followers of Thomas Helwys. 'Smyth derived from the Mennonites his belief that Christians should not take oaths or accept office as magistrates or marry outside the church. He was silent on military service, but article 85 of his long Confession

[1] Ibid., pp. 304, 321, 305, 309, 310, 316, 317; Wright, loc. cit., *passim*.

really rules it out for Christians . . . Helwys soon made it clear that . . . he was willing to take oaths and to accept the magistracy, though he completely dissociated it from the religious life of the nation.' The Waterlanders, incidentally, for all their liberalism, thought Helwys too liberal and made this clear to five General Baptist congregations in England with whom they stood in correspondence.[1]

The Quakers were no more able to withstand threats to their coherence, as can be seen from the epithets which were apt to add themselves to their name: Proud Quakers, Fast Quakers, Slow Quakers, Gay Quakers, Plain Quakers . . . The Proud Quakers, followers of Rice Jones and John Trentham, were a right-wing deviation. They did not approve of preaching in markets and demonstrations in churches. 'These people have taken up a belief that they may keep their inward unto God, and yield their bodies to comply with outward things,' William Smith said of them in his pamphlet *A Few Words unto a Peculiar People* (1669). Fox and his main-stream Friends loathed the lot for being outside 'sect fellowship', and even Braithwaite, writing in the twentieth century, reports with some glee that Jones died an alehouse-keeper and Trentham a drunkard.[2] In the Hicksite separation, to which we have already referred, the issue was, organizationally, how great the control of the elders over the rank and file should be, and theologically, what should bear more emphasis – the Word without or the Light within, the historic or the indwelling Christ. The conservatives were in both respects in favour of authority, the liberals in favour of freedom; the insistence of the latter that the Light within is the court beyond which there can be no further appeal is a form of libertarianism. In 1845, this conflict, with somewhat changed fronts, erupted again. John Wilbur's Slow Quakers were organizationally the conservatives (though they differed from the Hicksites by their greater emphasis on the mystical element – an emphasis which, however, blended well with their general traditionalism as the mystical element had loomed so large in early Quaker days). Joseph John Gurney's Fast Quakers were organizationally the progressives. They wished to bring the Friends more into line with Protestantism as shaped by the

[1] Underwood, loc. cit., pp. 26, 52, 53. Concerning the later split which brought about the emergence of the New Connexion, cf. ibid., p. 150 et seq.
[2] Braithwaite, loc. cit., p. 46.

evangelical movement – so much so that Thomas Shillitoe could call Gurney 'an Episcopalian, not a Quaker'. The situation was highly complex. The Wilburites were conservative with regard to Quakerism, wishing to keep it unchanged, but just for this reason they harboured a revolutionary element, namely belief in the supremacy of the inner experience. The Gurneyites were, as we have said, progressive with regard to Quakerism, wishing to see it transformed, but just for this reason they pushed in the direction of authoritarianism, for the written word was to them the last standard of judgement. More sharply expressed: the reactionaries in domestic policy were theologically revolutionaries; the reformers in domestic policy were theologically conservatives. Nevertheless, the fronts were clear. The Wilburite Slow Quakers were less advanced towards denominationalism than the Gurneyite Fast Quakers for they rejected some typical denominational features which the others accepted: a paid ministry, planned meetings, i.e. pre-arranged sermons, organ music and singing instead of the old-style waiting in silence, etc. The word 'worldliness' is applied to the Fast Quakers even by some whose sympathies are on the whole on their side.[1] In England, the tendency to split, inherent in the Quaker body, was not destined ever to bite so deep as in America. But when Joseph John Gurney was a boy, the Plain Quakers and the Gay Quakers were sharply distinguished. 'The "Plain Quakers", by their principles, were debarred from easy mingling with general society, but the "Gay Quakers" were just like other people, except for a stern barrier against intermarriage with "the world".'[2]

Among the Wesleyans, the most significant schism was the emergence of the Primitive Methodists between 1807 and 1812. (Alexander Kilham's Methodist New Connection of 1797 had been a rather mild affair.) Ostensibly, 'Hugh Bourne led a protest against the tendency to confine Methodist preaching to their preaching houses,' and 'attempted to restore the outdoor preaching of the "primitive" times'. But underneath this superficial, seemingly purely tactical, issue, there hid a deeper, a social, split. In their own historian's words, the Wesleyan movement 'was by now settled in its preaching houses and on its way to respectability,'

[1] Hinshaw, loc. cit., p. 37 et seq.; Brinton, H., *Friends for 300 Years*, New York 1952, p. 192.
[2] Whitney, J., *Elizabeth Fry: Quaker Heroine*, Boston 1936, p. 26.

while the Primitive Methodists undertook 'to minister to the working classes with whom the Wesleyans were losing contact'.[1] Obviously, the third and the fourth estate are breaking asunder: once more social history underneath ecclesiastical! Further secessions followed. To give but one more example: in 1815 another Bourne – Frederick William – started the Bible Christians, especially in Devonshire and Cornwall.[2] In America, the Methodist Protestant Church constituted itself as a body distinct from the Methodist Episcopal Church in 1828, the year when Andrew Jackson was elected President. The coincidence of the two events is not fortuitous. In both a lower, if not the lowest, stratum expressed its resentments and its aspirations, its desire for a total and consistent democracy.[3]

More recent sect movements have not, of course, had as much time for splitting as the older ones, but the fissiparous tendency can be seen at work all the same. Both Elimites and Christadelphians were affected by it. Indeed, even the Jehovah's Witnesses, though still held together by a fierce hatred of the world, have already spawned a sub-sect, the 'Servant of Yah', who regard the parent body as servants of Satan – no more, no less.[4]

Disruption came to Elim in 1939–40. The reason for it was that the movement had, in spite of its youth, already become organized, centralized, bureaucratized and routinized. Headquarters had become very powerful and had made its power-position permanent and more secure with the help of legal means. There was a revolt against this development on the part of those who desired to see Elim preserve its pristine localism, informality, lay administration and revivalistic-inspirational character. 'In 1938,' Wilson rightly says, 'Elim was at an altogether similar crossroads to Methodism

[1] Cameron, loc. cit., p. 75.

[2] Selbie, loc. cit., p. 191.

[3] Cameron, loc. cit., pp. 116–18.

[4] Concerning this interesting grouping which claims that the traditionally supplied vowel points of the Hebrew Scriptures falsify the text (so much so that the Devil's name, Jehovah, has become God's name!) and that a proper understanding of the Bible presupposes other vowel points which their initiates alone know, and which will never be known to more than 144,000 persons, cf. Whalen, loc. cit., p. 212. For the split of the Black Muslims which occurred in 1964 when Malcolm X broke away from Elijah Muhammad, cf. detailed reports in the *New York Times* of 26 February, 9 and 13 March, 8 and 10 May, and 4 October, 1964.

at the end of the eighteenth century.'[1] There was, however, also a parallel to the Quaker crisis of 1845, at least so far as the complication of the situation was concerned. Jeffrey, who fought denominationalization on the organizational plane, was himself pushing towards mental denominationalization in embracing a doctrine which shifted the locus of holiness away from the small dissenting group towards the wider, more inclusive society, as we shall presently see. Either way, by 1941, continued co-operation had become impossible. The Bible Pattern Church Fellowship broke away from the Elim Foursquare Gospel Church. We do not stay to inquire whether this was a case of secession or expulsion.

As for Christadelphianism, the history of its divisions and subdivisions is too complicated to be discussed in this book. Already 'in the first twenty-five years or so . . . no less than twelve different heresies had arisen'.[2] We cannot go into all this.[3] Suffice it to say that there *was* such a history, and a very unhappy one to boot, if unity is considered a value in itself. It is more pertinent to ask once again why such schisms have occurred in the Elim Tabernacle and in Christadelphianism, and also in all the other sect movements, old and new, which we have surveyed.

Bryan Wilson, who records details of the Elimite and Christadelphian disruptions in his book *Sects and Society*, has tried to explain them on a theoretical basis different from the one embodied in the present text. 'Division was on the question of power and institutionalization, not on the accommodation of the sect to the social practices prevailing in the world,' he says of the case of Elim. 'There was no suggestion that the schism was related to compromise with the wider society.' There was simply 'a struggle for control of the movement which may have been no more than a desire for power on the part of those intimately concerned'. And of the Christadelphians he writes: 'Clashes of personality, perhaps specifically concerned with the ambition to lead, appear to have been at the basis of most schisms in Christadelphianism, and not a differential desire to compromise with the world.'[4] Thus a kind of great-man-theory of sect-fissure is proposed, which stands in contrast to the social-movement-theory followed here.

It is obvious that leading personalities, and clashes between

[1] Wilson, loc. cit., p. 50. Cf. also, pp. 43, 46–9, 51–6.

[2] Ibid., p. 244.

[3] Cf. ibid., pp. 240, 242 et seq.

[4] Ibid., pp. 339, 340, 341.

leading personalities, are involved in any and every sect formation and sect dissolution. It is so obvious, indeed, as to be hardly worth mentioning in a book on the *sociology* of religion. The question is, however, whether the analysis and the etiology of divisive events leads us only to the personal, and not further down to a submerged, but underlying, social level. Wilson denies this; we would assert it still, and we can draw strength from Wilson's own, so splendidly informative, accounts.

In the case of Elim, one factor was 'the . . . loyalty of the leader to a gratuitous teaching, namely British-Israelism, and possibly his anti-pacifism based on this theory'.[1] This half-sentence is sufficient to prove that compromise with the wider society, and not only personality, *was* involved. For British Israelism is merely an extreme, grotesquely caparisoned version of religious ethnocentrism, religious nationalism; it teaches that all the British are God's chosen people, not only the sectarian Elimites. He who embraces these tenets is well on the way back to Anglicanism. He thinks in terms of his wider, rather than in terms of his narrower, culture. He is no longer a dissenter in the full sense of the word. And when he takes a step from pacifism to anti-pacifism, he advances powerfully in the same direction – towards acceptance of established society. A man who asserts that his country is worth fighting for and worth dying for is no longer a sectarian, for his country is holy to him now, not unholy. It is really difficult to see how accommodation of the sect to the social practices prevailing in the world can be denied in this case. Is the giving-up of conscientious objection to military service perhaps not such an accommodation?

The split in the Elim movement was therefore due to the fact, evidenced by the acceptance of a nationalistic theory and equally nationalistic practice, that some leaders (and members) had begun to contract back into the ongoing stream of inclusive national life and national prejudice and policy. An analysis of the case of Christadelphianism is equally apt to support the thesis propounded in this book. 'The very geographic incidence of many secessions suggests strong charismatic qualities in those who lead factions, and who have won allegiance from those who have been exposed to their charisma, rather than any economic divergence of interest between contending parties,'[2] Wilson asserts. The presence of

[1] Ibid., p. 339. [2] Ibid., p. 341.

charismatic qualities and their effect need not be denied; yet we would urge against Wilson that the geographic incidence of many of the secessions which he stresses, proves, and proves beyond the shadow of a doubt, that there *was* an economic divergence of interest between the contending parties. We need only turn to other of our fellow-worker's pages to see how true this is.

In the crisis brought on by World War I, F. G. Jannaway of London and C. C. Walker of Birmingham were the protagonists. Did they collect followings merely, or mainly, because they were strong personalities? By no means. The issue was how far a Christadelphian could become involved in the war effort without ceasing to be a true Brother of Christ. Was it lawful to accept non-combatant service? or to make munitions? 'The matter of non-combatant service was one on which the London Committee refused to compromise, in spite of an article by Walker appealing for the right of conscience in this matter since it was not covered by the Word of God . . . On the matter of munitions making, there were also divergent opinions. Walker wrote, "There is no law of Christ against it . . ."'[1] It is no exaggeration to say that the economic divergence of interest between the contending parties is obvious and undeniable here. Birmingham was a great centre of the armament industry; many of the Birmingham brethren earned their daily bread, and an increasingly large piece of that bread, in that industry; they followed Walker for a more tangible reason than his charismatic qualities . . . Beyond this all-too-human conflict, there lay the fact that the Birmingham community had become somewhat conservative all round, while the Londoners were as yet much more to the left – the familiar story of the withering of the green bay tree. 'Some brethren, notably Jannaway, and others in London, had always looked askance at the Auxiliary Lecturing Society [a body within the body], and Walker, its president, had acknowledged that compromise with first principles was involved in its organization,' Wilson explains.[2] And he continues, touching upon the crux of the matter and helping us in spite of himself to confirm our own theory: 'The protest was in some way associated with dislike of the increased affluence of some brethren . . . "Worldly habits are on the increase . . ."', a stern critic had complained. 'Birmingham in particular had been

[1] Ibid., p. 257.

[2] Ibid., p. 259.

accused of latitudinarianism . . .' 'All this,' Wilson himself states, 'may reflect a growing dissatisfaction with the relative comfort of the brethren compared to the earlier years.' It was because there was this relative comfort, because it did not come to all equally quickly and equally fully, and because some would have liked to hold this development back, while others wished to push it on, that the unity of Christadelphianism was in jeopardy, and not because of personal power struggles only. The latter are, on Wilson's own showing, merely secondary – symptoms of underlying causes rather than causes themselves. There is nothing in these materials which would force one to modify the thesis that the splitting of sects is an incident – near-necessary incident – in the process of sect decay, a result of the variation in the speeds with which sectarians travel back into the world.

The end result of all the fissions which occur, not to say, must occur, is truly amazing. In 1960, the House of Commons Standing Committee discussed a proposed amendment to the Charities Bill then pending, designed to grant religious bodies exemption from registration under the Act presently to be passed. The Joint Undersecretary of the Home Office, Mr. David Renton, gave on this occasion details of a Home Office register for marriage purposes and revealed that it contained more than a thousand entries. 'The position is nothing like so simple as one might think,' he pointed out. 'The Methodists, for example, are divided into about two dozen sections; . . . the Baptists into about three dozen; the Congregationalists into about the same number . . .' The older dissenting groups were thus anything but united, yet they accounted between them for only 10 per cent of the total. Ninety per cent was in all probability made up by tiny conventicles such as 'the Peculiar People, the Original Peculiar People, the Peculiar People (Liberty Section), and the Peculiars'. 'There were various brethren,' Mr. Renton reported, 'who objected to any specific designation . . . and about fifty [groups] who had to be described as "other bodies unattached".'[1] These latter were in all probability sects just struggling into existence, splinters that were splitting off of some stem, and themselves in all probability about to split again.

Even these statistics, however, amazing though they are, do not yet give us a full picture of the extent to which sect splintering and

[1] The Manchester *Guardian*, 1 June 1960.

attrition occur. They tell us nothing of the groups which have died and disappeared altogether, and their number may well be legion; they tell us nothing either of the groups which are too informal, or too self-centred, or too hostile to the State, to make their name known to the authorities. Mr. Renton's figures, it should be remembered, include only those sects which undertake to solemnize weddings, and not every sectlet need be active in this field. And, finally, the statistics given do not reveal how many names on the list are joint names of one-time hostile groupings that have buried the hatchet and are a unity once again. The process of sect-decay is not only a history of sect-separations; it is also, though to a lesser extent, a history of sect-reunions.

To restrict ourselves to three examples: in 1891 the General Baptists of the New Connexion fused with the Particular Baptists;[1] among the Methodists, there arose the United Methodist Church which embraced the Methodist New Connection, the Bible Christians, and the United Free Churches, the latter body having collected together such groups as the Protestant Methodists, the Wesleyan Methodist Association, the Wesleyan Reformers, the Arminian Methodists, and the Welsh Independent Methodists;[2] and in the Quaker fold, Rufus Jones exercised an effective healing ministry.[3] How was it that these reunions became possible? One need not look far for the answer. The original split had taken place because some had turned conservative while others had remained revolutionary; but the revolutionary wing regularly went the same way as their now divorced brethren, only a little later. The same cause, rise in the world, led to the same effect, fall from sectarian standards of the early days. When that had happened, when the temperatures of the two bodies had become adjusted to each other, there was no longer any reason why they should not join forces once again. Indeed, there was a reason why they should. Sect decay is a process of debilitation. The membership is apt to fall off; so is the ability to finance, or rather to maintain, the churchly apparatus; and beyond any concrete difficulties,

[1] Underwood, loc. cit., p. 202 et seq.

[2] *The New Schaff-Herzog Encyclopedia of Religious Knowledge*, Grand Rapids 1956, art. Methodists, vol. VII, p. 332 et seq., esp. pp. 339 and 340.

[3] Cf. Hinshaw's book, *passim*, but especially the illustration opposite p. 77 where Jones 'as the reuniter of Quaker groups' is bracketed with Fox and Penn 'to form Quakerism's great triumvirate'.

there is a general feeling of dysphoria. In these circumstances, a reunion is a great bracer, a shot in the arm. It creates an impression of progress, of upward development, where there is in reality a regress, an involution.

Reunions like the ones specifically mentioned do not as a rule alter the general picture, in fact, they do not even bring the total number of dissenting groups down, as one would expect them to do. This is once again due to the fact that history repeats itself. Just as the original movement had divided into a relatively denominational and a relatively sectarian, a relatively cool, and a relatively hot, half, so does the breakaway group which, when the first split occurred, was still all sectarian and burning hot. Some Particular Baptists were, after a time, 'particular' no longer, or rather only in name; others were as 'particular', i.e. as separatist-sectarian, as before. The crystallization of two communities within one community – the harbinger of the impending rupture – happened in and through a protracted public discussion of the question as to whether the Particular Baptists should stand for the principle of open, or for the principle of closed, communion. The champion of the former policy was Robert Hall; that of the latter was William Gadsby. Clearly, the difference between these two men, their convictions and their confrères, was that Hall was a sectarian no longer, whereas Gadsby still was one. Even a cursory glance at the biography of the two leaders shows that behind the theological contrast there was hidden a social one: Robert Hall had the privilege of a regular University education, whereas William Gadsby had no education worth speaking of, having been apprenticed, at the age of thirteen, to the craft of ribbon-weaving. It cannot be surprising for a reader of this book to learn that comfortably rich Mr. Spurgeon supported open communion, whereas desperately poor John Warburton decidedly did not. The sons of Gadsby and Warburton organized themselves as the Strict and Particular Baptists, an abiding, extreme, sect.[1] In Underwood's words, they 'declined to be drawn into the main stream of Baptist life'.[2] And thus the tendency towards fusion was counterbalanced and statistically countermanded by the persistent over-all tendency towards fission.

[1] Underwood, loc. cit., p. 169 et seq.; p. 185, et seq.; p. 242 et seq.
[2] Ibid., p. 242.

THE DENOMINATION

The logical end of a process of adjustment is a state of being adjusted, and when that is reached, the sect has finally become a denomination. 'Denominations,' so Howard Becker has defined these formations, and we subscribe to his definition, 'are simply sects in an advanced stage of development and adjustment to each other and the secular world.'[1] The word denomination is a good and expressive one, for it has in it the Latin *nomen* or name. The members of a denominational group are no longer distinguished from their fellow-citizens, as their forebears had been, by alienation, opposition, aggression and other negative sentiments; their attitudes towards inclusive society have become largely positive; they are different from the rest of society in name rather than in fact. Indeed, sometimes there is a certain embarrassment when the olden days of antinomianism and antipatriotism are recalled. Baptists do not like to be reminded of Münster and its communism; Quakers of Fox's performance at Lichfield, the 'bloody city' which he so uncharitably cursed; Methodists of the open spaces in and around London where so many of their co-religionists roamed on 28 February 1763, in expectation of the immediate end of the world. There is sometimes a subconscious fear on the part of these denominations and their individual members that their loyalty to the fatherland and other established values may be suspect. This is a new kind of inferiority complex, very different from the old, which they tend to overcompensate. If they do overcompensate it; if they speak with a particularly loud voice in defence of property, or in furtherance of a war effort; or of soberness and steadiness in all things, and so on, they prove how far their community has travelled from its starting point, how truly it has become a negation of its pristine self.

However, even this truth should not be overstated. Dissenting groups do lose their sectarian souls, but they retain their specific bodies; they therefore retain their identity and to some extent their individuality. They take their place in the world, but the world is not a simple monolithic whole; it embraces a whole gamut of variations, and the erstwhile sect adjusts to one of these variations which suits it, or adds itself as yet another variation to the existing

[1] Becker, H., *Systematic Sociology on the basis of the Beziehungslehre and Gebildelehre of Leopold von Wiese*, New York 1932, p. 626.

range. Comparison to another social process of adjustment may help to clarify what we have to say. There can be no doubt that the English polity has accepted the principles of modern democracy: the process of decision-making, which is what matters, is entirely democratic, or rather, to be careful about it, no less democratic than it is in other countries, for instance the United States of America. But this does not mean that England has become a country like the United States of America; it means only that she, also, is a democracy. She is – colloquially expressed – a democracy with a difference, and the difference is constituted by her specific history, and by the living tradition which carries this history from the past through the present into the future. So also with the denomination: in what matters, i.e. in the over-all attitude to the established values, it is no longer really a dissenting but substantially a conforming group, yet conformity can mean a number of different things. As D. A. Martin has expressed it in a truly ingenious and striking manner which will be readily understood even outside England: 'The sociological idea of the denomination is the idea of Her Majesty's Opposition, of disagreement within consensus.'[1] Just where-in the disagreements consist, is rather difficult to say, simply because men's mind-contents are never univocally defined. The closest investigation on the basis of the best questionnaires, though it might teach us something, would not reveal everything. A twentieth-century English Methodist does not himself know whether he is more of a Methodist or of an Englishman, and as he himself does not know it, we cannot expect him to enlighten others on this point. Indeed, even the word Methodist, as used in this statement, is of necessity obscure. Names remain, while the things which they signify alter. Methodist, in our sentence, would have to mean: modernized Methodist. But to what degree modernized? to what degree in the grip of Methodist traditions? All we can really say is that this man will not resemble, for instance, John Nelson, who refused to serve in the army because he thought arms-bearing contrary to the Gospel.

The substantive adjustment of Methodists (to continue to use them as a convenient example, although others would do as well) to English society and its constitutive values is clearly obvious from the fact that, for a long time, they have sided with the majority

[1] 'The Denomination', *The British Journal of Sociology*, 1962, p. 13.

of their countrymen in all questions of war and peace. But at certain crucial points a slight deviation from the main stream becomes noticeable. When, in 1943, the Royal Air Force bombed the Eder and Möhne dams and great damage was done to civilian life in the area, the measure met with little opposition in England. It was accepted as a sad necessity, and there was an underlying conviction, stemming not only from the consciousness that the war was a war against tyranny, but also from older conceptions, from the whole complex of religious ethnocentrism, that this action could not be wrong as it served a just purpose (Max Weber's *Erfolgsethik* – the ethics of utility). But the so-called nonconformist conscience gave a groan: it felt, to say the least, uneasy (a stirring of Max Weber's *Gesinnungsethik* – the ethics of principle). This uneasiness was due to the fact that there was a good deal less religious ethnocentrism in the circles concerned: perhaps we can even say there was a little bit of the spirit of John Nelson left. Washed down the stream of history since the 1740s, and watered down by a constant and copious influx of conservative ideas and ideologies, it was yet present, in the 1940s, as a definite and determinate trace-element (though no more than a trace-element) in the Methodist mentality. It is characteristic that the disagreement with public opinion at large, such as it was, was merely one about the means to be used in the war – indeed, merely one about one of the uses of one of the means; it was not a disagreement about the ends to be attained by the war. On that point, there was no conflict at all, not even the slightest, and this shows that the negativistic-revolutionary spirit had evaporated altogether. True sects, like the Jehovah's Witnesses, felt differently about means *and* ends.

Individual dissenters, even of the latter (denominational) days of their movements, have sometimes stood forth as open opponents of religious tribalism and thus retained, or revived, older attitudes. The Baptist John Clifford, for instance, condemned the Boer War, in spite of the fact that the waves of jingoism were running high in the whole country, in spite of the fact, also, that he was more or less alone in his own communion.[1] The question arises, however, as to whether, in the latter days, there were still *mass* protests against national policies; if so, the group concerned was still sectarian; if so, it had resisted the tendency towards accommodation

[1] Cf. Underwood, loc. cit., pp. 228 and 229.

to inclusive society. Here the continuing rejection, by Quaker youths, of armed service springs to mind at once. We must discuss it as is of crucial importance.

It goes without saying that this so-called conscientious objection, which is indeed a survival from truly sectarian times, must not be seen in isolation, as if the continued existence of one sectarian trait betokened the continued existence of all, of the whole negativistic-revolutionary outlook. John Clifford did reject the Boer War, but he did not reject appointment, in 1921, as a Companion of Honour – a sure sign that there could no longer be any question of all-round hostility to the establishment. But let us remain with the Quakers. If we widen the picture just a little beyond their refusal to carry arms, we see immediately that, even in the field of war and peace, Quaker attitudes are not now what they once were. One Quaker, Herbert Hoover, had no compunction about becoming commander-in-chief of the American armed forces; another, Richard Nixon, did not hesitate to be the running mate, and deputy commander-in-chief, of a general, Dwight Eisenhower, and he would have liked nothing better than to be made full commander-in-chief, atomic arsenal and all, himself; in England, Sir Samuel Hoare did not allow his Quakerism to stand in the way of deep involvement in diplomacy at a time when everybody knew that military conflict would be the end of that diplomacy. There were, however, many in the Quaker rank and file who looked askance at these activities and attitudes, and their case is really the most important here.

Were these conscientious objectors of the twentieth century, we must inquire, still animated by the sectarian spirit of the seventeenth? For the sociologist, the most appropriate search for an answer must be based on a total assessment of the Quaker community as it then was and as it now is. Then it consisted, as we have seen, mainly of small and uneducated men; now it consists, as everybody knows, mainly of rather comfortable and highly educated people. There has been a complete change in the recruiting area and consequently in the human type recruited, and with this change has come a transformation in the inner attitudes, even though one outer feature – objection to armed service – has remained. Perhaps we can best explain what has happened with the help of Max Weber's doctrine of elective affinity. Many intellectuals – for reasons which are fairly obvious – have felt attracted by the Quaker philosophy of life; it fitted some of them as a glove does the hand; but as they began to fill the benches of the meeting houses, the proletariat began to file out. Today, the Quakers are not at all a lower class grouping. Intellectuals are understandably opponents of war; it appears to them as *the* irrational form of international politics *par excellence*; pacifism, on the other hand, appears as a command of common sense. They feel (and this writer does not blame them) repulsed by religious ethnocentricity, and this is one of the incentives that drives them into the fold of the Friends. But a basically rationalistic is not a basically alienated mentality; it will criticize some traits of the social system, but hardly reject it *in toto*. By and large modern Quakers have found their place in the world; quite a few, indeed, a place at the controls, their pacifism notwithstanding – so much so that conscientious objection appears at times as no more than a fad. For this reason, the distance travelled by Friends since Fox's day is hardly less than that covered by Methodists since the day of John Nelson. Routinization has many forms and rationalization is one of them; rationalism is a reforming, at times, in fact, a politically revolutionary ideology; but it is certainly not a religious – i.e. a passionate, i.e. an irrational – rejection of the world. Even the most determined modern Quaker objector to military service will not go naked 'for a sign'! Even the most typical Quaker of these days does not quake any more.

There is no cause to doubt, then, that even the Quakers are, in this their third century, a typical denomination, and that denominationalization, though sometimes a delayed and sometimes a partial, is yet a universal, process in the area of religious dissent. Death, they say, waits for no man; it waits for no sect either.

The replacement of the sectarian by a denominational spirit draws after it certain consequences which, between them, impart to the dissenting – no longer dissenting – group a new and different social character and demonstrate the justification and necessity of distinguishing sect and denomination as two entirely dissimilar sociological types, in spite of the historical connection between them. In a book, concerned, as this is, with the *outer* relations of religious bodies, they can be of no more than secondary interest, for they involve the *inner* life of such groupings. A brief survey of them will, however, be of use for it will show – be it only by a consideration of symptoms – that the denomination no longer stands in the same sharp contrast to religious establishments (discussed in the first volume of this work) and to a universal church (to be discussed in the third and last) as does the sect.

The consequences of denominationalization of which we are speaking can be reduced to a common denominator by saying that they are all signs of a settling down into abiding forms. Max Weber has spoken of routinization, and the term is apt. Abiding form must here be understood as a contrast to dynamic life, and routinization as a contrast to spontaneity. More specifically, there appear set hierarchies or at least bureaucracies which replace the original equality of the members and the purely charismatic quality of the original leaders; set creeds which replace the purely experiential nature of the early religiousness, so hostile to rational formulation; and set rites which replace the formlessness of the true sect by a formality such as was once rejected and abhorred.

The denominationalization of sects is so obvious a development that it is not much of an exaggeration to say that even the blind can see it. The great German–Swiss novelist Gottfried Keller knew nothing about sociology; perhaps he had not even heard the name of it. Yet in his story 'Das verlorene Lachen', contained in the collection of stories entitled *Die Leute von Seldwyla*, he speaks of a small conventicle of poor people, washer-women, silk-weavers and the like, which undergoes in a very few years remarkable changes. 'During this time,' he writes, 'the community had secured toleration and achieved a certain respectability (*Stattlichkeit*); all the members were, supported by mutual aid and a well-ordered life, in a state of comfort; the preachers appeared already more like clergymen with some erudition and wore better clothes; the gatherings took place in a light and friendly prayer hall, and there was already a modicum of ecclesiastic politicking in relation to the official church and other sects with a tendency to spread themselves.'[1] This is a remarkable description: Keller may have known little about sociology, but he knew a lot about life.

In time, sects develop a definite class of ministers who are not, it is true, distinguished in a denomination, as they are in a church, from the rank and file by a special grace conveyed through ordination, but who *are* distinguished from it by a special function

[1] *Gottfried Keller's Gesammelte Werke,* ed. J. G. Cotta, Stuttgart und Berlin 1904, vol. V, p. 338.

through appointment. These ministers may not be priests, but they are assuredly more than mere laymen, however much this may be denied. This fact leads us, significantly, again back to the very inception of the sect. If the sect is to have any coherence at all, it needs some kind of office-bearers; some infringement of the principle of democracy is therefore unavoidable, if the group is to last. It is perhaps possible to imagine an organization without organizers, but experience proves that it is impossible to conduct one without them. In the end, a bureaucracy may be a deadening influence; in the beginning its formation is a response to the needs of life. In any case, there have in point of fact been few sects who have not found it expedient (to say the least) to single out a few of their members for special service: but a sect whose egalitarianism is broken has already developed one denominational, not to say quasi-ecclesiastical, feature.[1]

With the coming of an order of ministers, there is also apt to come a hierarchical structure. Occasionally, indeed, this is absent; but far more often it is present, notwithstanding the fact that it is at times disguised. The appearance of higher echelons of office-bearers is no less a response to the needs of life than is the appearance of simple office-bearers, of an office-bearing class. What regularly distinguishes a superior minister from an inferior one is the fact that he is concerned with a larger area: as a bishop overlooks a whole diocese, so does a superintendent (or whatever else the title which a denomination may give to its senior clergy). But without such a higher official who draws a whole district into a focus, the sectarian movement would in all probability dissolve. Each congregation would go its own way, and there would be nothing but splinters. Strict congregationalism means, and accepts, and values, precisely this. But strict congregationalism is at odds with the life-situation in, and out of which, a major sect movement develops. The weavers of Lancashire were no less inclined to accept Quakerism than the weavers of Yorkshire, the miners of Cornwall responded as fully to Methodism as the miners of Wales. What came to birth in such crises was a nation-wide wave of religiousness which called as much for nation-wide organization

[1] For illustrative material, cf. Wilson, loc. cit., pp. 43–6, 57, 58, 63, 64, 269–71, 273–80, 332, 334; Underwood, loc. cit., pp. 119–21, 125, 126, 129, 130; Cameron, loc. cit., pp. 102 and 103; Grass, loc. cit., vol. I, esp. p. 493; vol. II, pp. 325, 864, 869.

as the localized groups called for local organizers. In either case, unity demanded bureaucratization: in the latter case a more egalitarian, in the former a more structured, bureaucracy, a bureaucracy with merely restricted, and a bureaucracy with more than restricted, competence. In this evolution, the sectarian tradition acts as a definite, sometimes as a powerful, retarding force: D. A. Martin has emphasized that denominations remain largely democratic, though, as he admits, they possess no more than a 'delegated democracy'.[1]

True, a delegated democracy is still a democracy, but it is no longer a full one. And there have been thinkers of deep insight, such as George Sorel, who have expressed serious doubts whether a delegated democracy is a democracy in much more than name. There are, of course, great differences from community to community, but the over-all tendency is in common, and it is a falling away from the reality of egalitarianism.[2]

To these inherent and incipient causes for a drift from strict democracy, and hence from full sectarianism, others are soon added. As poverty recedes and well-being progresses, there arises a very understandable desire to exchange the dank and dark cellar or the dingy store in which the group has at first worshipped for some more dignified, or at any rate more suitable, premises. And when these premises are acquired, there follows the no less understandable desire to beautify them. The same onset of a more aesthetic attitude can be observed in the services themselves: with a better shell comes a hunger for a better kernel. The simple, often all too simple style of the lay-preacher is no longer satisfactory or acceptable: there springs up a taste for more sophisticated sermons, and this presupposes a trained predicant and, ultimately, as a secondary development, the foundation of training institutions. Thus the bureaucratization of the group is further promoted and doubled by a parallel intellectualization which destroys yet another feature of the sect: its hostility to learning, its belief in the supremacy of the innocent, child-like mind. A sectarian with a

[1] Loc. cit., p. 7. On the survival (sometimes stubborn) of sectarian features in the developing denomination, cf. Wilson, loc. cit., pp. 75, 76, 336, and esp. 327–30. But Dr. Wilson somewhat exaggerates the a-typicality of the Elim movement's development towards denominationalism. Substantially, its case is like that of other sects, as an analysis of Dr. Wilson's own graphic material would show.

[2] Cf. the literature given in the immediately preceding footnote.

B. Theol. is no less of a contradiction in terms than a sectarian with a large bank account: both will regularly be denominational in outlook, or have a tendency to drift, and to drive their fellows, into denominationalism. Nor can the sectarian spirit be expected to flourish or to survive in a grand and gaudy palace. There is what Max Weber would have called a *Sinnzusammenhang* between the poor man's sectarian religion and the poor man's slum prayer house: abolish the latter, and you tend to abolish the former; abolish the former, and you tend to abolish the latter. Cause becomes effect, and effect, cause: and both lead away from the spirit of the early days, the spirit of revolt.[1]

Once an intellectual *élite* is in existence, it will do what is natural for intellectuals to do: formulate what so far has been unformulated. But this means: transmute what has been fluid into something that is fixed. This alone is a giant step towards routinization: it adds another element making for stability and working against further forward development, further onward flow. Moreover, formulation will not and cannot be thoughtless verbalization. Deep thought will go into the now crystallizing creed, and so rationalization will join bureaucratization and hierarchical structuring as one more concomitant of denominationalization. But it is difficult to imagine a sharper contrast than that between experiential-emotional and rationalized-dogmatic religiosity. When the speechless rapture of the early days gives way to the relative reasonableness of the later period, the sect has finally declined into a denomination.[2]

The intellectuals, the preachers and teachers, are the instruments of that rationalization, yet it would be unjust to blame the resulting involution of live religious sentiment entirely on them. When we analyse this evolution, or rather involution, when we try to descend to its roots, we are yet once again pushed back into the very birth-act of the sect. The sect, as we have seen, is a group which feels itself in sharp contrast to the world, and therefore also to those churchly or church-like bodies which, in its opinion, are part and parcel of the world. But when it tends to set itself off against these institutions, it cannot help feeling that part of the

[1] For illustrative material, cf. Wilson, loc. cit., p. 73; Underwood, pp. 129 and 130.

[2] For illustrative material, cf. Wilson. loc. cit., pp. 221, 222, 243, 244, 252; Conybeare, loc. cit., pp. 177 and 176.

difference consists in its deviant theological conceptions. It is conscious of the fact that it singles out different passages from the Scriptures as being essential, and that it puts a different interpretation on those which it has in common with the rest of Christianity. Long before a denomination has an academic institution with professors to it, long before the naïve lay-preacher has yielded the pulpit to the learned predicant, a kind of canon will have formed, a sort of theology will have come into being. One thinks of the importance of Matthew XIX, 12, for the Skoptsy, and of John I, 9, for the Quakers. These verses were not later brought in to buttress a tardy doctrinal structure; they were much rather part of the seed-good from which the sects concerned have grown.

Finally, there is the matter of ritual. Whether or not there is any deeper truth to Pareto's assertion that all men have an indwelling drive to show forth inner states by assorted and appropriate outer acts (his 'residue' number III), one thing is certain, namely that even in informal services there soon tends to develop a core of set forms. We have a spontaneous process here which is akin to the folkway-forming process so splendidly analysed by W. G. Sumner. As the sect worships Sunday after Sunday, its members notice that certain arrangements are more satisfying than others, and it is no wonder that they are selected for retention and repetition, or at least for frequent re-enactment. For instance, there are hymns which express far better than any others the true feelings of an informal group. *Abide with me* springs to mind at once. For years it was sung in England at the close of 'Cup Final' football matches. These matches are predominantly patronized by working-class and lower-middle-class spectators, i.e. spectators drawn from strata shot through by denominationalism, and it was natural for them to break into precisely this song because it was spontaneously selected by them and their forebears as a splendid vehicle and verbal expression of their strongest sentiments. The sectarian past works here, as so often, as a brake. Fear of formalism prevents the too frequent singing of this and similar hymns. But it is true to say that *Abide with me* has nearly the position in English 'low church' or 'free church' hymnology which *O salutaris* has in Catholic. Repetitiveness is routinization, and it may in the end have debilitating effects; in the beginning it strengthens rather than weakens because it reinforces the feelings which are most vital to the movement and its mentality. Thus the firming up of the sect, not to say its formation, brings a formalization of the sect life which steers it, along with the other influences we have noted, from the whirlpool of revolutionary thought and conduct into the calmer waters of denominationalism.[1]

Other changes, however, would appear to be more characteristic, as well as more important, in the framework of a book on the outer relations of religious bodies, their relations to surrounding secular society, than the formulation of a creed or the growth of ritualism or bureaucratization (all inner developments). Above all others ranks the loss of the conviction that one's own group is the exclusive seat of salvation, the narrow gateway to the kingdom.[2] As D. A. Martin has so rightly emphasized, the adage *extra ecclesiam nulla salus* applies to churches and to sects, but not to denominations.[3] They have found out and they must acknowledge (however bitter this may be) that their group is not going to dominate society, that they will have to be satisfied with the conversion and control of a comparatively narrow circle of men; they therefore have learned to see themselves as religious organizations like others. They are tolerant, and though toleration is a virtue, it is a virtue destructive of fervour and enthusiasm. The denomination is a phenomenon of a religiously multifocal world, of a world in which religious multiformity is accepted. But the true sectarian can never accept this situation, for if he would, his claim to higher status in metaphysical terms, to exclusive election by, and nearness to, God, would vanish. So too would vanish the very significance which the sect has brought into, and bestowed upon, his life. Those who find membership in a denomination sufficient and satisfactory, are no longer men with an overpowering inferiority complex; they are no longer the lowest of the low and the poorest of the poor. For this reason a denomination must be neatly distinguished by the sociologist from its parent sect. In life,

[1] For illustrative material, cf. Wilson, loc. cit., pp. 24, 25, 34, 39, 71, 72, 74, 75; Grass, loc. cit., vol. II, pp. 786 and 787. Sometimes ritualism produces even the first signs of a beginning sacramentalism. 'The person who feels himself converted is invited to signify his surrender to Christ by raising his hand,' Wilson reports about Elim (p. 74). 'There is a tendency to regard the raising of the hand itself as the conversion, not only the indication of surrendering to Christ, but as the surrender itself.' Cf. also Underwood, loc. cit. pp. 268 and 269.

[2] On the fading of the apocalyptic spirit, cf. above, pp. 215 et seq.

[3] Loc. cit., pp. 4 and 5.

contrasting forms may meet and mingle, but in a scientific typology they have to be anxiously kept apart.

SECONDARY FORMS OF SECTARIANISM

Our study of establishmentarianism has revealed that there appeared, at the time of the French Revolution, a secondary (democratic) form of it which was both a continuation of, and a counterblast to, its primary (royalist) form.[1] Based on the concept of the holy nation rather than on that of the holy king, it was revolutionary so long as the nation was in subjection; but it bore in itself the seeds of a new conservatism which were destined to unfold as soon as the limited revolutionary programme of the bourgeois strata who carried it was fulfilled. The question now arises whether there existed a secondary form of sectarianism as well, and we can easily think out *in abstracto* what such a form would have to look like. It would have to be a kind of mirrored image, a photographic negative, of the sect in the proper sense of the word, just as Michelet's or Mazzini's or Mickiewicz's philosophy was of royalist religiosity. Its representatives would have to be upper class figures alienated from existing society, its spirit reactionary rather than progressive, a condemnation of the world for its abandonment of class divisions and class privileges rather than because of their existence and continuation, and so on. Even without a knowledge of the facts it must surely appear extremely likely, on purely theoretical grounds, that such a grouping or groupings did exist. When Louis XVI was guillotined, when the whole structure of the old régime crumbled, when what Burke called the swinish multitude began to rule the state and society, it was unavoidable that some should feel that the end of time had arrived. Would God allow such sacrileges to happen? Would He allow the wheels of history to grind on as if nothing had happened? Would He not rather come to destroy a world sunk in wickedness, to judge and condemn a generation which rebelled against all that was holy? The members of the so-called Catholic Apostolic Church were filled by precisely these sentiments. We shall study them here as a textbook case of secondary sectarianism. But before we do so, we must cast a glance at a few other religious formations which, to a superficial view, might appear as

[1] Cf. vol. I, pp. 136 et seq.

'upper-class sects', but which show a very different, much more narrowly sectarian, complexion if they are carefully considered and analysed.

What the sociologist must never forget is that there exists, in every upper class, a submerged stratum which shares one decisive feature with the lower classes even though it may share no others with them: the feeling of unhappiness, what one might call, with Miguel de Unamuno, a tragic sense of life. Sometimes this stratum may be no more than a number of disconnected individuals whose unhappiness is due to purely private reasons, and then they do not, *ab initio*, form a group. The term 'stratum' is then somewhat too strong, in the sense of too sociological, to describe them. But even such individuals may in the end join forces and form a community, if and when they look for consolation in the same source: when they attend the same séances, for instance, or the same prayer meetings, or seek out the same preachers or prophets. Such people are by some authors called a cult group, and the term is useful, if it is properly understood. A cult is the answer to some individual woe: the characteristics of the sect, recruitment from the lower classes and revolutionary animus, are absent. A good example is spiritualism. A loved one is lost; a heart bleeds; there is balm in the performance of the medium through whom the dead appear to come back into one's life. A séance may be attended by a dozen people; they may hold hands and so draw strength from the awareness that they may not be alone; there is thus a minimal element of sociality in the situation. But basically every one of those present pursues his own interests. They are not very different from twelve people who, when it begins to rain, open their umbrellas at the same time. They are acting in a parallel manner, but they are not (socially) acting together.

Sometimes, however, the submerged unhappy stratum is *ab initio* a group; sometimes, indeed, it is a sub-class of its own. In French history, the aristocracy certainly formed an upper stratum, *the* upper stratum even: but there was a difference between the nobility at the court or in the penumbra of the court, who could bask in the glory of the *roi soleil*, and the provincial nobility which was beyond the warmed and lighted circle and felt a little chill in the shadows. When they got together, what happened was not so very different from what happened when weavers assembled in a conventicle or in a sect. Their political outlook would be in a restricted, but yet definite and tangible, sense of the word revolutionary, and so would, in certain circumstances, their religious world-view and sentiment.

In his incomparable novel, *Anna Karenina*, Tolstoy shows with his accustomed mastery how a deep personal grief can bring even a rich young lady to search for comfort at the feet of a religious leader.[1] Pretty young Princess Shcherbatsky thinks in her childlike way that she is in love with dashing Count Vronsky; she finds to her dismay that he is indifferent to her. A blight falls on all her happiness, but in her darkest hour she makes the acquaintance of a certain Madame Stahl who knows how to soothe her lacerated heart. 'She found consolation in the fact that . . . an entirely new world was opened up to her that had nothing in common with her past, an exalted, noble world, from the heights of which she calmly looked down upon this past. What Kitty discovered was that aside from the life of instinct that she had hitherto given herself up to, there was a life of the spirit. This life was disclosed to her through religion, but it was a religion that had nothing in common with what Kitty had known since childhood, which had found its expression [in the official Church] in mass and vespers at the private chapel of the Widows' Almshouse where you met everyone you knew . . . This was a lofty, mystical religion that was bound up with beautiful thoughts and feelings that you could believe in, not only because you had been ordered to, but because you could love it.'[2]

At first blush, this might appear to be an entirely fictitious example not worth bringing up in a scholarly investigation, but in reality it has a good deal of fact behind it. All that we know seems to indicate that Madame Stahl is modelled on Madame de Krüdener (1764–1824) or Mademoiselle de Buxhöwden, better known by her married Russian name of Katerina Tatarinova (1783–1856), or indeed on both. The activities of these two curious women had their inception and perhaps their climax in the period covered by Tolstoy's first great novel, *War and Peace*. He must have encountered them when he prepared that work.

Inside the covers of the present book, it is the wife of Colonel Ivan Tatarinov that can best stand as an example of a personality around whom a religious, or rather cultic, group assembles whose

[1] Chapters XXXII to XXXV of Part Two.

[2] Carmichael translation, Bantam Books, New York 1960, pp. 236 and 237.

members are drawn into the circle, not by public, but by private woes. The 'Brotherhood of Christ' over which this exalted lady presided, was commonly regarded as an upper-class pendant to the Khlysty and the Skoptsy. Evil tongues asserted that there were the same sexual goings-on in her house as in any Khlyst ship; they also asserted the opposite – that there was the same unnatural sexual self-repression among her followers as among the followers of Kondraty Selivanov. The truth seems to be (so far as we can tell, for the group was, and still is, shrouded in considerable mystery) that the Tatarinov circle shared with both Khlysty and Skoptsy only one thing, namely their ecstatic religiosity, the production of states of exaltation (including glossolaly) by means of the round dance. Sexual deviations of a major order from the established mores do not seem to have happened – a high official in the Ministry of the Interior would hardly have allowed his wife to continue to frequent the meetings at Madame Tatarinova's if she had indulged in promiscuity there, or if she had promised to submit to a crippling operation.[1]

Why did some members of high St. Petersburg society become enamoured of this woman? Why did they allow their lives to be sucked into hers? The answer, in somewhat colloquial language, appears to be that the Tatarinov circle was a lame-duck-society, a club in which soothing plasters were applied to personal wounds. Madame herself was a deeply unhappy woman. She had not got along with the Colonel, her husband, who refused to reside with her under the same roof; and she had lost her one and only child.[2] No wonder she sought refuge in religion! As for her followers, the case of the most prominent among them, General Golovin, seems to have also been the most characteristic. Golovin went through a serious illness which brought him to death's door: he claimed that he would not have recovered if Madame Tatarinova had not interceded for him. The fact of the matter is that, after an 'inner revelation', she advised him to double the doses of all the medicines that the doctor had prescribed. As these happened to be emetics and sudorifics, the consequences can well be imagined. The good General was thoroughly cleaned out, and this seems to have done the trick. He claimed a miracle, and it is not surprising that other sick people began to seek salvation where he was supposed to

[1] Cf. Grass, loc. cit., vol. II, pp. 223, 255–7, 266, 267, 269, 754, 755.

[2] Ibid., pp. 224–6.

have found it.[1] This establishes a parallel between Madame Tatarinova and Mrs. Eddy: not indeed with the Mrs. Eddy of Lynn days, for then she was clearly a lower-class sectarian figure; not with the Mrs. Eddy of early Bostonian days, for then she was still the spear-head of a social protest movement, the protest of the refined upper class of decaying gentility against the coarser upper class of accumulating wealth; but with the Mrs. Eddy of her final stage in which she collected those unfortunates among the rich who were sick or thought themselves to be so.

General Golovin, however, did not only suffer from a physical sickness; he also suffered from a moral malaise. According to his own words, he had drifted into a 'criminal infatuation' for a chambermaid which 'totally destroyed the peace of his soul, tore his heart by unceasing self-accusations, and robbed him of the joys of family life'. Again Madame Tatarinova helped. In the language of the circle, 'she took the sins of another upon herself'. This was to be understood literally. Golovin claimed that the Tatarinova's sentiments, and indeed her conduct, towards the girl became exactly the same as his own had been before (one hopes they did not). Behind this liberation of the poor slave to sensuality there is, however, no more miracle than behind his liberation from ill-health. Madame Tatarinov simply removed the temptress by having her married to a suitable husband.[2] No matter how she healed the sufferer: the fact is that she did heal him. The case is really the same as before: moral debility, just like physical debility, is a weakness the flesh is heir to – the flesh of the rich no less than the flesh of the poor. In so far as this General was the victim of extraordinary difficulties, he was a depressed and not an exalted personality. He belonged to a disadvantaged, not to a privileged, class.

So far as her moral cures were concerned, the Tatarinova was parallel, not to Mrs. Eddy, but to Dr. Buchman, especially the Buchman of his Oxford period. Among the youngsters who attended this famous seat of learning, there were not a few who had failed to deal quite successfully with their youthful physical urges, and they felt as soiled and downcast after, e.g., masturbation, as General Golovin did when he could not break away from his liaison with a servant-girl. 'Oh God, help this young man to stop

[1] Ibid., p. 242; for another sick man's case cf. p. 241.

[2] Ibid., pp. 243 and 244.

his dirty habits,' is a prayer which literally came from Frank Buchman's lips. Something between an old-style Spiritual Director and a new-style Doctor Freud, Buchman had the answer and he dispensed it freely to the poor rich young men. The sense of sin, he knew, could be lifted from a boy's shoulders by confession, and as a Protestant boy (or girl – for female aberrations are not so different from male ones) had no other recourse, he would go to this practitioner-prophet. When, in 1961, Peter Howard published his adulatory book, *Frank Buchman's Secret*, two writers who knew the facts (R. H. S. Crossman, an Oxford don, and Wayland Young, a peer) revealed them and thereby exposed what the real secret was.[1] The tremendous loyalty which Buchman inspired – like the tremendous loyalty which the Tatarinova inspired – was based on retrospective gratitude to, and continuing dependency on, the healer who had healed many a sick soul, the liberator who had lifted the clouds from many a blighted life. Wayland Young has said that the 'guilt-ridden affluent' formed Buchman's main *clientèle*. In so far as they were affluent, they belonged to the upper classes; in so far as they were guilt-ridden, they did not. The cult which Buchman initiated was therefore both comparable to, and different from, a typical sect: comparable to it, because it ended in the removal of an inferiority complex, a feeling of defilement; different from it, because that complex was generated, not by underprivilege, but by lack of self-discipline, not by social reasons, but by reasons of an intimate and individual nature.

Charles Braden has called the clients of Frank Buchman 'up-and-outers', in contrast to the 'down-and-outers' who frequent, and fill the ranks of, sectarian groupings in the proper sense of the word.[2] But there may be up-and-outers who are out, not because of some personal and private, but because of some public, e.g. political, reason, and an important example of them were the Huguenots whom we have already half-introduced into our discussion. Many of them – for instance their leader, Admiral Coligny, Monsieur de Châtillon – belonged to the premier families of France and had no reason whatsoever to develop an

[1] Cf. Crossman's review in the *New Statesman*, 5 January 1962, and Young's in the Manchester *Guardian*, 22 May 1962. Cf. also Braden, Ch. S., *These Also Believe*, New York 1949, pp. 408, 409, 416.
[2] Braden, loc. cit., p. 409.

inferiority complex. Their blood was as blue as any. But they were a subclass out of power, and this irked them, so much so that they developed an alienation from the contemporary establishment and expressed it, *inter alia*, in a religious contrast to the court and the court circles. The Decembrists of Russia were a somewhat comparable case, though the religious differentiation was in their instance not as open and as extreme.[1]

The members of Katerina Tatarinova's Brotherhood in Christ and the members of Frank Buchman's Oxford Movement formed sect-like cult groups *in spite* of the fact that, generally speaking, they belonged to the upper classes. The members of the Catholic Apostolic Church, on the other hand, formed that body *because* of the fact that they belonged – and totally belonged – to the upper classes. Therein lies a deep difference. Whether or not the former groupings are brought under the concept of sect is merely a matter of definition: in their case, as in the case of true sects, it was a feeling of inferiority that induced a person to join. But the self-styled saints entered the Catholic Apostolic Church because they had a feeling of superiority, and therefore we have here a secondary sect formation, not a primary one, whether we define a primary sect narrowly or widely. The Tatarinov and Buchman circles were upper class only in appearance: the Albury crowd was so in fact and in truth. Why then should they have broken away from the Anglican communion which must have satisfied their status-inspired sentiments to the fullest? P. E. Shaw, the historian of the

[1] Two groupings which it would be most interesting to analyse in this context are the Seventh Day Baptists and the so-called Clapham Sect or Clapham Saints. The Seventh Day Baptists harboured such rich, educated and royalist figures as the Bampfields (Francis and Thomas), Peter Chamberlen, and the Stennetts (cf. Underwood, loc. cit., pp. 112, 113, 114, 115, 147, 148). The Clapham Sect (or rather quasi-sect, for not only were they well-to-do and conservative, but remained Anglicans) collected around the banker Henry Thornton. Only a detailed and searching inquiry could reveal what the social reasons for their religious peculiarities were. So far as the present writer can tell, the two cases are rather different. The Bampfields and Chamberlen were eccentrics: their deviance seems to have had personal rather than public roots. The Thorntons and their friends were decidedly not eccentrics: their deviance had a public and not a private background. The formation of the latter group – the so-called evangelical party – appears to have been part and parcel of the English reaction to the French Revolution. But of that reaction, the Catholic Apostolic Church, which we are about to discuss in the text, is by far the most colourful and revealing expression and incarnation.

movement, is frankly puzzled. 'Their . . . claims,' he writes, 'are immense: as the 144,000 mentioned in the Apocalypse, they are to be the rulers of the church. Were they a persecuted company of people, or such as had not made good in the world, it would be easy to account for it in terms of psychological compensation.'[1] But they were not that sort of person at all; they had nothing to compensate or overcompensate: why then did they develop their curious ideas? Let us see.

The whole thing started very much the way in which common sects ordinarily start. In 1830, two brothers, James and George Macdonald, 'men of humble walks of life', living in the proletarian township of Port Glasgow, 'became possessed of supernatural power'. Their sister, Margaret, too, 'was quite swallowed up in transport . . . heard unutterable things . . . saw the Lord coming in the glory of His Father and of all the holy angels . . .' One Mary Campbell was healed when she perused a letter from James Macdonald's pen, commanding her to rise and walk. Breathing pains and heart palpitations instantaneously ceased: 'I felt as if I had been lifted from off the earth, and all my disease taken from off me at the voice of Christ. I was verily made to stand upon my feet, leap and walk, sing and rejoice.' On the Friday and Saturday following this miracle, Mary Campbell started to speak in unknown tongues and the gift then jumped over from her to the Macdonald brothers. The local minister, the Rev. Robert Story, was at first impressed, but before long he changed over to a very unfavourable view of Mary Campbell, accusing her of vanity, a desire to please at all cost, and even plain deception. 'The very biography of Story seems to suggest,' P. E. Shaw writes more than a century after it all happened, 'that he was peeved that a working-class girl, instead of being content with the estate into which it had pleased God to call her, suddenly appeared dressed in fair raiment and silks; and that she chose her own idea of what her missionary call meant, based on the newer apocalyptic theories which had come to prevail . . .'[2] We are hardly sinning against the principle of scholarly objectivity if we suggest a second possibility, namely that the Scots levelheadedness and the Calvinistic rationality of Mr. Story reasserted themselves after a momentary eclipse. Be that as it may, there were some high up in the social

[1] Shaw, P. E., *The Catholic Apostolic Church*, New York 1946, p. 231.
[2] Ibid., p. 32.

scale – much higher than a poor country clergyman! – who did not doubt that the phenomena observed at Port Glasgow were genuine and that they foreboded, even initiated, the day of judgement and the end of the world. They came post-haste from London up to Scotland, saw and believed. Before long, what had happened in the hovels of Port Glasgow began to happen in their houses also. A Mrs. Cardale started to prophesy. A Miss Fancourt was mysteriously healed.[1]

We are not going to tell here the sad life-story of Edward Irving, the Scottish-born clergyman whose London church attracted many members of the *haute-volée* in the capital and became the scene of countless stirring events. In our sober context, he appears as no more than the intermediary between the proletarians on the Clyde and the society folk on the Thames. It is entirely wrong to speak, as is sometimes done, of an Irvingite Church. When this so-called Irvingite Church, or rather the Catholic Apostolic Church, was constituted, there was no organic place for him in it: he had to be content with a rather humiliating post (chief pastor or 'Angel' in his own congregation). He certainly was not made an 'Apostle'. But it was the Apostles who carried the movement, as pillars carry the vault of a cathedral. Who, then, were the Apostles? 'The Catholic Apostolic leaders do not manifest the variety of the group around our Lord, which ranged from fisherman to tax-gatherer and to fiery nationalist,' Shaw states. And he adds, understating rather than overstating the social prominence of the Apostles: 'They belonged to the upper or middle class, not to the poor or the underprivileged, and were perhaps not fully sympathetic with such . . . All were men of culture and of education, and most were persons of some social importance.'[2] There is no mistaking the class character of the whole phenomenon.

The Peter of the New Twelve whom God was supposed to have raised up to prepare for His Second Coming, was John Bate Cardale; we have already encountered the prophesyings of his wife; his sister, Emily, was a prophetess, too. Cardale is called the 'pillar of apostles', or 'the senior' among them, by the group. He is described to us as a man in whose moral make-up humility was signally missing, a man of imperious character and dictatorial

[1] Ibid., pp. 29–34.
[2] Ibid., p. 237.

habits. One contemporary said of him: 'He never seemed to hesitate or doubt on any subject; he had that decided look which would deter anyone from expecting him ever to change his mind about anything.' Another referred to him as 'a man of iron will and dominating character, which would brook no opposition'. There are several psychological explanations for this cocksure attitude: his father had left him 'considerable property'; his school was Rugby, one of the prime nurseries of candidates for the upper ten; before devoting himself to religion, he had been the head of a leading law firm[1] – all antecedents which would tend to make a person into a thorough-going authoritarian.

Linked with Cardale and made of the same stuff was Henry Drummond, whose country seat at Albury was the nerve-centre of the whole movement. The name of Drummond will bring up in many minds the famous banking firm, and the no less famous Professorship of Political Economy at Oxford. Henry Drummond was connected with both. Shaw calls him 'one of the wealthiest commoners in England'. His school was Harrow, his college Christ Church, both typical breeding grounds of aristocratic mentality. His daughter married a Lord Lovaine, later Duke of Northumberland, and through this connection he became kinsman to the Percys, one of England's most noble families. He was twice Member of Parliament, 'always known for loyalty to the Crown and veneration for the institution[s] of the country'. Thomas Carlyle met him[2], and there are several statements from his pen which, even though they do not perhaps err on the side of charity, appear to give a good picture of his character: 'This Drummond, who inhabits a splendid mansion in the west, proved to be a very striking man. Taller and leaner than I, but erect as a plummet, with a high-carried, quick, penetrating head . . . a singular mixture of all things, of the saint, the wit, the philosopher, swimming, if I mistake not, in an element of dandyism . . . abundant in speculation as well as in money . . . a sharp, elastic, haughty kind of man . . . a man of . . . pungent, decisive nature, full of fine qualities, but well-nigh cracked by an enormous conceit of himself, which, both as pride and vanity . . . seemed to pervade every fibre of him . . .' The costly Apostles' Chapel at

[1] Ibid., pp. 72 and 73.

[2] We mean, of course, the famous writer, not the other Thomas Carlyle, the advocate from Edinburgh who became one of Drummond's co-apostles.

Albury and a magnificent church in Gordon Square, London, were built by him.[1]

We have no room here to display all the details concerning the remaining ten apostles (though we may just mention, in passing, that one of them, Spencer Perceval, was the son of a British Prime Minister). As for the movement which they built up, it had above all one characteristic which sharply distinguishes it from sects in the primary sense of the word: its interest in, almost an addiction to, ritualism, artistry and learning, three preoccupations which are totally absent in lower-class dissent groups – and not only absent, but as a rule even execrated. There developed, in a short time, an elaborate and sophisticated symbolism to which neither deep meaning nor high beauty can be denied. One of the Apostles, John Tudor, was an artist. In this, there is a significant parallel between the Catholic Apostolic Church and the Tatarinov circle, for that, too, produced some remarkable works of art, more especially painting, and had Vladimir Borovikovsky, whose oils graced *inter alia* the Winter Palace and the Hermitage, as one of its prominent members.[2]

What was it that evoked in these men – nabobs, patriots and aesthetes – the belief that the end of the world was nigh? What was the wickedness and the blasphemy which convinced them that the day of wrath was about to break? The answer can be given in the words of one of the Apostles, F. V. Woodhouse: it was the 'wicked, blasphemous doctrine that all power is from the people'. Men like Woodhouse (or Cardale or Drummond) could not reconcile themselves to the fact that the age of democracy had arrived; even though their outlook was fairly internationalist, its coming to France might not have affected them too deeply; what truly shook them, what produced in them the apocalyptic mood and thereby indirectly the apocalyptic communion which they founded, was its coming to England. Dates are significant here. The great Reform Bill was introduced in 1831 and passed in 1832. It was in 1831 that the first 'manifestation of the spirit' occurred in Mr. Cardale's home; it was in 1832 that he was 'called' to be the

[1] Ibid., pp. 73–5, 83. Froude, J. A., *Thomas Carlyle, A History of the First Forty Years of His Life,* London 1882, vol. II, p. 177; Carlyle, Thomas, *Reminiscences*, ed. J. A. Froude, London 1881, vol. I, pp. 297 and 312.

[2] Cf. Shaw, loc. cit., p. 194 et seq.; Grass, loc. cit., vol. II, pp. 234, 235, 264.

chief Apostle . . . These coincidences are not fortuitous; they reveal a causal nexus. These men, we may perhaps say, had not become alienated from society; society had become alienated from them. This, at any rate, was the light in which they saw recent developments. It was the lurid glare of the infernal fire, no longer contained in hell, which lay over the land. Surely, the trumpet call would come before long? The hundred and forty-four thousand white-robed ones of the Apocalypse had to be ready: the Catholic Apostolic Church would make them ready. The twelve thousand of the tribe of Reuben would assemble behind Francis Woodhouse; the twelve thousand of the tribe of Naphtali would assemble behind Frank Sitwell . . . It only remained for God to do his bit.

A study of the political opinions prevailing in this circle amply confirms our interpretation. The two great sources of apocalypticism, Daniel and Revelations, were so explained as to yield condemnations of democracy. In Nebuchadnezzar's dream unravelled by Daniel, the great statue seen had a head of gold, but feet of iron and clay (II, 31–3). According to a spokesman of the group, Basileutos (*recte* William Bramley-Moore), 'this seems to be the teaching of Daniel's prophetic image: the head of gold setting forth the autocracy of Nebuchadnezzar, as contrasted with the miry clay and iron of the ten toes, the democratic government of the people'. In other words: the rule of one is the highest, the rule of all the lowest, form of the state. According to this way of thinking, the end of sacred monarchy must also be the end of an aeon, the beginning at least of the end of the world. This is what the members of the group tried to prove in much the same manner in which sectarians of lower class origin usually make use of the figures mentioned in Revelations. The 1,260 days of Revelations XI, 3 were taken to mean 1,260 years; most characteristically, they were seen as the interval between the appearance of Justinian's Digest and the execution of Louis XVI. The choice of the *terminus a quo* of this stretch of time may be a little puzzling (though a case may be made out for the proposition that holy rulership began in 532), but it is fully explained by the *terminus ad quem*, 1792, the year of outrage, *minus* 1260 yielding 532. Louis' death was to Cardale and to Drummond the angular point of universal history, the sin after the commission of which God simply *could not* allow the world to go on. The guillotine was the

Devil's engine, as democracy was the Devil's idea of government. As for the spread of 'mob rule' beyond France, it was connected with Revelations XIII, 'the beast with seven heads', i.e. Antichrist: 'And power was given him over every tribe and people and tongue and nation.'[1] Characteristically, it is not only political democracy that is anathematized. Trade Unionism, also, is condemned.

While the small American wing of the movement tried somewhat to mute and mitigate these Tory sentiments, they were driven by the two Canadian leaders, George Ryerson and Adam Hood Burwell, to almost hysterical lengths. Burwell, to use his case as an illustration, came from an 'intensely loyalist family, devoted to the British name and institutions'. He was in Anglican orders, his charge being Christ Church at Bytown (since turned into the Cathedral of Ottawa). As editor of *The Christian Sentinel*, he filled the pages of his journal with violent and sometimes abusive attacks, not only on Jacobins, but also on Dissenters and Anti-Episcopalians. In *A Voice of Warning* he wrote: 'A democrat hates kingly rule because God is a king.' 'Democracy is pure atheism.' In *The Doctrine of the Holy Spirit* he called the proposition 'that the people . . . are the only true source of legislature and government' a 'lie of Satan', twin-sister to another lie, namely that everybody had the right to serve God as his conscience dictated. The abolition of the Test Act and the removal of Catholic disabilities appeared to Burwell as a devil's triumph under the mask of political reform.

Burwell described his contemporaries as a 'sinful, wild, rebellious, contentious, cruel, deceitful, treacherous, bloody-minded race', in the 'doleful and devil-possessed condition of essential enmity against God'. What led him from the Church of England to the Catholic Apostolic Church was the conviction that the open reign of Satan, the first act of the drama of the last day, had arrived and that the rest was presently to follow. 'It seems as if despair at the non-success of the conflict against the evil forces of democracy and the like turned him . . . to the expectation, perhaps the desire, for a divine interposition and judgment,' writes P. E. Shaw, and he is correct. In 1836, Burwell turned to the Cardale-Drummond communion and became 'Angel' of the believers at Kingston, Ontario. A Bytown poet recalls the event in these words:

[1] Shaw, loc. cit., pp. 165, 166, 223; Knox, loc. cit., p. 552; Basileutos' book (of 1903) was called *Divine Government*.

'Adam Hood Burwell is the man.
An English Churchman he began,
But ended a most shining light,
A mystic full-fledged Irvingite.'

Before he died in 1849, his pen produced many statements of the Catholic Apostolic faith, among others a poem entitled: 'Nebuchadnezzar's Vision of a Tree, or Human Rule contrasted with the Rule of Christ'. In Burwell, the mental roots and political motives of the whole movement can be seen with all desirable clarity.[1]

The word 'Irvingite' in W. P. Lett's poem just mentioned is a mistake. Irving was, and in spite of everything remained all his life, a Presbyterian. Burwell, and of course Cardale and Drummond and the rest of them, were impassioned Episcopalians. How could they have been anything else? Authority and aristocracy were the watchwords of these men. They could suffer democracy as little in the church as in the world. Irving was bound to be an outsider in their circle. It is most amazing how far this Episcopalianism went. Bishops were prayed for in the Catholic Apostolic Church, even Anglican bishops, but not nonconformists.[2]

We can take leave of these men by quoting once again from a poet, T. W. Dove, whose volume *The Silent Pool* refers to a lake in Albury Park, near the Apostles' Chapel:

'. . . No sect is here, nor names
Of men held up for fickle crowds to follow.'[3]

The first part of the statement will hardly be accepted by the sociologist as it stands (though we do admit that the movement was a sect merely in a secondary or transferred meaning of the term). But the second part is certainly correct. There was indeed nothing here that ordinary men may have found congenial. What is a little distressing about the whole movement is the indifference it showed to the social problems of the day. Shaw says, finely but perhaps a little too gingerly, that this church was 'letting others show the compassion and concern for the multitudes which we find in the Gospel'. Stronger language might have been allowable in view of the fact that there was condemnation of the temperance

[1] Shaw, loc. cit., pp. 122, 123, 125, 126, 127, 128, 129. Cf. also pp. 118 and 119 (*re* Ryerson).

[2] Ibid., pp. 89, 90, 225, 205, 206.

[3] Cit. ibid., p. 243.

movement as an attempt to help those who were hardly worth helping. The tendency to use Acts V, 4 as well as Matthew xx, 15 and xxvi, 11 as a defence of private property and capitalism generally, might also find rather few nods from Christians.[1]

The decline of this secondary sect took place in much the same way in which primary sects decay. There was disruption, and there was in the end dissolution, so far as England is concerned. The years in which the second Advent was supposed to come about were 1835, 1838, 1842, 1845 and 1866. By 1860, six of the twelve Apostles were dead, yet the remaining leaders refused to fill up the number. A German member, the 'Prophet' Geyer, thereupon 'called' the required six to round out the circle, claiming to act under inspiration by the Holy Ghost. The 'Apostle' Woodhouse excommunicated him and Geyer replied by forming a breakaway movement, known at first as the Universal Christian Mission, and later as the New Apostolic Church.[2]

In 1960, the New Apostolic Church was still in a flourishing condition, claiming about 550,000 members. This may, *prima facie*, appear surprising, but the surprise wanes when one learns that nearly four-fifths of this membership lived in Germany, a country whose unhappy history since 1934 may well have inspired an apocalyptic mood in many souls. In England, the Catholic Apostolic Church had entered its death throes much earlier. The Manchester *Guardian*, while asserting that there was no lack of devotees, reported on 12 December 1934: 'The Catholic Apostolic Church now awaits dissolution within ten years . . . All the surviving ministers are either elderly or aged. The youngest in London is sixty-five. The one in charge of . . . Paddington . . . is eighty-nine, and one who conducted services in Gordon Square last week was ninety. These men are carrying on because there is none to succeed them, and it is realized the time is approaching when there will be none to do the work.' The reason given for this fading out of the hierarchy is that the last Apostle died in 1901, so that there is nobody left who could lawfully ordain. But this, surely, is a lame excuse. The hard fact of the matter is that the movement is dying off, or has died off, from below; the recruit-

[1] Ibid., pp. 219–21 and 233. Matthew xx, 15: 'Is it not lawful for me to do what I will [with my own]?' Matthew xxvi, 11: 'The poor you have always with you.'

[2] Algermissen, loc. cit., pp. 25, 27, 28.

ment has dwindled and even retainment has become difficult. The ashamed stalwarts refuse to discuss the situation. Since Francis V. Woodhouse closed his eyes, they say, they are 'under silence'. But, when the truth is told, this silence is less a sacred duty than a sad necessity. In a movement that believes in the revival of the gift of tongues, the disappearance of ordained priests would, in principle, still leave in existence potential prophets. But, as Shaw tells us, 'the prophets who might have had some living message to meet this emergency [simply] have nothing to say . . . The freedom and frequency of their utterance has been checked . . . until now it has become almost extinct . . . and stillness reigns over all'.[1]

Underneath this involution, there are two explanatory facts, the one microsociological and less important, the other macrosociological and more important, indeed, decisive. The microsociological and less important aspect is the repression and suppression of the prophetic office by the priestly class which parallels, in primary sects, the replacement of lay preachers by a learned clergy. Cardale's *Short Discourse on Prophesying and the Ministry of the Prophet in the Christian Church* (1868) marked a definite step on the road from free inspiration to deadening formalism, a step on the road downhill. But even if there had been no discouragement of tongues, the end would not have been different. The truly death-dealing process in this secondary sect has been a macrosociological evolution, an evolution in the wider world – the adjustment of the rich (or rather of the no longer quite so rich) to a democratic dispensation, as in a primary sect it is the adjustment of the poor (or rather of the no longer quite so poor) to a capitalist society. Sects, whether primary or secondary, are not destined to live long: they are creatures of crises, songsters of a season, and the doom they like to predict for others has invariably fallen upon their own heads.

THE CASE OF SOVIET RUSSIA

The great adversary of the sects has always been the sanctified state. The sects are, as we have seen, the religious version of revolutionary sentiment, and as such they run parallel to, even if they are clearly divided from, the irreligious version of revolutionary effort, the radical party. We have noted, especially in

[1] Shaw, loc. cit., pp. 2, 3, 241.

connection with the Old Believers of Russia, but also in connection with, e.g., the Primitive Methodists of Britain, how easy it is for men when a general secularization takes place, to slip out of the revolutionary sect and into the revolutionary party. The transition is very simple, almost without difficulty, because the two have their main enemy in common – another confirmation of the old adage that politics makes strange bed-fellows. The fall of the Tsar-Autocrat in 1917 was, in principle, no cause for regret to the dissenters, though in practice they may well have felt that the new masters might not, in the end, turn out to be much more tolerant or tolerable than the old. What, in fact, has been the relationship of the Soviet state to the sectarian communities? No general answer is possible. We must distinguish three periods, each of which shows a different complexion: the embryonic form of the *régime* up to 1917; the decade of search, on its part, for appropriate policies, which lasted from 1917 to 1927; and, finally, the period which started with the last-named year, the period of a conscious drive for more clearly envisaged goals.[1]

It is in no way surprising that the Bolsheviks looked at first upon the dissenters, including even the Old Believers, as potential, if not indeed as actual, allies. Not only were there obvious tactical advantages in co-operating with other enemies of the established government, but such co-operation could even be shown to have a sound theoretical basis. Lenin took the view that the pattern of history demanded that feudalism should be ousted by a bourgeois revolution, and that the bourgeois society thus created would only later be overthrown by the proletarian forces, although he hoped, of course, that the halt on the road, the capitalist interlude, would not last long. Even the denominationalized Old Believers were bourgeois in social character and liberal in political affiliation; even they were therefore worthy of support, and support from them was logically to be welcomed by the Communist Party. There was not, all told, too much cynicism involved in taking their money, for instance. Lenin accordingly accepted for purposes of financing his paper *Iskra* an annual grant of 24,000 rubles from the Old Believer industrialist Morozov who has figured in these pages before, and it is said that the 60,000-ruble life insurance

[1] Cf. on what follows the useful article by Ethel and Stephen P. Dunn, 'Religion as an Instrument of Culture Change: The Problem of the Sects in the Soviet Union', *Slavic Review*, September 1964, p. 459 et seq.

payment made upon Morozov's death ultimately also reached Lenin *via* the wife of Maxim Gorky, a trustee. It was specifically Lenin's close collaborator V. D. Bonch-Bruevich, a student particularly of Dukhobor life, who insisted on the reasonableness of a comradeship-in-arms between Communists and sectarians; it was under his influence that a Party Congress in 1904 acknowledged that 'the sectarian movement in Russia is in many of its manifestations one of the democratic tendencies directed against the existing state of things'. All sects, Bonch-Bruevich felt, would fight for the liberalization of the Russian state; some sects might even fight for the destruction of that state and for the abolition of private property. There was thus no reason for alienating, and every reason for accommodating, these forces which were pressing forward in the right direction.[1]

The comparatively favourable attitude towards the sects continued long after the Soviet seizure of power in October 1917, but it was a different aspect of sectarianism on which the emphasis was now laid. What made them appear valuable in the new circumstances was not their revolutionary animus, but their communal forms of living. Uprooted by the tsarist authorities and resettled in remote regions, quite a few dissenting groups had developed co-operative colonies not too different from the communistic experiments which their cousins-german had undertaken in North America. The Communists in power at that time were still strongly idealistic: they believed that the good of humanity demanded the transition from competitive to more co-operative arrangements in production, to a human solidarity which would oust the specific vices of capitalism and generate the specific virtues of socialism. Some sectarian settlements appeared in this context almost as models of communal living. A statute of 19 February 1919, therefore, sanctioned the foundation of communes of all sorts and thereby set the seal of official approval upon them. It was again the research of Bonch-Bruevich which served as a justification for this policy. His description, for instance, of the Dukhobor communes near Tiflis proved that a truly united brotherhood could be an economic success in spite of extremely adverse natural conditions, and this was taken as a good augury for the success of socialism as a whole. After 1917, Bonch-Bruevich subjected the commune 'Sober Life', situated near

[1] Ibid., pp. 464, 462, 463.

Moscow, to a searching analysis and found it entirely worthy of preservation, if not indeed of support. The members had been jailed during the war (because of their pacifism), they had been freed by the Revolution; they had delivered grain in the darkest days of the famine, though they had to go hungry themselves; they even had a confused idea that their general aims and those of the new *régime* were identical. Then there was, of course, their rejection of the principle of private property: this made them at least half-Communists, notwithstanding the fact that their religious creed made them wholly 'obscurantist'. Could such men not be induced to replace their religious by a rational world-view? Could their half-communism not be changed into a full communism by a little propaganda, by a little enlightenment? Bonch-Bruevich and his friends felt it could, and they hopefully arranged in the winter of 1920–1 for the institution of an administrative unit called, in the jargon of the system, ORGKOMSEKT, whose task would be the organization of communistic sect settlements. We know of the Molokane (who numbered about two million and thus were not a negligible factor) that they responded favourably to such moves on the part of the government. Their all-Russian congress at Samara in the fall of 1924 offered its support for the 'construction of Communism'. More practically, their thirty-nine brotherhoods in the Northern Caucasus formed themselves into the 'Hammer and Sickle Agricultural Co-operative of United Molokan Communes'. This was partly self-administered and partly administered by the village Soviets. All seemed to be harmony between state and sect. It is a tell-tale detail that some of the Molokan enterprises were named after Party leaders.[1]

But this honeymoon was not destined to last. By 1927, there was a sharp turn-about, and the friends became foes. The idealistic delusion that post-revolutionary men would prefer the warm comforts of communal production to the cold comforts of individual consumption died overnight, and the new realism demanded goods for Russians, not the good of mankind. But sectarian communes were not delivering the goods; they had a rooted tendency to use up what they brought forth; from the point of view of the national – and especially the urban – markets, they were next to useless. All of a sudden, the fact that they were experiments in communal living was forgotten and only their

[1] Ibid., pp. 464–70.

addiction to religiosity was remembered. Indeed, the communality of living was made into a prime argument against the sectarian settlements: it was said to be an obstacle to progress, and this is not as illogical a shift in attitude as it might seem, for progress meant now advancement in technical efficiency and not advancement towards human integration and brotherly love. Against the reality of the communes there was now pressed the ideal of the *kolkhozy*, of the wheat-factories that would help urbanization and industrialization by freeing people from agricultural labour and village life, not fixing them there, as communes (especially the successful ones) did. The fact that many sectarians were pacifists did not help them either in an increasingly militarist state. History was re-written: it was asserted, with much too much insistence to be convincing, that the sectarians had never been on the side of the Communist *régime*. The League of the Godless, led by Kalinin, went into action against them. They were said to be a kind of opium for the people more difficult to deal with than the Orthodox poison. And so, by 1929, the same relationship between government and dissent groups had been reached as the one which had existed in 1829, or 1729, or 1629. It was an entirely negative relationship. The authorities did their best to break up the sectarian colonies by forcing Orthodox and Communist elements into them, elements which could not but ruin the whole spiritual principle on which they were originally based. Opponents of this policy were deported. The new tsardom thus returned to the methods of the old.

The renewal of persecution in 1927 did not affect all the sects in the same way. The more radical ones had taken no notice of the apparent friendliness of the Soviet leaders *à la* Bonch-Bruevich: they knew, and they had quietly continued to believe, that the state was an instrument of the devil, whether its ruler was called tsar or commissar. The Khlysty, for example, simply remained in their position on the margin of Russian society, and so, as we have seen,[1] did the Stranniky. But the less radical sects who had flirted with the government were thrown into a deep crisis. They had become contaminated; they had, to say the least, evinced a lack of common sense. Many of their members abandoned them and joined other movements. It is very interesting to see what movements they joined: the Baptists, the Adventists, the Pentecostalists,

[1] Cf. above, p. 260.

the Jehovah's Witnesses, all Western-born and Western-oriented groups. In the circumstances, it was *these* groups, these *sorts* of groups, which satisfied the spirit of opposition, and not the Molokane who had allowed themselves to be caught in the Communist snare. With the return to form by the ruling powers, the sectarians returned to form also: they proved themselves anew as alienated men, men in conflict with established society.

Today, nobody knows how many sectarians there are in Russia's sixth of the world. For the Baptists, the figure of three millions has been mentioned. It is based on their own estimate. On the other hand, it has been claimed by government supporters that the drift towards them and towards other Western-oriented groups became bogged down after 1931 or so – an assertion which is not necessarily irreconcilable with the other. By and large, the whole phenomenon of sectarianism appears to be on the decline in the Soviet Union. This is hardly due to the fact that there is little to complain about under the *régime*, but rather to the far more important fact that opposition movements are apt to reflect the general character of the establishment which they oppose. An official image of a god-like or godly tsar will be countered by the assertion that the tsar is devilish or a devil. A secular government is more likely to be criticized in secular terms. It is not surprising, therefore, that such information as is available shows the sects composed predominantly of ageing people. It is not surprising, either, however, that the same information shows that the females heavily outnumber the males. Here we have a factor of continuity rather than of change. All propaganda assertions to the contrary notwithstanding, women are still substantially underprivileged in Russia, and so have a much stronger tendency to align themselves with protest movements than have the still substantially overprivileged men. Even more important is another point. Women are everywhere the natural upholders of family life, and they see its values threatened by the Communist Party[1] – not only in Russia, but also in such countries as Italy and Chile, where the recent stagnation in the Party's fortunes is due mainly to the resistance of the women voters. The defensive position transmutes itself here as everywhere into an aggressive one, and thereby something akin to a sectarian mentality is engendered in women's minds.

[1] Ibid., pp. 466–77.

THE CASE OF THE UNITED STATES OF AMERICA

In the foregoing pages we have taken our illustrative material not only from Russia and England, the classical countries, as it were, of caesaropapism and therefore at the same time of sectarianism, caesaropapism's shadow and negation, but also, on occasion, from the United States. We have implied, therefore, that the religious situation in the United States is at least comparable with, or kindred to, that of the typical caesaropapist cultures. Indeed, we have already given part of our proof that this is in fact so: we have shown the presence, in America, of an ideology of messianism which, as we know, is part and parcel of every typical 'established' religiosity. Yet America is in this respect, as in so many others, a country with a difference, an important difference. The Constitution forbids all linking of government and religion: a state church is out of the question. Established religiosity must therefore have developed here in devious ways, and sectarianism, too, must exhibit certain characteristics of its own, a certain Americanism, so to speak. Let us investigate, then, the *differentia specifica* of the American culture, so far as the relation of conservative and revolutionary sentiment in religious life is concerned.

We can best do justice to the facts by following the historical thread. In the beginning, the constellation in the thirteen colonies was substantially the same as that in the mother country. In Virginia, and other states south of the New York boundary, it was exactly the same, for here Anglicanism was firmly established and dissatisfaction tended to express itself in sectarian dissent, as it did on the other side of the Atlantic. In New York, Anglicanism was not formally established, but it was greatly favoured by the authorities who – to give but one revealing detail – consistently refused the Presbyterians permission to incorporate themselves and thereby prevented them from leading a normal collective life. To the north of New York, and especially in Massachusetts and Connecticut, things were indeed different. A form of Calvinism, of Congregationalism or Presbyterianism, was the accepted creed. Not technically established, i.e. not fused with the State, it was yet acknowledged by the law, i.e. linked with the social pattern. But it would be wrong to see the New England states as states in isolation. They were painfully conscious of the fact that they were dependencies of the English Crown; the English Crown threw a very long shadow across the sea, a shadow long enough to make the people of Boston and Hartford feel a chill. Thus, though the contrast between Anglicanism and Dissent was virtually absent in one sense – Anglicanism was too weak to matter locally – it was very much present in another. The tension between Old England and New England was after all a continuation of the conflict between High Church and Low Church, between Laud and Cromwell, Erasmus and Calvin. So even Massachusetts and Connecticut showed, *mutatis mutandis*, the same situation as Virginia and, indeed, England herself.[1]

If the situation had been static, perhaps the Puritans would have forgotten all about it. But it was not. The Church of Old England – conceiving herself definitely as the Church of *all* England or of all *Englands* – had no intention of abandoning New England. In the Society for the Propagation of the Gospel in Foreign Parts, she created a powerful battering-ram which, it was hoped, would break down the locked door of the Puritan strongholds. Characteristically, the first intention was to establish an American episcopate; characteristically, too, the New Englanders regarded such a move as the introduction of a Trojan horse into their citadel. Carl Bridenbaugh has told the story in his book, *Mitre and Sceptre (1689–1775)*. What interests the sociologist most is the prominent link between the religious and the socio-political aspect. A bishop would have been a nobleman of a kind: were the English bishops not members of the House of Lords? To accept such a type would have been to admit the thin end of a wedge which would before long split American society in two and bring in all the evils of the Ancien Régime as seen in Europe. After the Lords Spiritual would come the Lords Temporal: Governor Francis Bernard's plan for 'introducing temporal dignities' was only too clear an indication of what was afoot.[2] All through the struggle which ended in 1776 with independence, the battle-cry was 'civil and ecclesiastical liberty'. 'Civil and ecclesiastical' should be connected by hyphens, for, as ever, the religious form carried a socio-political content, and that content, to say the least, mattered very much. Indeed, form and content were hardly distinguishable at the time. As the

[1] For references, cf. next footnote.

[2] Bridenbaugh, C., *Mitre and Sceptre* (1689–1775), New York 1962, p. 250 et seq. Cf. further ibid., pp. 20, 26, 27, 54, 55, 75, 76, 100, 118, 131, 138, 213, 217, 256, 257, 306, 312, 313. But the reference should really be *passim*.

St. James's Chronicle of London tersely expressed it: 'The stamping and episcopizing our colonies were understood to be only different branches of the same plan of power.'[1]

With the achievement of independence, the Anglican incubus was removed. The Episcopalian Church had to take its place alongside other churches, an equal among equals, as was right and meet in a country like America. What would the future bring? It was clear that religious multiplicity was there to stay. But multiplicity did not necessarily mean invidious discrimination. There could in principle be many churches without some of them being conservative and others revolutionary, without some of them catering to an upper class and others to a lower. The hope on the morrow of the Declaration of Independence was that, as American society in general would settle down into a libertarian and egalitarian pattern, so would religious life. The scandal of the old world – not just differences in worship, those were harmless, but division of the worshippers along socio-economic lines, with establishments for the upper income brackets, and sects for the lower – would be banished for ever from the new world.

But things were not destined to develop in this way. The United States had no established, privileged, respectable religious organization against which the dissatisfied could have reacted, and which, in their mood of protestation, they would have rejected. However, there were other forces at work which led to the formation of sects, or of religious movements very much like sects, in the country. The two most important of them were, first, the appearance of a contrast between settled and frontier society, and second, the immigration of masses of men who could not, overnight, be turned into well-adjusted citizens. In so far as settled society – the eastern seaboard – felt itself, and was rated as, superior to frontier society, the settlements west of the Alleghanies; and in so far as the old inhabitants – the Anglo-Saxons – felt themselves, and were rated as, superior to the new-comers, the 'Guineas' or the 'Bohunks',[2] there was a situation very much like that in a class-divided society. Social contrast led to religious conflict. Thus it was that a land which had rejected the principle of religious establishment, which, in the First Amendment to its Constitution,

[1] Cit. ibid., p. 289.

[2] Guineas=immigrants from Southern Europe (Italians or Spaniards); Bohunks=immigrants from Central Europe (*Bo*hemians or *Hun*garians).

had made a state church, or even anything remotely like it, for ever impossible, drifted in the same direction in which England had developed after the Henrician settlement – the direction of a division, in religion, between those up above and those below.

Whatever one may think of Frederick Jackson Turner's general thesis, the facts displayed in support of it in *The Frontier in American History* must surely be accepted by all. When, even before the War of Independence, the population began to spread from the shore-states into such inland-territories as Vermont, the pristine unity of the American people was over and in its place stood two conflicting societies of which the younger, feeling itself underprivileged, developed in contrast to, not to say in resentment of, the older and more respectable. 'By this time,' Turner says, referring to the middle of the eighteenth century, 'two distinct New Englands existed – the one coastal and dominated by commercial interests and the established congregational churches; the other a primitive agricultural area, democratic in principle, and with various sects.' Further south, the situation was the same. 'In Virginia . . . in the governorship of Alexander Spotswood, we find a contest between the frontier settlers and the property-holding classes of the coast . . . The small landholders, seeing that their powers were steadily passing into the hands of the wealthy planters who controlled church and state and lands rose in revolt,' even before Spotwood's day. Again, 'the Declaration of Grievances which the back counties of the Carolinas drew up against the aristocracy that dominated the politics of those colonies exhibits the contest between the democracy of the frontier and the established classes who apportioned the legislature in such fashion as to secure effective control of government'.[1]

It is interesting to note that Turner speaks of this clash between geographically divided societies as if it were a class conflict; and, indeed, the parallel is unmistakable. Some of the coast-dwellers had secured property rights in frontier regions ahead of the settlers; they were thus absentee landlords in a proper class contrast – owners *versus* non-owners – with the landless or at least still landhungry pioneers. Other features, though not directly con-

[1] Turner, F. J., *The Frontier in American History*, ed. New York 1962, pp. 78, 79, 247, 248. Cf. the parallel troubles of Brazil, the conflict between seaboard and sertão (the backlands). Freyre, G., *The Masters and the Slaves*, ed. New York 1956, pp. 157 and 181.

nected with the control of the means of production, were also economic in nature, for instance the confrontation of the debtor interest of the frontiersmen with the creditor interest of the older regions, or the frontiersmen's call for a paper currency, opposed, in the older regions, by a defence of the metallic circulation. The detail is complex and need not be unravelled here. The tension existed and dominated life as is demonstrated with all desirable clarity by the political cleavage which soon rent the continent. 'One can trace a distinct belt of democratic territory extending from the back country of New England down through western New York, Pennsylvania, and the South,' Turner states. 'In each colony this region was in conflict with the dominant classes of the coast. It constituted a quasi-revolutionary area . . . and . . . formed the basis on which the Democratic Party was afterwards established.' Jefferson and Jackson were children of its soil and champions of its ideals. Jefferson came from western Virginia, from the edge of the Blue Ridge; Jackson came from the backwoods of the Carolinas and grew up in distant Tennessee. Their call for individual freedom expressed an attitude which was bound to assert itself in religion as much as it did in politics. It engendered the sectarianism of the frontier settlements.[1]

It is not to be overlooked, however, and must be emphasized, that the developing religious differentiation between the East and the West was due, in part at any rate, not to conflicts in economic interests and political intentions, not to a kind of class war, but simply to the different religious needs of the two societies. It would have appeared, even if there had been no tension at all. Turner's analysis has to be completed, if not corrected, on this particular point. Old societies have a well-integrated social life. Folkways are firmly in control; the sanctions which support them are vigorous and effective. The fact alone that the people of the East were small-town-dwellers ensured that they conducted themselves in accordance with local norms, and their lawabidingness was further strengthened by their Calvinistic upbringing, a fierce system of repression if ever there was one. New societies, on the other hand, are apt to be lawless. It was not without reason that the West was known as the Wild West. The uphill struggle of the Sheriffs against the bad men is part and parcel of the frontier epic.

[1] Turner, loc. cit., pp. 248, 250, 252; cf. also p. 109 et seq.; but, again, the reference should really be *passim*.

Religiously expressed, there was much open sinning in the backlands – but where there is much open sinning, there is also great need for much open repentance. The fierce paroxysms of fear and remorse, reassurance and exaltation, which characterized the camp meetings of the frontier regions were the direct result of a deep-seated elementary need which simply did not exist in the staid communities of Connecticut and Massachusetts. Their inhabitants viewed its manifestations with dismay and disgust; such things simply were not decent. Unavoidably, therefore, the West had to create a religious style of its own. It was near-sectarian in its nature.

Speaking broadly (and that is all we can do here), Episcopalianism and Congregationalism remained characteristic of the East, while Methodism and Baptism conquered the West. In so far as the two latter variants of Protestantism were successful in the Atlantic shore states, they were successful among the proletarians, not the bourgeois – an important indication of the fact that the pioneers felt themselves as proletarians of a kind. Even more significant, however, than the apparently geographical, but really socio-political, distinction between the Episcopalian–Congregational East and the Methodist–Baptist West was the split which rent the Presbyterian Church. Not so closely identified with the existing social pattern of New England as their Congregationalist fellow-Calvinists, they could venture out into frontier regions: but when they arrived there, they found that they drifted further and further away from the brethren whom they had left behind. Schism was the unavoidable result. In addition to these imported and adjusted movements, the West spawned movements of its own, the most significant being the Disciples of Christ and the so-called Mormons (*recte* Latter Day Saints). To discuss them fully would mean writing a volume. We can but say in a line that they largely conformed to the sectarian type.

To be more precise, they conformed to the sectarian type while they were yet young. Like other sects, they soon turned into pure denominations. The frontier in due course ceased to be a frontier: it became settled in more senses of the word than one. With a more settled state, socially and intellectually, the feeling of antagonism towards the respectable East ceased. Religion in the West could, and did, become conservative.[1]

[1] On all this, cf. Niebuhr, loc. cit., p. 135 et seq., and the literature adduced there.

In discussing the differentiation between coastlands and backlands, Turner has pointed out that the latter harboured many people who were not English in language or at least in culture. 'The Middle region, entered by New York harbor, was an open door to all Europe,' he writes. 'The tide-water part of the South represented typical Englishmen, modified by a warm climate and servile labor . . . New England stood for a special English movement, Puritanism. The Middle region was less English than the other sections . . . The Scotch–Irish and the Palatine Germans or "Pennsylvania Dutch" furnished the dominant element in the stock of the colonial frontier.'[1] It contributed not a little to the multiformity of American religious life. But greater still was the impact which later non-English immigrants were to have – the Irish, the Italians, the Poles; the Danes, the Norwegians and the Swedes. Their case is very different from that of the Pennsylvania Dutch.

When the Irish and Italians and Slavs arrived, the frontier was no longer quite what it had been. The continent, if not yet crowded, was already well settled. The new-comers, or many of them, had perforce to remain in the towns, and there they had to be contented with low-paid and low-prestige jobs. They became, in the narrowest sense of the word, a class of bottom dogs. This was not at all what they had expected when they left their homelands. Turner calls the contrast between hopes and fulfilment in the 'hordes of recent immigrants from southern Italy . . . almost pathetic' – a classical understatement.[2] Unavoidably, they developed the resentments which go with disappointment and humiliation; and these resentments in turn tended to express themselves in religious terms. There was a situation very much like the one from which new sects normally arise. But here, there was no need of new sects; the old, imported religions were at hand and could do the job. Will Herberg, in *Protestant-Catholic-Jew*, has explained that the immigrants' churches gave the immigrants 'identity'.[3] It would be even better to speak of solace, reassurance, self-assertion and self-respect; indeed, of the 'overcompensation of an inferiority complex'. The 'Bohunk' was a Bohunk only in the strange secular world into which he had been propelled; when he knelt at the altar-rails he could feel that he was a man superior to those who beat him on the labour market, for did he not have 'the

[1] Turner, loc. cit., pp. 27 and 22. [2] Ibid., p. 264. [3] *Passim.*

true faith'? Thus churches which are not in themselves sects – Roman Catholicism, but also Greek Orthodoxy and Lutheranism in its various incarnations – came to do the office of sects. Nothing is more significant than the secondary developments which ensued here. The Italians came a generation or so after the Irish; in other words, the Irish were already well-established citizens when the Italians appeared and had to go through the depressing experiences which are every immigrant's lot and make him hostile to his new society, or at least to its upper strata. Great tensions sprang up within Catholicism, of which the plan to split the Church into national divisions, known as Cahenslyism, was a dangerous symptom.[1] The spasm passed, but not without damage. Some Italian-centred criminality may have been due to a lack of outlet for feelings of hostility against the hard host society in the bosom of an insufficiently sympathetic – 'too Irish' – church. In the case of the Poles, a major schism ensued, which removed a considerable number of souls from the ranks of the faithful.

A good deal of the often asserted vitality of religion in contemporary America is due to the fact we have just discussed – the fact that, not so very long ago, church membership helped many new Americans through the dark valley of depression. But the malaise of the immigrants was a malady which automatically mended with every day that passed, and so we get again a process of denominationalization. From vessels of dissatisfaction, the churches concerned changed into vehicles of conservatism. What is most characteristic here is the language question which soon became a hot issue in the Lutheran camp. A second generation desired abandonment of German or Swedish or Danish as the medium of worship, but newly immigrated members, who had not quite managed to find their niche in American society, passionately opposed transition to English as a kind of betrayal. Needless to say, English won in the end, if we disregard a few splinter groups in social (often geographical) isolation. Once again, adjustment brought denominationalization and conservative convictions.[2]

To sum up, then, the Anti-Anglicanism of colonial days; the conflict of the frontier society of the West with the old-settled society of the East; the re-invigoration of the European-born,

[1] Cf. Herberg, W., *Protestant-Catholic-Jew*, Garden City, N.Y., 1955, p. 158 et seq.

[2] Cf. Niebuhr, loc. cit., p. 200 et seq.

brought-in churches in response to a specific psychological need of the immigrants; and, finally, to mention one more feature, just to show that we have not forgotten it, the formation of Negro sects and the division of the white man's churches over the slavery and colour issue, have, taken together, created a condition in America which can perhaps best be described as a multi-denominationalism *sui generis*. Denominationalization has proceeded along a very broad front and with amazing speed. For this, there are two decisive reasons. The first is the open character of American society, its 'melting-pot' quality. An immigrant's children have not the insecurity of the immigrant himself, and his children in turn feel so secure that they can even take a lively interest in grandfather's antecedents.[1] To the third generation, if not the second, all doors are open; they feel 'in', not 'out'; and so the *de-facto* sect becomes a denomination. The second reason is the unique success of American society as a whole. To the individual immigrant's ascent in well-being is added the collective ascent of the whole country in the scale of wealth. True sectarianism is thinkable only in the remaining pockets of poverty.

But what pattern has denominationalization followed in America? The question must be asked, for here lies the true *differentia specifica* of American development. In England a sect becomes a denomination when it grows more similar to the established church. In America this was not possible. Our last task in this section, and our most interesting one in this context, is therefore to analyse the specific process whereby ever-recurrent religious alienation, on American soil, has turned into all-round religious conformity. Expressed in a nutshell, there has been progressive adjustment, not to one particular form of Christianity, but to an outside ideology which threatens to become its successor without being even recognized as its foe.

What has happened can best be understood, and can most quickly be explained, by starting from the birth-act of American culture – the revolution of 1776. Like her younger sister of 1789, this revolution was inspired by an all-round mentality whose great formulators were men like Rousseau and Leibniz, believers not only in the goodness of God, but even more in the goodness of man, deists with a leaning in the direction of a non-dogmatic, but basically optimistic, creed. It is that creed, duly developed, and

[1] 'Hansen's law', cf. Herberg, loc. cit., p. 201.

somewhat sobered up by an antecedent Calvinism, which has taken possession of all the denominations in the country and has brought about a far-reaching mutual adjustment of all religious groupings. Within each one of the one-time sects, the original negative attitudes have waned and given way to an increasingly positive philosophy, an acceptance of things as they are, a feeling that all is well with the world. There is nothing at all surprising in this. The country has found an appropriate mental form, ideas and sentiments, symbols and rituals in tune with its historical experience which has, on the whole, been one of peace and progress. The fact must be faced, however, that this evolution has led Americans away from traditional Christianity, and especially from that particularly hard and harsh form of Christianity, Calvinism, which dominated the pre-history of the United States. The fact must also be faced (we beg the reader's forgiveness for introducing what looks like a value-judgement at this point – we are not really going beyond the limits of sound definition and sober fact) that this underlying mentality, which has crept under the mantle of all denominations, is a pseudo-religion rather than a real religion because its concept of the deity is vague (as it is in all deism) and its understanding of the human condition less than realistic (as it is in all optimistic humanism if and in so far as it closes its eyes to the more discouraging aspects of existence). A partial and exceptionally favourable life-experience can hardly be expected to generate a total and entirely convincing metaphysic.

The deism and humanism of American religion as represented by the large denominations has clearly emerged from recent investigations. Americans believe in God: '97 per cent according to one survey, 96 per cent according to another, 95 per cent according to a third'. But 'when nearly thirty outstanding Americans were asked not long ago to rate the hundred most significant events in history, first place was given to Columbus's discovery of America, while Christ, His birth or crucifixion, came fourteenth', and 'tied with the discovery of X-rays and the Wright brothers' first plane flight'. This is no longer personalistic theism in the full sense of the word: it is, in fact, the near-pantheism which emerged from the French Revolution and found expression, as we have seen, in writers like Michelet and Mazzini (as well as artists like Manzoni with his *I Promessi Sposi* and Beethoven with his Ninth Symphony). Like Michelet and Mazzini, the votaries of the new creed indulge in a glorification of man. According to one poll, 90 per cent of those asked asserted that, looking within themselves, they could honestly state that they were obeying the law of love; while, according to another, only 5 per cent confessed to any fear of going to hell.[1] But no polls are needed to prove that the doctrine of original sin is virtually abandoned and replaced by a doctrine *à la* Rousseau of original goodness. American education, the least repressive in the world, is based on the assumption (alas, less than justified) that the naturally growing child will develop into a naturally kindly adult; that an 'internalization of culture', or at least educational pressure towards it, is a work of supererogation. This all-round optimism (a true metaphysic – *see* Leibniz) finds its final expression (some would say, its last *reductio ad absurdum*) in the desperate attempt to impress, through the mortician's art, a smiling look even upon the features of death. It has inspired (if this is the right word), inspired by way of revulsion, Evelyn Waugh's *The Loved One* and Jessica Mitford's *The American Way of Death*.

As a substitute for religion, such a philosophy is a failure, as this unavailing attempt of dealing with men's end amply proves; but as a pragmatic code, a guide in life, it has been a success. Following upon, but progressively displacing, the Calvinist mentality, it has added to the workmanlike habits bred up by the latter a confidence in the future, in the worth-while-ness of taking any and every risk. This outlook upon life has triggered a process of material ascent for which hardly any epithet is strong enough. It is not surprising, therefore, that it should have won hearts and minds, but it is difficult to reconcile with Christianity. 'It marks a radical break with the fundamental presuppositions of both Judaism and Christianity, to which it must appear as a particularly insidious kind of idolatry,' Herberg writes in sorrow.[2] Yet it co-exists in most American denominations with both Christianity and Judaism. Why should it not? Men simply are not logical. They have lived for many hundreds of years under a mythology which mixed the fire of the Gospel with the water of ruler-deification. Why should they not live under a similar mixture now, especially

[1] Cf. Herberg, loc. cit., pp. 85, 13, 14, 89, 86. Cf. also pp. 207, 211 (with note 5 on p. 224), 247, 279, 280.

[2] Ibid., p. 102. He also speaks of 'man-centredness' (p. 284) and of a 'religiousness without religion' (p. 276).

as they have become entirely absorbed in practical pursuits, in 'deeds, not creeds'?

We have pointed out above that the working faith of Michelet and Mazzini was a revolutionary ideology which bore in it, however, a conservative kernel, the design of a new 'established' religiosity to be realized in the democratic age to come. America has developed it – probably so far as it ever will be developed. Everything has been of one piece. History has shown much more consistency than has the collective mind. Just as the United States are the fullest unfolding of the civic society dreamed of and hoped for by the revolutionaries of the eighteenth century, so the indwelling mentality of its citizens is the fullest unfolding of their inherent mood and creed.

Herberg has characterized this *de-facto* religion of the model American of the twentieth century as a belief in the American Way of Life.[1] 'The American Way of Life,' he explains, 'is an organic structure of ideas, values, and beliefs that constitute a faith common to Americans and genuinely operative in their lives, a faith that markedly influences, and is influenced by, the "official" religions of American society. Sociologically, anthropologically, if one pleases, it is characteristic American religion, undergirding American life, and overarching American society despite all indubitable differences of region, sections, culture and class.'[2] It is the orthodoxy that has drawn many different denominations together which, in earlier days, were far apart. It is the democratic counterpart of the monarchical religions of yesteryear. It is also the *pièce de résistance* of those who still find life as it is unacceptable – Negroes above all, but also men in alienation like the members of the newest sects, Pentecostalists, Jehovah's Witnesses, and whatever else their proper names may be. With its emergence the country has drifted into very much the same situation which prevailed in the great caesaropapist civilizations: an official – a civic – faith on the one hand; anti-official – revolutionary – sects on the other. The only difference is that this official and civic faith is, for historical reasons, not formally connected with the government, but more factually with the people. It is parcelled out among many different religious bodies, each of which presents its own

[1] See his chapter V, 'The Religion of Americans and American Religion', loc. cit., p. 85 et seq. Cf. also pp. 211 (with note 65 on p. 224), 247, 279, 280.
[2] Ibid., p. 90.

particular variation of it. This, however, does not prevent them from labouring a common theme.[1]

Christianity, properly so called, was once merely an ingredient in a compound mentality in which the monarchical religion, the belief in the sanctity of one man, prevailed. Christianity, properly so called, is now merely an ingredient in a combination in which the religion of democracy, the belief in the goodness of all men, is paramount. The Christian must hope that the faith of his heart will as successfully survive the embrace of the new ideologies as it did that of the old.

[1] Cf. Berger, P. L., *The Noise of Solemn Assemblies,* Garden City, N.Y., 1961.

Index

For Product Safety Concerns and Information please contact our EU
representative GPSR@taylorandfrancis.com
Taylor & Francis Verlag GmbH, Kaufingerstraße 24, 80331 München, Germany

www.ingramcontent.com/pod-product-compliance
Lightning Source LLC
Chambersburg PA
CBHW070546270326
41926CB00013B/2218

* 9 7 8 0 4 1 5 6 0 5 5 9 5 *